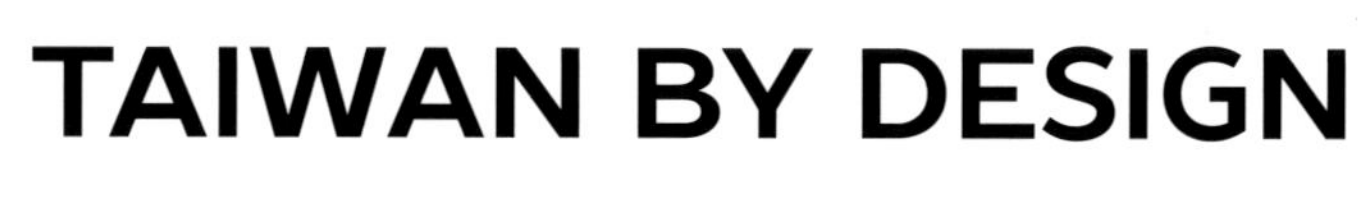

TAIWAN BY DESIGN

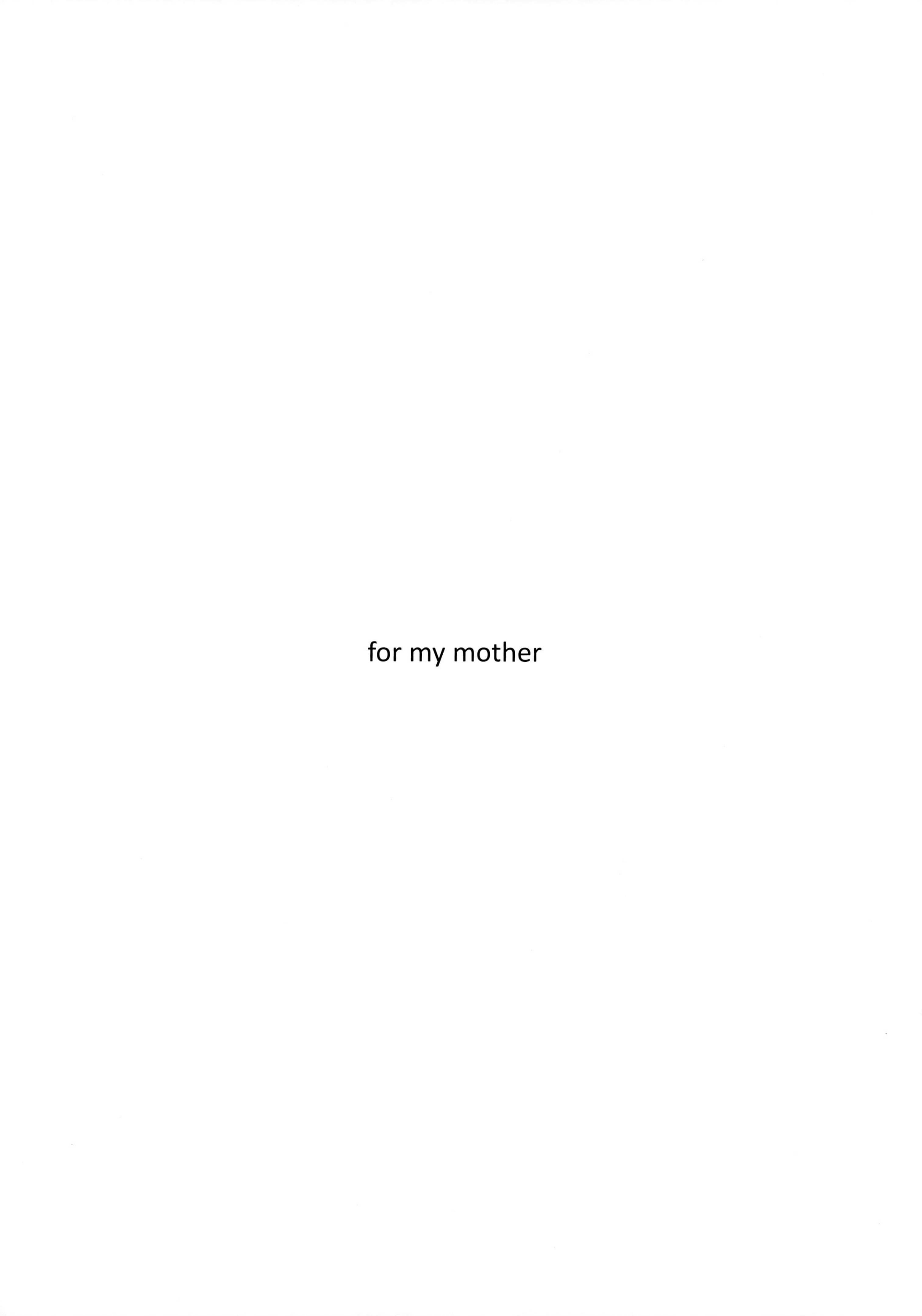

for my mother

NOVAMEDIA
Sydney • Melbourne • Taipei

TAIWAN BY DESIGN
88 PRODUCTS
FOR BETTER LIVING

ANNIE IVANOVA

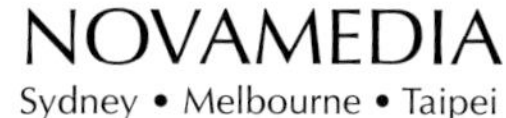
NOVAMEDIA
Sydney • Melbourne • Taipei

ANNIE IVANOVA is an award winning curator and entrepreneur, and one of Australia's leading proponents of cultural diplomacy. She has extensive experience in creative exports and has worked with some of the world's most influential institutions, including: Ars Electronica, Centre Pompidou, Beijing World Art Museum, Ars Electronica, ZKM Center for Art and Media, Shanghai Zendai MOMA, Taipei 101, MOCATaipei, and the Australian Centre for the Moving Image. Since 2010, Annie is the first international curator to be based in Taiwan.

www.annieivanova.com

First published in 2016 by
NOVAMEDIA LTD PO Box 877
Sydney NSW 2147 Australia

Worldwide release by
INTELLECT LTD
The Mill, Parnall Road, Fishponds
Bristol BS16 3JG UK

www.intellectbooks.co.uk

USA distribution by
University of Chicago Press
Distributed Presses USA

Community
www.taiwanbydesign.net
www.facebook.com/taiwanbydesign

National Library of Australia Cataloguing-in-Publication:
Ivanova, Annie. (author & editor)
Taiwan by Design: 88 products for better living
1. Industrial design--Taiwan.
2. Design--Taiwan--History.
3. Product design--Asia.
4. Taiwan--Civilization.

ISBN: 9780975199848 (hardback)
745.20951249

Produced by Studio IVANOVA
Directed by Annie Ivanova
Graphic designers: I-Chen Huang, Pei-Hsuan Kuan
Typeset: Prosto Sans Bold, Optima
Forward translated from the Chinese by Tsung-Yi Lin
Printed by Round corner books case maker / 圓典股份有限公司

Printed in Taiwan

TAIWAN BY DESIGN
88 PRODUCTS
FOR BETTER LIVING

ANNIE IVANOVA

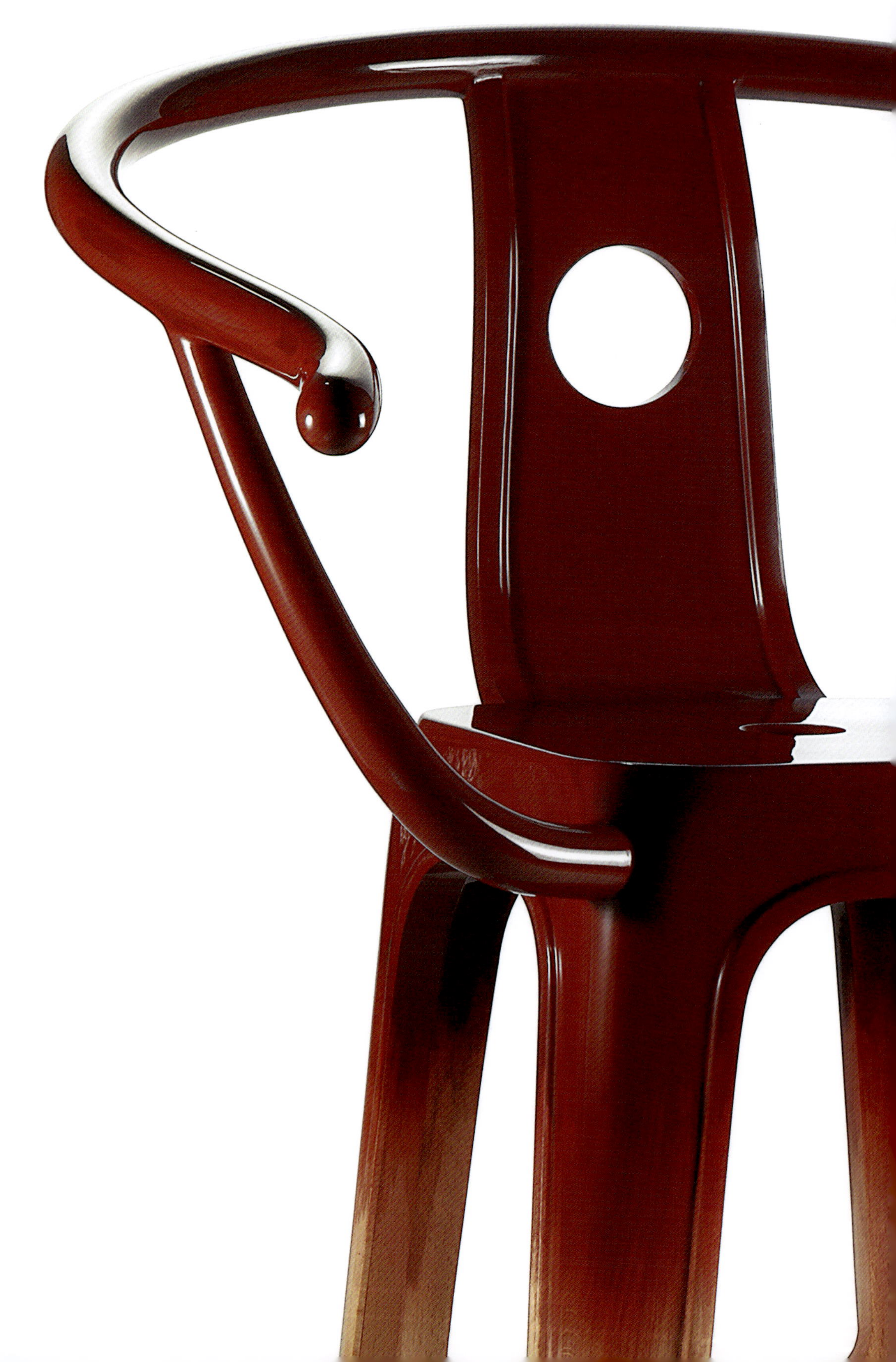

CONTENTS

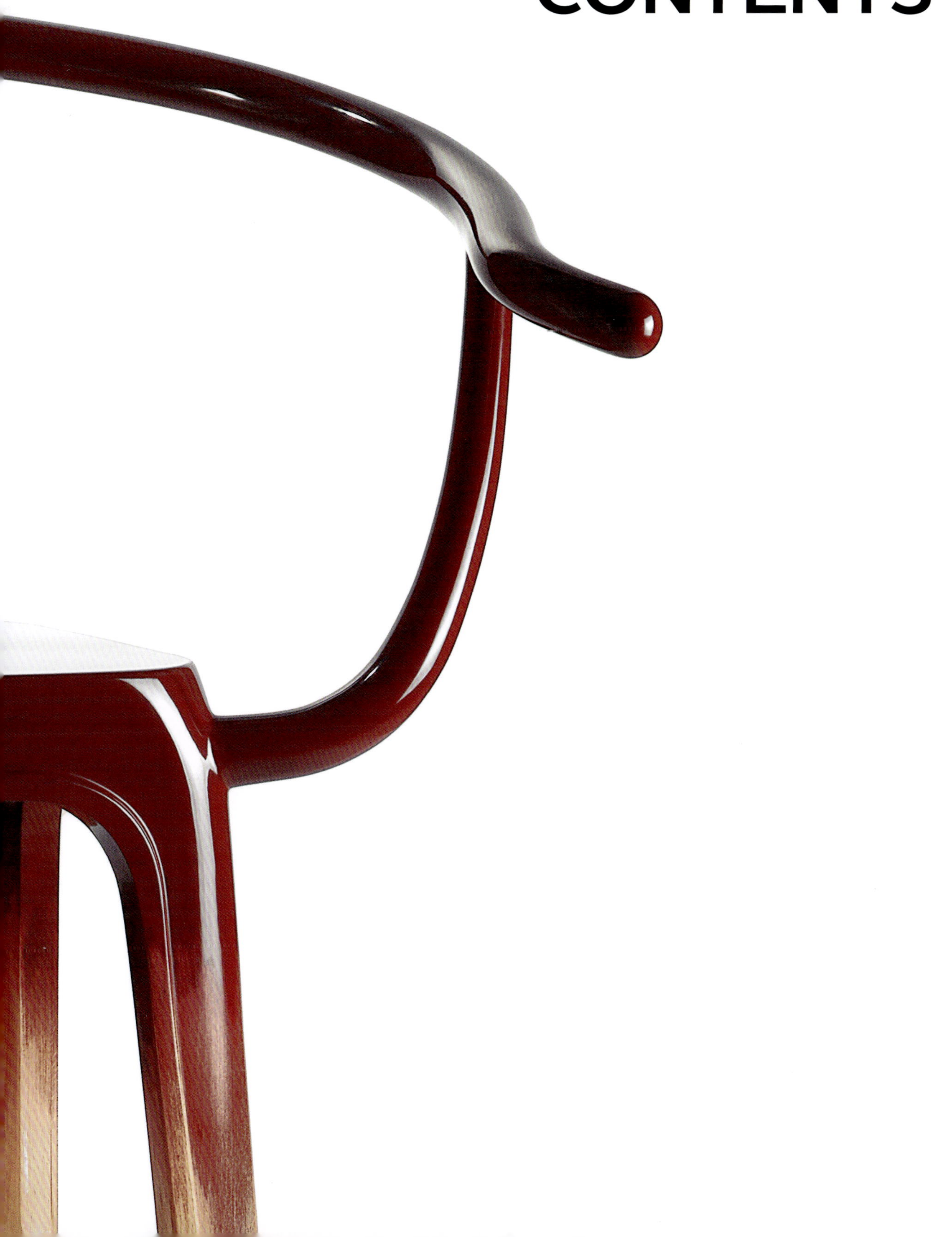

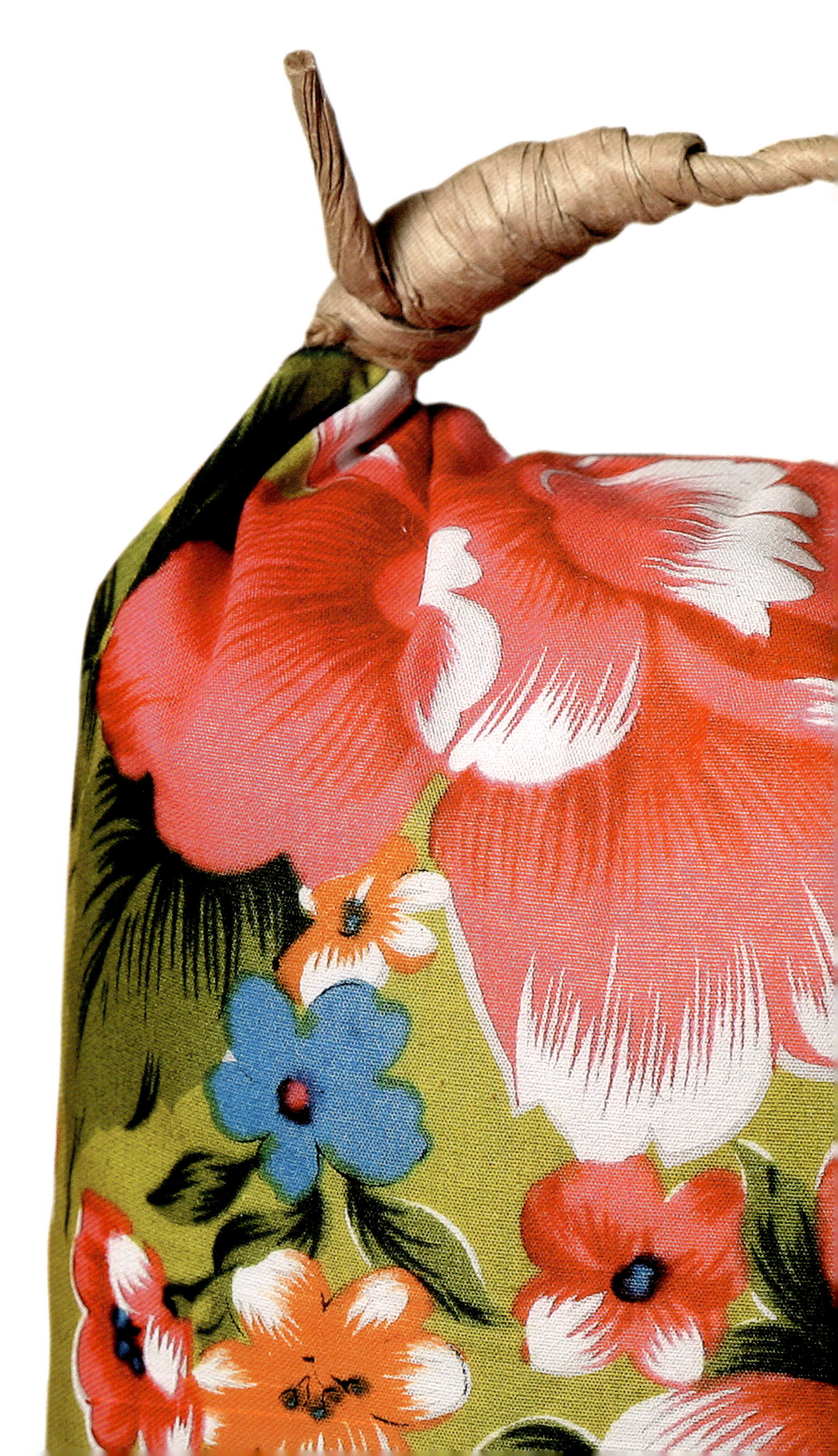

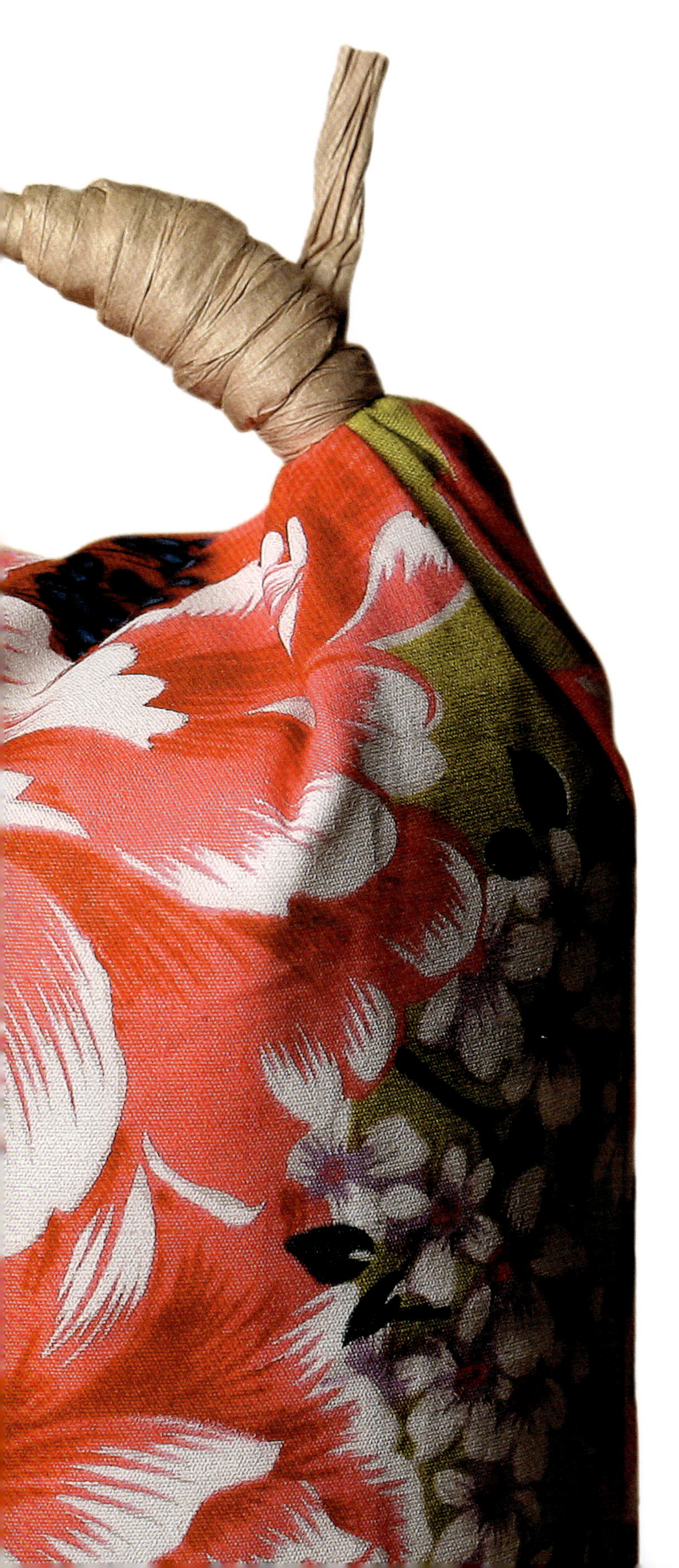

ESSAYS

FOREWARD

It is an immense joy to be holding the first book about Taiwanese product design and to know it will reach readers all over the world in the English language. For us, coming from a place with such a complex history, being able to communicate with the West who we are as creators is an enormous hurdle. We are all indebted to Annie Ivanova for giving us the gift of her talent to bring this amazing project into being.

I met Annie Ivanova at Taipei World Design Congress gala dinner in 2011, which she was attending with an Australian delegation. Her knowledge of Asian culture and her enthusiasm to collaborate with Taipei design circles made a lasting impression on me. We maintained contact and I introduced her to members of the Taiwan Graphic Design Association, an organisation I founded in 1994. In Taiwan such associations are the real drivers of the creative sector. We lobby the government to improve its policies, hold training programs and work to connect designers with peers from abroad. Through our events she met other leaders, gradually expanding her network.

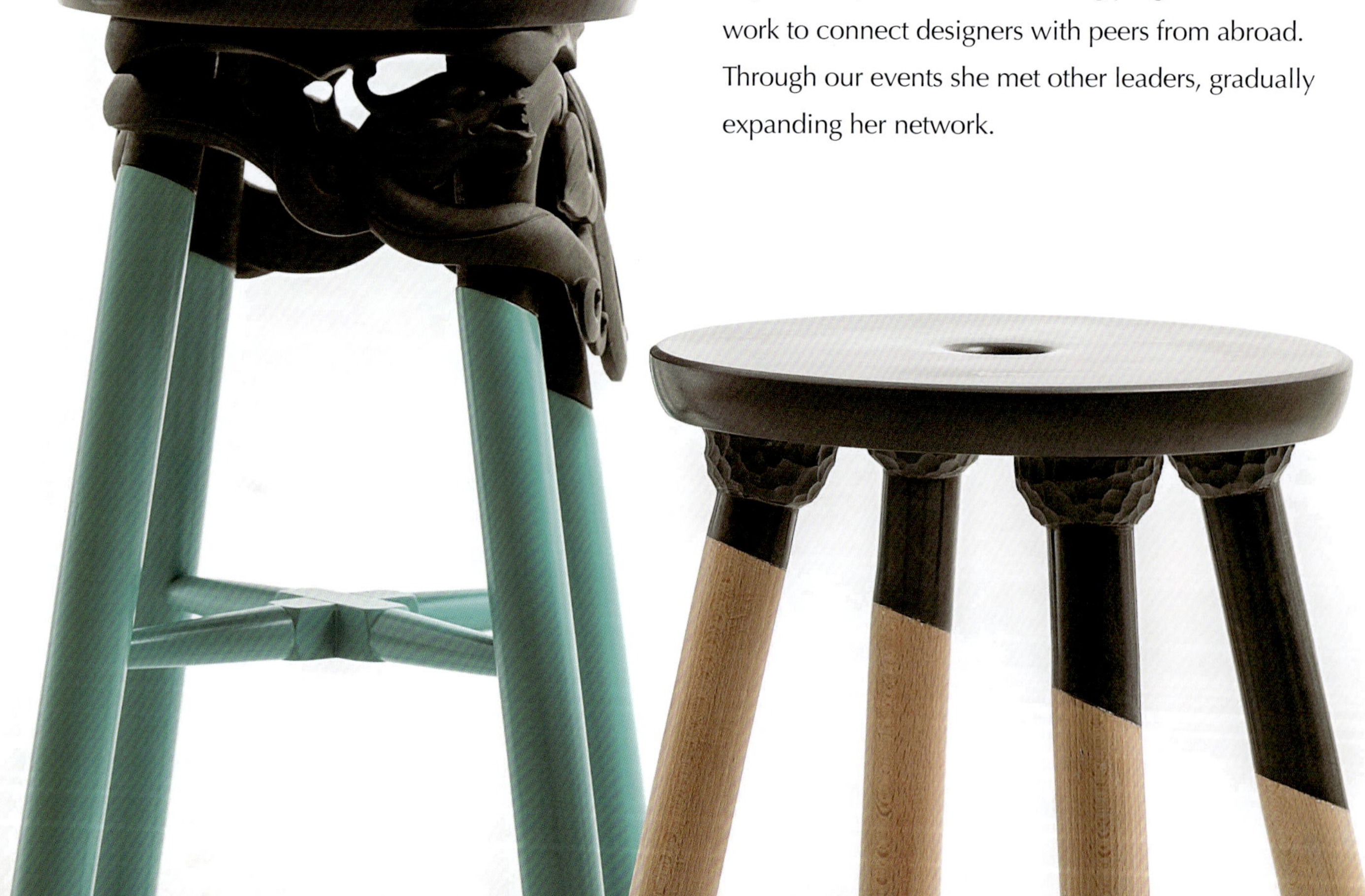

Through her broad international perspective Annie could see value in our way of thinking that we, ourselves, often overlook. As the first and only international curator to be based in Taiwan, she has travelled extensively around the island to visit companies. Not only this, she is also the first foreign curator to travel to remote Aboriginal art communities, something even the Taiwanese rarely do.

Her unprecedented exhibition Vibrant Vision, staged in Taipei in 2013, displayed the amazing diversity of over 60 contemporary works representing all tribes. Annie's vision was for the public to develop a deeper appreciation of local Indigenous knowledge and, as she puts it, learn to 'respect its contribution to the common heritage of all humankind'.

In Australia, her initial efforts were to present Taiwanese designers at Ideas on Design (previously agIdeas), one of the most prestigious international design festivals taking place in Melbourne. I had the honour to participate in the 2013 Creative Masters forum and must admit was only too eager to share my reverence for my homeland. The audience had no idea of the cultural context of Taiwanese design, but judging from the curious responses there was a lot of avid interest to find out more. There, in the backstage 'green room' of the event, the idea for this book was born. Annie felt, and I agree, it was too slow a process to shine the spotlight only on one designer at a time. 'A hundred would be great', we

thought, and so the curatorial brief for this book was set in motion.

Returning to Taiwan, Annie made it her goal to research and identify 100 iconic products through which to tell our design story. As she admits, the book became a mammoth project. What she sought out was diversity of representative ideas and excellence of practice that encompasses craft traditions, design classics and innovation. I sincerely admire the tenacity with which she committed herself to this initiative, executing her curatorial work incredibly thoroughly and with pronounced sensitivity.

In our culture the number 88 signifies great fortune and it is especially lucky for business. For this reason the book breaks away from the Western 'top 100' convention. We hope the number will add a bit of extra magic to this wonderful project!

Given *Taiwan by Design* has been compiled through hundreds of interviews in a Chinese-speaking environment, the book is an exceptionally courageous achievement. The stories gathered here are glimpses into what influences our creative work, what fires up the imagination and what touches the heart. Through this significant collection we are all eager to share with you the spirit of our Beautiful Island.

Stony Cherng

INTRODUCTION

Taiwan is a mystery as it is a miracle. A small island in the Pacific Ocean constantly swept by the changing tides of civilisations, it emerged at the turn of this century as one of the four Tiger Economies of the East. Primarily it achieved this by riding on the 1990s digital boom: the 'Electronics Kingdom' has been manufacturing affordable gadgets and computers of all kinds imaginable, tens of millions of which are shipped around the world each year. The unprecedented wealth created during this era is praised as the backbone of Taiwan's development—although the success has been long in the making, and involving a lot more than Forbes financial charts could ever reveal.

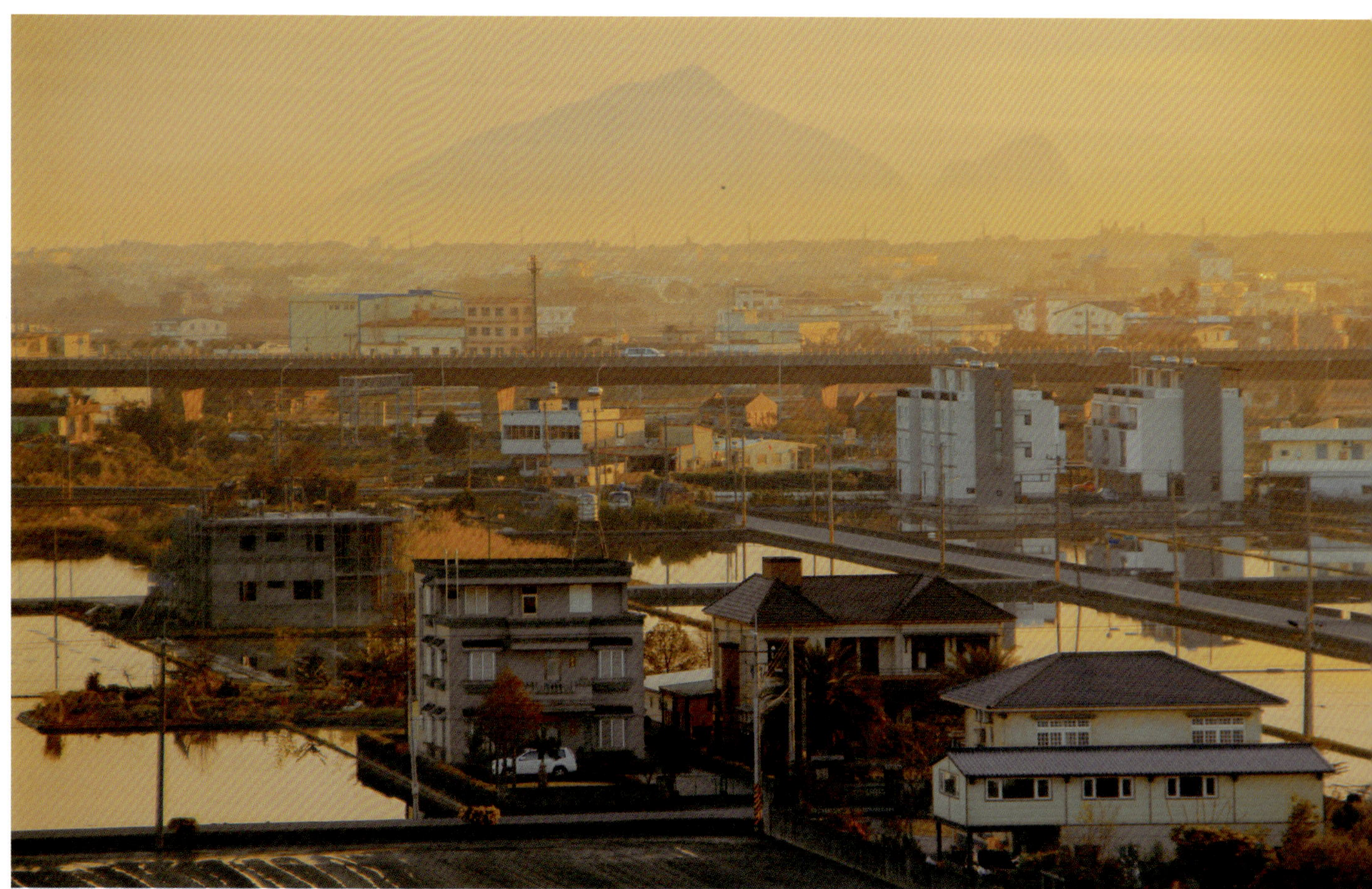

Yilan County in the early morning, with guardian beast: Turtle Island

It is the intention of this book to introduce a different view of Taiwan, as seen through the eyes of a new generation of creative people passionately concerned about its future and its heritage. The objects featured here piece together a story of the island's fascinating cultural make up and traditions. They also introduce local design excellence, which despite being on par with the 'best of the best' in international practice is relatively unknown outside of specialist circles.

Taiwanese designers have a big challenge ahead of them. As most manufacturing has recently relocated offshore, industrial design has needed to move away from traditional low cost production to high-value creation of original products that make people's lives easier, happier and more enriching. Perhaps success is to be found in design hybridity: a peculiarly Taiwanese remix of high-tech and hand-made, high-class and mass-produced, old and new.

Looking through a local design prism, we discover creative inspiration amongst the vanishing worlds of night markets and temple squares: the places and times when people lived in harmony with nature and artisans were recognised for their mastery of materials. Classical elements from colonial architecture and the warmth of the traditional home are reimagined anew, and contemporary objects are infused with the stories of elders who remember life before urbanisation. Generosity of heart, history and ideas abound.

In this context, *Taiwan by Design* is the first comprehensive book of the elements and influences shaping a new Asian design aesthetic: hard to define, easy to delight.

TAIPEI: AN ARTIFICE OF CREATION

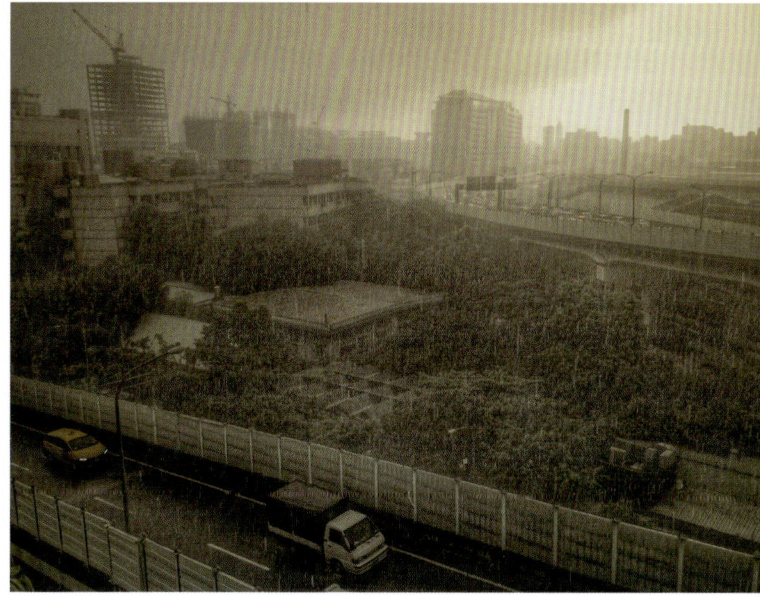

Taipei morning after typhoon

The small island is located in the Taiwan Strait along the Tropic of Cancer, with China to the west and Korea and Japan to the north. The land consists mainly of mountain ranges sprawling along the east coast and the central plateau, with some flat plains to the west where the world's most densely populated cities are built. The tectonic boundary that formed its magnificent landscape is still active and tremors are felt frequently. As if this is not enough drama, tropical storms and typhoons crash the shores each year. To shield people and property from nature's fury concrete reinforcement is present everywhere, especially in Taipei.

A futuristic-style metropolis, Taiwan's capital is an artifice of creation. All its modern structures are built in accordance with seismic building standards and prepared to withstand years of torrential rain and humidity. They are solid and safe but rarely aesthetically pleasing. The ride from the international airport to the city snakes for an hour's drive along the massive colonnades of a double-tier highway. In the down town districts, with the exception of a few tree-lined boulevards, the presence of vegetation appears as an after-thought: hanging from roof gutters, squeezing through cracks in pavements, or decorating construction sites in what the locals call 'green cemetery walls'. Not surprisingly, first time visitors find the endless stretches of Brutalist architecture an assault on the senses (page 36). But this is just the surface. Give Taipei a bit of open-minded attention and it soon reveals its hidden treasures.

The streets are tightly packed and every bit of space is utilised. Underneath the towering commercial buildings, merchants' displays spill onto the sidewalks with a pandemonium of all kinds of goods imaginable. Once a month tables laden with snacks, drinks and incense are set up onto the pavement, and paper money is burned as offerings to various gods for good luck. Behind the main boulevards are mazes of narrow alleys where community life pulses around local shrines and cramped markets. As most city dwellings are relatively small, neighbourhood gardens have become a semi-private domain where local folk take their portable furniture to and socialise.

Despite the constant attack of urban pollution, private spaces are kept clean and dust-free. The Taipeinese are early adopters of new technologies, and every home has a bundle of machines to maintain comfortable living standard: dehumidifiers and kitchen ventilators ensure the air is breathable, while air-conditioners percolate ceaselessly to keep the intolerable summer heat at bay. Luckily for its residents, the city is surrounded by green hills and a nature escape is just a short drive away. Hot spring bathing, cycling, and group picnics are popular pastimes. Active leisure time is a relatively new trend, one that has attracted the attention of designers (page 184). From filter bottles and portable kettles to gears, bicycles and wheelchairs,

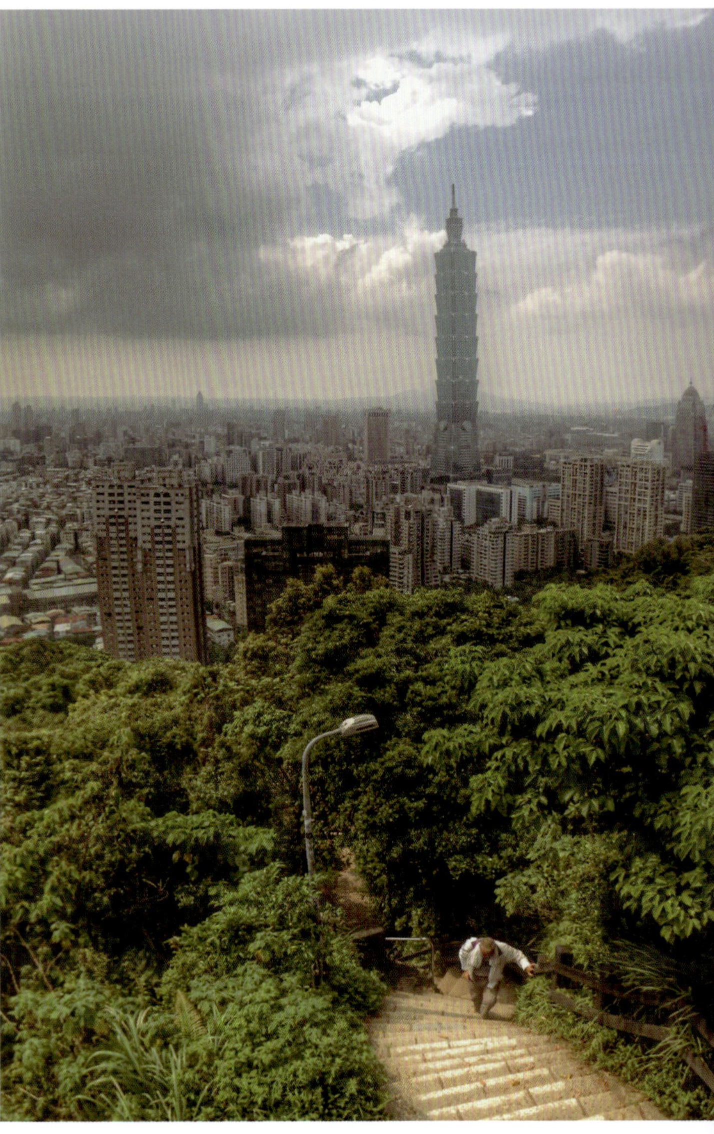

Xiangshan, mountain lookout

many new products are developed with a 'happiness factor' in mind.

Cycling is perhaps the most popular leisure activity. Since the 2007 film Island Etude by Taiwanese director Huai-En Chen—a spirited story of a young man's cycling adventures around the island—getting 'into gear' has become fashionable again. People of all ages riding all kinds of bicycles, spill onto the roads on weekends. Of course local companies such as Giant and Merida have been making bicycles and exporting them all over the world for decades. The entire Taiwanese bicycle industry has become highly successful by adopting the '3 Ns' of design—new materials, new functions, and new uses—reinventing the two-wheeler time and again into a versatile vehicle. With more than 30 per cent of Taiwan's people living in greater Taipei, the city's population density is now amongst the highest in the world. The limitation of living spaces is a major everyday conundrum that needs to be solved through clever design. Anything that is foldable, stackable, collapsible or miniaturised and easily portable is valued here (page 76). A positive aspect of living in a compact environment is that everything one needs is within close proximity, allowing for efficient use of time. Taiwan's plethora of convenience stores is estimated to be over 10,000—about 1 every 500 meters in residential areas! Convenience is so much embedded in design that it has become a lifestyle.

HYBRID CULTURES

Contrary to popular perceptions, Taiwanese culture is exuberantly hybrid, malleable and adaptable. Against the dramatic backdrop of mountainous wilderness the clashes and confluences of vastly different political ideologies have been involved in shaping it. It is a not a widely-known fact that the traditional custodians of the land are the Taiwanese Aborigines, who have been living here for over 6,500 years and who continue to assert their traditional rights. Historical records suggest they belong to the Austronesian people, who migrated as far as Madagascar and New Zealand.

Amongst the 16 officially recognised Indigenous groups there is a rich heritage of objects: from delicate embroidery and beadwork to fine stone-masonry and elaborate bamboo weaving. Some of these objects are created to decorate the homes of the nobles; others have been handed down as part of ceremonial practices. Up-and-coming Indigenous designers are now giving the ancestral colours and patterns new forms of expression, particularly in contemporary apparel.

The first Europeans to come in contact with Taiwan were the Portuguese sailors en route to Japan in the 16th century. Amazed at the lush green landscape seen from the sea, they named it *ilha formosa* or 'beautiful island'. The place entered cartographic records as Formosa, and it was known in the West by this name until the mid 20th century. The name is still found on some brand labels as a mark of local pride.

During the period of early global exploration by the Europeans, the Dutch were the first to establish a colony here in 1624 as part of Holland's (The Netherlands) expansion plans along the Spice Trade Route. The Dutch East India Company maintained a strategic base in the south from where mercantile exchanges with Japan and Qing Dynasty China flourished. Its activities turned the unknown little island into one of the most important trade destinations in Asia at that time.

The legacy left by the Dutch (1624–1662) is best exemplified by a group of picturesque ruins and a city citadel remaining from its Fort Zeelandia. Built from imported red bricks the fort is Taiwan's earliest civic

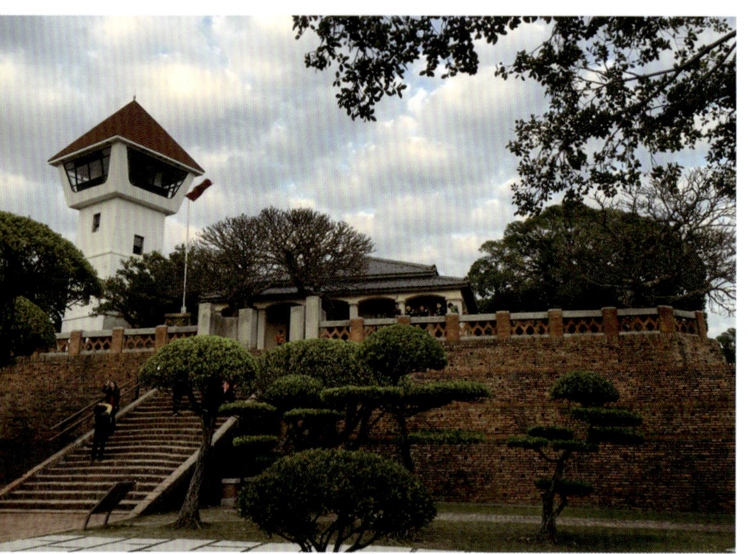

Tainan, Fort Zeelandia ruins

compound located in its oldest city, Tainan. 'This bewitching place might be a relic from the times when East and West first came in contact but we have absorbed it as our own. For me the terracotta bricks radiate a nostalgic feeling of how Taiwan used to be before urbanisation. I'd like to think of this kind of architecture as local', laments Rock Wang (page 54).

For a brief time, parts of the island were ruled by the Spanish conquistadores (1626–1642) and pro-Ming Dynasty settlers (1661–1683), each etching their mark onto the landscape. But it was when the Dutch conceded to the Qing Dynasty (1662–1912) that history took on a radically different turn for Taiwan. Mainland settlers, mostly ethnic Hakka and Fujianese from Southern China, started arriving en mass. They acquired land, took over property and began to actively exchange Formosan agricultural produce for speciality goods from their ancestral homes. As a result, new objects of great refinement in blue and white porcelain, jade and lacquer were introduced to the island. *Gong-fu cha*, the ritualised preparation and appreciation of tea, became a major part of local culture (page 158). As tea plantations grew so did the popularity of Formosan Oolong Tea, peaking at one time as Taiwan's most profitable export good.

Another interesting development took place around the newly founded temples. Artisans from the mainland were brought in to work on temple decorations. From the brick-and-tile work on the floors and embroidered murals on the walls, to the meticulously carved altars and ostentatious stone-sculpted pillars, temple architecture became a rich

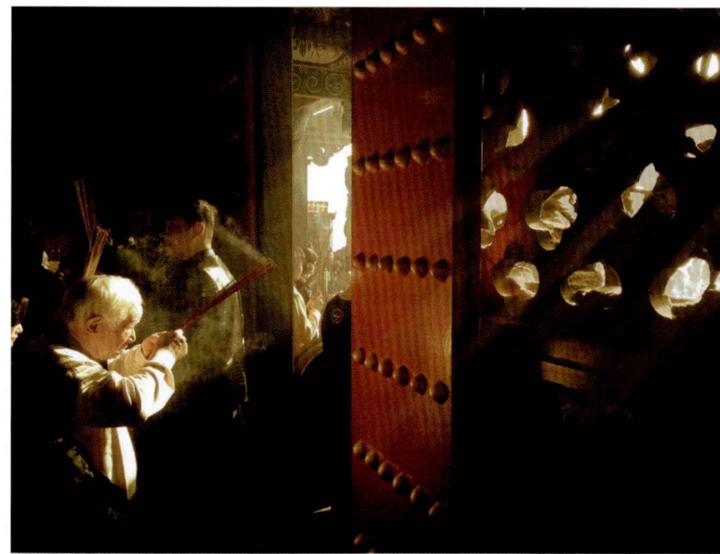

Worshipers at Dali Temple, Yilan

repository of some of the best examples of traditional crafts. Being at the heart of community life, these were also places where traveling troupes entertained and educated villagers, and civic matters were publicly debated.

Confucius teachings, syncretised with Buddhist and Taoist thought, spread as the dominant norm from which all social values would be derived, even today. The most enduring of these, the reciprocity of family and societal harmony is considered key to civic cohesiveness. This is more evident in the traditional homes where the centrepiece of the living rooms is a large table, often made from a single long piece of timber. Extended family members gather around it to spend time together. The essence of strong family bonds within today's living and dining environments is reflected in the numerous home-ware products introduced in this book.

Towards the end of the 19th century Taiwanese society was confronted by another political calamity when the Qing Dynasty government gifted the island to Japan as a trophy in the First Sino-Japanese War. To the gaze of Japan's emperor, Taiwan was an attractive opportunity where a 'model colony' could be built. His ambition set forth an expansive plan to radically transform the newly acquired territory into a sophisticated modern society (1895–1945).

This is significant because while other Asian countries modernised through Westernisation, here the process was more complex as it evolved through Japanese influences. The primary evidence is Taiwan's magnificent colonial architecture, which catalogues some of the finest examples of Early

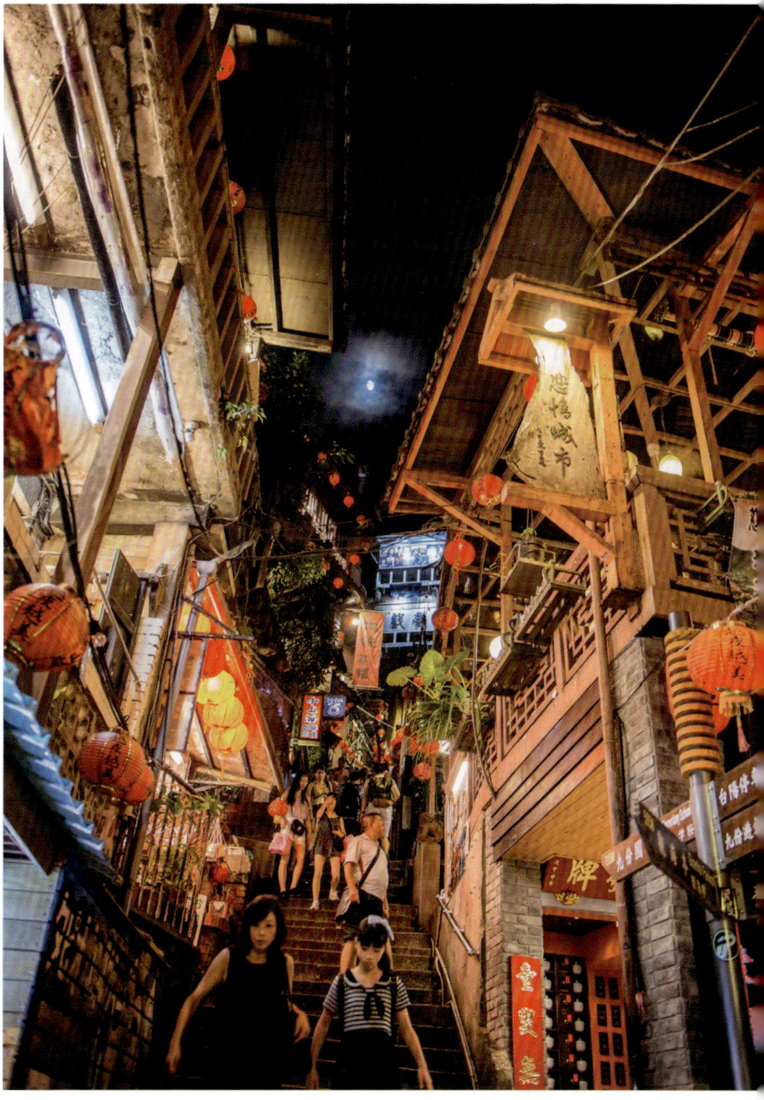

Juifen at night The mountain town north of Taipei was developed during the 1900s gold rush. Its architecture reflects the Japanese colonial era.

Japanese Modernism. Furthermore, during this period an advanced education system—based on studying the arts and sciences—was implemented. Taiwanese intellectuals were urged by Japanese officials to define pictorial and literary representations of the new society by exploring local subject matter. Through various assimilation programs, known as *kominka*, people adopted Japanese as the official language, favoured Japanese diet and even turned to Shintoism for spiritual guidance. Consequently, the cultural shift that occurred shaped and defined Taiwan as distinctly different to the mainland—a matter that continues to be hotly contested.

The hallmarks of Japanese aesthetics are emulated in the works of many designers. For example, packaging design follows the Japanese approach of it being an extension of the product. As the Taiwanese tend to place great importance on enhancing the appreciation value of gifts, packaging often presents visual stories, decorations, or folding intended to make products more adorable. So much so that sometimes the wrapping is more enticing than the contents!

After Japan's capitulation in World War II, Taiwan was returned to the mainland but the reunion was short lived. With Mao Zedong's Communist Party founding the People's Republic of China in 1949 (and thereby changing the political system), the republican nationalists had no other option but to retreat to Taiwan where the jurisdiction of the Republic of China was established. The split between these two doctrines marks the beginning of what would become at times a treacherous, at others an opportunistic, relationship between the mainland and the island. Despite being the first Asian country to hold a democratic election and to be self-governed, Taiwan is an autonomous state without a broadly recognised nationhood. This is, in itself, remarkable.

HOME OF WORLD TREASURES

With the civil unrests of the early 20th century leading to the abdication of the last emperor of China, a large portion of the artefacts of the Forbidden City in Beijing had to be evacuated and eventually brought to safety to the island. Taiwan became home to one of the world's most important cultural institutions: the National Palace Museum in Taipei, or *Gu-gong*. Its permanent collection assembles almost 700,000 pieces of the most significant Chinese artefacts from the Neolithic era to the last Dynastic emperor. These fascinating objects not only record past generations' relentless search for spiritual sustenance—derived from the teachings of Eastern philosophy and the cultivation of the arts—but they also illustrate the development of new techniques and aesthetics.

In dynastic times, under the patronage of the imperial court, artisans expended great efforts to perfect the making of ritual and everyday objects using a variety of materials such as porcelain, lacquer, enamel, ivory, wood, and bamboo. Furthermore, Gu-gong holds precious artefacts brought to the emperors by foreign emissaries. The similarities between these and the objects made in the imperial court reveal that outside influences have contributed to advancing the Chinese civilisation, and that its character is cumulative and pluralistic from its very beginning.

Amongst the museum's most popular exhibits are the curio boxes from the Qing Dynasty period. Their striking designs are intricately constructed of tiny sections intended for safekeeping and hiding miniature valuables. The exquisitely carved inner compartments were usually made of sandalwood with porcelain or mother-of-pearl inlays. Some display delicate ink brush inscriptions. The exterior is finished in lacquer and gold leaf. Visually stunning, the boxes also are wondrous examples of space design efficiency: no cavity is left hollow or unused. Such old inventions are great inspirations for product designers who constantly aspire to find a balance between form, function and beauty.

The museum's director, Mrs Ming-Chu Fung, has championed opportunities for Taiwanese designers to study its vast collections. 'In 2009 we held our first Cultural and Creative Development Camp and opened our galleries to artisans and designers interested in trying out new pathways for interpreting old artefacts. What they came up with was really marvellous! Some created digital and interactive experiences; others imprinted home decor and furnishings with stylised details from famous calligraphic works; contemporary jewellery designs emerged, amazing new tea-ware, stationery, even mobile phone accessories were made. Our sincere wish is that such training programs enhance the productivity of related industries. It is a good way to support and promote Taiwanese design', says Mrs Fung enthusiastically.

One of Gu-gong's key business initiatives has been the special licensing program through which several local companies—Tittot, Franz, NewChi, Chullery and others, as well as Italian company Alessi— have developed products based on famous pieces from the collection, several of which are featured here. Specialising in fine porcelain, Franz has graced dining tables around the world with its ornamental plates, cups

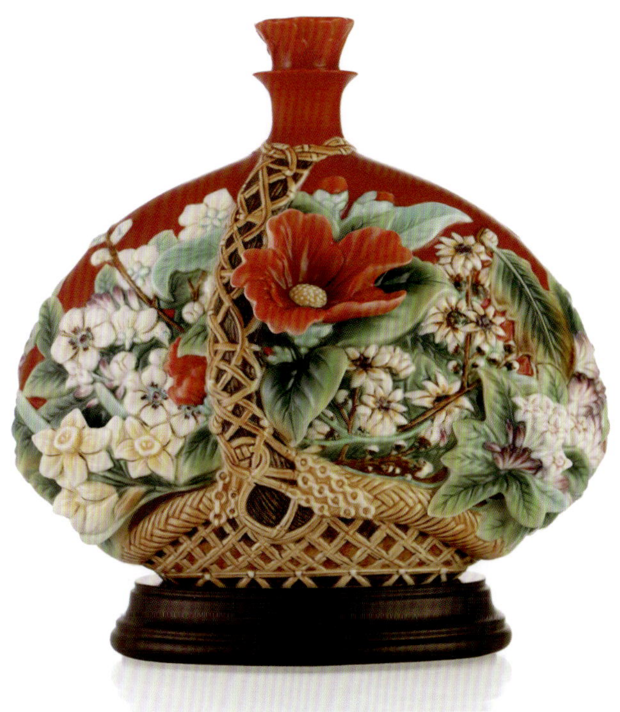

Amidst the Flowers a Jug of Wine, National Palace Museum 90th Year Anniversary Wine Bottle

and vases decorated with sculpted flowers, lovebirds and animals. World leaders have exchanged its objects as messengers of good will. 'Our mission is to revive classical art into objects that suit contemporary tastes', states Franz Chen, founder and CEO. 'We are successful because we strive to combine the best of Eastern and Western decorative design knowledge. But to me it's not so important if the company has a long-term longevity or not. What's at the heart of our work is to bring into the world products that could withstand the test of time, that are substantial and, dare I say, have some impact to humanity. Would they last 100 years? That's the real deal!'

INDUSTRIAL BOOM

In Taiwan the period from the 1950s to 1980s was a harsh era ruled by martial law during which all forms of cultural expression had to be re-framed within a Han Chinese context and anything distinctly local became taboo. The regime suppressed all political opposition, ruthlessly tracking down even the faintest hint of dissent. The legacies of the Japanese colonial time were overwritten by a new vocabulary of classical Chinese themes and imagery. Mandarin Chinese replaced Japanese as the official language while the local Taiwanese language, spoken by the majority of the population, was pushed into the private domain.

Because of its strategic position during the looming Korean War (1950–1953), Taiwan signed a mutual defence treaty with the United States, as it was leading the UN troupes to defend the South of the Korean peninsula while China backed the North. Needing a powerful regional allay, America poured foreign aid and investment into the local economy. This suited the technocracy-centred planning of the government as it spearheaded Taiwan's industrialisation through engineering based on the US model. By adopting American know-how, many businesses expanded rapidly and profitably. An illustrative example is the massive turnaround of industrial giant Tatung Co. (est. 1918). In a landmark overhaul strategy, the steel manufacturer set forth to diversify its operations into designing and producing all kinds of new electrical appliances, including refrigerators, air conditioners, television sets, radios and more. At first, the in-house technicians worked in its prototyping centres but as

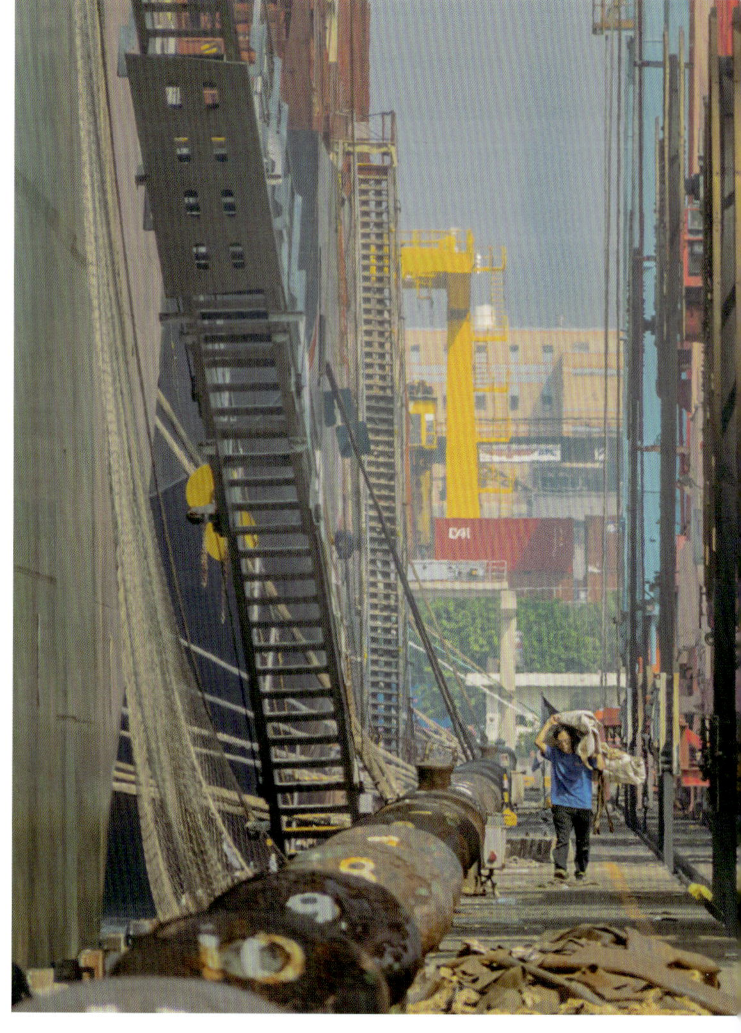

Port of Kaohsiung

market demand grew, in 1971, a specialised industrial design department dedicated to product development was formed. Soon after Tatung became a benefactor of a technology university and a vocational school, both established to provide specialist training to prospective employees and to drive Taiwanese product design innovation forward (page 178).

During the martial law time—primarily out of fear that with the importation of radios people would listen to communist propaganda beamed from across the Taiwan Strait—restrictions were imposed on radio components from the mainland. As a result many local assembly plants started to make the needed parts. By implementing US and European industrial processes and utilising cheap domestic labour, these businesses became highly self-sufficient and capable of producing almost anything demanded by overseas clients. Taiwan became a manufacturing hub for some of the world's most powerful brands. But this good fortune was a double-edged sword because working for others meant little concern for design value: counterfeiting was widespread. The lack of copyright protection wreaked havoc on the marketability of Taiwanese goods and demotivated designers from developing original projects. As an intervention measure the central government made an ambitious move to turn the economy around once again: the beautiful island was set to become technology island.

During the 1980s a national platform for advancing the broader benefits of industrial design through technology was established. Taiwan became one of the founders of the International Council of Societies of Industrial Design (ICSID) alongside the most powerful design nations of the region: Japan, Korea and Australia. Government-supported organisations started to offer specialised training and staged expositions for international buyers. Across the tertiary institutions industrial design became recognised as a discipline in its own right, distinct from engineering. Inaugurated in 1981, the Taipei International Design Exhibition, Taiwan Design Expo's predecessor, grew into a launch pad for local products.

The second wave of the industrial boom brought empowerment. Some of most robust technology companies in the world—Acer Inc, ASUSTeK Computer Inc (page 208), Quanta Computer Inc, Taiwan Semiconductor Manufacturing Co Ltd, and Datex Systems Inc (later D-Link Corp)—were established during this era. These powerhouses of the IT industry produced a vast range of items: from desktop computers, tablets, flat screens and smart phones, to motherboards, graphic cards and servers. 'Made in Taiwan' became the brand.

NEW ERA OF INNOVATION AND CREATIVITY

With the advancement of the global market economy of the 1990s Taiwan found itself at a new crossroad. Market liberalisation enabled companies to trade globally, but it also challenged the very factories that had created its prosperity in earlier decades. As these could no longer offer competitive advantage, their foreign investors started relocating. Many previously thriving industries slowed down; places once vibrant with activity sunk into ghost towns.

Cultural reinvention and economic renewal arose through a new wave of design thinking. Companies willing to evolve their operations from original equipment manufacturer (OEM) to original design manufacturer (ODM) gave themselves a chance to emerge from the depths of the downturn relatively unscathed. In addition to making goods for overseas buyers, these companies focused on investing in their own IP and started releasing products under their own brands, as recounted in some of the stories here.

Today Taiwan's patents registration per capita is exceeded only by the US and Japan, ranking it amongst Asia's most knowledge-driven economies. Designers are conscious of the need to develop their reputation on the merits of their own original work. They have learned from previous generations that adaptability, matched with efficiency and high quality, is essential to remaining relevant in a highly globalised industry.

The self-initiative of the creative community is especially commendable. In 2006 a group of designers working at ASUS, together with peers from other design houses, started meeting after hours in a cafe in Tamsui, a historical district north of Taipei. Dissatisfied with the lack of creative outlets in their daytime jobs, they pondered: What would it take for Taipei to have a design exposition similar to those of Milano and Tokyo? They were convinced that if the industry was to mature, an open and free cross-disciplinary dialogue about design had to be stimulated. They knew designers had

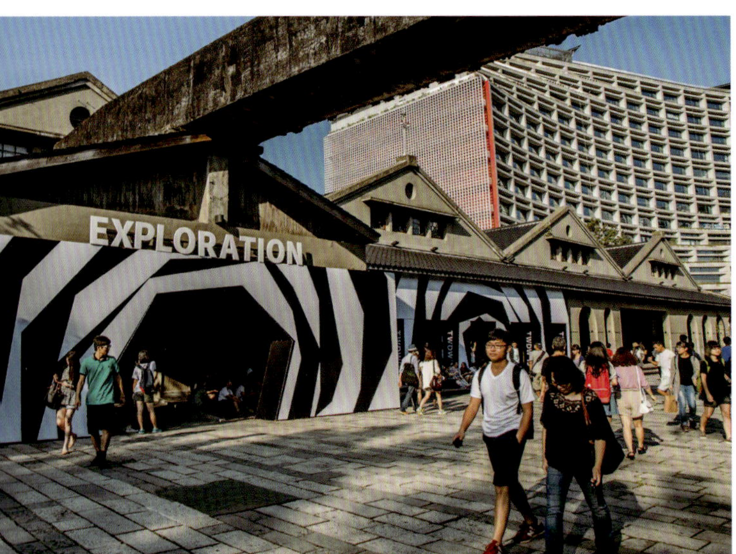

Taiwan Designers' Week 2015

to proactively use their skills not only to service the corporations but also to start their own businesses. The concept for Taiwan's own designer's week eventually emerged.

The designers pooled personal resources to stage their first exhibition of at the prestigious Eslite Bookstore. Curated collaboratively under the theme of '50 Benches', it featured as many examples of the popular item of furniture. At a time when Taipei's trendsetters were keeping up with the latest fashions coming from Europe and Japan, the show was big news because everything on display was local. In the following year the group staged another exhibition at the heritage listed Japanese Military Barracks, also in Taipei's Xinyi district. Visitors were pleasantly surprised by the diversity of objects and the confidence with which designers referenced local themes.

What began as a brave experiment grew into a substantial and influential project: in 2007 the group registered Taiwan Designers' Web as a studio, which become the official organiser of Taiwan Designers' Week (TWDW), with Timothy Liao taking over its management as a full-time director in 2009. 'We have come a long way since those coffee shop meetings. When Huashan Creative Park partnered with us to mount our first ticketed trade show we didn't even have floor plans! Exhibitors just brought in their products and set them up themselves', recalls executive director Ben Chiu. 'Today we have more than 200 studios participating with over 500 products on display. Tens of thousands of visitors come to TWDW and we're internationally recognised. In spite of this tremendous popularity, the principle of designers supporting design has remained our core value.'

The government stages its own initiatives aimed at encouraging design excellence. It rebranded its design competition into Golden Pin Design Awards and designated 2011 as the 'Year of Design', commencing with the inauguration of Songshan Cultural and Creative Park in Taipei. Located at the former Songshan Tobacco Factory, the site is one of the jewels of Japanese colonial architecture. Because the complex was originally envisioned to be an exemplary 'industrial village', in addition to its warehouses there are also a neo-baroque garden, nature pond and recreational facilities. The beautifully restored factory site is now home to Taiwan Design Museum, Taiwan Design Center and several creative associations.

2011 Year of Design presented two major events: Taipei World Design Expo and World Design Congress, both of which have been unprecedented in scope and international reach. The Expo covered 47,000 square meters of exhibitor spaces showcasing some 58 enterprises, 50 design studios, 43 promotional agencies and 25 schools of design. 'When we were planning our show, many questions came to mind about the role of design', explains Sean Hu, curator of In Bliss, one of the exhibitions in the Expo. 'We were asking ourselves: if design is used to solve problems, why isn't society made better? And whilst the world is still excited about the latest commercial opportunities, the planet is breaking down in ways that are unfathomable. It seems we're living in denial, can design wakes us up?'

Shedding light on the big questions of our time, the Expo emphasised the importance not only of environmental protection but also the necessity for

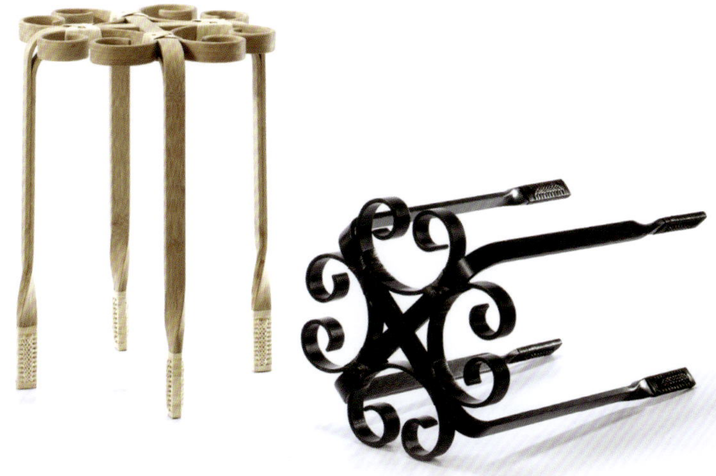

Bamboo stool by Sally Lin

sustainable living for local communities through the rejuvenation of cultural traditions. Design is regarded as a means to build meaningful connections between individuals, communities and nature through which a more spiritually oriented society could evolve. According to a survey conducted by the Ministry of Education, there are 70 types of crafts still being practiced in Taiwan, including paper cutting, knotting, woodblock printing, jade stone carving and paper lantern making . A small group of artisans continues to diligently use this knowledge to keep the traditions alive for future generations.

As part of its mission to protect cultural assets the National Taiwan Craft Research Institute in Nantou, together with Taiwan Design Centre, devised a pilot project for matched collaborations between artisans and designers titled Yii Craft & Design. In Mandarin Chinese the meaning of yii has a special connotation. It is made up of three characters with the same sound *yi*: the first 易 refers to the belief that transformation is an underlying law of Nature; the second 意 is the character for

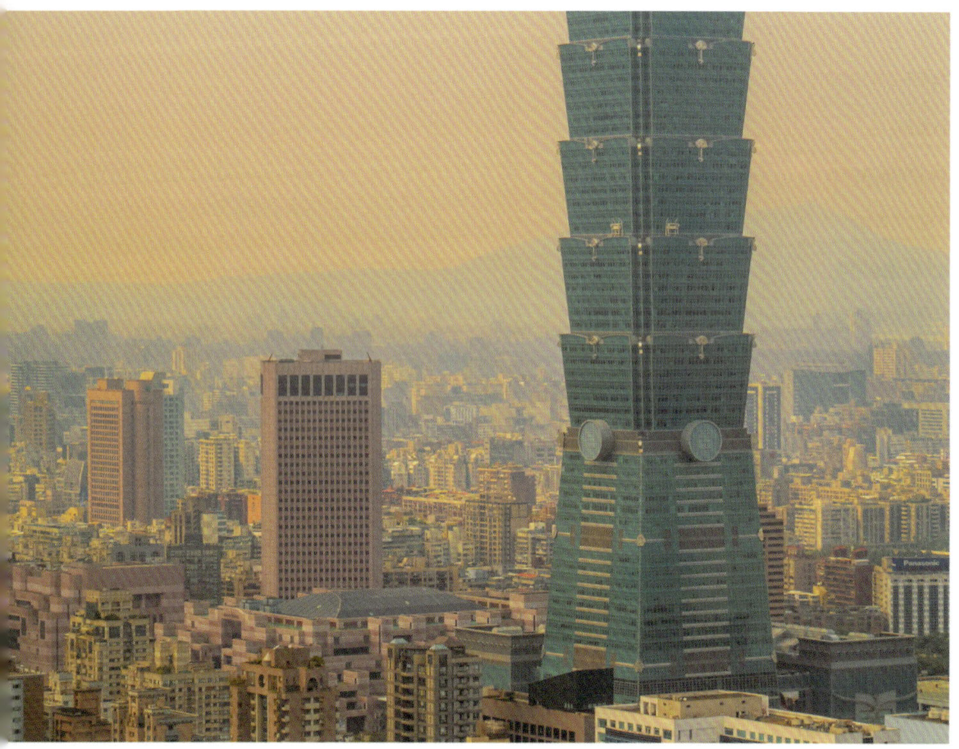

Taipei twilight

architectural masterpiece towering one hundred and one floors above the city. Until recently the tallest building in the world, the tower was designed by C.Y. Lee and partners to represent a symbiosis between ancient wisdom and the evolution of our technological times. An extraordinary engineering marvel that can withstand typhoons and earthquakes, it is also the world's largest 'green' building. The tower commemorates the arrival of the new century and alludes to a future underpinned by technology. The main structure comprises eight segments of eight floors each, with the number 88 signifying great fortune. Stylistically, Taipei 101 resembles a pagoda, the traditional connector between Heaven and Earth, as well as a bamboo stalk surging with growth and strength.

'meaning', 'idea' and 'wish'; the third 藝 refers to 'artistry'. When transcribed in this way the concept behind Yii Craft & Design is understood as an expression of a deeply held desire that through meaningful ideas and creativity Taiwan's crafts can be revived into beautiful products or decorations. Forty different items were developed during the program. Among them, a hybrid chair by Pili Wu (page 120) and a sofa assembled from 999 hand-woven bamboo balls by Kevin Chou.

DESIGNING EVERYTHING EVERYWHERE

No other landmark expresses more breathtakingly Taiwan's dream for the future than Taipei 101, the

This eagerness for renewal and prosperity is felt everywhere around the capital. Since 2011, its creative community together with the local government campaigned hard to win the bid for Taipei's appointment as the 2016 World Design Capital. Themed 'Adaptive City: Design in Motion', the program aims to embed design thinking into every aspect of the city's governance, balancing modernisation with environmental protection and sustainability.

'Taipei has its own unique character: old night markets can still be seen right next to ultramodern buildings. We are very international, yet totally local. In the process of preparing the bid we discovered that if it were to provide better services for residents and visitors our city's public administration has to embrace design thinking across all levels', comments Tony Chen, former director of Taiwan Design Centre. 'We enjoy a world-class metro system but most facilities need to be made universally accessible. There is a lot of scope to improve the green credentials of our capital. I hope one day design permeates every aspect of how we live in Taipei.'

The 88 inspiring products featured in this book demonstrate that this wish can be realised. For a place which has had to adapt so many times, and which in some way still struggles to define its identity, the high reputation of Taiwan's manufacturing and design is a hard-earned achievement. The objects presented together here tell an authentic story: about a place where centuries of crafts traditions continue to be practiced alongside the latest developments in digital media. Today it is no longer 'Made in Taiwan' that matters. Instead, the deep worth of this work is that it is designed on the Beautiful Island.

Annie Ivanova

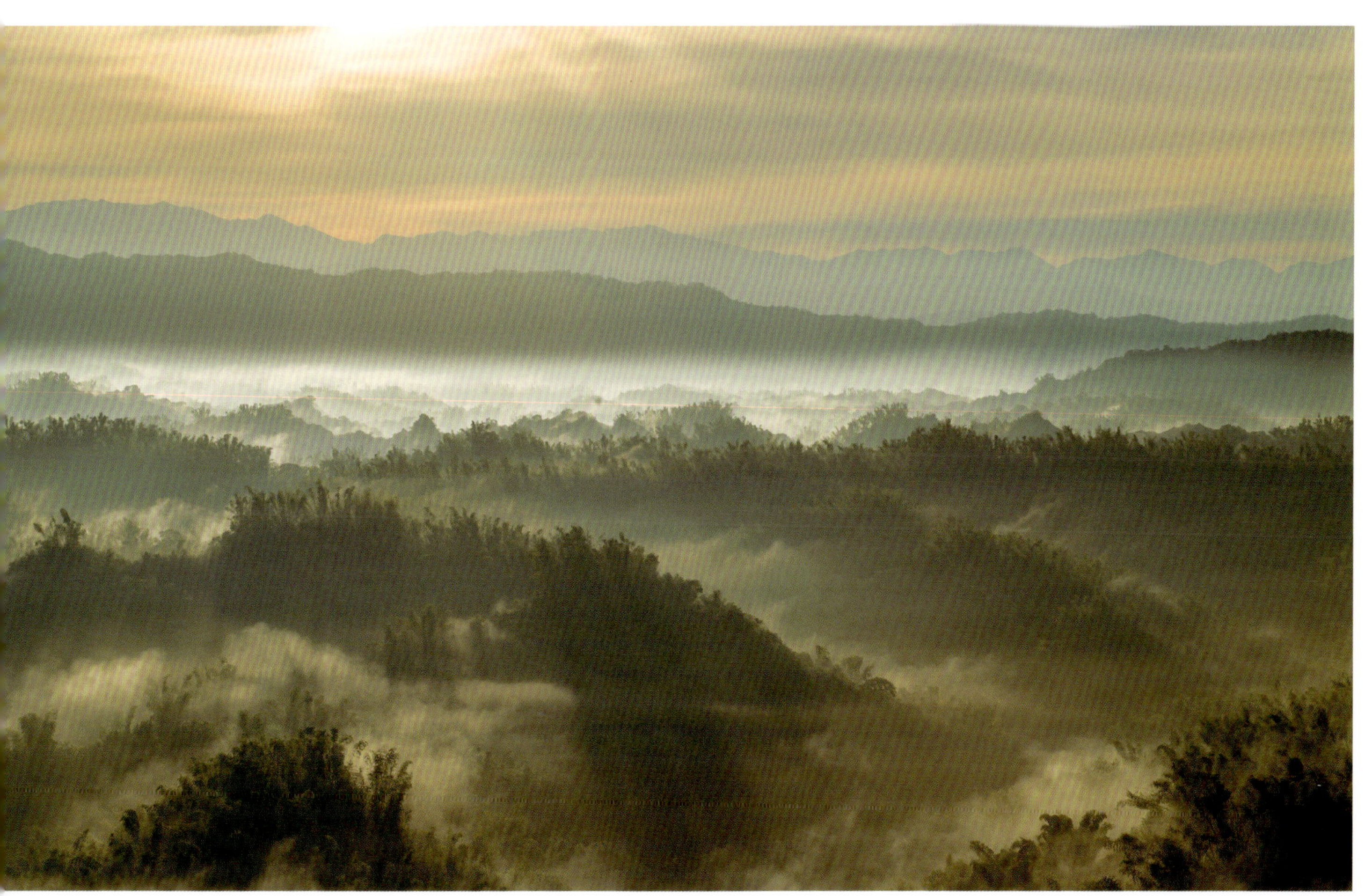

Tainan, Erliao Mountain Sunrise

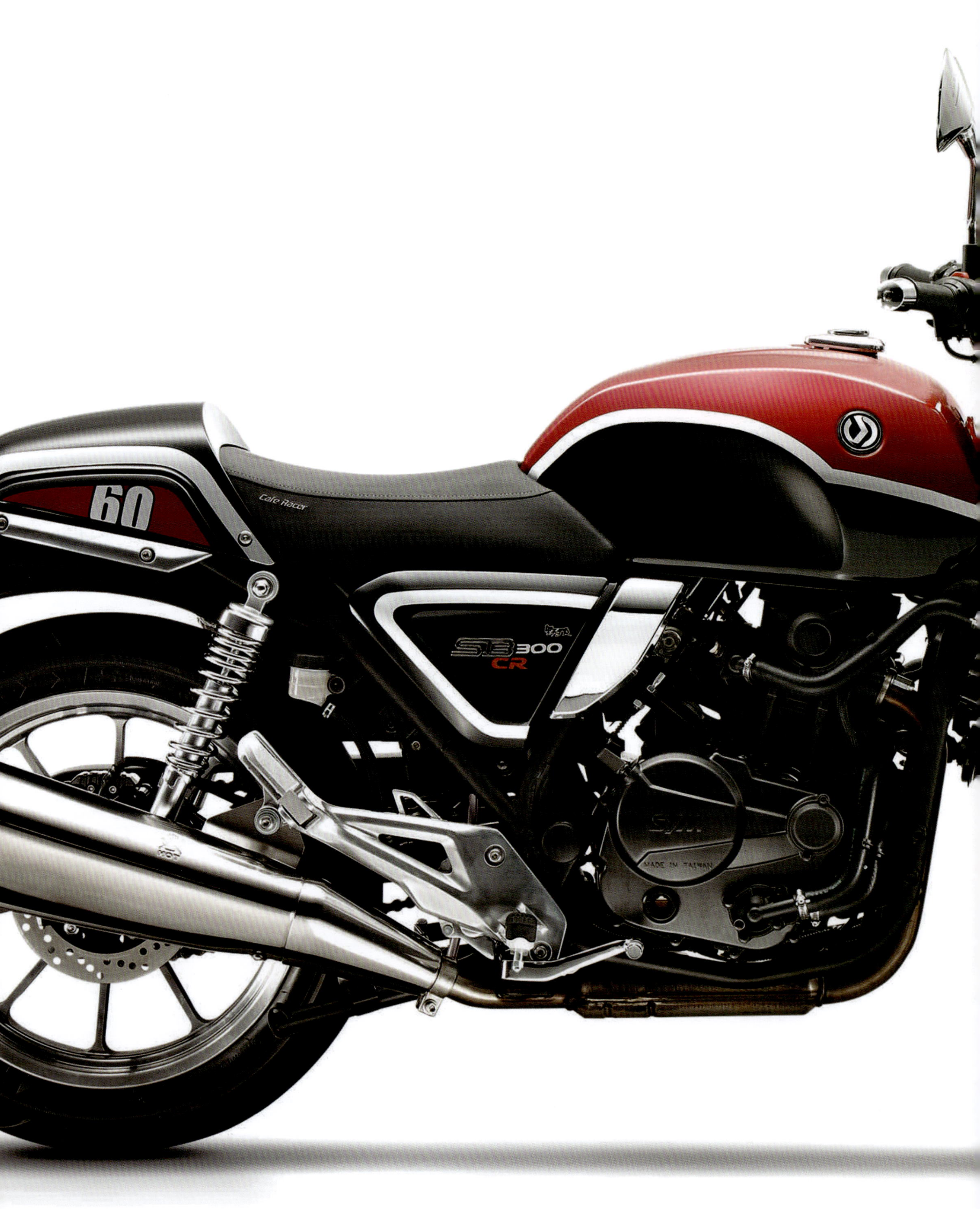

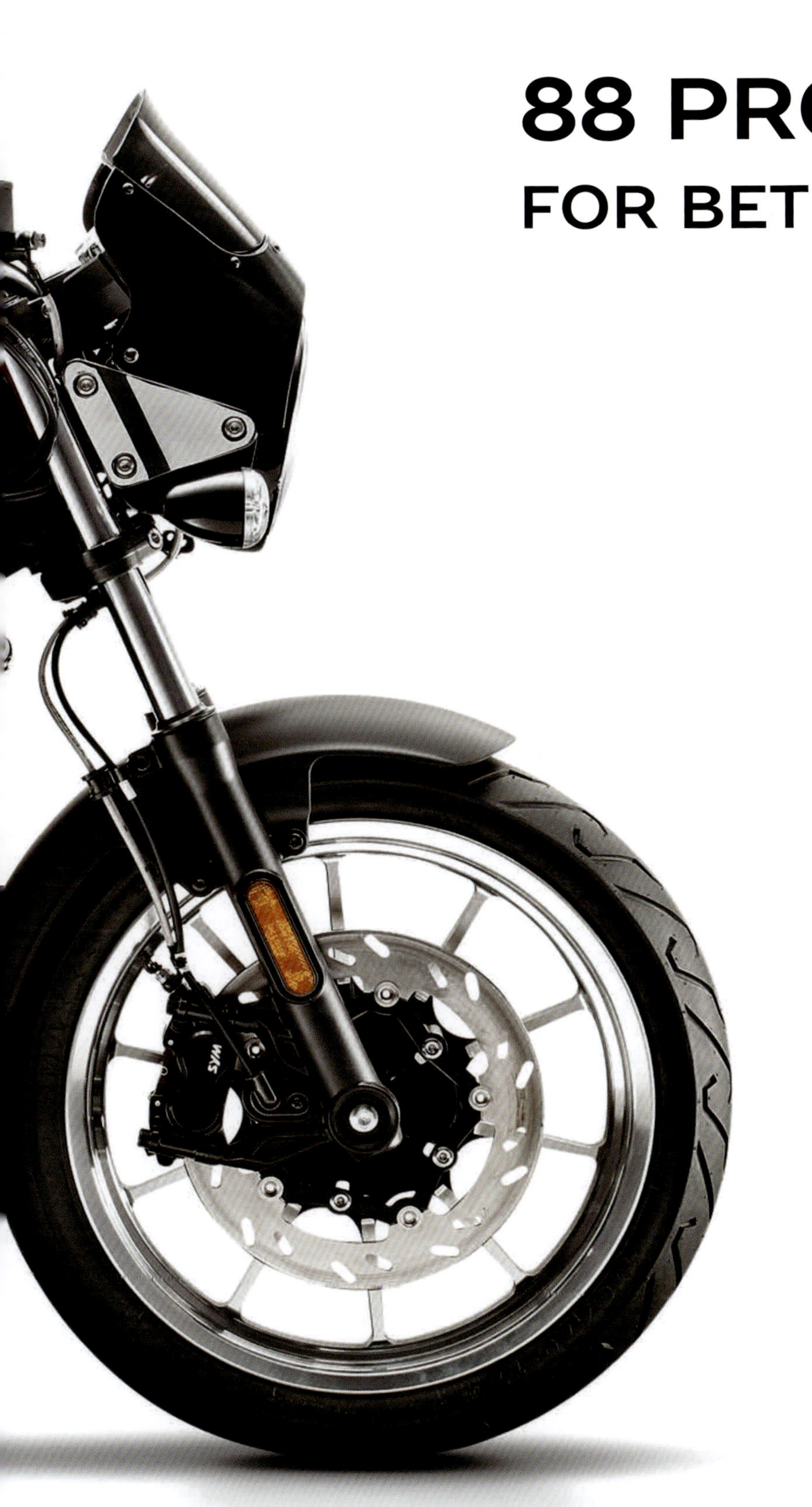

88 PRODUCTS

FOR BETTER LIVING

01

3 X 3

Module Flower Pot

3+2 Design Studio | Chiu Tong Plastics

In densely populated cities like Taipei, portable landscaping spontaneously sprouts around residential areas: building entrances, narrow lanes and alleys often overflow with potted plants. These mini oases of delicate greenery cover up the concrete sprawls, but they can be easily repatriated to shelter from menacing storms. Indoor spaces, no matter how compact, also accommodate the potted garden phenomenon.

'Gifting a miniature plant in a small brown plastic pot is the kind of thing Taipei hipsters would do. It's a little gesture of affection', says Eason Xie. 'But plants aren't toys; they need care. Most of us get lazy looking after them: for sure, I'm guilty of many plant crimes! So we wondered what if we designed a pot system that could help urban-garden enthusiasts organise their hobby better.'

3x3 is a plants basket that fits three individual small pots, with a chassis water tray attached to its base. If plants need to be taken outdoors, the pots can be detached from the basket and anchored into soil with a clip-on peg. This prevents them from tipping over when the weather becomes windy, or if pets jump over them. The cylindrical core of the module functions as a stand for the accompanying set of gardening accessories, such as a plant label, magnifying glass and scissors.

'We made the basin tray attachable so it can be moved together with the basket. This frees up one hand to be able to open a door or turn on a light when a person carries the module. The system also drains excess water, which is important. In Taiwan mosquitoes are rampant and very annoying because they tend to get attracted by stagnant water. The way this product is designed makes it more difficult for the potted plants to become a breeding ground for mosquitoes.'

The eager gardener can stack sets vertically or line them up to form a variety of potted landscapes. Breaking away from the traditional earthy brown pot, the product comes in seven candy colours that mix well with nature's pallets of luscious green leaves and flower blooms. It is an invitation for creative enjoyment ... in a mini pot!

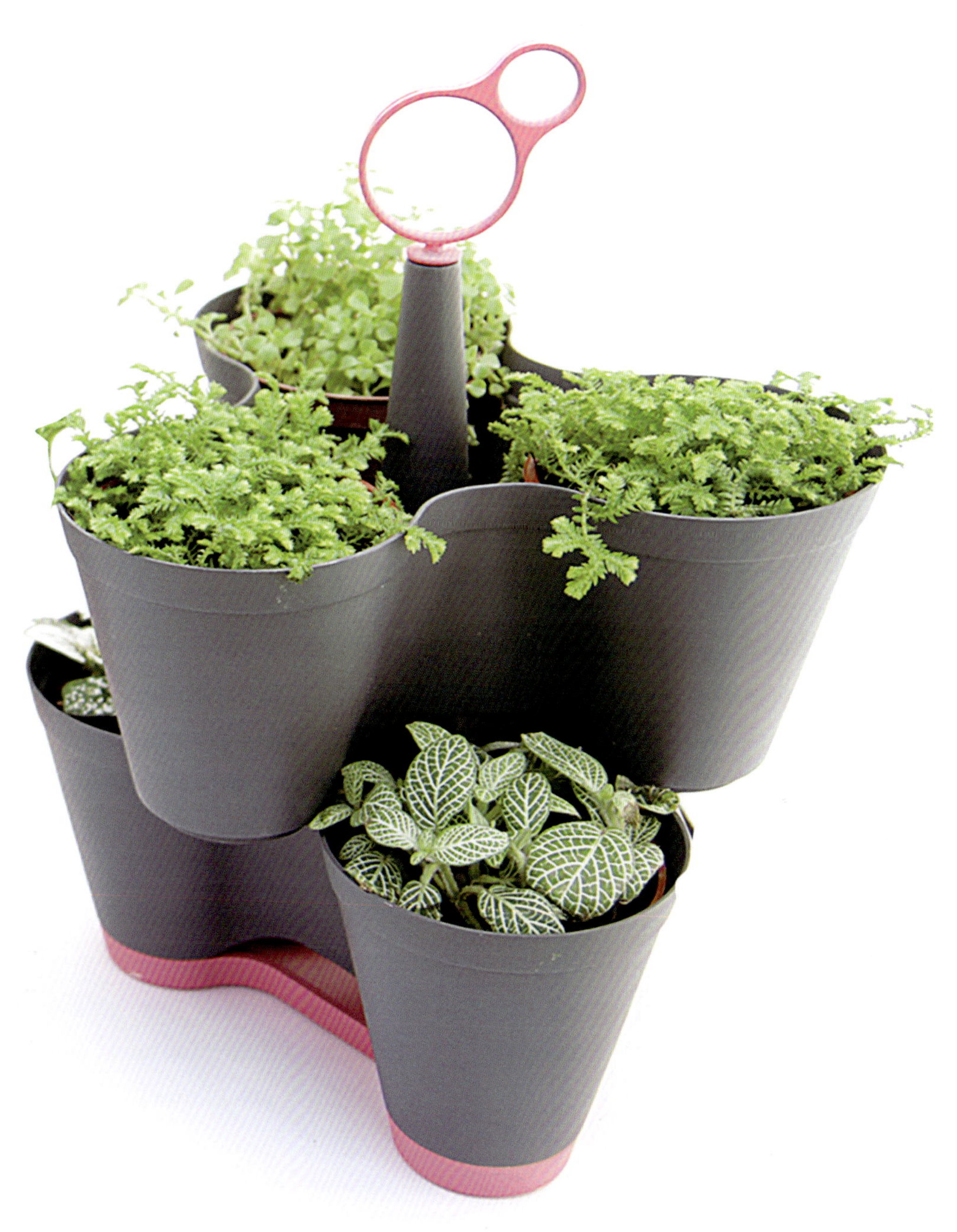

02

4TH DIMENSION

Wall Clock

22 Design Studio

The *4th Dimension* wall clock is a conceptual piece created as a visual representation of the space-time phenomenon. Made of concrete, a key feature of the clock is its miniature staircase held inside a sculptural cylinder. Instead of numbers each hour is represented on the dial as an ascending segment on the spiral interface, with the two ends overlapping at the 12.00-hour point. A tiny gap is intentionally left between the upper and lower ends of the spiral as a way of alluding to the infinitude of time.

Set against a grey wall the clock can be almost indistinguishable from its architectural surrounds. Only the smooth movement of the three thin handles indicates its function as a silently ticking timepiece. Sean Yu, founder with Yiting Cheng, credits his admiration of the great Japanese architect Tadao Ando as having had profound influence on how he resolved the form of this object.

Although critical of the way concrete is used throughout Taiwan—'some buildings just look awful', he admits—the young designer finds concrete an interesting material to work with. 'I went to Japan on a personal pilgrimage to some of Ando's sites. What I recall most vividly from the trip is the way he has made concrete walls function as projection screens upon which light and shadows are constantly interplaying ... This image of time passing pushed me to think critically about my clock. It had to capture a *feeling of time* not merely count it.'

The geometry and simple mechanics of the clock perfectly convey this idea primarily through the application of concrete as a material of architectural durability that also weathers as the days pass. But crafting concrete by hand on a tiny scale can be fickle, as the makers soon discovered.

Sean explains: 'In the beginning we couldn't get the concrete's viscosity right: it needs to be sufficiently low to be moulded yet viscous enough to take form. It's like baking cake; the mixture has to set. Occasionally air bubbles would get trapped, or the surface may not turn out completely even. We like such small irregularities because they are a natural feature of something being crafted by the human hand. We are mindful, though, the clock needs to satisfy diverse tastes and some customers prefer the industrially polished finish.'

4th Dimension is one of the most popular products made by the studio. Perhaps feeling pressured by a seeming lack of time, busy urbanites enjoy its philosophical twist: time may not stand still, but at least it is set in concrete!

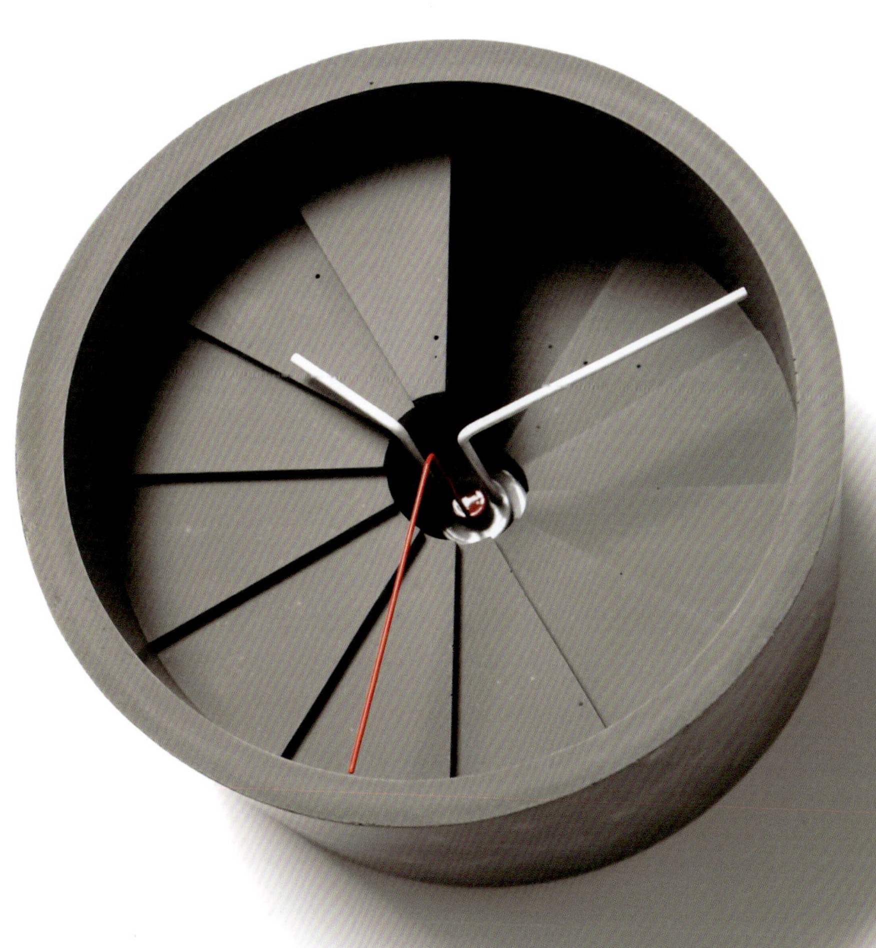

03

ADER CHAIR

Ergonomic Chair

Ader Chen | Xcellent

Not all office chairs are created equal. Those with superior ergonomics are favoured as they can support the body maintain a good posture over prolonged periods of seated activity. There are plenty of choices, of course, with some classic designs enjoying a cult status. To bring something new into a crowded market space is not easy. For its part, Xcellent has been commended by the furniture industry.

Named after its creator, the design of the *Ader Chair* has taken into account functionality, user lifestyle choices and price. Company design director Ader Chen shares his concern about working in an advanced economy where the struggle for any business is efficiency: finding more cost-effective solutions to fabricate a product without compromising its special features and qualities.

'Sitting at a desk day and night slouches the spine and it is not good for our overall wellbeing. The problem with good ergonomic chairs is that their price is still out of reach for the average customer. The question then is how to innovate with the materials and technology we have at our disposal to produce high quality office furniture that is also affordable.'

The first thing a user notices when testing the *Ader Chair* is how uncomplicated it is to operate. Its height and reclining angle can be adjusted intuitively.

The shoulders remain relaxed and well supported by the arm rests, which are positioned low enough to fit under a desk. The chair can be manoeuvred smoothly around the office so different tasks can be performed without one needing to get up.

The backrest is moulded through a plastic injection tooling process. It is slightly bendable in order to flex around the body when it takes back, forth and sideway stretches. 'We invested considerably in the production process of the curvilinear lines of the backrest to ensure it gives maximum lower back support. Even when a person wants to take a power nap in the chair and reclines the back to 40 degrees, the lumber support is still excellent', explains Chen.

The seat is padded with a thick foam cushion, factory-moulded and punctured with small holes for aeration. This hidden yet essential detail feels like a blessing during the sweltering summer months, when every office worker complains about the unbearable humidity. The calligraphic lines of this piece make it blend well with both Asian and Western interior spaces. Its elegance is inviting and its comfort addictive. In Chen's words, to be sitting on his chair is to 'enjoy a warm embrace and a good feeling that all is well in the world'.

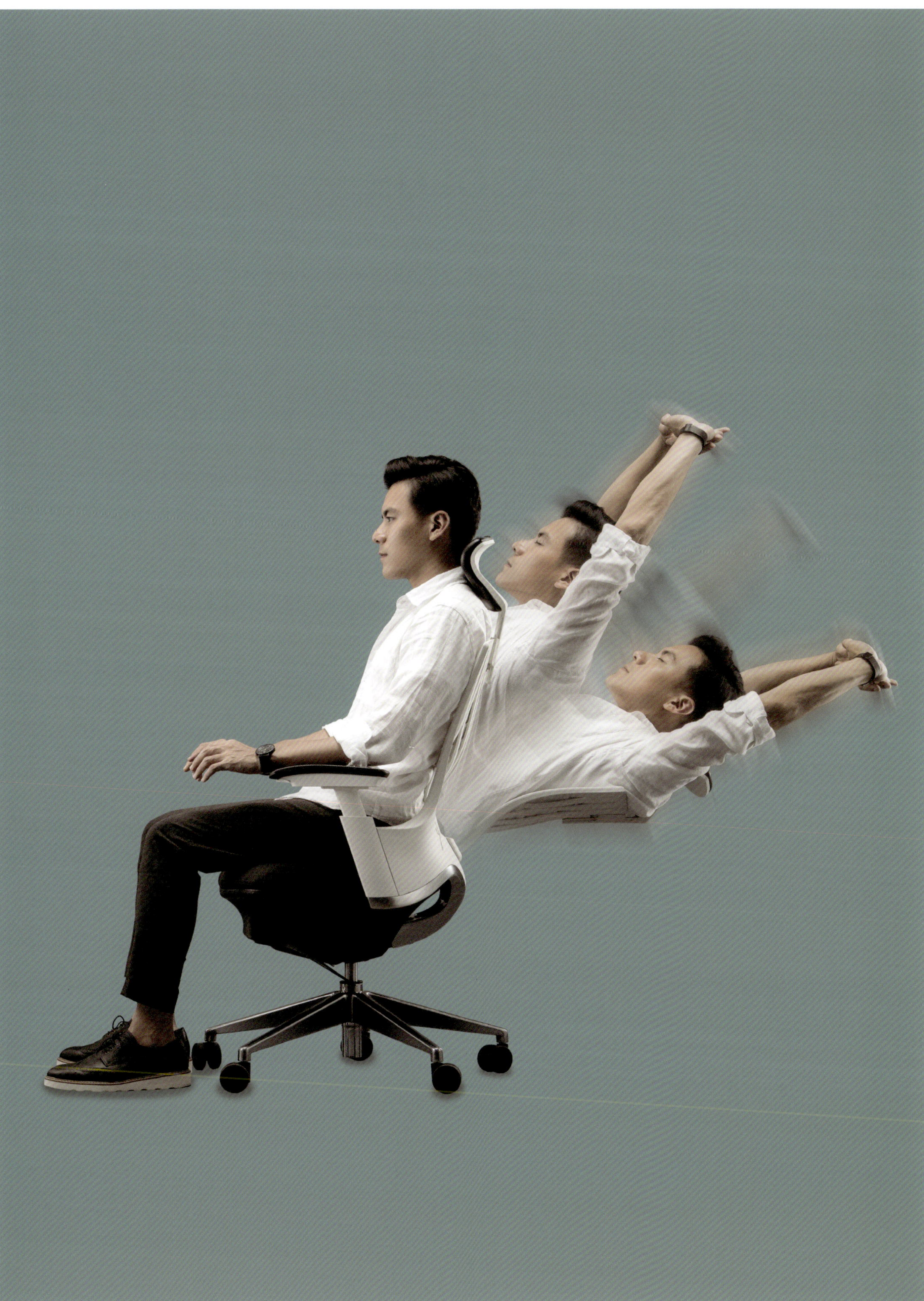

O4

AEOLUS

Shoulder Bag / Windbreaker

Taiwan Textile Research Institute

Named after the ruler of the winds in Greek mythology, *Aeolus* is an adaptable shoulder bag designed to double up as a fashionable windbreaker with a hood. It was developed at the internationally renowned Taiwan Textile Research Institute (TTRI) where product designers work alongside scientists to devise alternative applications for high-tech fabrics.

As a bag *Aeolus* is big enough to carry a mobile phone, wallet, cosmetic pouch, and set of keys. When opened up the bag turns into a pocket that is tucked into the inner backside of a jacket with all valuables still safely kept. The fibre nylon is derived from plant oil as its raw material. The fabric's structural design keeps the wearer shielded from the wind, and relatively dry. 'This product is suitable for Taiwan. The weather here is quite temperamental … one minute it's sunny, the next it rains. It is helpful for a cyclist or a walker to have a small item on them that can offer some temporary protection from the elements until the person reaches shelter', explains Wei-Hung Chen.

Scientist by training and working as a senior materials researcher, Chen is often asked to crossover into the field of industrial design, constantly sketching ideas that potentially could be developed into smart products. 'The first jacket was made in a reflective yellow colour because we were thinking it's better for road safety. The problem was that when folded into the bag it crinkles and some people felt self-conscious wearing clothing that's not ironed. It may sound a small thing but it had to be addressed. One of our cloth designers, James Hsu, came up with a graphic solution replacing the fluoro colour with a patterned print. The geometrical design is quite fashionable and it masks the wrinkling.'

Many of the of products developed at the Institute use fibre derived from castor oil, also known as bio-based fibre, as opposed to the petroleum-derived equivalents. It is his area of expertise, and one he passionately promotes the ecological benefits of. 'Oil is a finite resource while anything growing from the earth can be replenished. It is a smarter choice', he concludes.

The current challenge with bio-fibres is to advance the manufacturing processes so that the materials and derived products become more affordable to more people. Like many of his generation Chen hopes that makers and consumers can join efforts to be a part of the bio-solution for protecting the ecological balance of the planet.

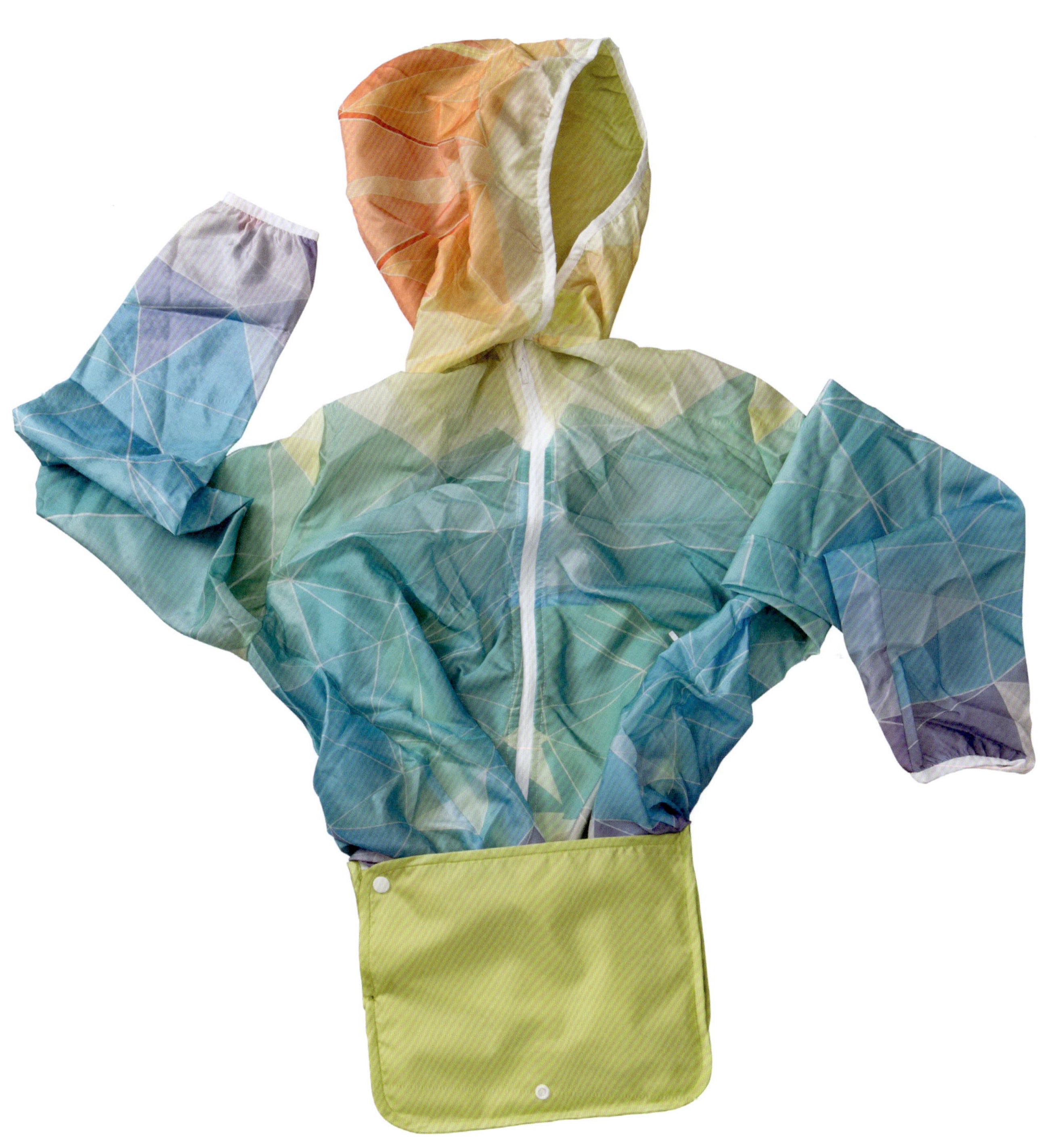

05

AKIAK

Greenland Paddle
GEARLAB

For the love of Nature: paddle or peddle! With a shared passion for the great outdoors, Henry Chang and Chung-Shih Sun love to design products for adventure sports enthusiasts and to promote human powered, zero carbon footprint modes of mobility. 'Spending time in nature is an inseparable part of our way of living. We have a designer's instinct to seek to improve the gears we use so we can make our own experiences more enjoyable', says Chang.

This is how their company was created: out of necessity. As avid kayakers, the two friends were using European style paddles, the only models available in Taiwan. These are built for Caucasian anatomical proportions and are not quite comfortable for the Asian body. The European paddles are also good for sprinting as they propel considerable power but are not suited as lifestyle gear for daily expeditions because they can cause muscle strain.

Being a Taiwanese-Canadian, Chang decided to research the indigenous kayak making techniques of both Taiwan and Canada, which unexpectedly took him all the way to Greenland. Throughout the centuries the Greenlandic Inuit have developed unique sea-kayaking techniques using a specially shaped gear known as the Greenland paddle. The gear is lightweight and narrow yet it can generate excellent hydrodynamic glides with amazing efficiency.

Based on the Greenlandic wooden model, the two designers spent three years developing its modern cousin. The unique feature of *AKIAK* is that it is moulded in carbon fibre. It has a narrow body with its extreme width being just enough to allow the paddler to grasp it between the thumb and the forefinger in a tight grip. This allows for over 35 paddle scrolls to be performed based on the Nordic paddling style.

The advantage for the paddler is that a quick shift can be made to an extended grip, thus, extending the paddle for braces, rolls or sweeps in response to changing environmental conditions. The design considerably improves the effectiveness of each stroke and the amount of air pulled down along the blade. The lightweight material floats on the water surface, making the paddle a versatile tool in various situations. Its slim blades are easier to manoeuvre by smaller bodied paddlers. The range comes in five grip sizes which can be taken apart with the click of a button for easy storage.

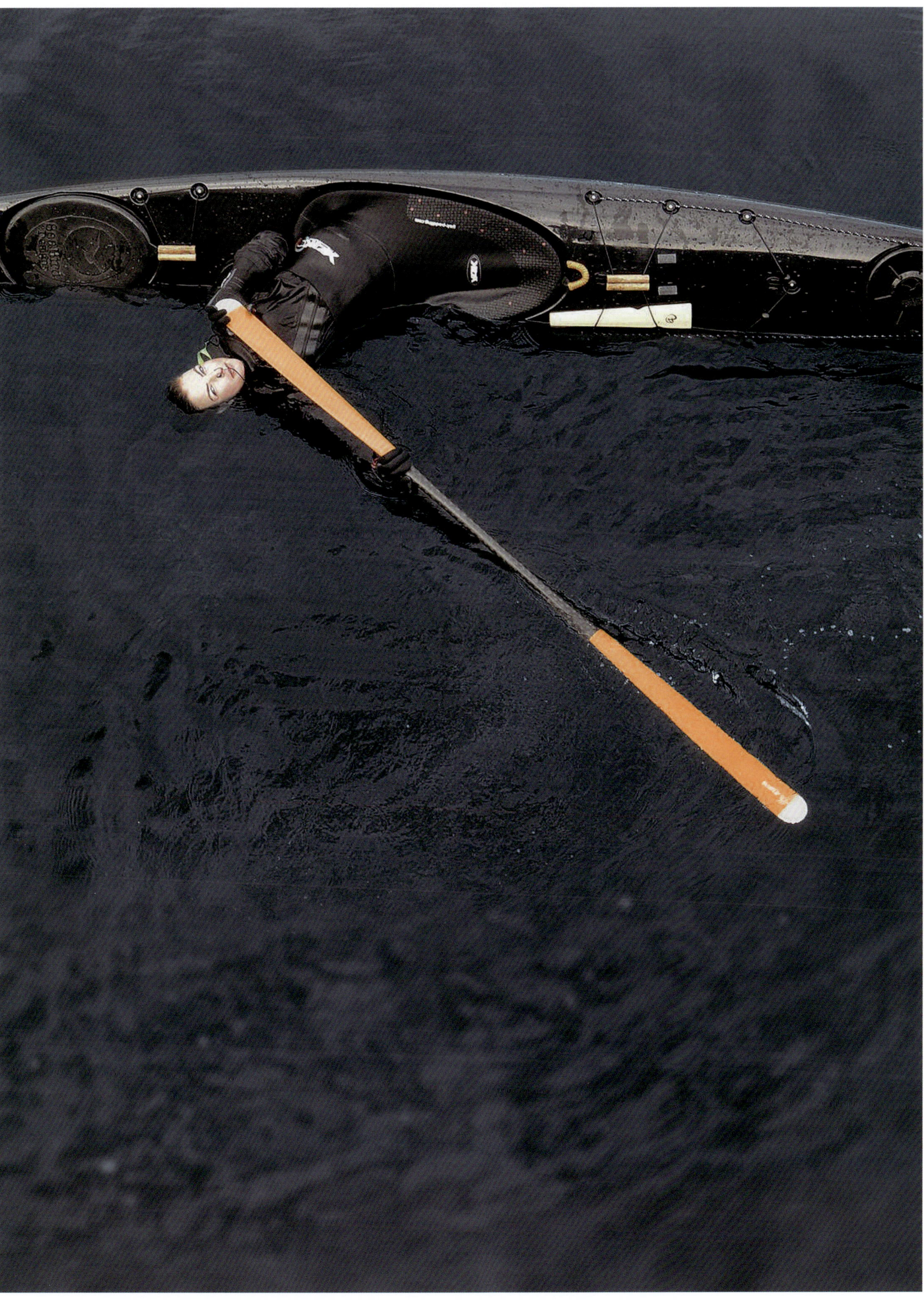

06

ANIMAL CHAIRS

Stools

biaugust

With expertise in visual communication Cloud Lu and Owen Chuang have a quirky approach towards product design: 'We're a bit obsessive about how things look. We really care if an object creates a good atmosphere or not, function comes later. Products needn't be high tech to be great, just clever enough to bring a lasting enjoyment. A chair can be a straight piece of furniture or a comfort creature, it all depends on how it is designed.'

The future business partners started working together while both were living in Japan, and named their company biaugust as both are born in the month of August. Being immersed in a different culture inevitably made them look at their own heritage with renewed curiosity. 'We needed to find our own authentic voice and differentiate our practice. For us, it meant going back to our cultural roots. At the other side of the equation, our craftsmen need alternative avenues for applying their skills to survive. Small companies like ours can be a link between the workshop and the market', explains Lu.

The company's big breakthrough came out of the blue. In 2011, leading luxury goods brand Hermès discovered their work in a magazine and invited them to participate in its annual campaign celebrating the 'spirit of craftsmanship'. The duo came up with a fun concept to create a series of animal furniture—an elephant cabinet, a pink flamingo lamp, a piglet stool—upholstering each piece with silk scarves from the brand's collection. After months of hard work, 42 fantastical creatures appeared at 6 signature stores in Taipei. The designers personally styled each shop window as a seamstress atelier. 'The project was a mega hit but not without difficulties', reminisce the designers. 'What we enjoyed the most, was seeing our work connect local furniture makers with textile artisans from France. We kept going with the concept and made *Animal Chairs* and *Animal Family*, released under our brand name.'

Animal Chairs are four stools shaped after the form of four animals. With a little bit of imagination one can see a poodle dog with fancy-styled fur, a gracefully alert pony, a lucky buffalo, and a friendly little lamb. They are all made of natural timber, with padded seat cushions and soft furnishings. All pieces have hand-stitched head covers which can be removed and interchanged like puppets. The series is available in coloured fabric combined with natural wood, and in all black. The extended collection includes a mini cabinet, bedside table, and storage box that would live happily as furniture pets in any home.

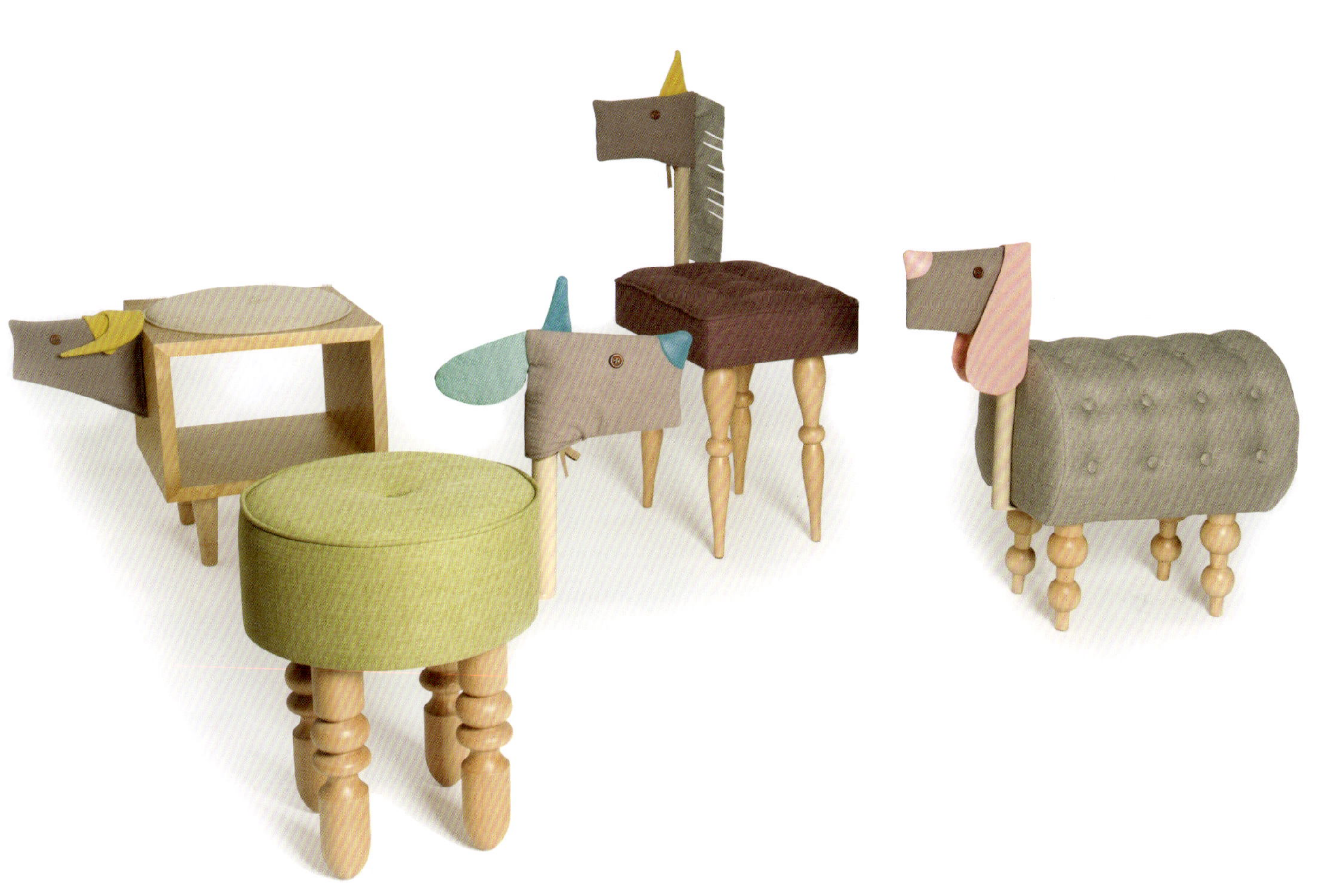

07

APERITIF TIME

Snack Box Set

Kate Chung | JIA Inc.

In Chinese, the word *jia* means 'home': its character 家 is made of a rooftop symbol with an abstract image of a pig underneath it that in the old days meant abundance in the household. Derived from this cultural context, the brief given to JIA designers is to develop tableware that pays homage to old materials whilst it transfers the good feelings of the traditional home into today's dining environments.

Being the company's 'employee 001', and even though one of its youngest, Kate Chung has already left a legacy as the creator of some of its most heart-warming products. Her *Aperitif Time* is a contemporary set of boxes described as party-ware that can be conveniently used for serving, storage and stacking. During the Ming Dynasty (1368–1644 AD) such items were called *quán* boxes. Back then sweets were offered at festive times as a way of celebrating something coming to an end. This is where the label *quán*, meaning 'completion' and 'together', comes from. The custom is practiced today especially during the Luna New Year holidays, one of the few occasions when families gather together.

Drawing inspiration from old baskets used by farmers during harvest time, Kate transferred the hexagonal weave pattern into 3D geometric models. These eventually resulted in the unusually angled lid of the set. Being a party-ware the box has three sections of removable trays functioning as plates. The product is made of degradable EPA melamine to which food-safe compounds have been added for greater weight and thickness that give the box an almost ceramic feel. Practically, melamine has heat-insulating properties: if the box is first cooled in the freezer, it can keep cold snacks chilled for a longer serving time.

'Even though I borrowed some elements from old objects, I really wanted the product to look fresh. I took time to develop the colour pallet. Each pigment was tested many times until I got the hues I wanted. For instance, the terracotta red references roof tiles and it is quite different—warmer and quieter colour—compared to the rather intense reds prevalent in our culture. Also, to enhance the tactile appeal of the box I applied two surfaces [gloss and matt] and the rim is finely polished, which give the product a luxurious finish. These details may be imperceptible but they've been carefully thought of.'

Chung hopes that through this degree of sensitivity her objects will create associations of homecoming, so that *Aperitif Time* is cherished as a 'special times' companion for years to come.

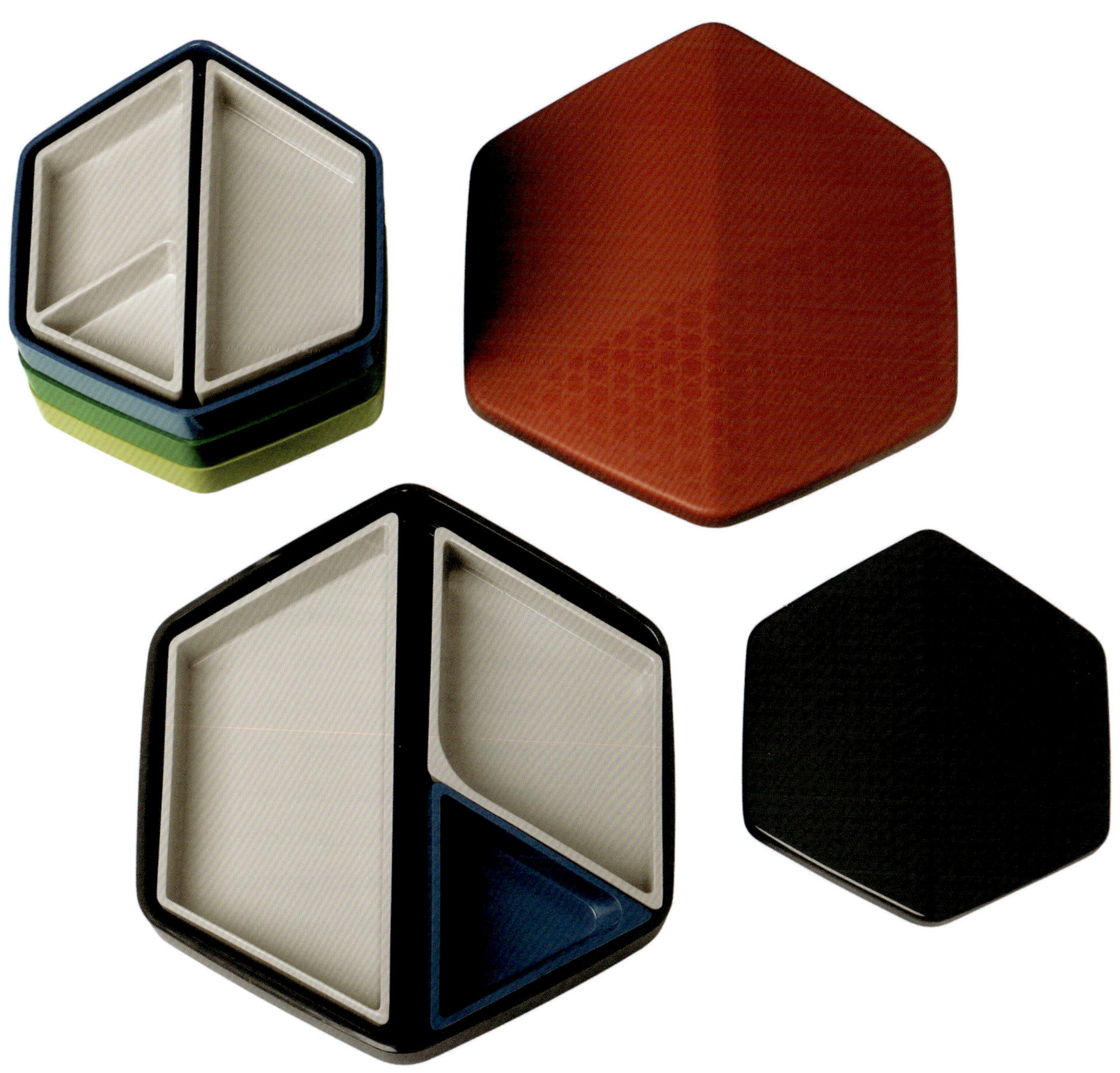

08

ATOM 2.0

3D Printer

Lawrence Lee | Layer One

ATOM 2.0 is a smart machine that renders visual designs as 3D objects. It combines the immediacy of printing with the prototyping benefits of injection moulding. An architect by training, Lawrence Lee found the slow moving pace of the construction industry frustrating and so decided to divert his career towards 'building on a micro scale'.

'In 2012 I bought a 3D printer for $3,000 online. At that time only a handful of such machines were available in Taiwan, so I began printing for clients. Naturally I wanted to learn more about the technology and the best way to find reliable, free information is to join the Open Source community. At some point I realised I'd build a printer myself!'

Lee's curiosity grew into an all-consuming obsession. He found Open Source solutions for many technical challenges and together with his two collaborators—a programmer and an engineer—successfully assembled his first machine. They named it 'Atom', a building block on the path of realising a creative idea. Even though it was operational the printer was not market ready. Major financing was needed to develop it into a fully-fledged product.

'We were doing our own thing, and wanted to control it too. We decided to stay away from investors', recalls Lee. With the support of a crowd-funding company, the young entrepreneur launched an online campaign hoping to pre-sell a dozen pieces, 'sufficient enough to cover all production costs'. What happened exceeded his wildest dreams: over 120 printers were ordered. 'This really jump-started our business. It seemed the 3D tribe needed us', he says excitedly.

Lee explains: 'The essence of a good print is an evenly thick extrusion of the right temperature that is good for smooth bonding. The hot end is a CNC machine, milled from titanium, coupled with an aluminium heat sink to ensure the heating is localised for maximum temperature control and better filament integrity. The layers are so fine they're almost indistinguishable to the unaided eye!'

ATOM 2.0 is sold in a flat pack with all parts and electronics separate, and a step-by-step construction manual. It is like D.I.Y. furniture for geeks, taking about 6 to 8 hours to assemble. The instructions must be followed methodically and accurately. Once assembled, the printer stays completely rigged down to the effector. In addition to the solo hot end, dual hot end configurations and a laser engraver are possible. But for all 3D printing fans, the most satisfying thing about this product is that it can be built from the ground up.

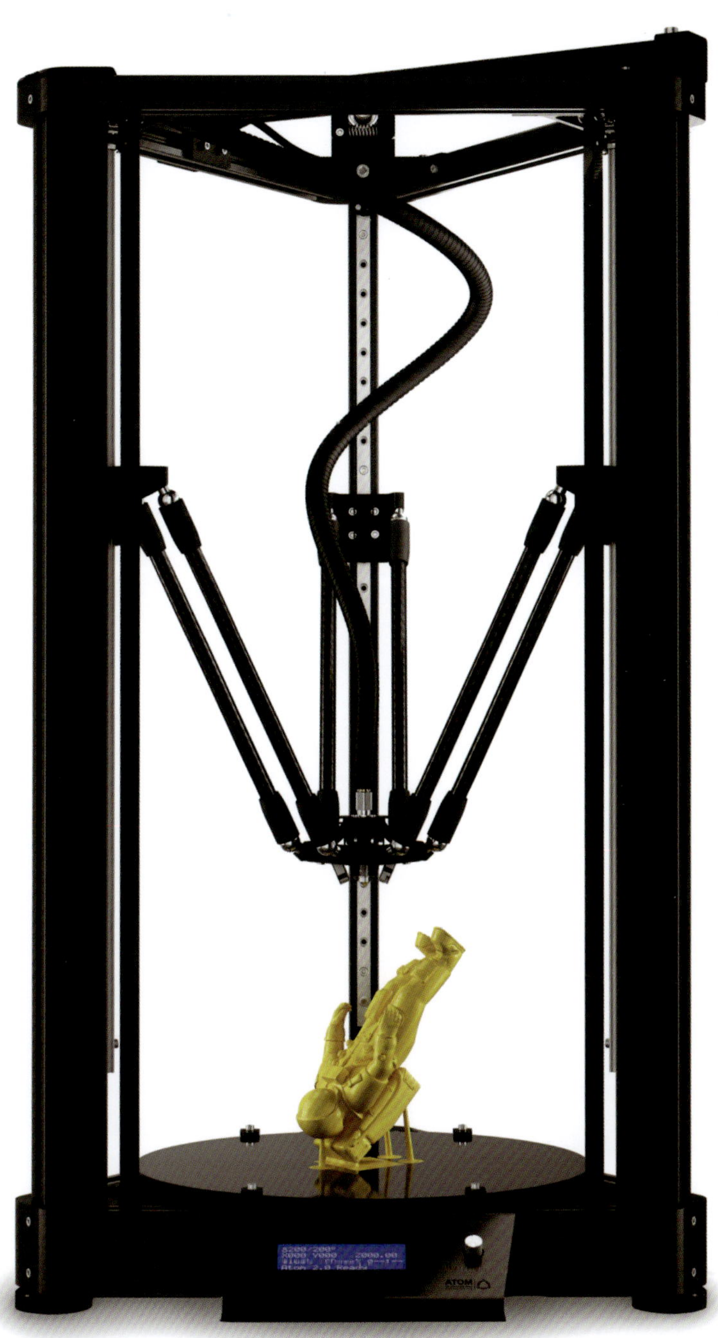

09

BENCHES CHAIR

Furniture

Elvis Chang | Homer Concept

The most critical challenge for designers today is to develop sustainable products the manufacture and recycling of which can be holistically integrated into Nature's ecosystems. In furniture production the wide spread use of toxic chemicals is not only detrimental to the environment, it also poses risks for both the makers and consumers.

Homer Concept was founded on the premise that furniture must be made long lasting with no side effects to human or environmental health. The studio's lead designer Elvis Chang describes its products as Art-Eco (after Art-Deco)— eco-friendly limited editions of furniture. 'It's beyond trend … it's a necessity. As designers we have a social responsibility to promote conscious consumption. We have to educate consumers to be reasonable with their choices', he comments.

Benches Chair is an ingenious bench that can be folded into a backrest chair. According to Chang, the product was created in response to a design conundrum: 'Can natural resources be conserved by making multi-functional furniture out of the one object?' The single unit not only has a dual function, it can also be split into two halves that are easily joined back together and locked in place with snugly fitting magnets. This makes the furniture especially well suited for smaller living spaces as it can be temporarily split in half to make extra seating available.

The idea-to-product process was a long and arduous one. True to Homer Concept's sustainability principles, the ancient mortise-and-tenon joint woodcraft technique was applied to connect the two folding parts at an angle, without nails. The slope of the backrest of the chair had to be designed for comfort. At the same time it had to be positioned precisely to ensure maximum stability when it is flipped over to become a bench leg. The product is polished with organic linseed-based oil, and made in two variations of natural timber and bamboo.

With its simple yet sturdy structure *Benches Chair* is a clever adaptation of the popular country bench, demonstrating maximum use of materials with a minimal intervention. By making versatile and durable furniture, the revolutionary design studio introduces products of lasting value for a lifestyle that respects Nature.

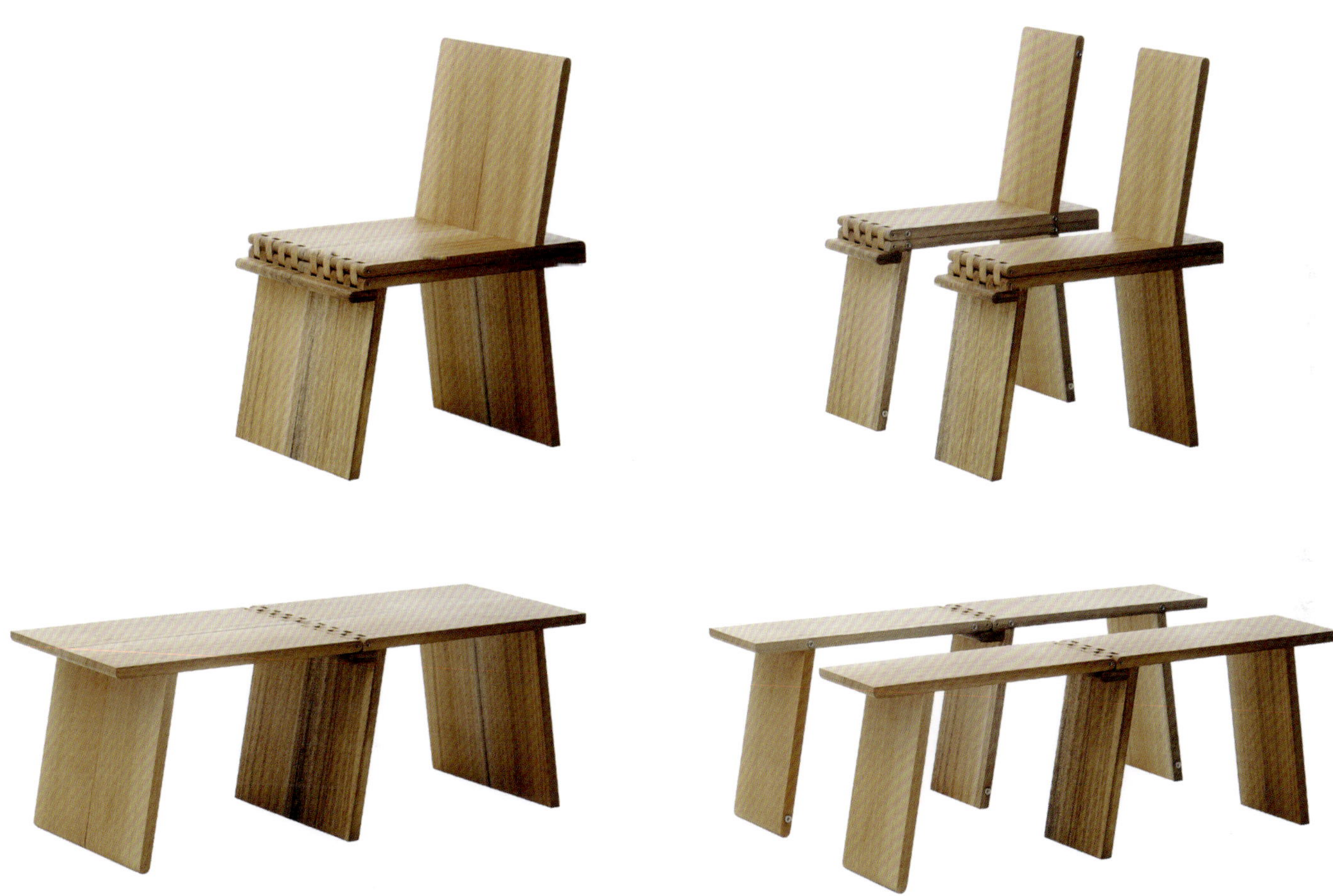

10

BI.DU.HAEV

Cold Brew System

[bi.du.haev]

In a country famous for its bubble teas, cold-pressed coffee is still a novelty. But this ultra slick *bi.du.haev* cold brew system has a cult following amongst the trendy café owners in Taipei. Looking more like an experiment in alchemy than a coffee machine, the system is extremely easy to operate—no electricity or hot stove required—and it produces an exceptionally flavoursome beverage.

Made from a high-grade laboratory glass, *bi.du.haev* consists of three main sections fitted together to form one streamlined mechanism. Covered with a petri dish-like lid, the upper cylinder is the container for iced water. A glass valve attached to it regulates the water drips. For best extraction results, it is recommended that the valve is set at 1 drop per every 2 seconds.

The water sieves through the ground coffee beans and passes through a microfiltration fritted glass filter. The pressed coffee is collected in the base cylinder, which has a pouring spout and it can be used as a serving carafe. It takes about 8 hours for one litre of coffee to be made using this system. To maintain the flavour fresh the brew should be kept in the fridge in the same carafe for 3 to 5 days. If it tastes too concentrated, a little bit of warm or cold water can be added to dilute it to a desired consistency.

The system is packed in its own safety case, and is suitable for travelling.

Iron Wang jokes that he bets on being a good designer more than a good barista. 'This may sound strange but I didn't like coffee that much, it always tasted bitter to me. Then I read somewhere that cold pressed coffee is better for health because it is less acidic. As I was learning how to make it, I could see potential for improving the existing systems. For example, the frame that usually supports the larger versions is stripped away in my model. I also replaced the regular paper filter with glass', explains Wang.

The reductive design of *bi.du.haev* not only minimises the use of resources, it is also quite seductive. A friend of the designer experimented embedding a small LED light into its wooden base. When lit from below the brewed coffee reveals an intensely rich iron-ore gradient of colour. This quirky presentation adds a touch of scientific allure and upmarket cool to the coffee extraction process any caffeine connoisseur would find enticing.

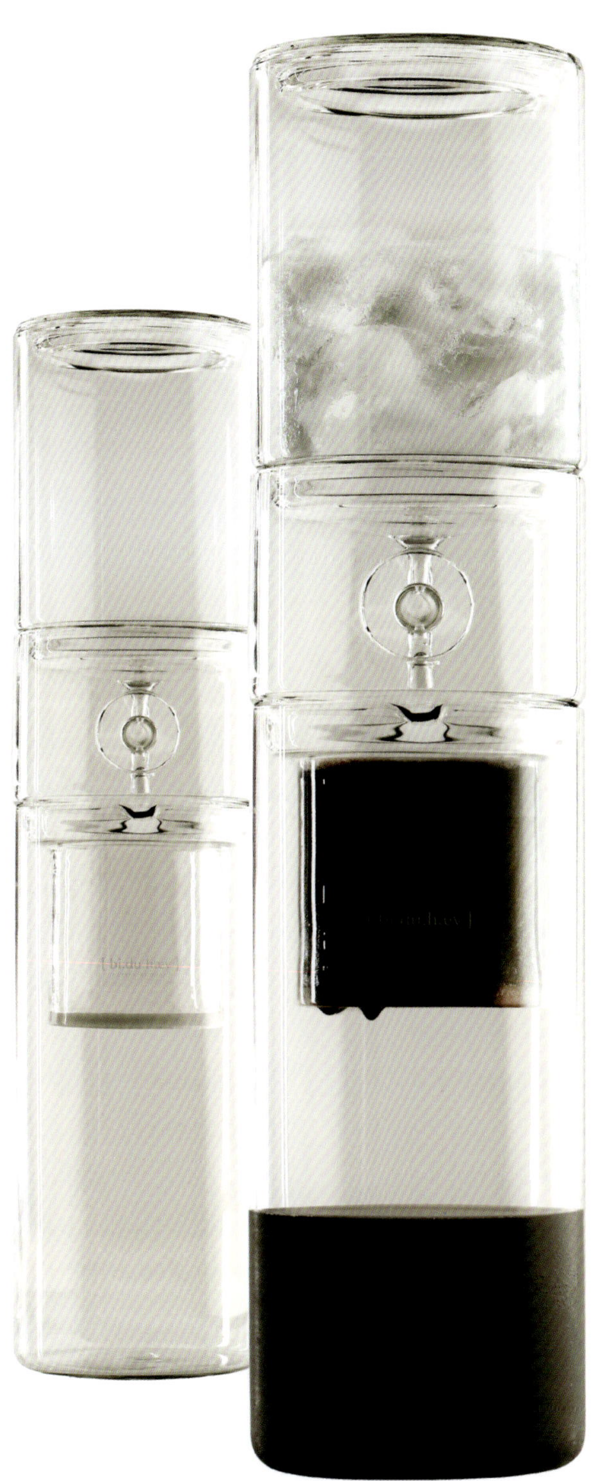

11

BRICK PLAN

Earthenware

Rock Wang | Studio Qiao

The word *qiào* holds a special meaning for the Taiwanese: it can be translated as 'having an insight' into the nature of things. The principle of 'design as insight' is central to the work of Taipei-based Studio Qiao. Lead designer Rock Wang believes that whenever possible objects should express the cultural confluences of their place of origin. This often determines the studio's unconventional choice of materials. Silkworm cocoons, woven bamboo and rocks found on the beach are all regarded as potent transmitters of people's deeply felt associations with particular places.

This belief has led to some interesting outcomes such as the *Brick Plan* series of bowls, vases and trays developed around the history of bricks as a cultural material. The red brick is a distinct feature of Taiwan's colonial architecture. Introduced to the island by the Dutch in the 1600s, the natural polished terracotta brick was used specifically for military defence structures and government buildings. In a later period bricks were adopted for building affluent merchant neighbourhoods as well as temples.

Rock Wang comments that the red brick is now so much a part of the vernacular it is considered Taiwanese. 'May be I am a dreamer, but I really wanted to recreate the feeling of touching the sun-warmed wall of my childhood home rubbed countless times by us kids playing outside. It's fascinating to see a person feeling moved by holding this product ... it can really touch someone's heart. This is not easily achieved through design. With *Brick Plan* it took us two years to get it right.'

Most of the efforts were concentrated on finding a precise formula to bind the bricks and inlayed cement together without compromising the object's function. Wang wanted the brick patterns to be visually intriguing rather than layered the regular way. When he tried this, however, the two materials kept separating and the form collapsing. The expertise of a local master-builder with knowledge of old bricklaying techniques came to the rescue. He suggested the bricks and the cement be made into blocks first and then carved out. Finally a solution was found! Once hollowed out and shaped into its form, each object was then polished with precision tools to achieve a silky smooth surface texture ... just as the designer remembered it from his childhood.

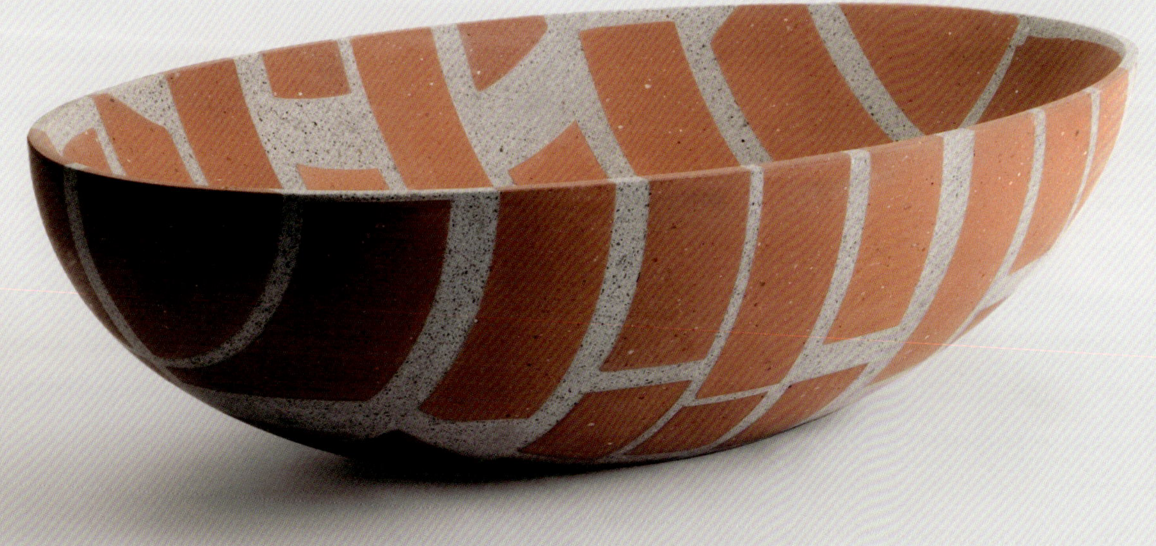

12

CENTERPIECE

Table Lighting

Bonnsu

Every day tonnes of fresh blooms are couriered across the world from major export regions to the doorsteps of local florists. The truth about the flower trade is that this pretty industry is delivered with a choking carbon footprint. But if the sustainability conscious consumers find supplementing flowers with their plastic copies not so desirable, they may be pleased by this solution from Bonnsu.

Centerpiece brings together ornamental concepts from floral and candle-lit decorations merged into one piece. More of a magic lantern than a bouquet, its main body is a candle-shaped core with an LED light defusing an even glow. Around it an abstract floral arrangement is created from seven 'petal films'. These are sheets of clear film with lovely patterns printed on them, each folded and slotted around the core to generate soft shadows and shimmering refractions when the light is on. To enhance a particular interior mood the films can be interchanged with a variety of available patterns.

The long-life rechargeable battery makes the product an ideal accompaniment to both indoor and outdoor entertainment. Although its main purpose is as table decoration, the light has a small hook attached to its screw-on top so it can be hung from umbrellas or trees to add a touch of romantic atmosphere to garden parties.

Unexpectedly, it was the designers' own wedding that sparked the original idea. 'Naturally we wanted our big day to be gorgeous and memorable. At the reception banquet each table was adorned with fresh flowers and everything looked picture-perfect. We then found out the beautiful arrangements had travelled from far away places to last just for the afternoon. Beside the expense it all seemed a terrible waste of resources', exclaims Adam Bonnier who, together with his wife Ai Su, founded Bonnsu. Eager to solve the problem, the newlywed couple quickly returned to the design studio. Development hurdles were plentiful, yet they remained faithful to their original motivation to 'develop special occasions décor that minimises consumer waste of flowers'.

Bonnsu believe mindful consumerism begins with responsible design. The key to their product is its longevity, 'keeping it away from ending up in landfills'. If an inner component wears out it is replaceable with a new one. None of the electronics is fused with the plastic in order for it to be recycled separately. Better for the Earth and brightening the spirit, *Centerpiece* is ideal for discrete lounges transforming any gathering into a joyous event.

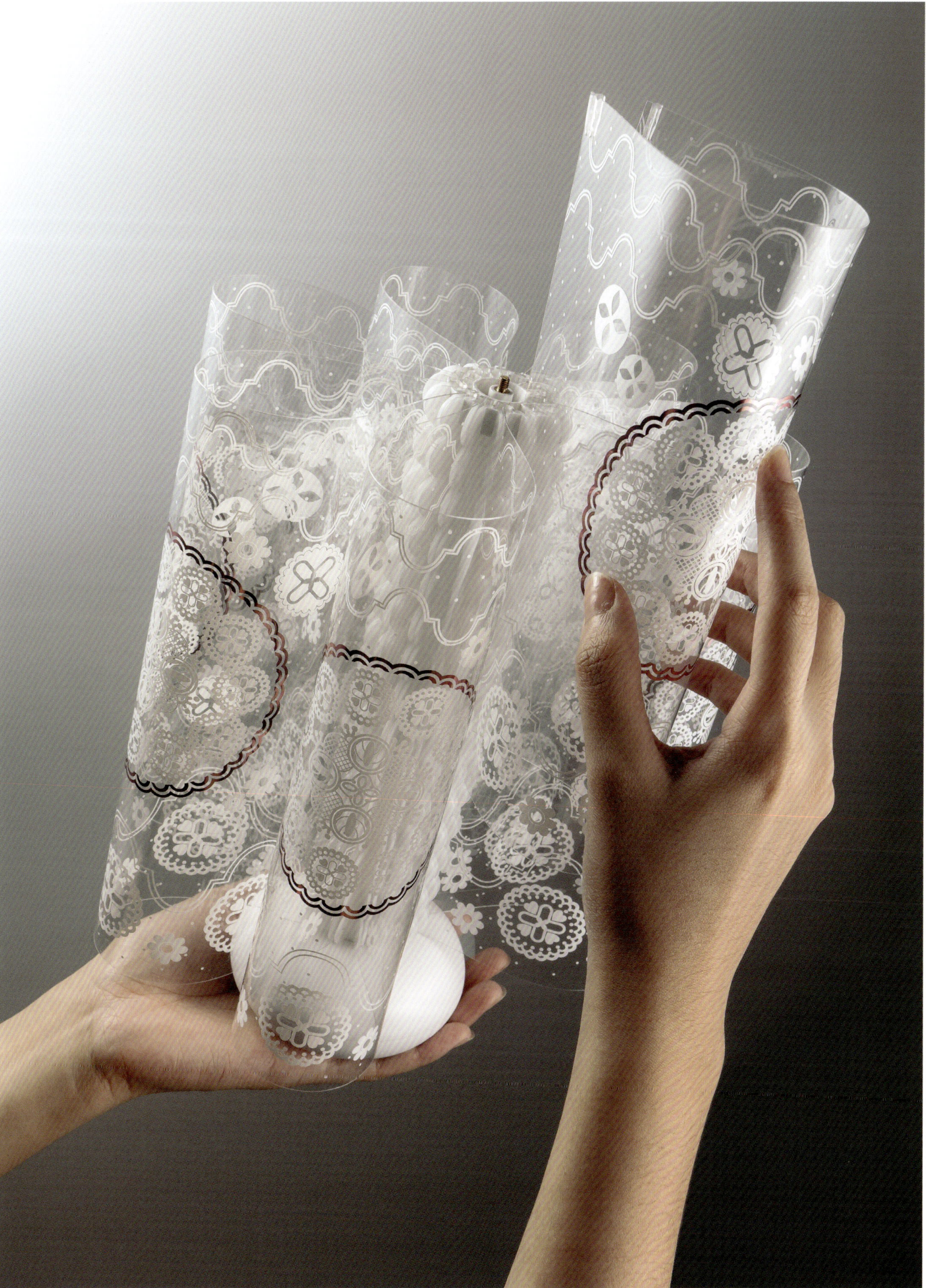

13

COLLAPSIBLE KETTLE

Stovetop Kettle

RiCCO Engineering

The Taiwanese are accustomed to disposable products, which in a crowded society amounts to a lot of waste. Like many new businesses emerging on the island, RiCCO is on a mission to improve consumer habits through smart design. 'We want people to become proactive about conserving resources. This is our core business objective', says Ronald Tuan.

It all started with a clever idea for a reusable and durable coffee filter that can be packed flat in a backpack. This may sound simple, but for the engineers it felt like the Mt Everest of product design, taking two and a half years to climb. The key challenge was how to make the filter collapsible yet safe. It had to be foldable and at the same time one hundred per cent functional when it pops up back into shape. Most importantly, it had to be made of heat-resistant and non-toxic material.

The engineer's prior experience in the aviation industry sparked an interesting idea. It occurred to him that an aircraft and a coffee filter might have something in common. Silicon has excellent mechanical properties because it is a hard yet flexible material with high chemical resistance and can withstand extraordinary temperatures of up to 250°C. 'Few people know this, but it's actually used for the manufacture of military missiles as they change temperature sharply and need to be heat-resistant. I was thinking ... If silicon can withstand that much heat, surely it could be adapted for kitchen appliances? It all started from there.'

The coffee filter was well received and so the company combined its patented technology with other materials o broaden its product range. To date, 25 different items have been released on the market, all of them designed around the same principle.

The revolutionary *Collapsible Kettle* is RiCCO's most praised invention. Unlike the regular 600-watt stainless steel models, which conduct heat fast but also lose it fast, the silicon kettle traps the heat and thus keeps the temperature of boiled water for much longer. According to laboratory tests, it can save up to 50 per cent more energy than a conventional kettle. It can be collapsed half way for single serve use or expanded if a full kettle of hot water is needed. It is one of the company's next generation semi-collapsible products, which cannot be pushed down: it remains in an upright position, but it can be folded flat if picked up with both hands.

By encouraging consumers to save on their electricity bills, the *Collapsible Kettle* indirectly helps them to reduce their carbon footprint.

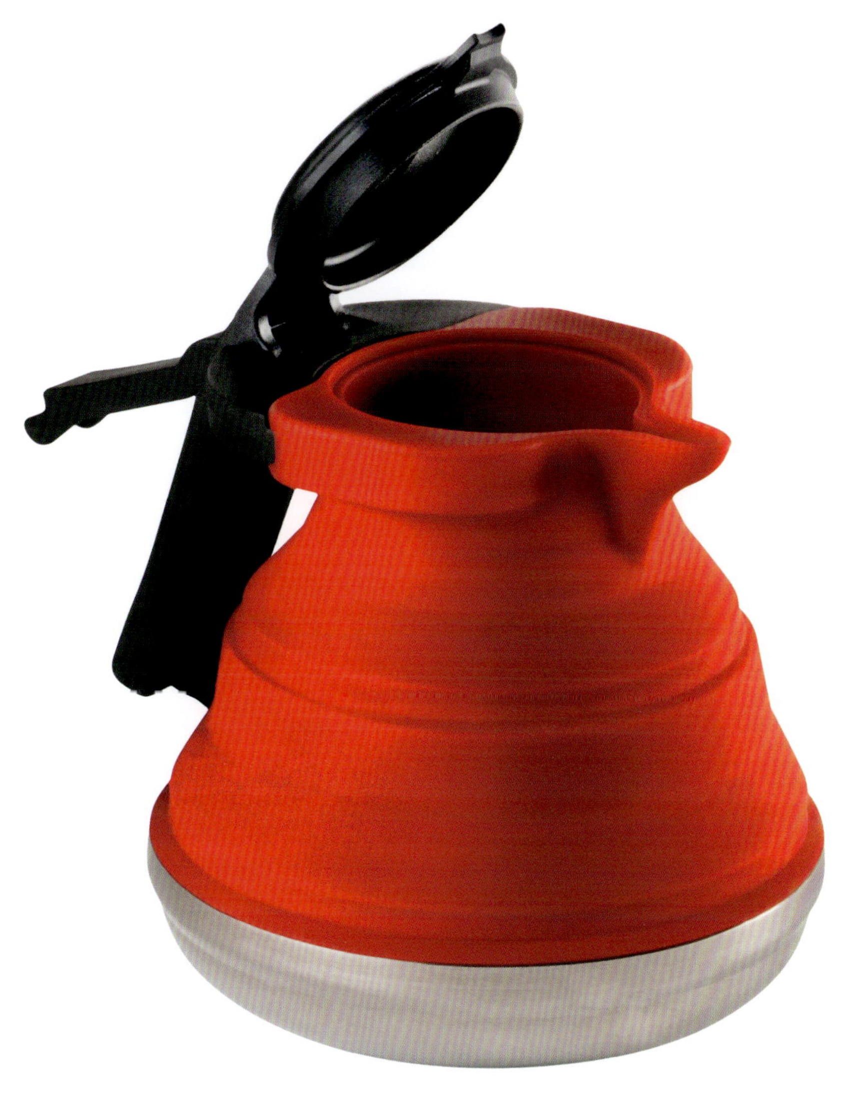
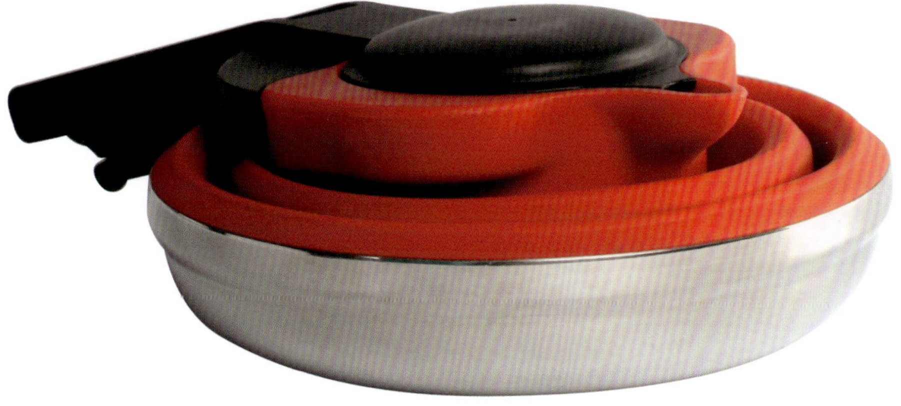

14

COLORUP

Colour Responsive Table Lamp

PEGA D&E

PEGA D&E is the creative off spring of Fortune 500 listed PEGATRON Corporation. It is a dynamic team of seasoned innovators who push the boundaries of design through cross-disciplinary approaches and quick responses to emerging trends. 'It's a hothouse here', says Ann Chou, spokeswoman for the team. 'Sometimes we make one-off pieces that are more like digital artworks; sometimes projects may never leave the studio, and it's all ok.'

ColorUp is a funky lamp that can mimic the colour of any surface it touches. It was initially made for the company's Present Perfect exhibition to showcase the team's interactive design capabilities. 'People loved the playfulness of the lamp', says Chou. 'We got lot's of thumbs up for it. So the business department directed us to keep working on the product and bring it to market. Everyone was really happy because one of our more experimental ideas was given the go-ahead.'

What users find most enjoyable about this product is that they interact with it by capturing colour hues from surrounding objects. When the base of the lamp is pressed against any object, the colour frequency of its surface is absorbed and the lamp changes to shine in that same colour. Green grass turns the light green, blue bathroom tiles switch it to blue, and so forth. When users squeeze the top of the lamp they can also recall the collected colour frequencies to be beamed by the lamp.

The main body of the lamp is made of silicone because its elasticity is suitable for fabricating the squishy bulb. Unlike an ordinary bulb, the interactive version posed several functional obstacles that the designers and engineers had to resolve. A balance between the thickness of the silicon body and the brightness of the light element had to be achieved. If the emitted light was too bright a larger battery may have been required, which in turn would influence the size and cost of the product.

ColorUp playfully reconfigures preconceived ideas of how lighting objects should function. A user can intuitively redefine the ambience of a room by gently squeezing the lamp. The convenience of being able to change the interior light without having to redecorate a space is what captures the imagination. It can be done simply, and literally, with a light touch.

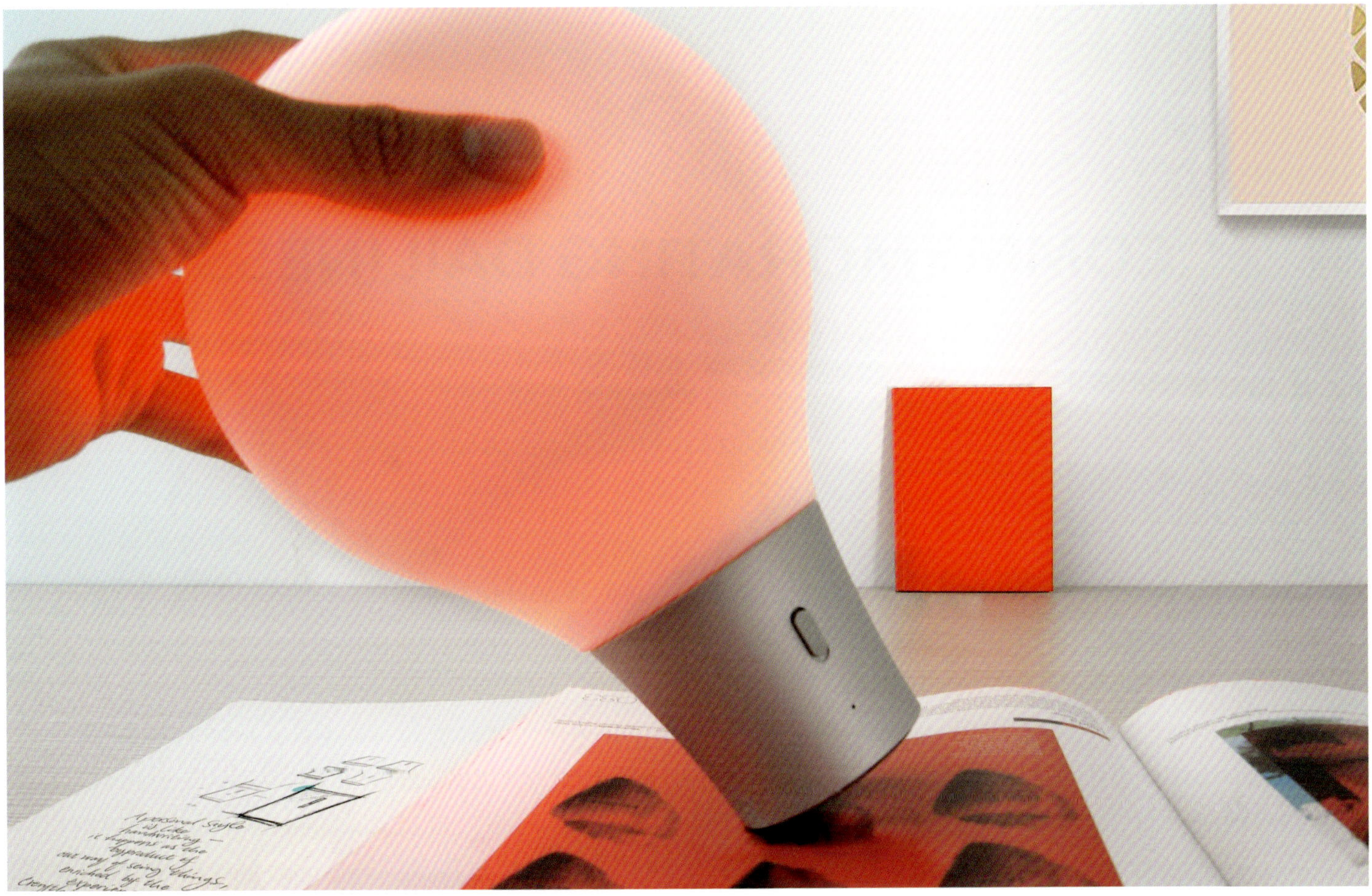
A personal style
is like
handwriting –
it happens as the
byproduct of
one way of seeing things,
enriched by the

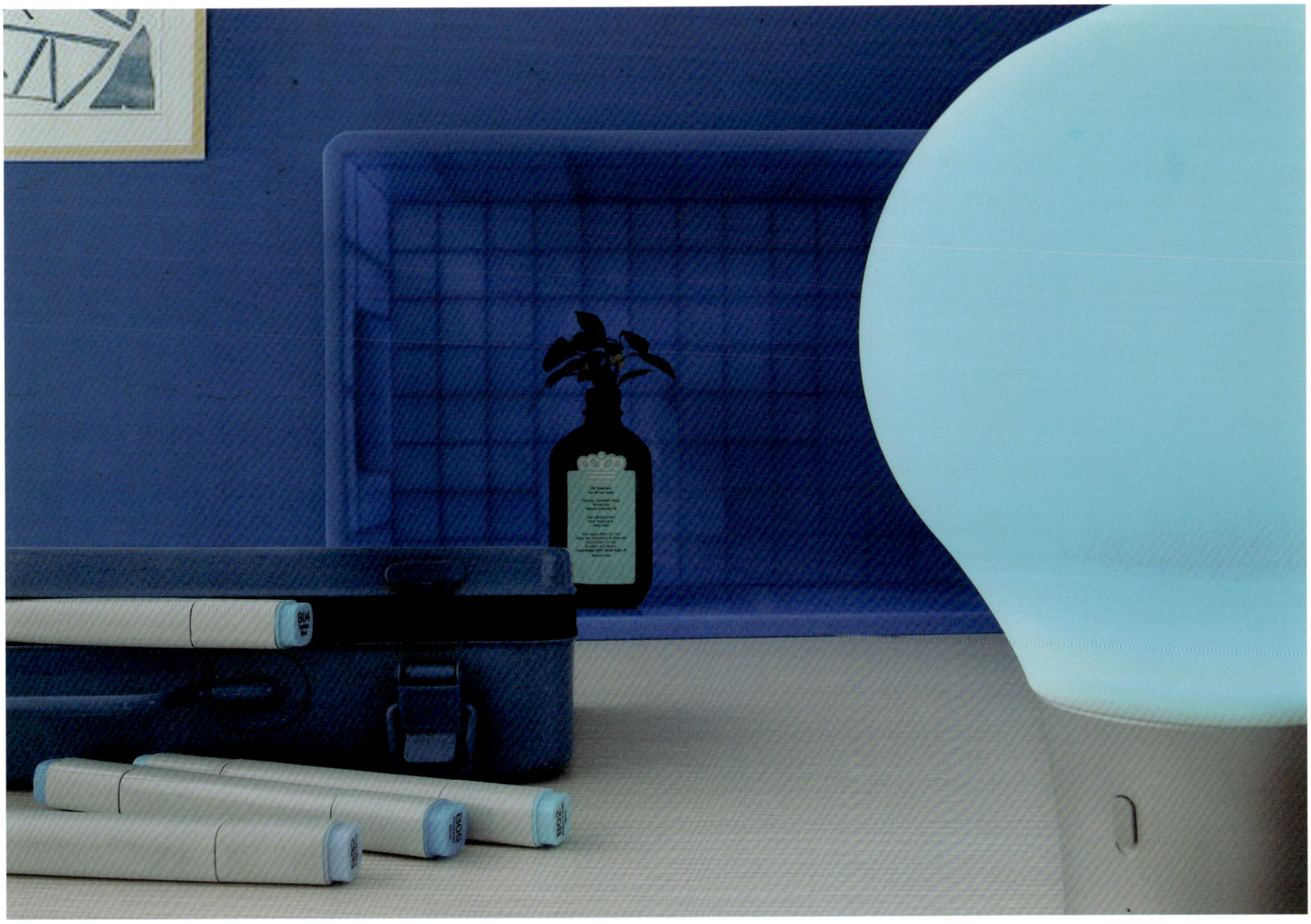

15

COMMEMORATING DAILINESS

Stool

Studio Co-Fusion

The ancient skill of stone masonry has its own traditions in Taiwan. The widely available black limestone was first used by the Aborigines as a building material for house walls and fences made from stacked hand-cut slates. With the arrival of Buddhism and Taoism, new techniques were introduced to serve the needs of temples. Large stones began to be chiselled into pillars, hollowed out, and then with great artistry transformed into three-dimensional carvings of birds, flowers, and mythical creatures to illustrate religious scenes.

Che-Chen Kuo was researching the various uses of the material when he made a curious observation. 'Local temples are like civic squares where older people still enjoy hanging around. In the shade of temple gates grandmas and grandpas sit around on these little wooden stools chatting all day long, sometimes may be even having a little nap. There is something very comforting watching the simplicity and ordinariness of this way of being, just sitting there watching everything pass by.'

Inspired by the atmosphere, Kuo began to redesign the beloved stool in a way that it could bring some of this peaceful presence into the city apartment. He decided to merge the form of the stool with decorative details found on temple pillars and, for a more contemporary functionality, to elongate the legs. As a starting point the designer made sketches from stone carvings, which he then refined by stripping away any obvious religious connotations. The combination of wood and stone brought together into a single piece of furniture had to be made with engineering precision. For this he partnered with master stonemason Pei-Tse Chen, who is skilled in stone carvings.

By combining industrial design and craft technique they made two versions of the stool: one with a simple top of finely polished limestone, and another featuring an elaborately hand-carved dragon wrapped around the base of the seat. The legs of the stool are painted in a non-traditional turquoise blue.

Such successful collaborations between designers and artisans have become an excellent platform for revitalising traditional craft techniques that are disappearing due to modernisation. 'We were both very pleased with the final result. I hope that through experiments like these the essence of our culture can be revived', reflects Kuo about his work. 'I named the product *Commemorating Dailiness* as a reminder of the origins of the stool. Even if it ends up in a trendy bar or a hotel lobby, it will still have a story to tell.'

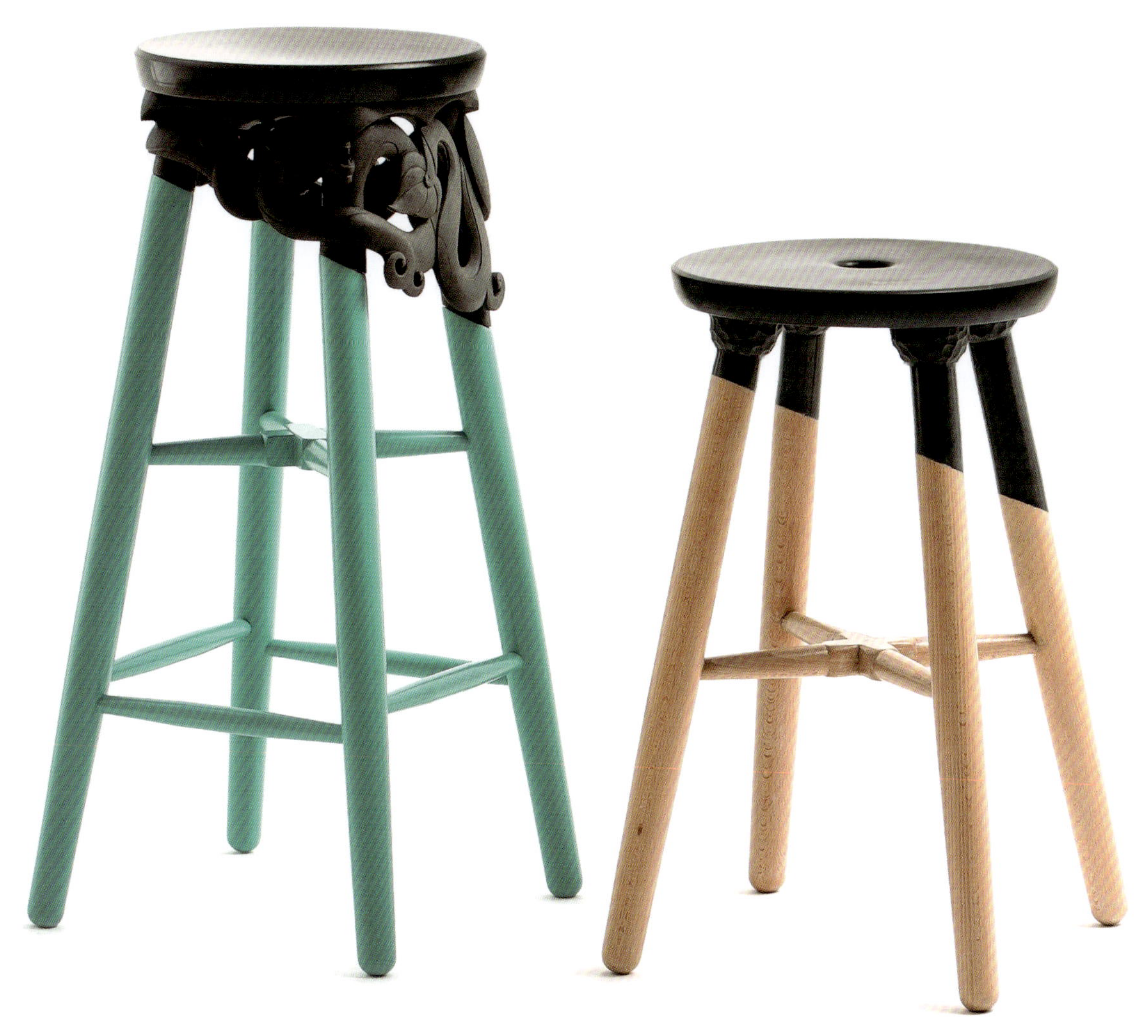

16

CRANE

Umbrella Stand
Liberté

If Taiwan were to be named something other than 'Beautiful Island' it would have to be 'Island of the Drifting Clouds', for like elsewhere in the subtropics it rains a lot here. Sensible locals always carry a portable umbrella or pack a long raincoat under the seat of their scooters. In summer, the ladies still use umbrellas to safeguard their youthful complexions from the blazing sun. In the metro, for instance, next to the ticket checking machines there are stands with left-behind umbrellas available for anyone to use: they get passed on like batons from one person to the next in a free-exchange system.

It is not surprising, therefore, that Liberté would invest time and creative energy to produce a modern umbrella stand. After all, keeping everyone's little rain shields neat and tidy in a household is a common nuisance. The designers explain: 'We wanted our product to be highly stylised and not look like a stand. When it's not being piled up with umbrellas, it won't stick out or feel empty. Instead, its visual presence remains decorative on its own.'

Indeed, *Crane* looks more like a shadow wire work of art than an umbrella stand. It is constructed from quasi-geometrical polygons outlined with thin iron rods welded together. The designers' credit enjoying folding origamigot the first impressions of their product. The paper animals are then rendered as computer models. Exact measurements of the length and angle of each wire segment are calculated to ensure that the form is well balanced.

The product is fabricated in a small factory in the southern city of Changua, where all segments are precisely joined together in order to render the bird's geometry. Folded long umbrellas can be propped up between the wire frames. The base tray is designed to structurally stabilise the stand as well as to collect runoff raindrops. There are two versions of the product: one with the crane leaning forward touching the base, and one with it looking up.

Crane is a playful creature. The wire bird takes on different personalities depending on its surrounds and the angle of its silhouette. 'Everyone complains about the rain so we hope when a person reaches out for their umbrella seeing the stand makes them happy', says Pei-Chun Shih with a beaming smile. Liberté now service other homeware brands in Taiwan and Japan. Their expanded range of shadow-wire animals can be found in design stores throughout Asia.

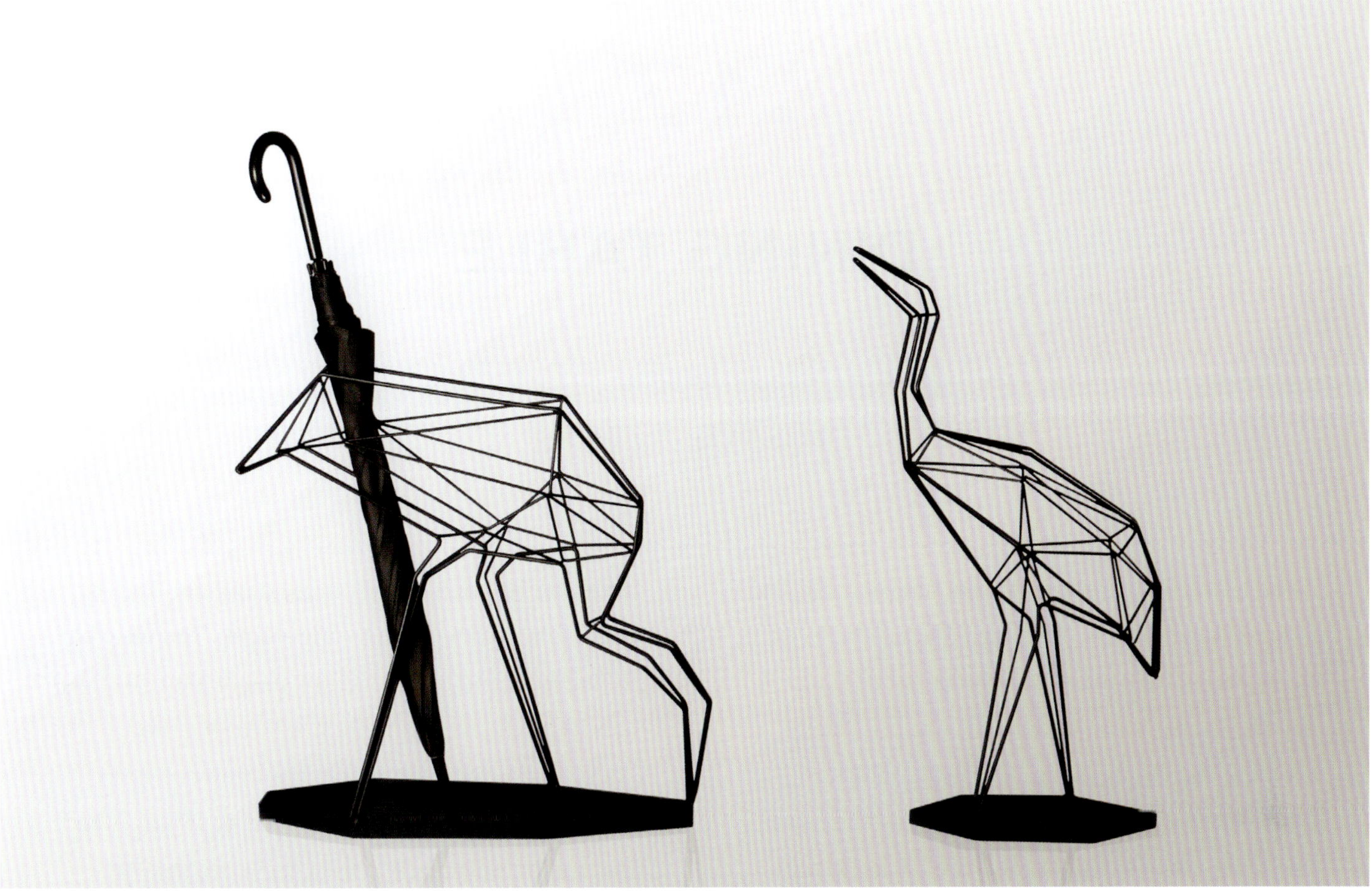

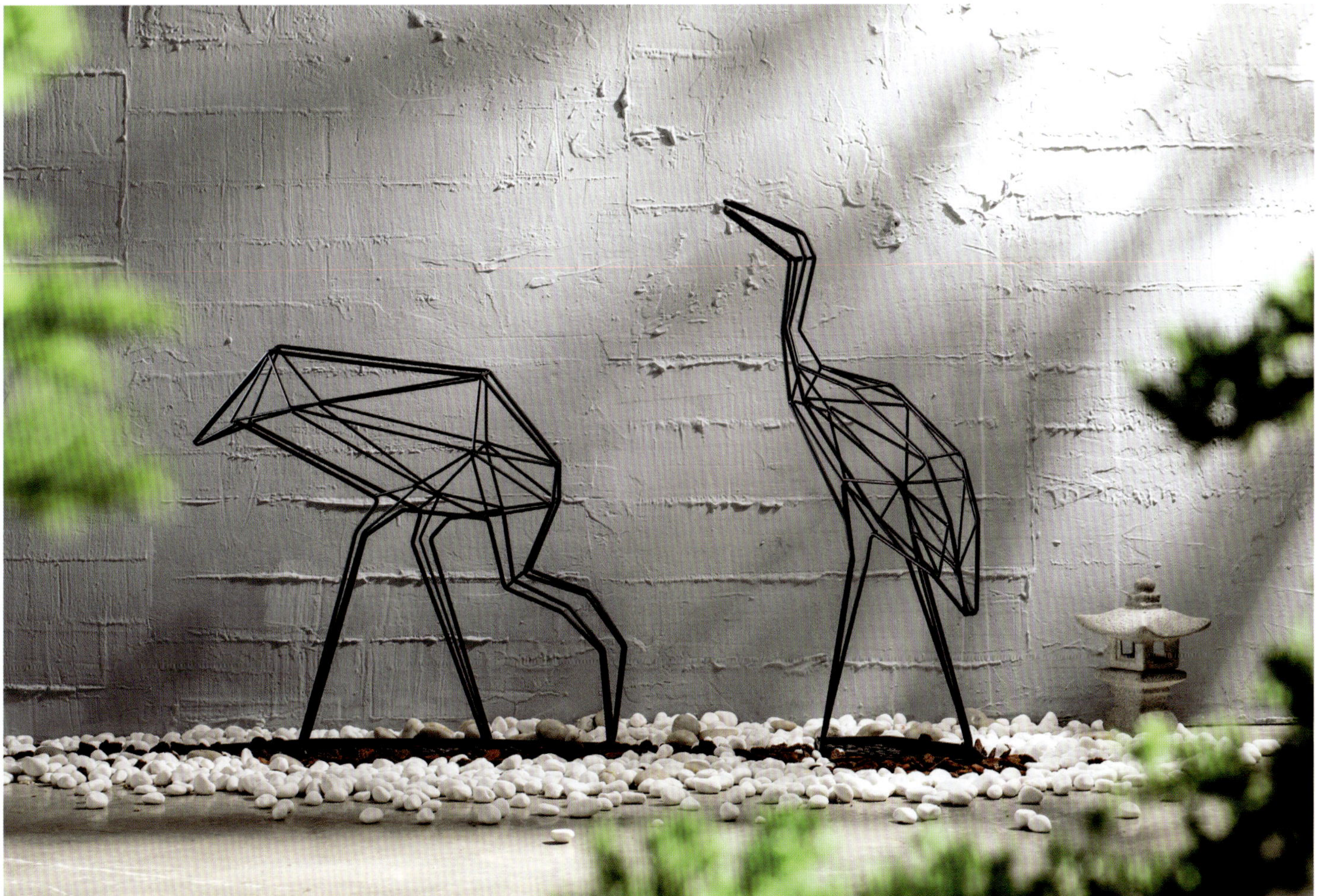

17

DINING TABLE

Table

Yang-An Lin | anLiving

Dining Table was created as a bet between son and father cabinetmakers. Positing a playful challenge to his demanding master-carpenter father, Yang-An Lin wanted to demonstrate it was possible to produce a stunning piece of wood furniture and be environmentally responsible at the same time. The table mimics the assembling of wood blocks deployed as a decorative technique in traditional cabinetry, yet it is produced at a fraction of the cost.

Applying his proficiency in marquetry Lin used contrasting colour strips of exotic wood veneer to design the table's surface. Cut with minute precision and delicately interlaced at particular lengths, the strips are matched to form a visually rich pattern. The crisscrossing lines appear as if woven, giving the top a natural cloth look so that meals can be set directly onto it. The surface is hand sanded and varnished with a protective coating that highlights the wood grains. The top and legs are made of concealed lumber core plywood, making the table light to move around. The clever design up-scales similar pieces found in department stores that the Taiwanese often use for playing Mahjong games.

Coming from a lineage of carpenters, the young designer can quickly evaluate the quality of timber by looking at its density and hardness. He can assess its price based on its colour and can work a plank of wood into any shape. 'Timbers like sandalwood and rosewood are sought after because trees like that take a hundred years to mature. Blackwood furniture is a priced investment. But cutting down ancient forests to feed demands is bad. It's a contentious point in the family because my father is old fashioned and can't yet appreciate my work.'

Despite his creative rebellion, Lin maintains the practice of traditional calculus. The system was devised by Lu-Ban, a legendary carpenter who lived in the fifth century B.C. Its standards for geomancy continue to be adhered to by master builders and carpenters to this day throughout in many parts of Taiwan. The proportions of *Dining Table* are determined with a *Lu-Ban ruler*, a complicated tool of numbers and characters by which it can be calculated if a measurement is auspicious or not. The marquetry pattern is designed to form a continuous surface when two or more tables are lined up, with the added up proportions remaining lucky *ad infinitum*. This may seem pure superstition, but for some this object intertwines design with spirituality and cosmological beliefs as a way of welcoming good experiences into the home.

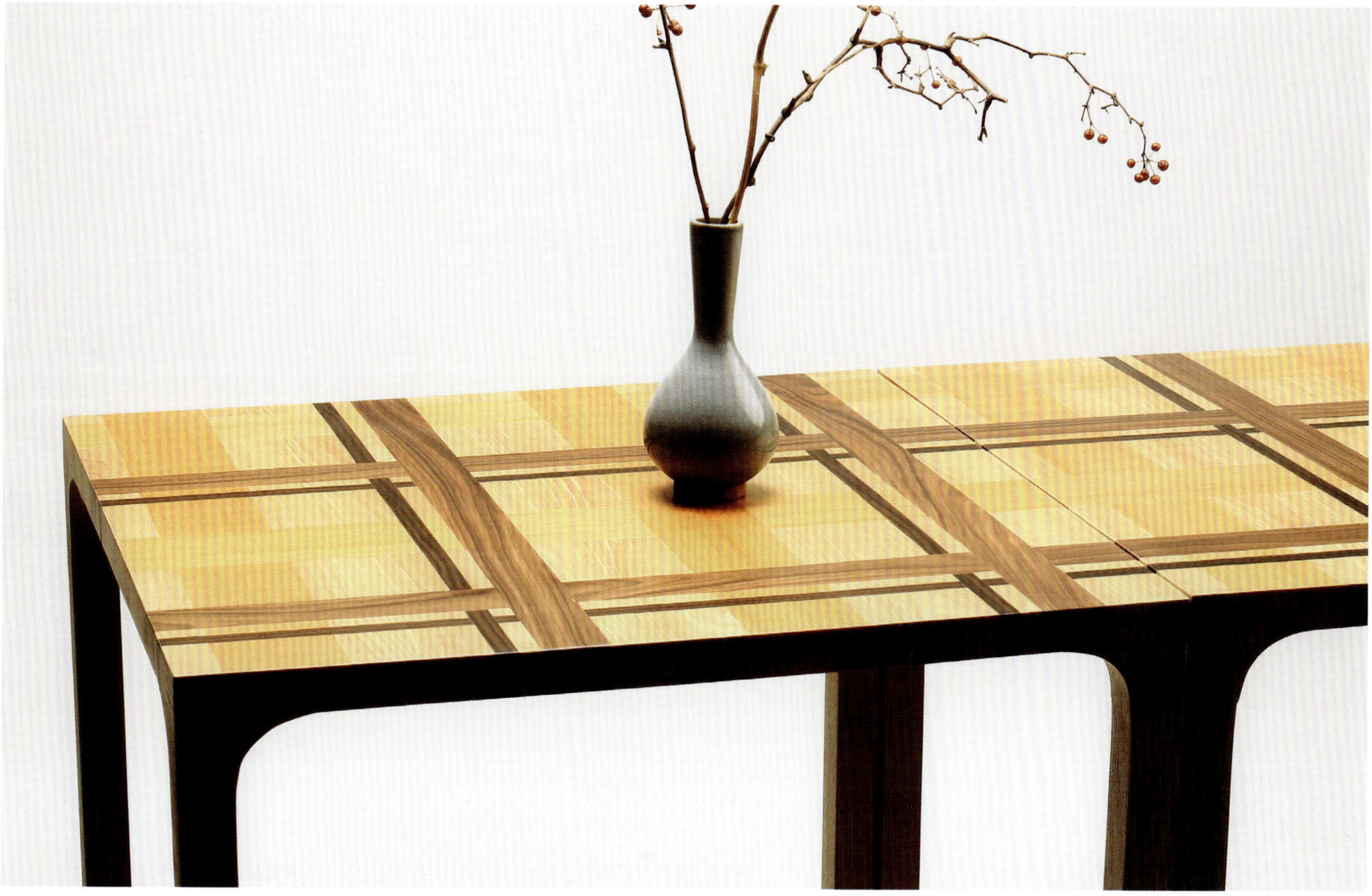

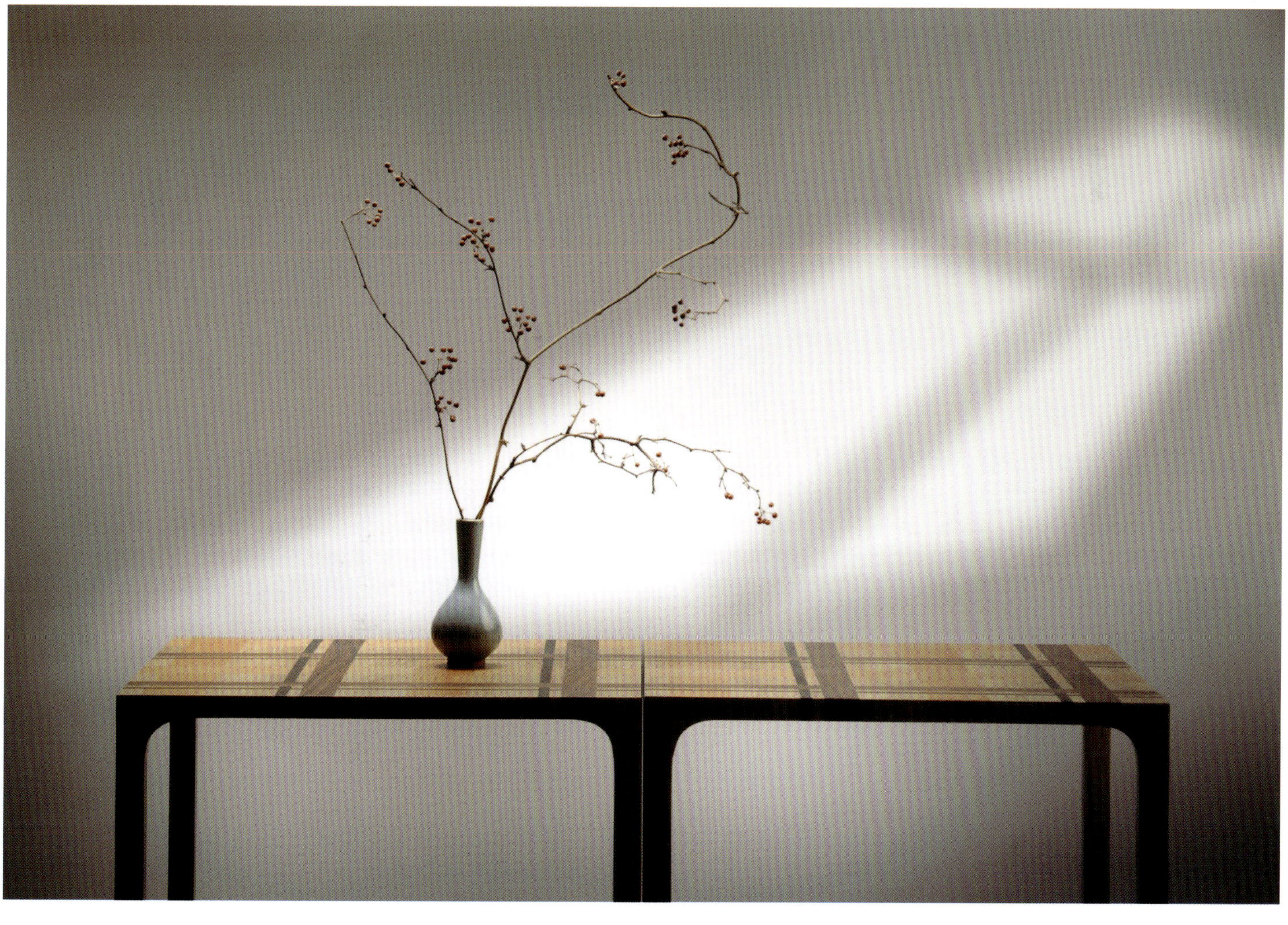

18

ECO BLANKET

Blanket

DA.AI Technology

Founded on the Buddhist principles of compassion and environmental protection—as taught by Dharma Master Cheng Yen—and utilising the latest advances in science and technology, DA.AI is the first company in Taiwan solely dedicated to promoting eco-friendly polyester products using 100 per cent recycled PET (polyethylene terephthalate) bottles.

In Chinese *dà-ài* literally means 'grate love' in the spiritual sense of the word. It is an expression of the belief in universal love that is also the company's core business value. The design team takes pride in the fact their job is to turn garbage into a precious resource and in doing so spread a message of caring co-existence with the Earth. Through smart engineering they regenerate tonnes of consumer plastic waste into clothing, bedding, footwear and luggage.

Eco Blanket is the first recycled fabric product in Asia to be certified by the Cradle To Cradle Products Innovation Institute. Over seven processes are involved in its making: from collecting and sorting PET bottles, crushing them into flakes and melting the PET chips, to spinning yarn from the raw material and weaving it into fabrics. The product derives its distinct light green or white colour from the original dies of the recycled plastics.

The value of *Eco Blanket* is measured by the restoration of resources and the replenishment of natural capital. Interestingly each blanket is recorded in a unique labelling system. It is tagged with a production history chart and a QR code, which enables the user to trace the recycling process back to the collection depot (from over 5,400 stations!) and see the origins of their own blanket. The chart also includes technical information and a story about the particular volunteer involved in the sorting and cleaning the PET bottles used for the item.

At DA.AI net profits from corporate and product sales are reinvested in charity and disaster relief projects. To date the company has distributed over 500,000 blankets through organisations working in disaster areas in 90 countries and regions, becoming a world champion of the idea that it is possible to make a significant contribution to society while also taking care of the earth.

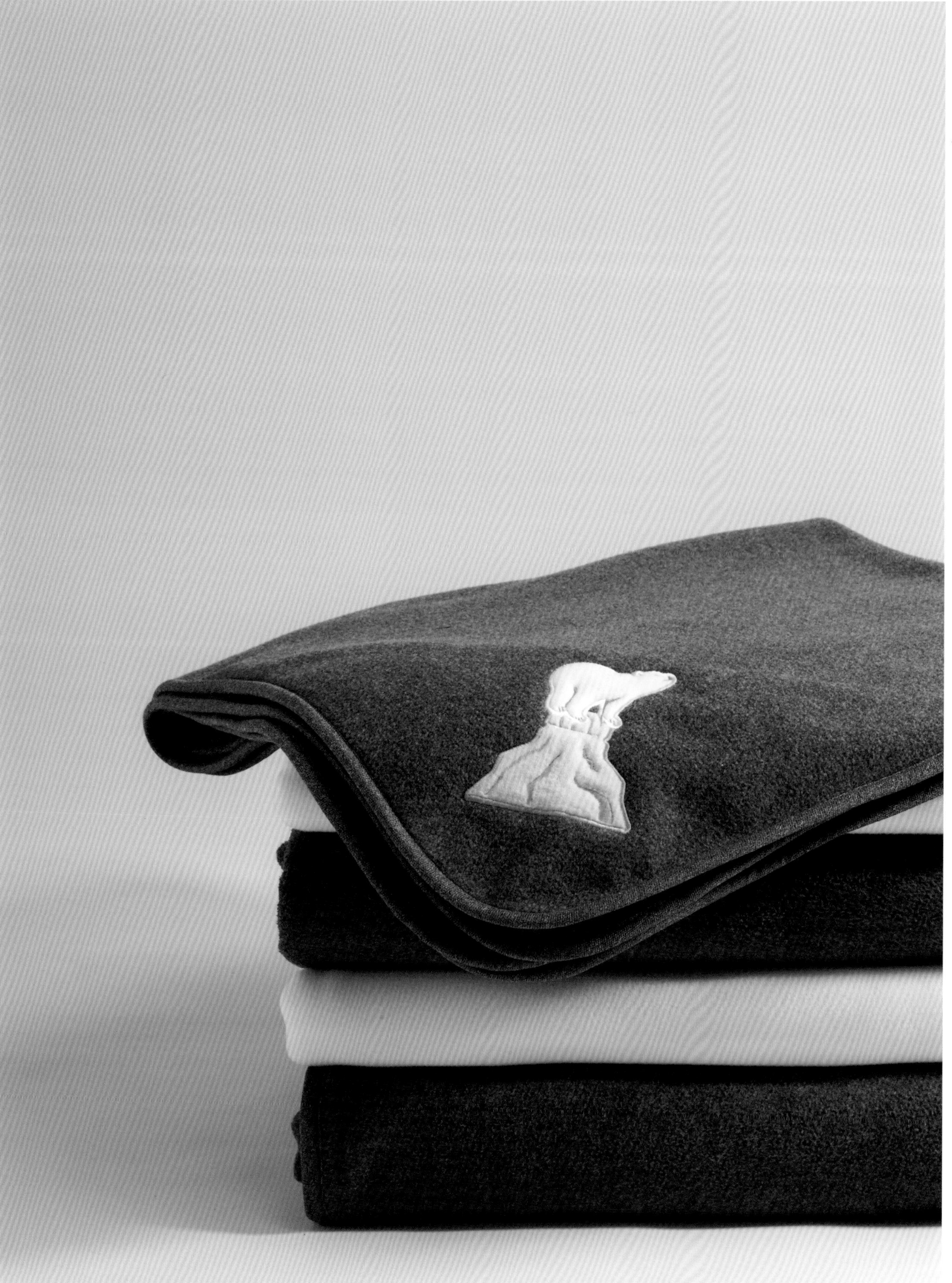

19

ESPRESSO

Urban Bicycle

GEARLAB

Mitigating the effects of traffic pollution and managing transport congestion is a pressing challenge for most urban planners. Representing the concerns of their generation, GEARLAB have invested their design knowledge in the pursuit of niche solutions for such problems. Their *espresso* urban bike is a prime example.

Asked what motivates them to put yet another bike on the road, design director Henry Chang explains the rationale for this product quite simply. 'Most bikes are built for power: put them on any road or rocky terrain and off you go. But actually these may not be the best alternative for getting around places like Taipei. Urban cyclists need not only to quickly accelerate or stop at intersections. They also need to feel confident and comfortable wearing a nice outfit or carrying an office bag. So the challenge is how to have an elegant riding experience in the city … It's a kind of a fashionable way to travel, the old fashioned way.'

Growing up in Vancouver, Chang has been commuting by bike since he was 12 and has an embodied sense for the two-peddler. He has also travelled overseas to research the bike systems of some of the world's most bike-friendly cities. This broader perspective has generated new ideas to be introduced to Taiwan. As with the cultural differences of its *Greenland Paddle* (see p. XXX), they regarded the European bikes as being great for places like Amsterdam or Copenhagen but too high for the average Taiwanese and too heavy to turn around Taipei's narrow laneways. 'We came up with an urban bike that we enjoy using around the neighbourhood. It's for a niche market that the big manufacturers wouldn't touch. All the better for us!'

Characteristics of this unisex bike include smaller wheels, lower frame and front basket. Compared to sports bikes, its leaning angle supports a more upright position intended to give a rider a wider view of the road and the traffic lights. Attached to the main frame is the basket that can safely carry a 15-inch computer satchel or a grocery bag. This helps the cyclist conserve energy and maintain balance.

The integrated styling gives the bike a retro-romantic appearance. The patented lock is stowed away by being wrapped around the frame, so it can never be lost. It is also long enough to loop through the wheels. The custom-made bell has a charming ding-dong tone for friendlier interaction with pedestrians. The designers say that lifestyle cycling has to feel natural and easy. They hope *espresso* becomes the bike most people enjoy around Taipei.

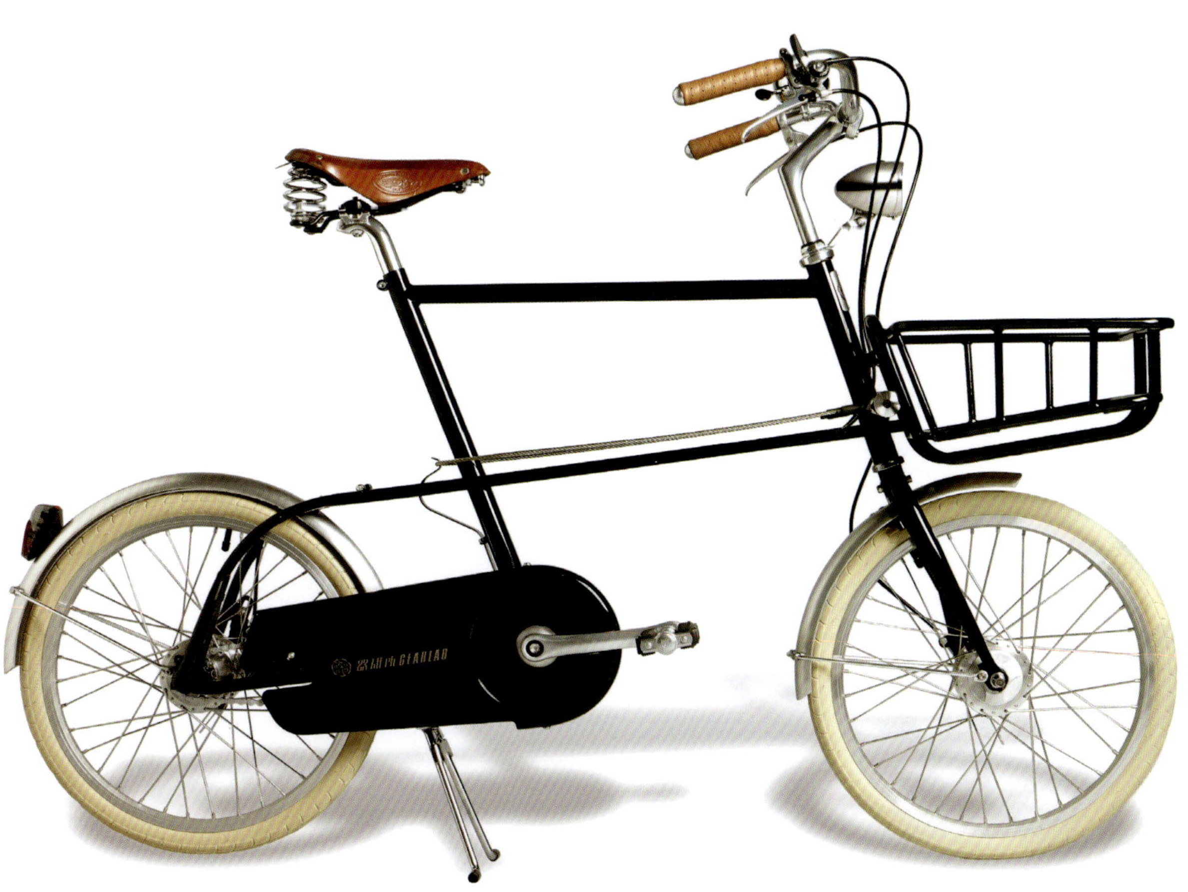

20

FABRIC GARDEN

Textile

Tom Cheng | TTRI

Fabric Garden is the world's first 3D curved surface textile designed as a soil substitute. Its composite fibres can be used for planting anything: from herb gardens on the balcony to greening up building facades to farming. Dr Huang, senior researcher at Taiwan Textile Research Institute (TTRI), jokes that the idea behind this product was quite simple. Recalling school botany lessons, he says: 'Kids learn about plants by doing home experiments like seeding green beans in cotton submerged in water. If the temperature is right and there is a bit of sunlight, they can observe the gradual sprouting of new bean shoots. *Fabric Garden* is based on the same experiment, only that it's more robust and sophisticated than cotton pads.'

The product is constructed of two layers of woven material made from recycled PET bottles spun into yarn. Sandwiched in-between is another layer of reused fibre. The top surface is slightly porous, enabling water and air to flow into the inner side. Nutrients remain trapped inside and slowly seep to the plant roots. The grey fabric can be seeded with any kind of vegetation. All that needs to be done is for tiny insertions to be made into the top layer in order for shallow pockets to be made for seedling.

The texture is adaptable to any surface it is attached to. It can be spread out flat, similarly to laying turf for a lawn, or it can be curved into sculptural forms to support fantastical hanging gardens. As it is a relatively lightweight material, the fabric is also suitable for greening up the exterior of buildings (which requires the construction of a special irrigation system). An encouraging example of this is a government department in the southern city of Chiayi that greened up 1,350 m² of its office buildings with the fabric.

Of course, the idea of hanging gardens is as old as ancient Babylon. However, the designers and scientists at TTRI have produced a new generation building product that also can be adapted for humanitarian purposes. 'While working on the project, I was thinking of all the people living in dry regions, like Sub-Saharan Africa, who cannot grow food crops because there is no topsoil around. Our product can be a blessing for them. Also, it can be a part of floating aquaponics systems in other places where poverty is rampant and there isn't enough food', enthuses Tom Cheng. 'But even if in the end the only use is to make Taiwanese cities prettier, I'd still feel happy we are putting design to good use.'

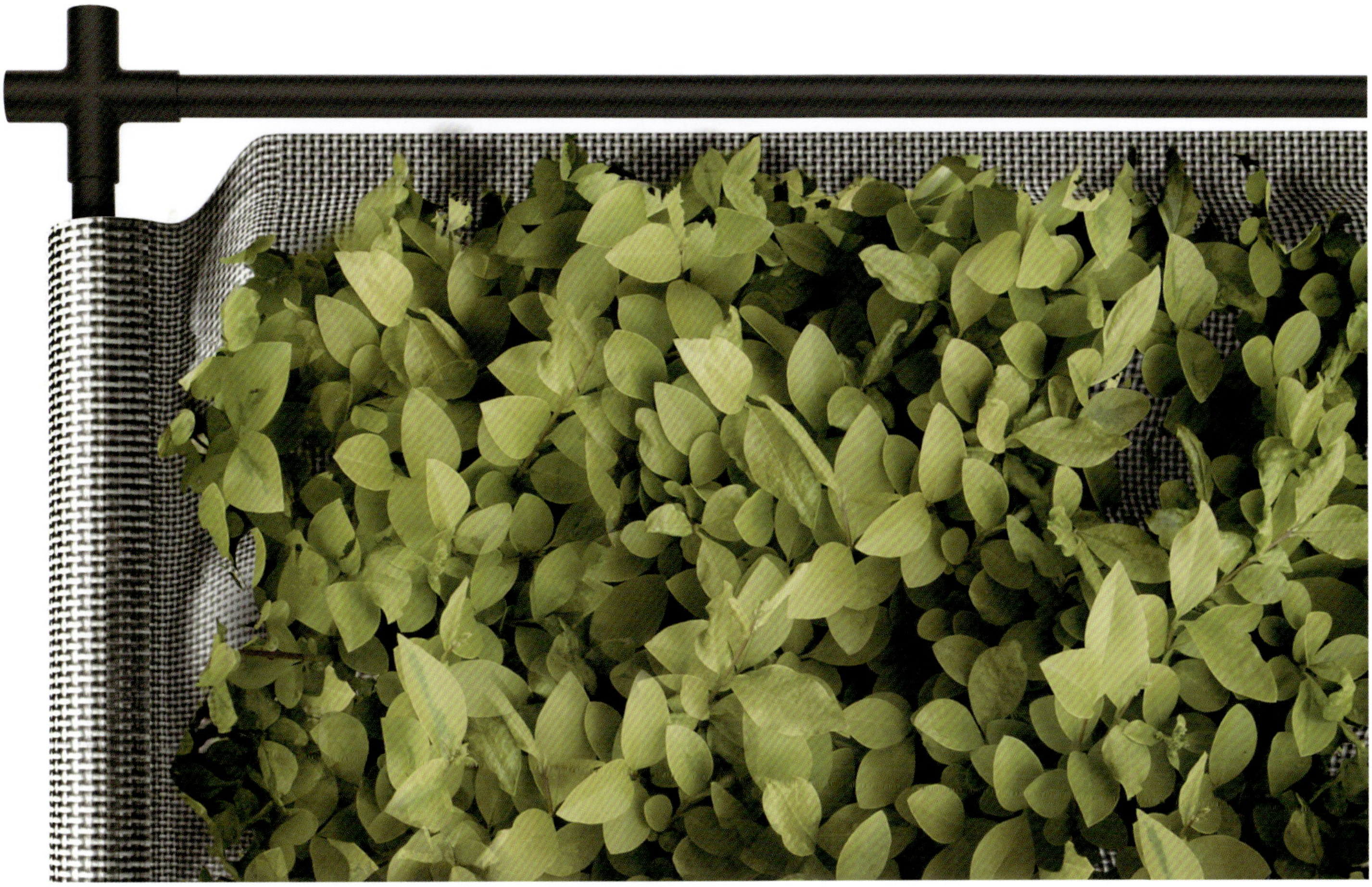

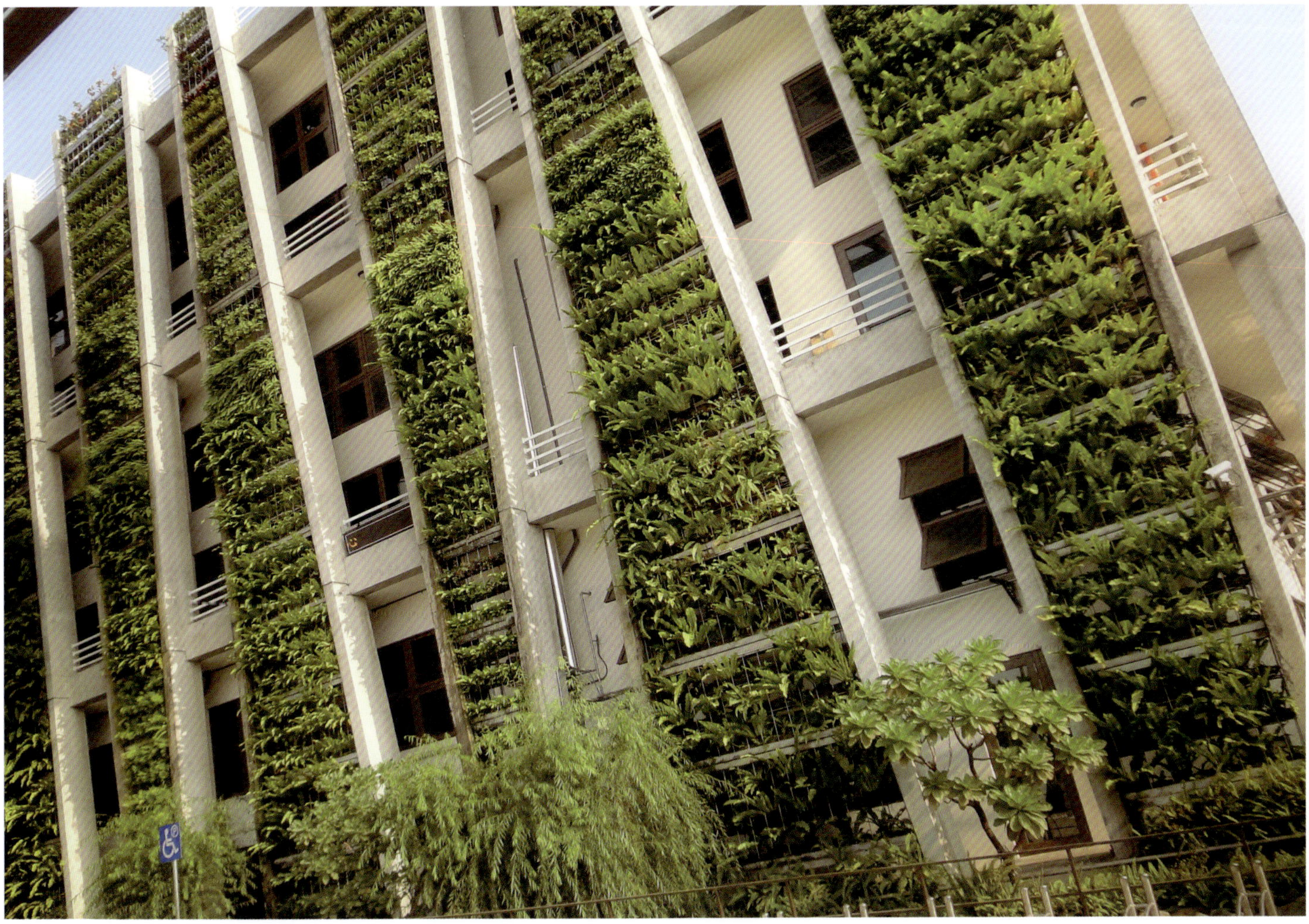

21

FLAMENCA

Ambient Light

Jennifer Chen | QisDesign

Despite its reputation as a city that never sleeps, with markets and clubs packed with people socialising late into the night, Taipei can be a lonely place. 'Everyone tends to be busy and personal contacts are hard to keep. I often work until late and when I get to my apartment I look for something to welcome me', confides Jennifer Chen. 'I was thinking about this when I was assigned to develop Qisda's next generation lighting products. They had to bring some joy to people who work hard and don't have time for simple pleasures.'

An admirer of Spanish folk music, Chen is fascinated by flamenco dancers and their ability to express depth of emotion: 'I wanted to find a way to plant the seed of that kind of passion into my product. At first, I made sketches from flamenco costumes then abstracted lines and shapes of 'liveliness' as represented in their movement. My flirty *Flamenca* has playfully captured this concept by throwing an ambient light of dancing shadows and colourful reflections.'

The lamp looks deceptively simple, but many steps were undertaken by engineers, designers, and manufacturers to produce this product. The body is made from two mirroring segments of ruffled transparent acrylic held together at the core by a cylinder with embedded tiny LED lights. The direction of each light points vertically towards the acrylic part, then it refracts along its curves in horizontal beams. The top of the lamp is a metallic disk made of conductive silver attached to a touch sensor. This allows for the light to be controlled via a gentle tap of the fingertips.

To enhance its rhythmic form, the acrylic halves are each tinted in warmer and cooler hues. The designer credits her sensitivity towards the blending of colours, and light and shadow to her prior practice as a painter. 'The end product is wonderful ... even more so because it's completely recyclable. When I was testing the final prototype, the manufacturer suggested that the acrylic be sprayed with a protective coating as a standard practice. I refused. I'm sure *Flamenca* has a happier existence because of it', says Chen, visibly pleased.

The lamp could be adapted as a cardholder or a bowl for serving complimentary sweets at reception desks. Because of its unconventional shape it has been dubbed 'Buddha's lotus', a fair description of its full-of-vitality blooming form.

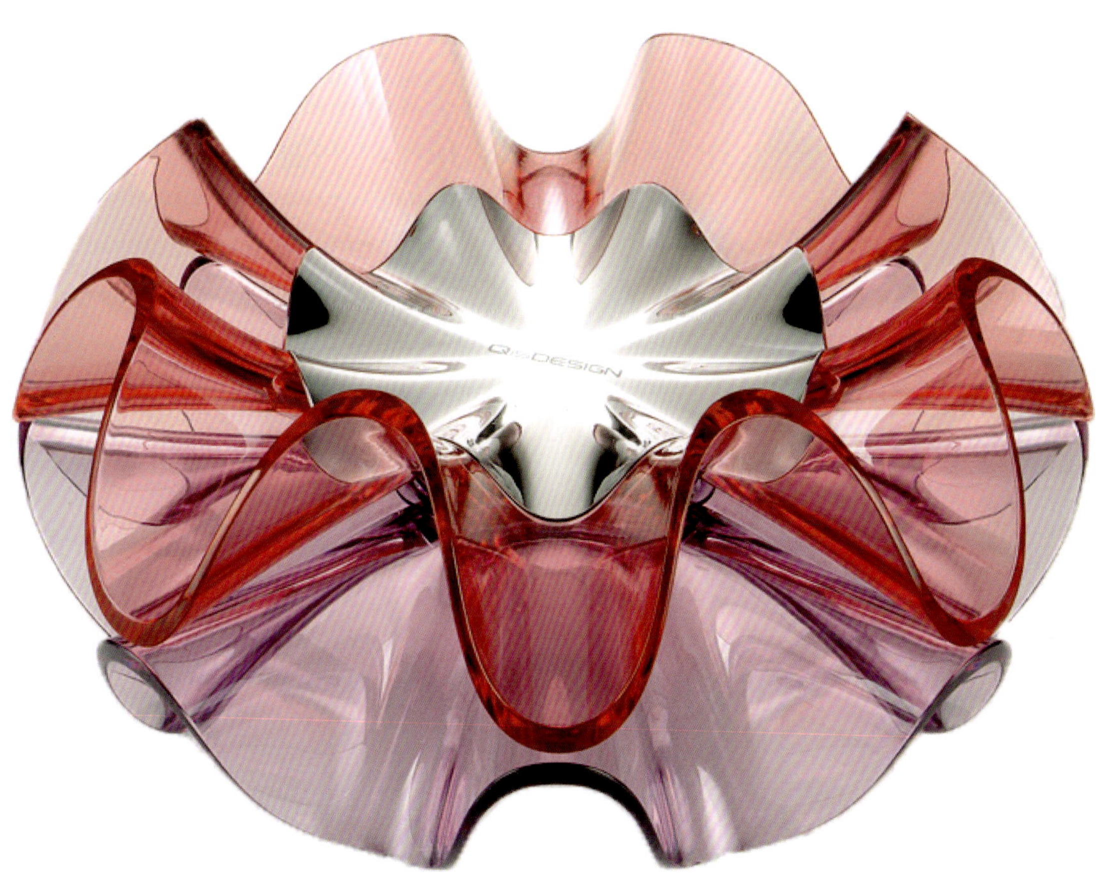

22

FLEXIBLELOVE

Expandable Seat

Chi-Shen Chiu | Pinzaan

FlexibleLove is a unique piece of furniture with a stiff seating made from a paper honeycomb. The concept was sparked when Chi-Shen Chiu discovered a local manufacturer making honeycomb paper pallets instead of wooden ones. The geometrical structure of a honeycomb is Nature's own intelligent design. Its strength-to-weight ratio is especially valued in the aerospace and automobile industries where raw materials must be light whilst providing maximum support. Thinking about its amazing properties to hold up heavy cargo, the designer made a logical connection with furniture.

Another interesting aspect of his work is that Chiu grow up in a family manufacturing religious objects and was encouraged from an early age to study the Buddhist Scriptures. The belief in the ever-turning wheel of life and the Japanese *wabi-sabi* concept of finding beauty in the imperfection of things, have significantly influenced his creative thinking. These principles are evident in every aspect of the aesthetics, functionality and technical specifications of *FlexibleLove*.

The seat functions similarly to an accordion: it has two flat supporting sides joined together by an expandable honeycomb paper body. When stretched out the seat can accommodate up to 16 persons and support a weight load of about 1,900 kilos. Yet it can be collapsed and packed into a large size suitcase. This practical product is especially well-suited for limited spaces as it can be temporarily expanded to sit a small party, after which it can be stowed away under another piece of furniture.

The side panels are made of medium-density fibreboard manufactured from 100 per cent post-industrial wood chips, while the seating is made of 100 per cent post-consumer cardboard. With frequent use the top edge of the seat naturally levels off into a velvety smooth surface. As with all natural fibre products special care is required, so jumping on it is not recommended!

A special quality of *FlexibleLove* is that with time it gradually moulds its form around the body shapes of the people enjoying it: each seat becomes a unique object inscribed by its owner's habitual use.

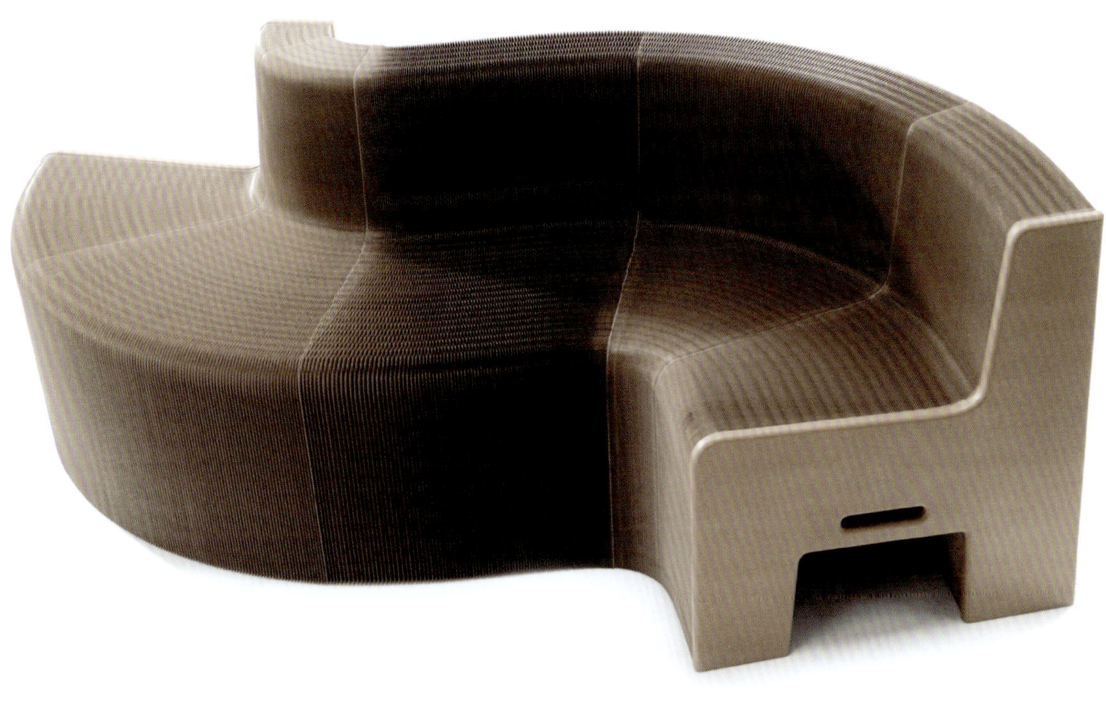

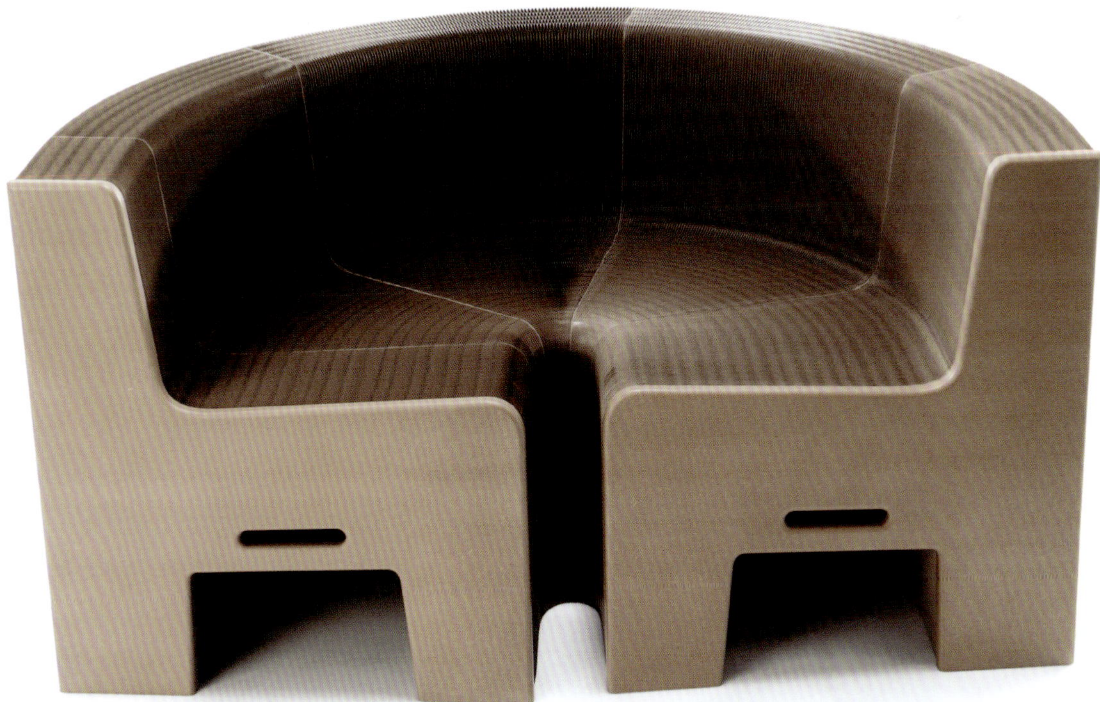

23

FLOW

Lounge Seat

Cheng-Tsung Feng & Kao-Ming Chen

Appreciated for its flexibility, toughness and versatility, the bamboo has been used throughout Asia as a building and product material for centuries. In Taiwan the endemic Moso bamboo is regaining popularity as preferred timber due to its conservation properties: its short growth cycle allows for a high yield of bamboo to be harvested sustainably.

Cheng-Tsung Feng embraced Taiwanese bamboo crafts as an integral part of his practice whilst still a student at the Design Academy Eindhoven in The Netherlands. At the academy budding designers are encouraged to find their own creative approaches and philosophy, which are a very new experience for the Taiwanese. Returning home Feng decided to challenge himself to live in *Zhu Shan* (Bamboo Mountain, Nantou)—famous for its bamboo groves and community of skilled craftsmen—and sign up as a furniture apprentice.

Under the guidance of master Kao-Ming Chen, the young designer learned carving, heating, smoking, and bamboo shaping techniques. 'The way bamboo furniture is made in Taiwan is based on a regular grid filled in with neatly woven patterns. This is desirable structurally because it makes the furniture durable but I felt it didn't express the nature of the material aesthetically. I wanted to try something else.'

Fortunately, master and apprentice had a good understanding, and, careful not to seem disrespectful, Feng convinced his teacher to break away from conventions. His idea was to create a visual illusion of floating bamboo by designing a form that balances the positive and negative spaces in a piece of furniture.

A superb outcome of their collaboration, the *Flow* lounge seat presents an unorthodox yet sophisticated use of bamboo in furniture design. The seat is formed from an irregular pattern of finely polished bamboo strips bundled together at one end but let loose at the other. Lightweight and floating in appearance, hollow round balls serve as the seat's legs and backrest support. These are tested for weight resistance and strength, and fitted precisely for maximum seating comfort.

'At the beginning, masters in Nantou were a bit sceptical of my idea. But when I let them take a seat and test for themselves how wonderful my bamboo couch is, they were satisfied that it works well. *Flow* turned out to be quite a sensual piece of furniture. It has captured a feeling of being in a bamboo forest; reminiscent of stalks bending and yielding as the wind rustles the leaves of the high tops ... free and flowing.'

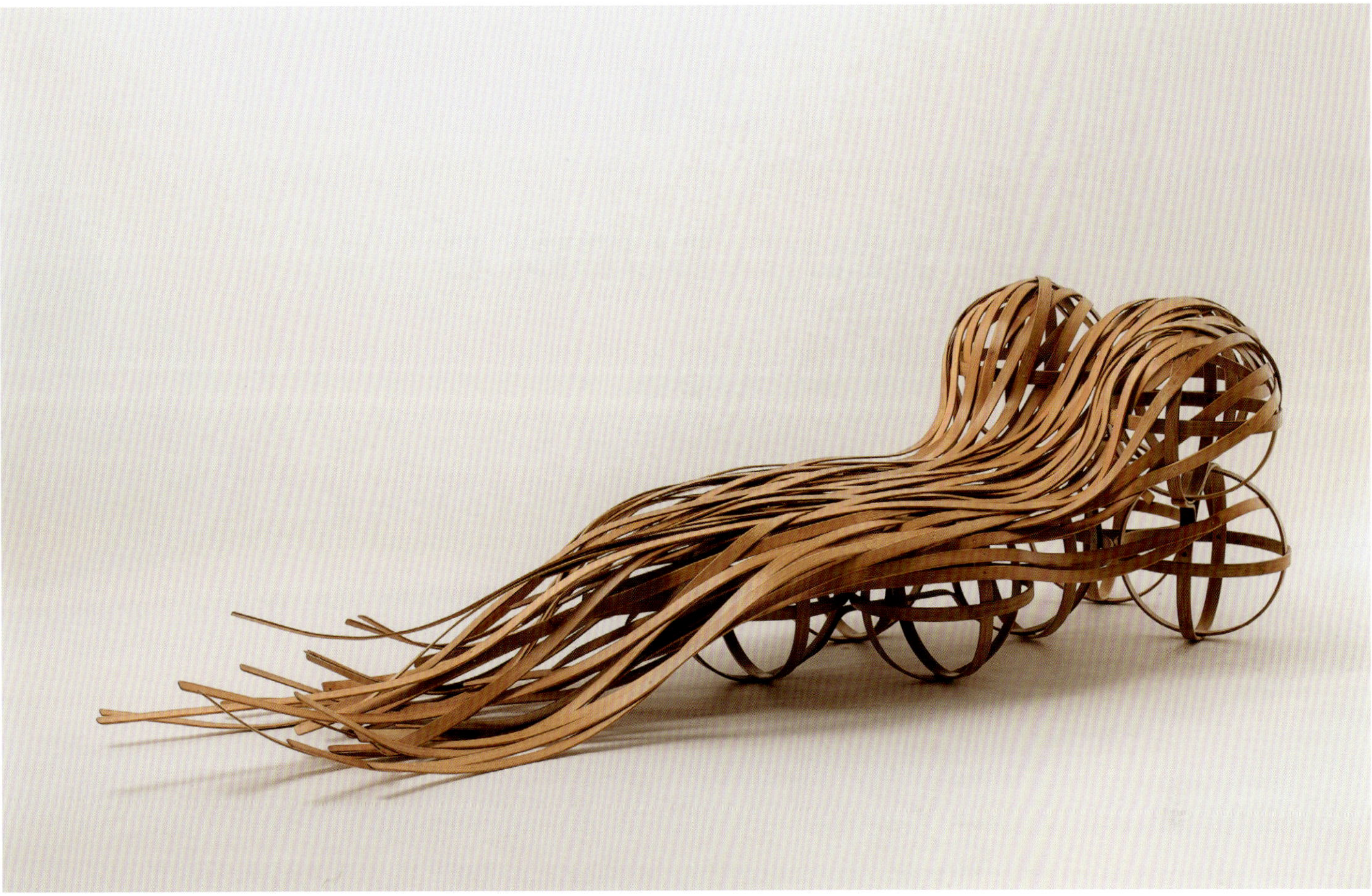

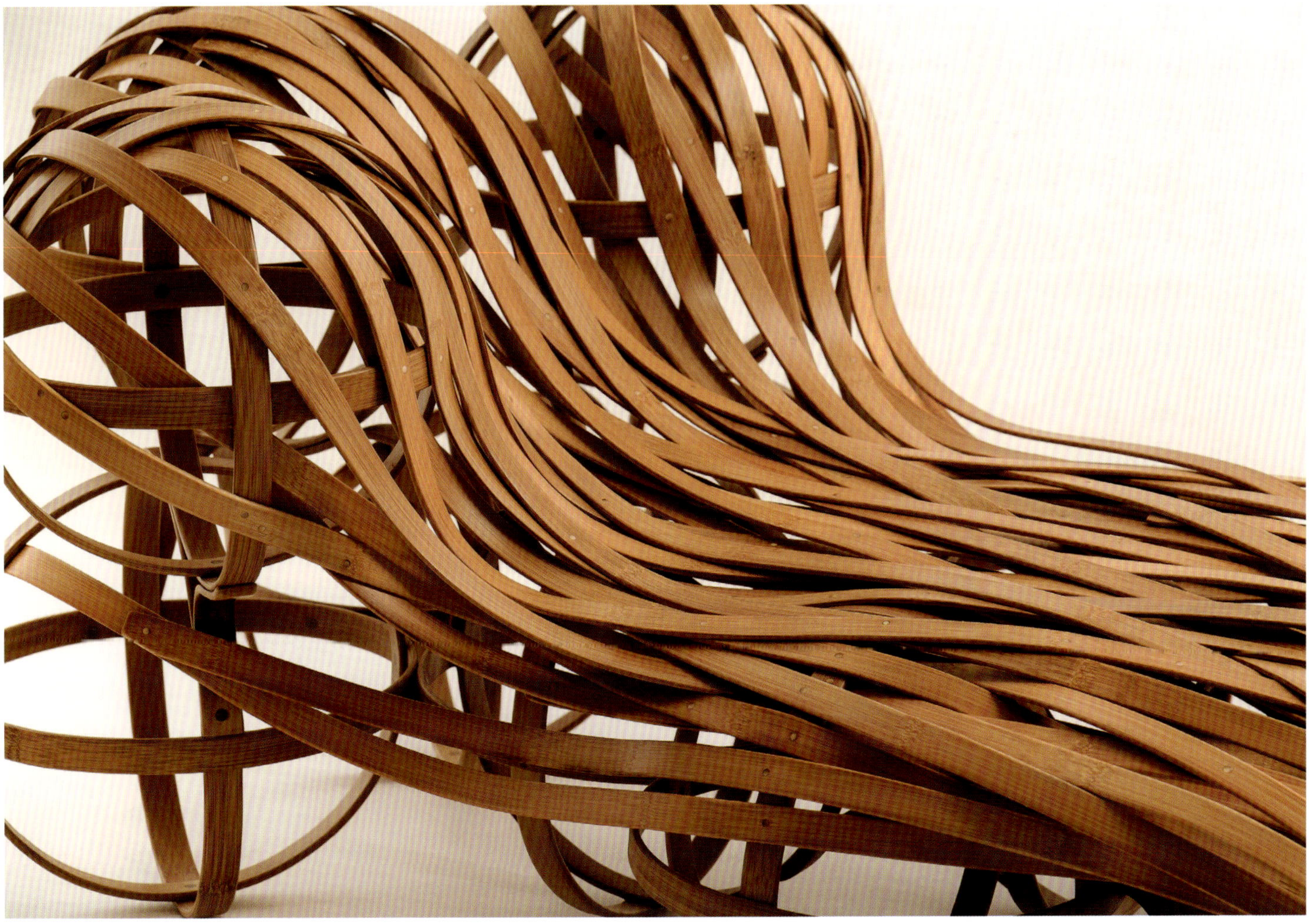

24

FLUID BUBBLE

Fishbowl

Camo Lin | Drii Design

Considered a symbol of prosperity, water is widely revered throughout Asia as one of the five elements of the eternal cycle of creation. In Taiwan, a water feature can be found in every living room, restaurant or public building, and *yú* (fish), which sounds similarly to *yù* (abundant), is offered at social gatherings as a blessing for good fortune and longevity.

Camo Lin's initial intention was to design a fishbowl as a lucky object that could enhance the good energy of a living space. 'My thinking was that if the product is to have a positive qi, an interaction between the bowl, the fish and the people had to be encouraged somehow. As a starting point I researched traditional ink brush paintings of fish. It's fascinating how with just a few strokes an ink painter can capture the lines of a fish, its lightness and movements in the water. The images can be deceptively simple yet meaningful. The challenge for me was to find a way to express that kind of fluidity in a three dimensional object', he recalls.

One day, Lin was playing with a magnifying glass in front of an aquarium. As he watched the swimming fish appear distorted, a captivating idea came to mind: if he was to enhance the qi, it was the energy of oxygenated water that needed to be visualised. One way this could be done was by introducing the optical illusion of floating air-bubbles in glass.

Not being familiar with the varied properties of glass, Lin approached glassmaker Shu Liu to help him develop the new product. On Liu's advice they selected borax glass to make the fishbowl. Borax fitted the concept perfectly because its heat and chemical resistant properties can be made thinner and more transparent than regular soda glass, the kind that is usually used for bottles, jars and drinking glasses.

The fishbowls were first blown into elongated vessels. Then 1,600°C heat was applied to particular spots of the glass body and with great care the air was sucked out from the melted spots. Through this process fine and deep outlines of bubbles were formed inside the object. The outside surface of each bubble spot feels hollow, while its extremely thin inner wall (less than 1 mm) makes the water almost palpable to touch. Holding the fishbowl with two hands and turning it around is particularly pleasurable as the optical illusion morphs the bubbles into different shapes. If tradition is to be true, having two gold fish swim in *Fluid Bubble* will bring plenty of luck.

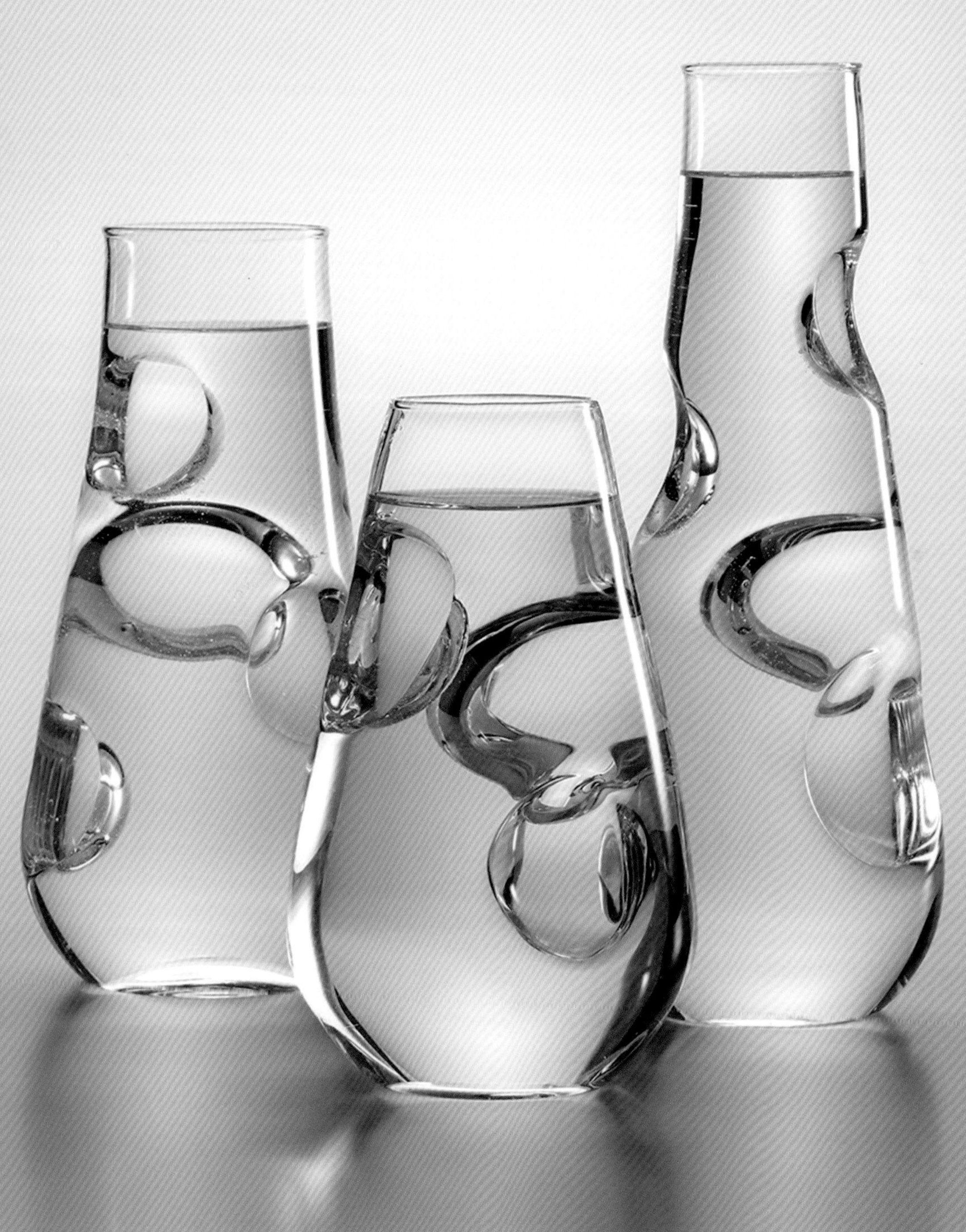

25

FOFOCUP

Reusable Takeaway Cup
FOLDnFOLD Engreeneering

Everyday conveniences have become a way of living for the Taiwanese. Nowadays not only the cafes but also corner stores and small goods shops are equipped with a coffee machine to offer rushing shoppers a cup of tea or coffee. But this customer care has started to generate another problem—one that the *FoFoCup* is trying to solve.

Back in 2010 when *Cyc* Chen was first tinkering with the design of this product, reportedly 1.5 billion takeaway cups were being thrown away in Taiwan. Despite the introduction of various reward schemes intended to encourage people to use their own containers, by the time the product was launched that quantity exceeded a staggering 3 billion. Reluctant to carry a bulky flask in their bags, most people continued to be uninterested in making the switch. No more excuses! The remarkable space efficiency of the *FoFoCup* presents a great alternative, especially its 8 oz version that packs down to a cardholder size.

The invention has the shape of a cup yet it can be collapsed flat and folded like a milk carton. The best way to unfold it is to hold it with the bottom up, then pull the two folded edges out and squeeze the cup into form. To keep it in shape a holding sleeve can be slipped on. The top is a sealable lid. To open it for hot beverages, the security tape should be positioned to the side. For iced drinks there is also a slot for a straw. The product is made of recyclable and 100% food-safety certified polypropylene. If good care is taken it can be used 5,000 times!

Manufacturing a container for hot and cold liquids, which also has to be collapsible and reusable, is not easily done. Paper lends itself to being shaped through folding but the more it is creased the weaker it becomes. Using plastics solves the durability problem, yet fabricating it without breaking the material is challenging. Finding the middle ground was the biggest hurdle.

'We had to be precise with the folding otherwise the product wouldn't last. In the beginning the melted resin just kept hardening too quickly. It was a major headache. I changed three factories until I found a place capable of fabricating the cup based on specifications', admits Chen, whose strong belief in green engineering kept him motivated. 'Convenience has gone too far; we've become too self-absorbed. It takes the pulp of one tree to make 2,500 disposable cups. Translate this to how much we consume each year and you will see a forest being swallowed up just in takeaway lattes!'

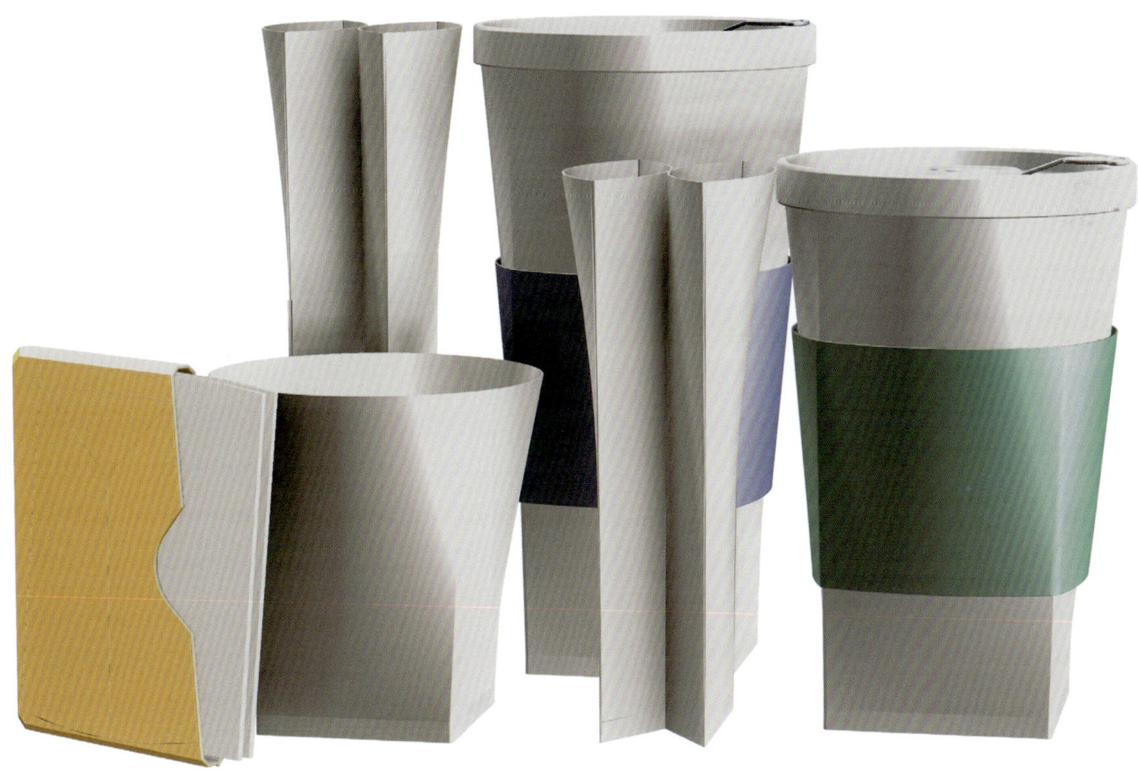

26

FOLDING NOTEBOOK

Notebook

Kevin Lin | Mr. Sci Science Factory

Imagine if a book had a secret message encoded between its covers: a message that could only be revealed when the corners of all pages were folded, one by one, along some magic lines. Filled up diaries that are no longer needed or old books that no one wants to read can be morphed into works of art by simply folding them. It is an idea Kevin Lin stumbled upon on Pinterest and was instantly captivated by.

'I found a folded copy of The Bible and purchased it for our Mr. Sci Science Factory shop as décor. We are a design and retail business specialising in educational toys with a scientific bend. Trickster gifts, if you like. One of the earlier products we made was a set of playing cards with a magic eye image on the back that revealed the number on the front. When I saw The Bible on the Internet, I became fascinated that a person would spend hours hand-folding God's word, turning it into a heart-shaped symbol of love. It was very cool. Unfortunately ... one day the precious object vanished from our store. Someone must have liked it as much as I did', jokes Lin. 'It was a bit upsetting and to comfort me a colleague suggested we should try designing something similar ourselves. It all started from there.'

In a typically Taiwanese manner, Lin felt that he had to find a technical shortcut to folding pages. 'We did try to manually draw the folds for an airplane but when we folded the pages the shape looked more like a banana than anything else. For a product to be commercially viable, rather than just exist as a crafted art object, precision and mass production have to go hand in hand. The secret to the 'secret' inside the *Folding Notebook* is a computer program we wrote specifically for it.'

Applying a special algorithm, the program calculates where the folding lines need to be drawn so that a beautiful 3D shape can be achieved once folded. The original version of the notebook contained a total of seven sets of patterns with a small icon printed next to each as a guide. The icon is a hint as to which visual image will show up in the end. The notebook has a vintage style hard cover, and once its pages are all folded it can stand alone as a decorative piece.

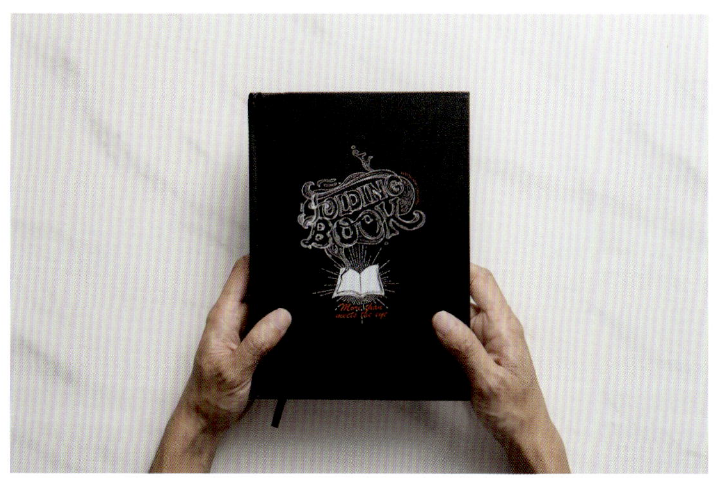
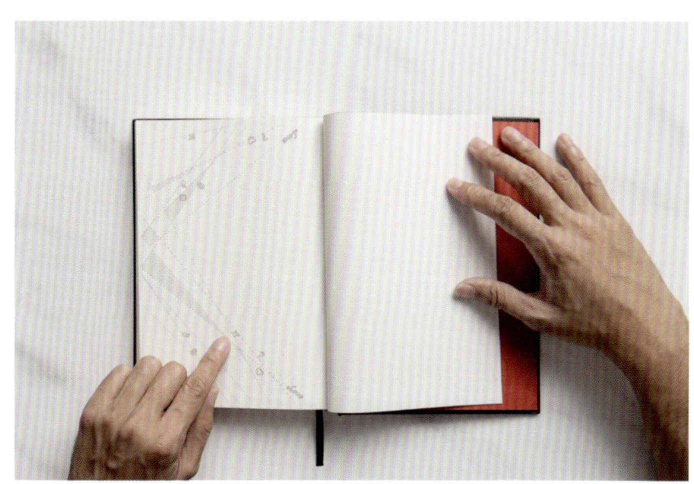
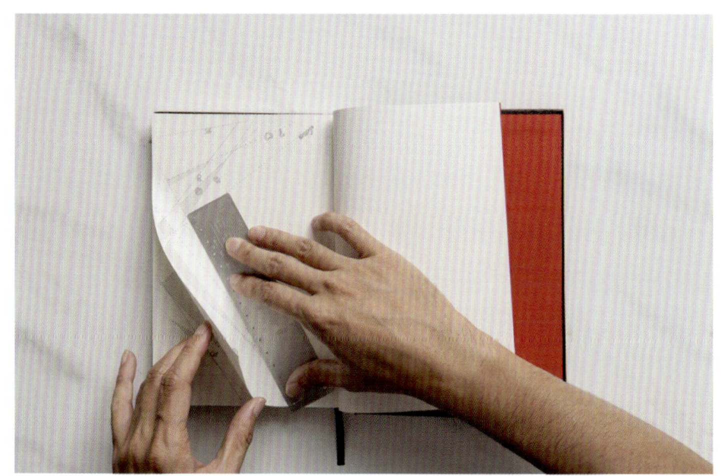
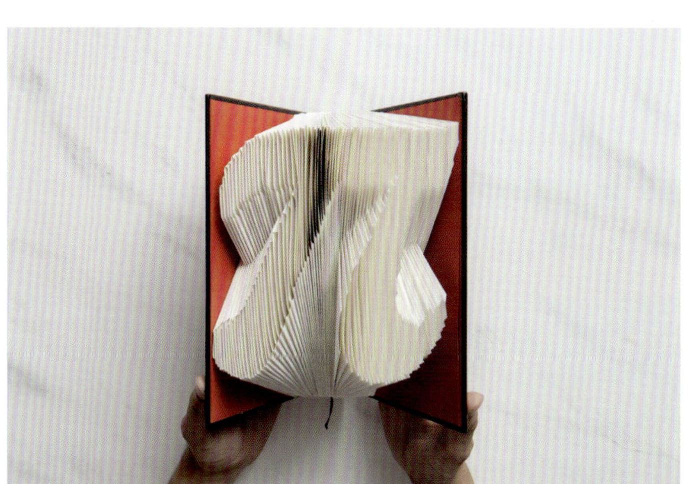

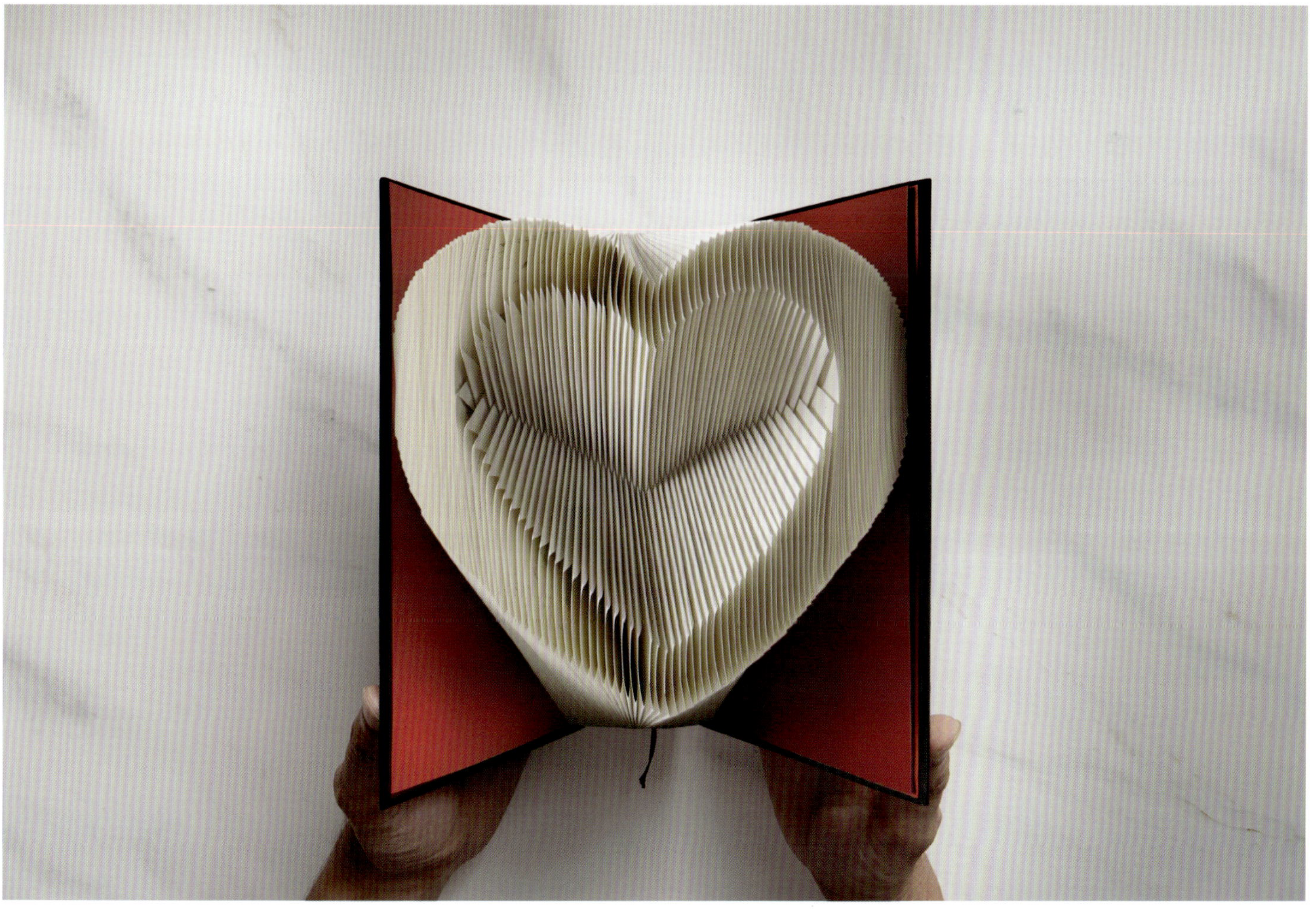

27

FORWARD

Bio Bonsai

Taiwan Phytoculture

A sign of things to come, this biotech bonsai is nurtured via a soil-free capsule housed in its own ceramic *Forward* pot. It is an innovative concept for plant cultivation pioneered by Taiwan Phytoculture. The miniature tree is grown at a biotech nursery where seedlings are germinated under quarantine control. Once they reach a scale of 1/100 to the mother tree each bonsai is transferred into its capsule and placed in a pot ready for delivery.

About seven years ago, while still a director in the electronics industry, Shi-Xian Tai was at a crossroads. The sector was shrinking and it was time for an exit strategy. He decided to hire himself with no immediate rewards guaranteed. 'When travelling I'd stay at nice hotels and it dawned on me there were no fresh plants in the rooms. It was something to investigate: opportunity is often hidden in a problem', says the creative entrepreneur.

Tai had read about an old Japanese professor in Kyoto cultivating tree seedlings using a super water-saving method. 'Good potential for hotels!' he thought, then packed his suitcase and visited the professor. The commercialisation of the technology was promising and so he acquired the rights to one of the biotech patents.

'Converting a patent into an enterprise is an enormous challenge', he admits. 'There is no "how-to" manual; I still had to engineer all the tooling. It took 4 to 5 years until the equipment and laboratory were fully operational. Then the "no bugs–no worms" technology and value had to be developed to make the product compliable with sanitary standards. It was an enormous business undertaking.' The unique feature of the product is the sealed roots-feeder dipped in a fixed amount of water rather than soil. The water is kept in a small plastic capsule and it is topped up once every 30 to 180 days. The technology takes care of the tree, and the tree owner.

The *Forward* ceramics container was designed to commemorate the survivors of the 2011 Fukushima Japan tsunami disaster. Touched by a story of how people in one village, having lost everything, had started to sing a popular ballad rhyming 'forward ... forward', Tai created a new product inspired by their stoicism. The tilted base of the pot is reminiscent of a peg-top toy, with the curved indent of the upper part allowing for a smooth handgrip. The plant is completely concealed and water will not spill even if overturned. The wooden rim creates a visual connection between the bonsai and the container. It is a living work of art evoking a universal sense of hope for the future.

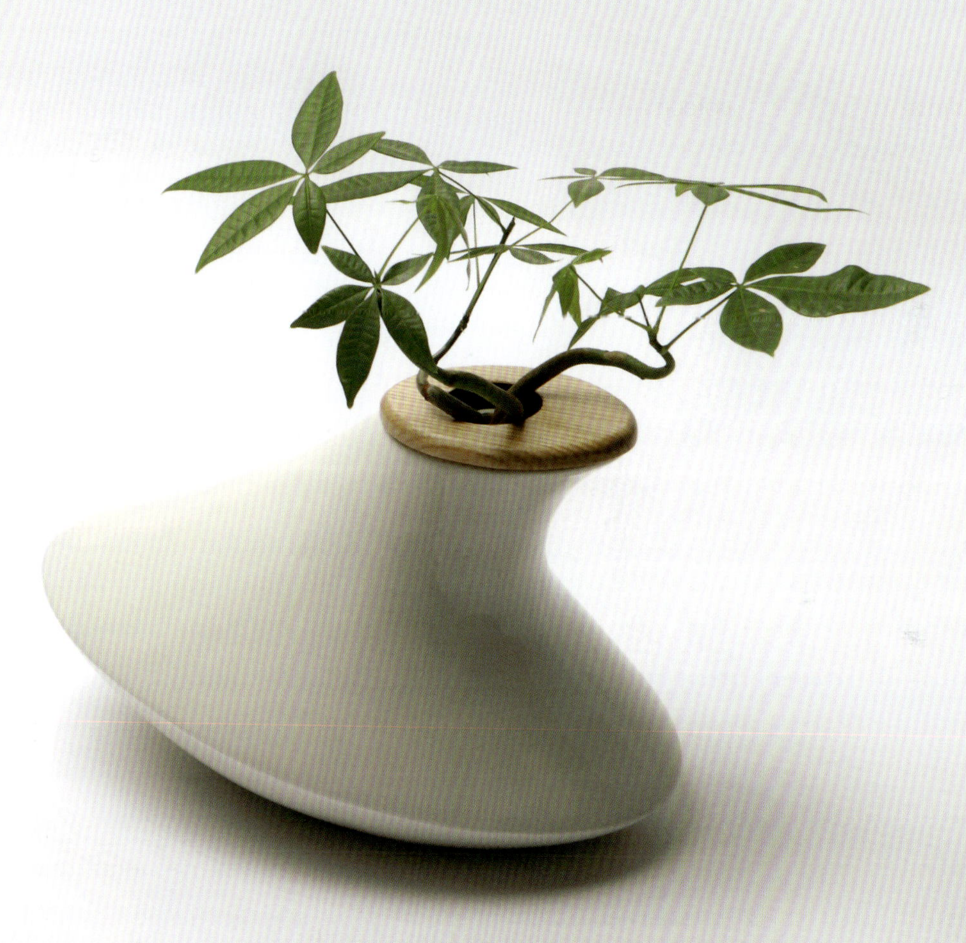

28

FRUIT & VEGETABLE PEELS CUPS

Porcelain Cups Set

Vii Chen | HNH LIVING

Vii Chen was working for a major corporation designing motorcycles when she gradually came to the realisation that all she wanted to do was make objects for the home. The inkling persisted until one evening it all crystallised in her mind as she wandered through a local market feeling overwhelmed by the sight of farm produce on display. 'The stalls were overflowing with fresh fruits and vegetables of an amazing variety of shapes and aromas. All sold directly by the hands of farmers growing them', she recalls. 'It was such a contrast to the supermarket sterility most of us are now accustomed to. That evening my thinking about design shifted: it was no longer about consumption but appreciation.'

Soon after, Chen left her employer and returned to university where she invested her time in developing the *Fruit and Vegetable Peels Cups*. Her interest was in the emotional affect that could be derived from holding a cup with a serve of fresh fruit. She researched the means by which ceremonial and memorial touch can stimulate insight, and 'how through tangible objects a subliminal sensory experience can be encouraged'.

Inspired by her visit to the local market, she wanted to link the visual representation of select fruits with a strong tactile impression. 'It had to trigger some associations even if the user hadn't had a direct experience of the fruit's place of origin', explains the designer. The peels texture of six iconic Taiwanese fruits and vegetables were selected for the surface. She made stencil impressions and sketches, then wrapped the drawings around computer models to get the first concepts. The objects were then sculpted in ceramic and further textured by hand to achieve a realistic transfer of the peel surface. 'The product is cast at one of the last remaining factories specialising in fine porcelain. Every cup is carefully checked for quality before it is hand-packed for the shops. We only make limited editions.'

The collection comes in a glazed and unglazed white porcelain. The unglazed cups are particularly warm to touch and their surface colour would slightly change its patina with use. The collection has become a popular souvenir for the promotion of local agricultural produce, but Chen still sees them as her 'message of gratitude for Earth's plenty'.

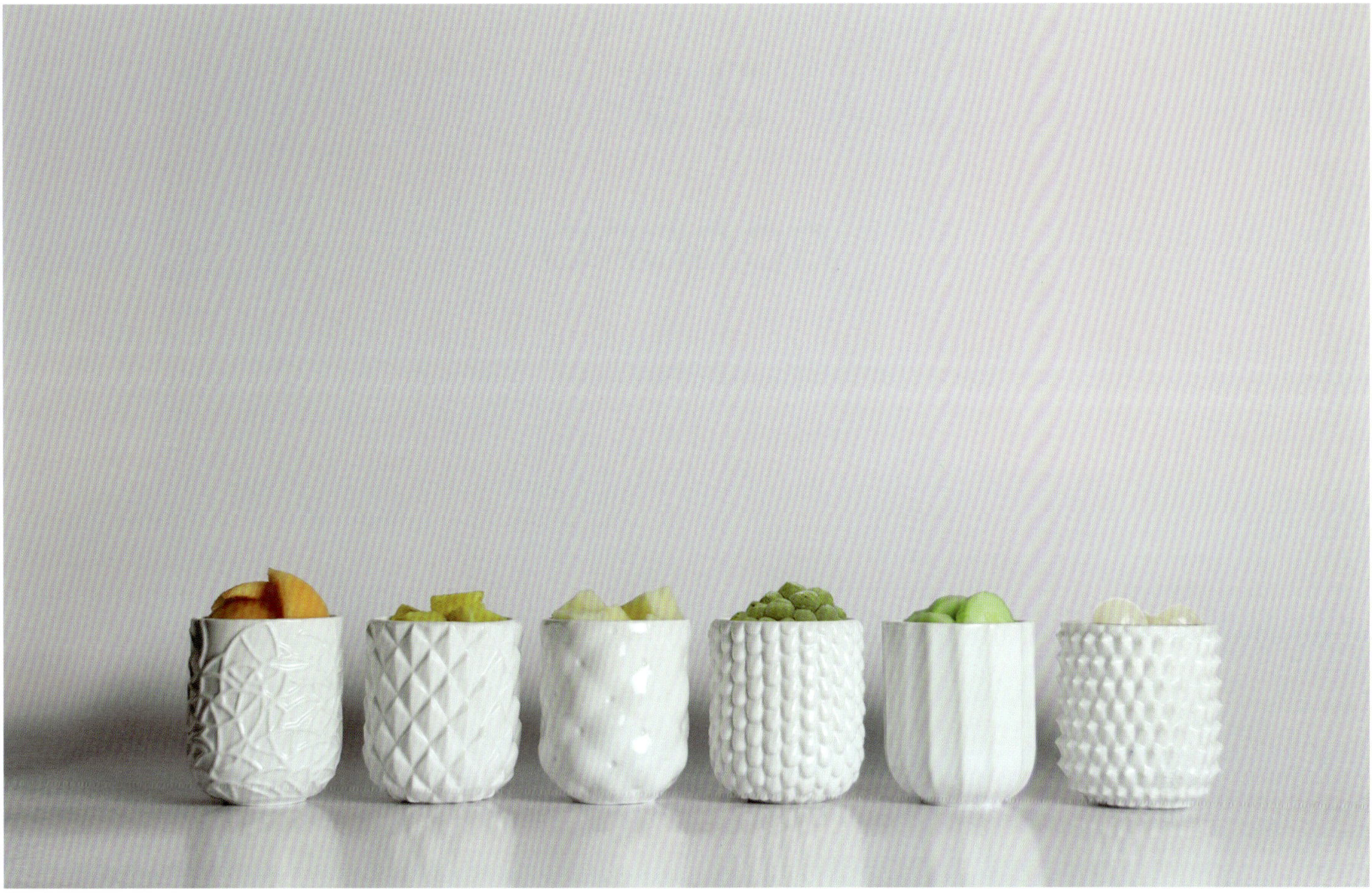

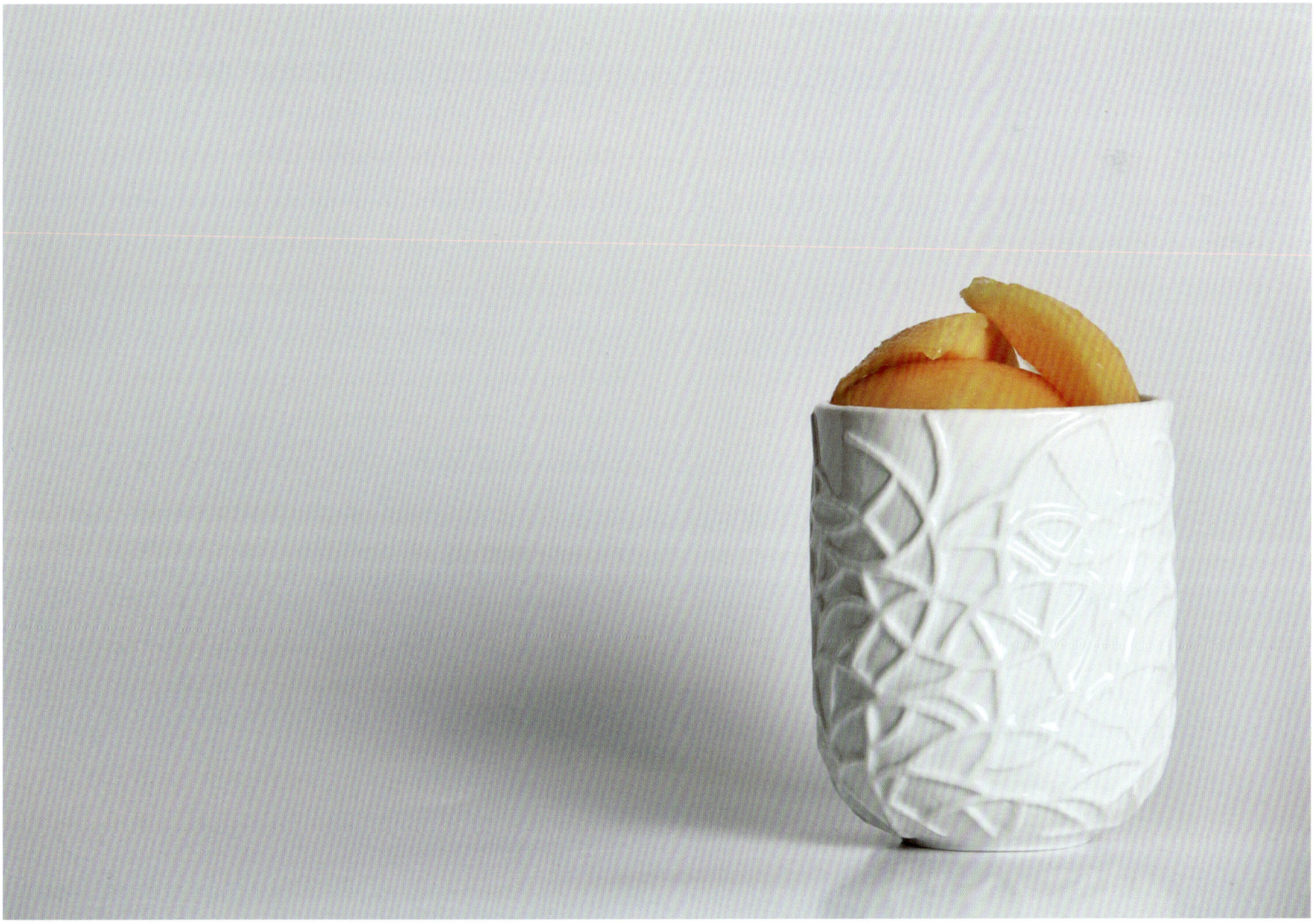

29

GOGORO

Electrical Scooter

Horace Luke | Gogoro

Gogoro is the latest street warrior with a mission to fight environmental pollution in mega cities. Engineered to operate similarly to the mini Smartcar, the world's first Smartscooter is an electrical two-wheeler powered by rechargeable batteries. It doesn't generate green gas emissions and it is super quiet.

The company's co-founder, Horace Luke, is a multi-talented designer who started out as a jeweller, then worked for an architectural studio, and was once a brand manager for a global sportswear company until he eventually joined Taiwan's telecommunications giant HTC as Chief Innovation Officer. Luke professes a sustainable energy future. 'It is the job of our generation to reduce pollution!' he says passionately. 'During peak hour the air in Taipei is unbreathable ... The motorcycles fly like wasps in all directions making a terrible racket. We have the technological means to switch from gasoline to clean energy right now. The challenge is actually changing people's mindsets about energy consumption and value.'

The smart and easy to operate *Gogoro* introduces a much-needed alternative design for the ubiquitous Taipei scooter. Visibly proud of his team's achievement, Luke reveals that the combination of the aluminium chassis, motor, and racing suspension was 'inspired by jet fighter landing gear to enable the vehicle to attain balance when the rider is in position. The compact motor delivers drive to the rear wheel and it can remain cool for longer. We used aluminium because it's a light yet tough material, which requires less energy for acceleration. But it's not a racing bike! It's for urban commuters and it is operable within our network of GoStations.'

Soon after its launch in early 2015, Gogoro had installed over 150 battery-vending stations around Taipei at which riders swap power cells within seconds. The batteries have a range of 60 miles and a lifespan of about five years. Riders do not own them—once expired the company takes the batteries out of circulation, and any unused power is fed back into the city grid. 'The scooter collects travel and performance data via 25 sensors. This helps riders determine the optimal energy. We also built a cloud connectivity for data sharing via our App.

The company takes its environmental credentials seriously: it audits the impact of its suppliers, and each component of the scooter is recyclable. The long-term vision is for the scooter to become a key player in the concerted efforts to get the world off gasoline. Performed, of course, in style that is quintessentially Taiwanese.

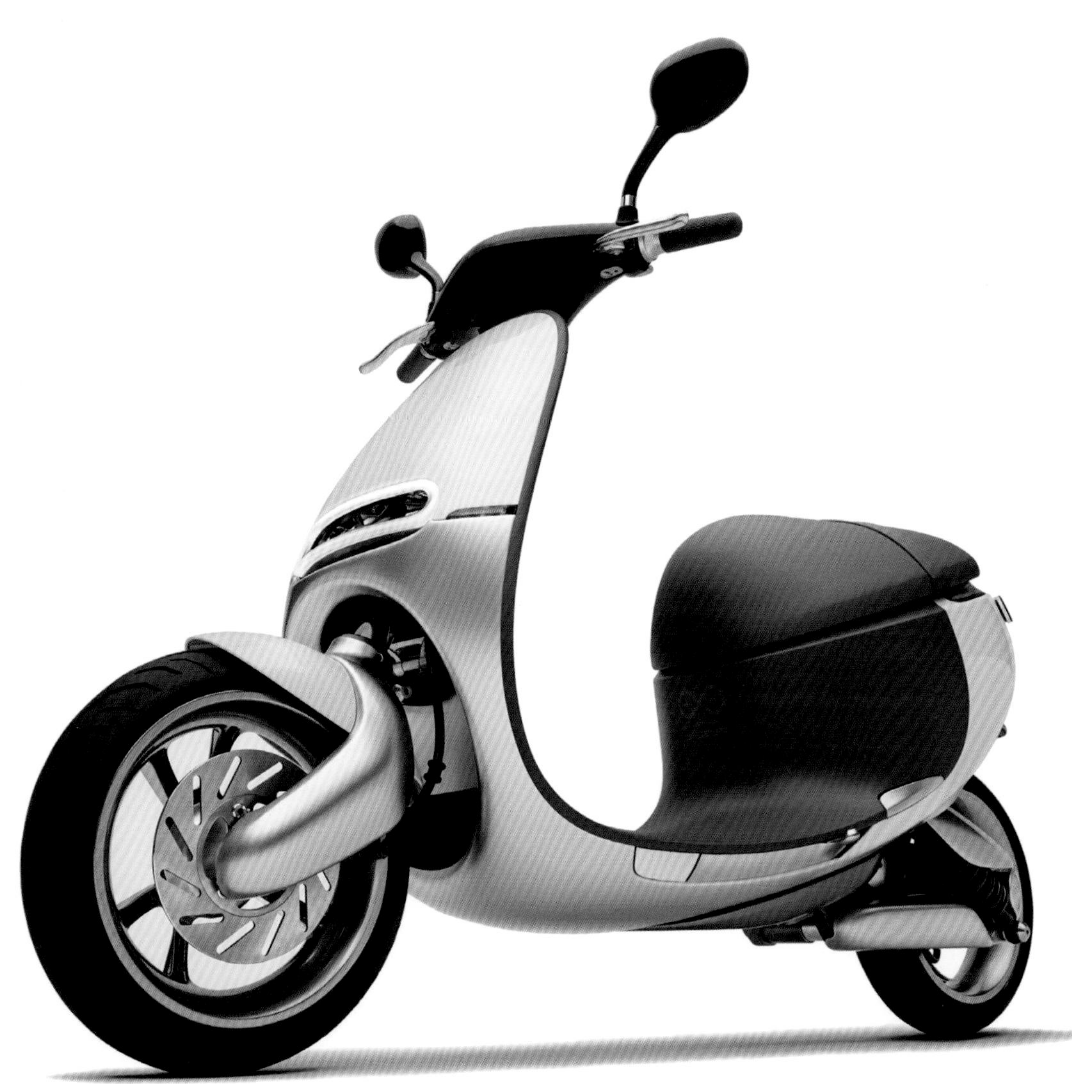

30

HALFWAY

Folding Bicycle

Cheng-Chung Kuo | GIANT

In the history of product design, GIANT's iconic folding bike is perhaps as legendary as the famous Taiwanese rice cooker. Since the debut of its first model in 1997, this smart transportation solution for urban dwellers has weathered fashion trends and withstood tough competition. *HalfWay's* introduction into the market was a lifestyle changer: people treated it as a reliable companion to take among other outdoor activities. City folk had a newfound liberty to pack their bicycle into a car and travel to the countryside for the weekend. Multimodal commuting became more convenient. Storage was less of an issue as its compactness suited the typically small city apartments.

'The challenge was in achieving portability with a quick folding action. Back in the days of developing the first prototypes, we observed that as people moved to live in the city they were becoming lazy about cycling. The question was how to turn the culture around through a conceptual change', recalls Kuo, one of Taiwan's leading industrial designers.

For Kuo, engineering a folding bike for GIANT was an unprecedented project, one full of technical challenges. 'We're the leading global bicycle manufacturer servicing diverse sub-groups. I was sent to different parts of the world to study the cultural context of user experience. It was essential to have such a broad grasp of human and social psychology. Sometimes designers have to foresee where and how human needs manifest ahead of them becoming a trend. As was case with the bike.'

Technically, *HalfWay's* geometry and riding position are similar to the racing/city bicycle. The folding method follows the classic structure of the diamond frame to which a hinge point is added to allow the bike to be folded in half. The patented quick-release clamp is the first fast folding structure in the world. The universal design of the clamp makes it easier for kids or not very strong riders to operate it quickly and accurately. Its overall design has had several reincarnations over the years but its core function has remained the same.

The 2015 model is packed with practical features such as a rear rack, fenders and a kickstand, and it comes with a special mount. Advances in material innovation are introduced in the Aluxx SL aluminium frame, which is simple and light (less than 10 kg) yet it can bear weight at the same safety standards as the regular bike. The new chain-stay structure also allows the bike to fold narrower. With its one-size-fits-all design *HalfWay* has become a great bicycle for the whole family.

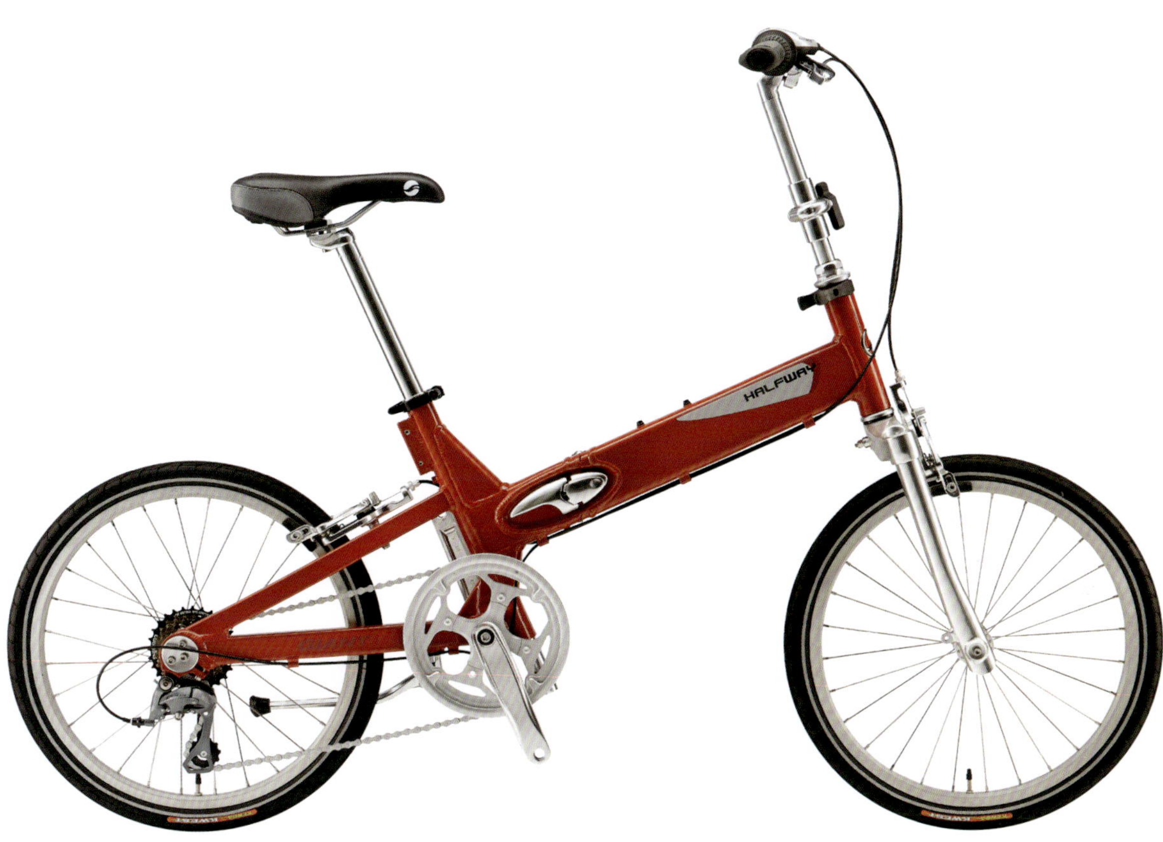
HALFWAY

31

HAPPINESS

Ceramic Casserole

3+2 Design Studio | Cocera

A short train ride from Taipei City, the small town of Yingge is on the itinerary of most tourists as a must visit destination. It is not the scenery that attracts tourists, but rather the town's Old Pottery Street. A century ago the ceramics industry was flourishing in the district and many pioneering pottery studios, such as Cocera, have their roots in Yingge. Despite the necessity to keep moving with the times many businesses have tried to preserve the local style of fine porcelain and ceramic collections. Their colourful shops and galleries now line up the old merchant quarters, making the street a fantastic place to hunt for gifts.

When 3+2 Design Studio was approached by Cocera to design their new ceramic casserole, the brief they were given was for tableware that could 'present a harmonious relationship between the dining table and the family' in line with Yingge's ceramic traditions. 'For us what this really meant was sharing', explain the designers. 'We thought it would be interesting to experiment by bringing together two common ways of dining—the hot pot and the turntable—and shrink them conceptually into one product.'

Typically in Taiwan, hot pot restaurants have the cooking pot embedded into the middle of the table with a mini gas stove attached underneath it. Pieces of sliced meats and vegetables are dropped into the bubbling broth to stew. When ready, long chopsticks are used for serving everyone from the same pot. The challenge for the designers was how to convey this common experience in a portable casserole suitable for dining at home.

The special feature of *Happiness* is the wooden tray ring that is hooped over the top to rest on the handles. Meals are served straight from the dish. Cooked pieces can be placed on the tray to cool and then rotated around for all diners to help themselves. In this way the meal is shared fairly and everyone gets a bite without making a mess on the table. The wooden tray can also be used as a heat insulating matt and a chopstick rest.

The *Happines* casserole is made from pottery clay to which gravel sand is added. The composite material spreads heat evenly, keeping the pot hot and the served meal flavoursome. The product is kilned under 1,200°C without generating toxic emissions. It is produced in black and white with lovely-to-touch rustic texture. Slow cooked dishes presented in this casserole make for a perfect family meal on a cold winter night.

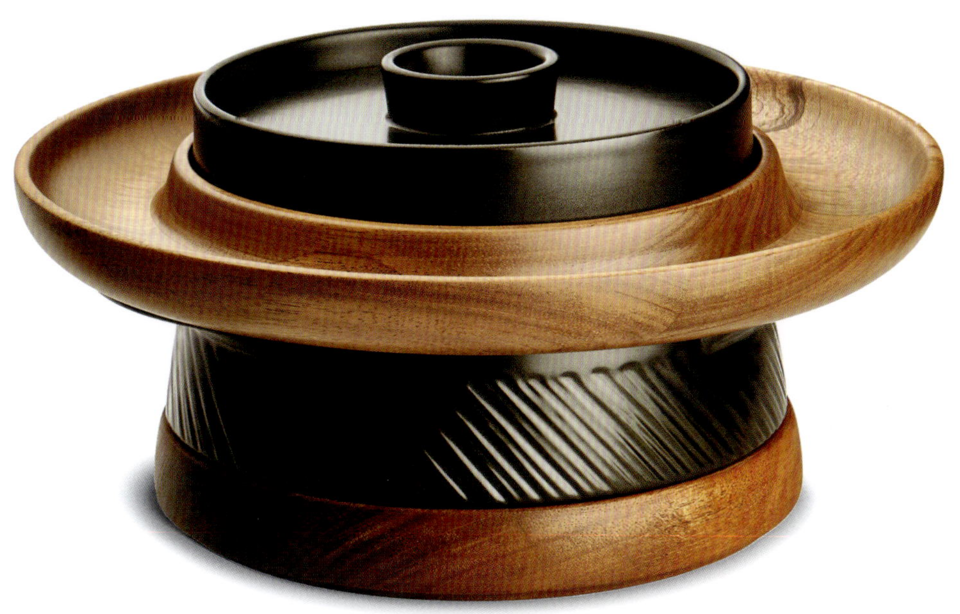

32

HERE I AM!

Sticky Note

Rebecca Chang | Miccudo

With today's innumerable ways for information aggregation and social-media sharing, the solitary activity of reading a book seems a little old school. Yet, despite being born in the electronic age, and regarding her mobile phone as an extension of herself, Rebecca Chang pays close attention to how our relationship with the printed word is changing.

'I encounter many little inconveniences every day, which trigger ideas for new products. I've always had trouble organizing my reading. There are too many things that excite me when I read a book or a magazine—interesting things pop up from the pages all the time. I was trying to find a tool to assist me organise printed information the way I do it on my laptop. Because I couldn't find anything satisfying, I took it as an opportunity to design one', she says with excitement.

Cheekily named *Here I Am!* the product consists of six functional markers, or information system tools as Chang describes them, some of which can be turned into 3D notes through folding. The comment bubble is similar to notes used in electronic documents such as PDF. Rather than writing in the margins of a book and defacing the pages, the sticker assists with short memos that can be incorporated into the text. Similarly, the underlining note can be applied to important passages instead of marking text with a highlighter.

The *vertical marker* can be folded into a 3D mini signpost and used as an analogue map pin. Readers who habitually fold the corner of a page can take better care of printed materials by sticking *a book corner*. The different colours of the stickers help organise the reading into chapters or topics. 'My favourite sticker is the *mini notebook*. I first thought of it as a useful addition to cookery book pages, because when I'm trying out a recipe I like to keep track of my progress. It's a bit like noting experiments in a laboratory onto the extra writing space. It's a useful tool for diary entries as well', she says.

Besides the practicality of *Here I Am!* Chang's wish is that using the product will make reading a more imaginative activity—one that is not so much from cover to cover, but rather a way of discovery or maybe a friendly conversation.

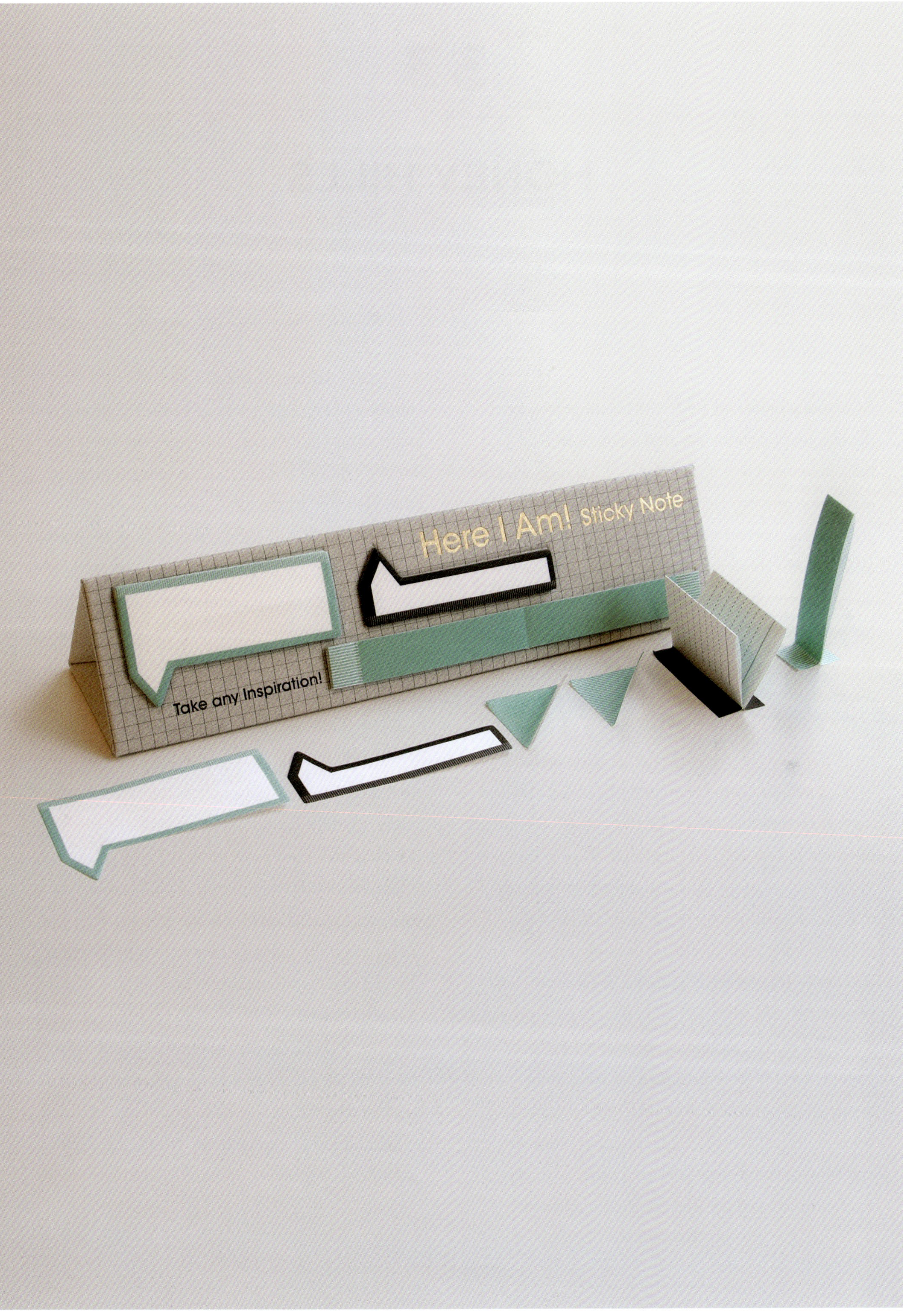
Here I Am! Sticky Note
Take any Inspiration!

33

HONEY HILLS

Educational Equipment

Weplay

As a young university professor of early childhood development, Wendy Wu had a dream to help Taiwanese kids access the best learning methodologies enjoyed by their little friends abroad. She had no idea how to design products; all she cared about was supporting the cognitive development of the next generation. Professor Wu's husband needed little convincing that this was what they were destined to do, and in 1987 they founded a company for the importation of educational toys.

The early years of operation were invaluable for harnessing business knowledge and capital, leading eventually to the launch of Weplay. 'When we first entered the Taiwan Design Awards the judges assumed our product was a modified copy. This was in the heydays of the digital boom when everyone was profiting from making gadgets. Our toy was unfashionably analogue but kids really loved it. And you know, it's was what mattered the most, so we persevered', recounts Mrs Wu's son, Elton Chiu, now a director of the company.

One of their most popular educational systems is *Honey Hills*. Modelled after a natural honeycomb, its twin-hexagon building block combines a tactile container and a step/seat with a soft anti-slip surface. The container can hold materials like sand, water or pasta. Additional sorting bags can be purchased making it easy for children to interchange and play with whilst keeping all materials tidy inside the container.

A set of six twin-hexagons can be stacked or lined up together to form a path of various heights. The system challenges children to find their balance by relying on their own awareness when climbing it. The product is made of durable plastic tough enough to withstand daily use but also soft enough to keep noise at a minimum when dropped by the little ones.

The equipment encourages kids to play together. This is especially important in the early stages of human development as it teaches foundational communication skills and it fires up cognition. 'Kids have plenty of imagination of their own and love to apply it when playing. They don't really need the latest electronic toys to have fun. To them these are mountains to be conquered and fields to be harvested ... with endless possibilities.'

Indeed, unlike the entertainment industry toys that are often turned into trash as they get replaced by successive editions, Honey Hills has a long life cycle and is loved for the wonderful memories of growing up happily amongst friends.

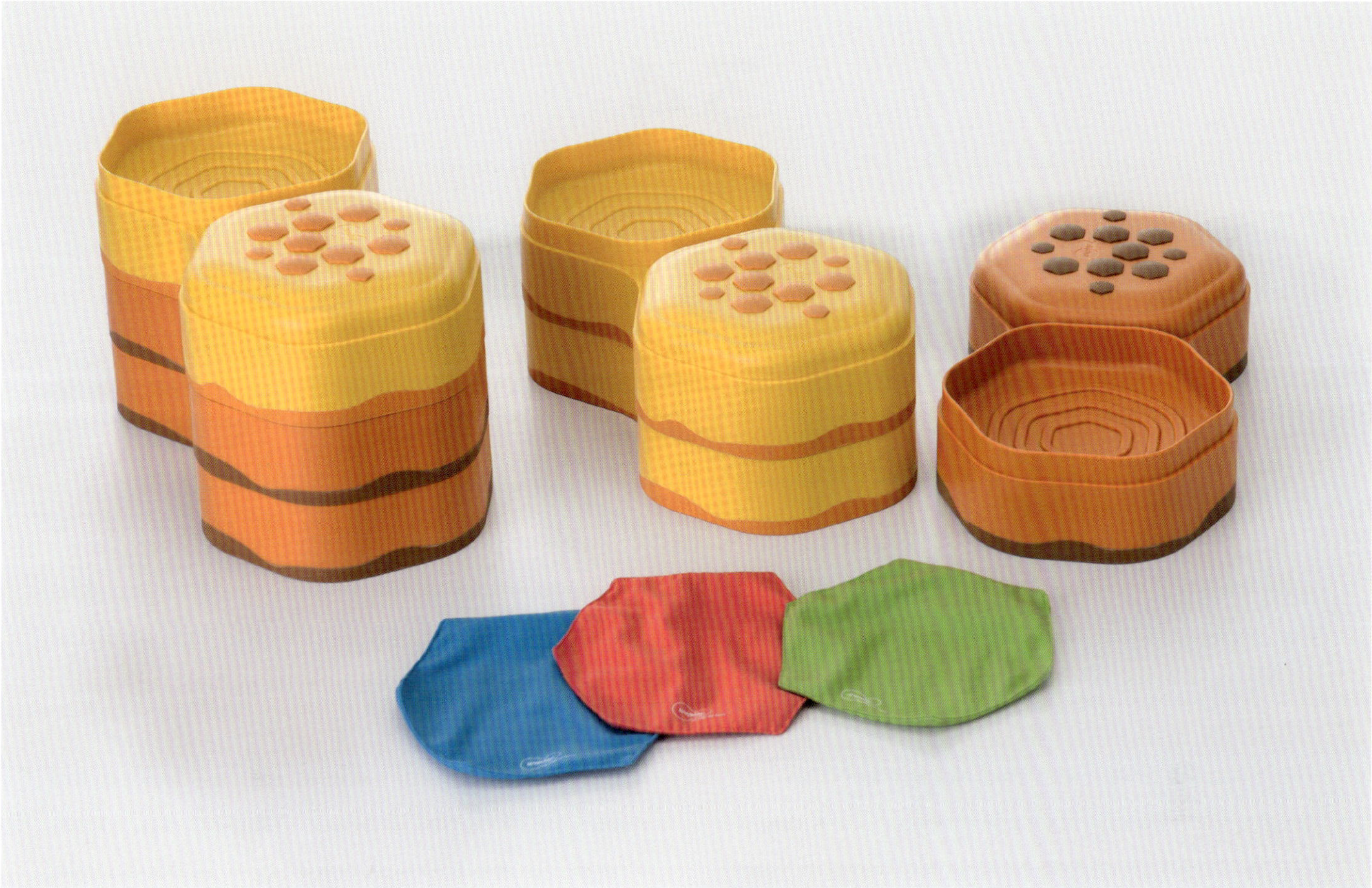

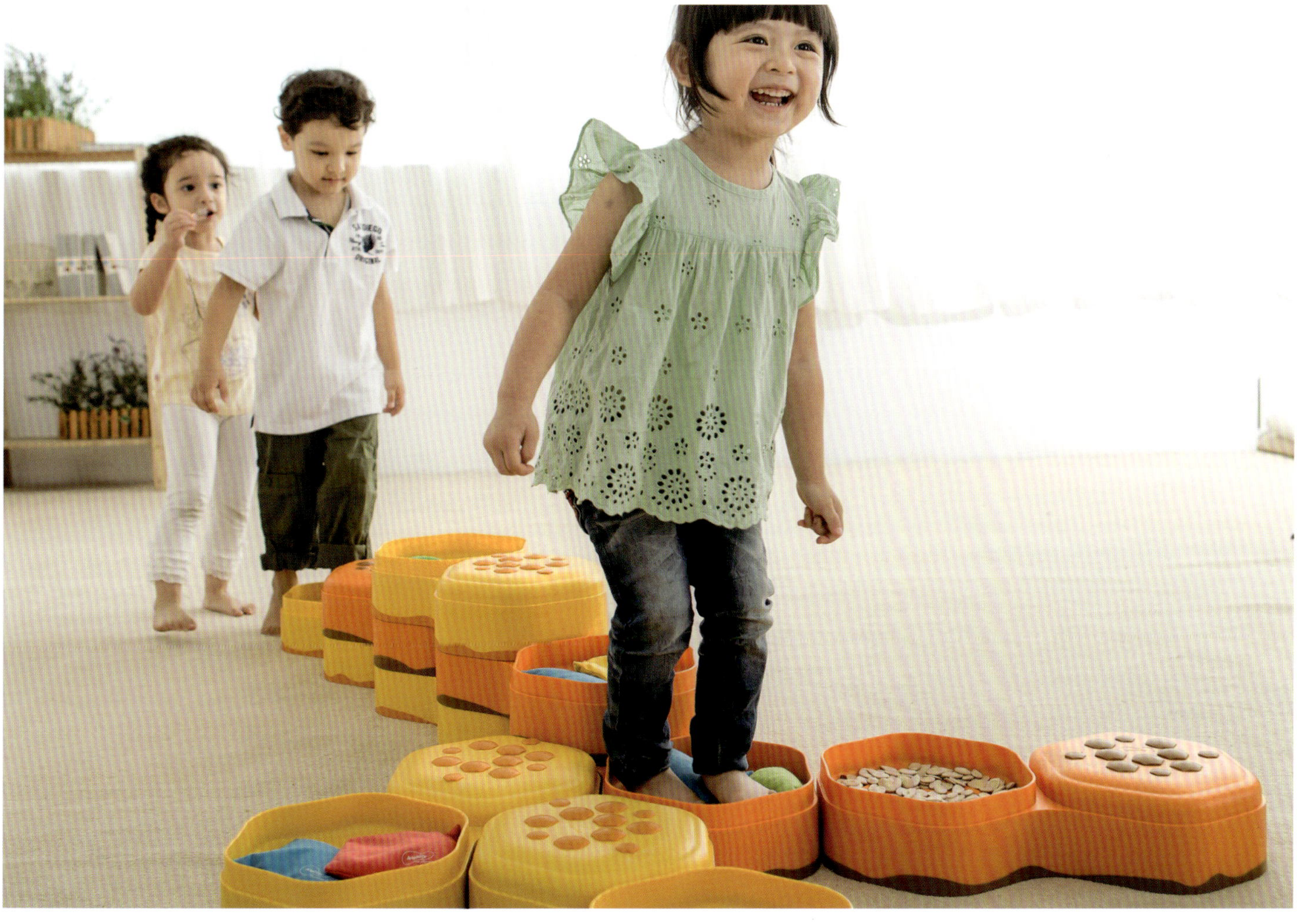

34

IN YOUR TIME

Interactive Clock

Chia-Ying Lee | studio if

Time is such a complex idea. From the simplest sun clocks to the most sophisticated horological instruments, humans have observed its cyclical nature and tried to record it. When Chia-Ying Lee was given the brief to design a clock rather than developing a purely mechanical object, she thought long and hard about how to capture a sense of time as an indicator of presence of life. Lee belongs to a new generation of designers whose interdisciplinary approach to product development results in novel interpretations of age-old concepts. By incorporating electronics and other mechanisms she gives traditional objects some alternative applications.

In Your Time is a pendulum clock device that presents the concept of measuring and displaying time in a highly personalised way. 'Time is often an elusive concept to me. Creative people tend to be dreamers, we get lost in our ideas and visions, and then ... "where did the time go!"', muses the young designer. 'I sometimes get frustrated with this whole notion that "time is money" or that "time is lost". To me time "is", just the way human beings just "are".'

Her clock is designed to tick at the speed of a person's heartbeat. A pulse sensor embedded in the product records a person's heart rate and translates it into hours and minutes. By setting the seconds interval to the duration of one heartbeat, the length of a day changes from 24 hours to the length calculated from a proportion between the heart rate and heart beats per minute (bpm).

For instance if the heart rate is at 90 bpm this makes the clock run 36 person-hours per day, while a heart rate at 60 bpm will clock up a 24 hours cycle. It is possible to see 32 hours and 47 minutes as the day's length, which corresponds to a heart rate of 82 bpm, and so forth. Individual users leave a different day record on their personal clock.

The four rows of numbers on the interface show the current time as well as the heartbeat day length, while the pendulum swings at the recorded heartbeat. When setting the clock the user needs to press one fingertip against the sensor for 20 seconds. Once the pulse is recorded, it automatically shows the heart rate and changes the time accordingly. The clock becomes a tool of remembrance of being, ticking one heartbeat at a time.

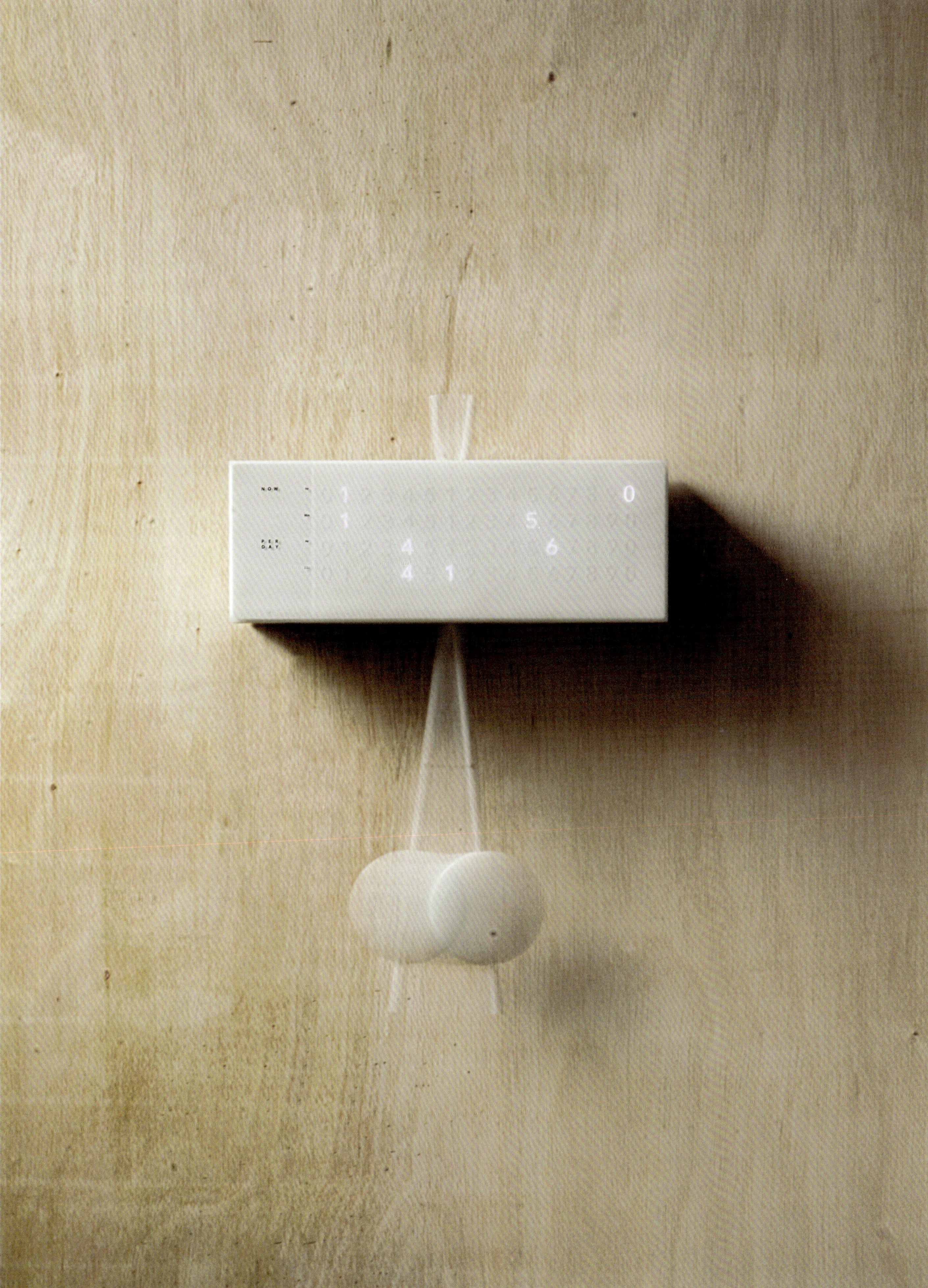
N.O.W.
P.E.R.
D.A.Y.

35

INTERLACED

Light Screen

Vii Chen | HNH LIVING

To appreciate the creativity vested in *Interlaced*, it is worth making a brief historical reference. In traditional culture vertical wooden screens were an essential element of interior design. People used them not only to partition a space but also to prevent drafts or dust entering a room, or to create private walkways along corridors that led to the inner sanctum of a house. In Taiwan the smaller versions of the foldable screen were used as table dividers. These were made of wooden frames mounted with fabric and were intended to display wealth: the richer the household the finer the silks and more delicate their embroidery.

Vii Chen has created a new product that subtly enmeshes such references. She has borrowed from tradition only to deconstruct it. *Interlaced* is comprised of three individual objects arranged together to create a semi-transparent visual barrier with a light source in the middle. Each of the three metal mesh screens—framed in a circle, oval, and round-edge rectangle metal frame—is balanced on a wooden quadrapod.

All fixtures, locally manufactured in Hsinchu, are easy to assemble at home. The wooden legs are attached to a metal platform, which is also the base of each individual screen. There are two small holes in each of the metal platforms. In the first one, closer to the frame, a second frost glass circle screen—the size of a hand-held mirror—can be installed. The second hole is for a light source. Instead of being hinged together, the three screens are free standing and can be configured in a variety of ways.

'I think of it as a light filtering apparatus. During the day the meshes can be stacked in front of one another to diffuse light coming from a window, and to reduce glare from a computer. I made the legs to be about table top high so the screens can be also placed between two work desks and function as a partition without actually boxing people in', says Chen thoughtfully.

'The screens introduce some strong graphic lines to a space, while keeping it well organised with the overall atmosphere remaining open ... which is better for creative environments anyway. If people see them more as a light object, then the light bulb can be installed just behind the small glass screen. I've kept all lines clean and minimal because I want the product to stand alone as a decorative piece, too. Whichever scenography an individual chooses to adopt, *Interlaced* would happily lend its presence to a tasteful interior styling.'

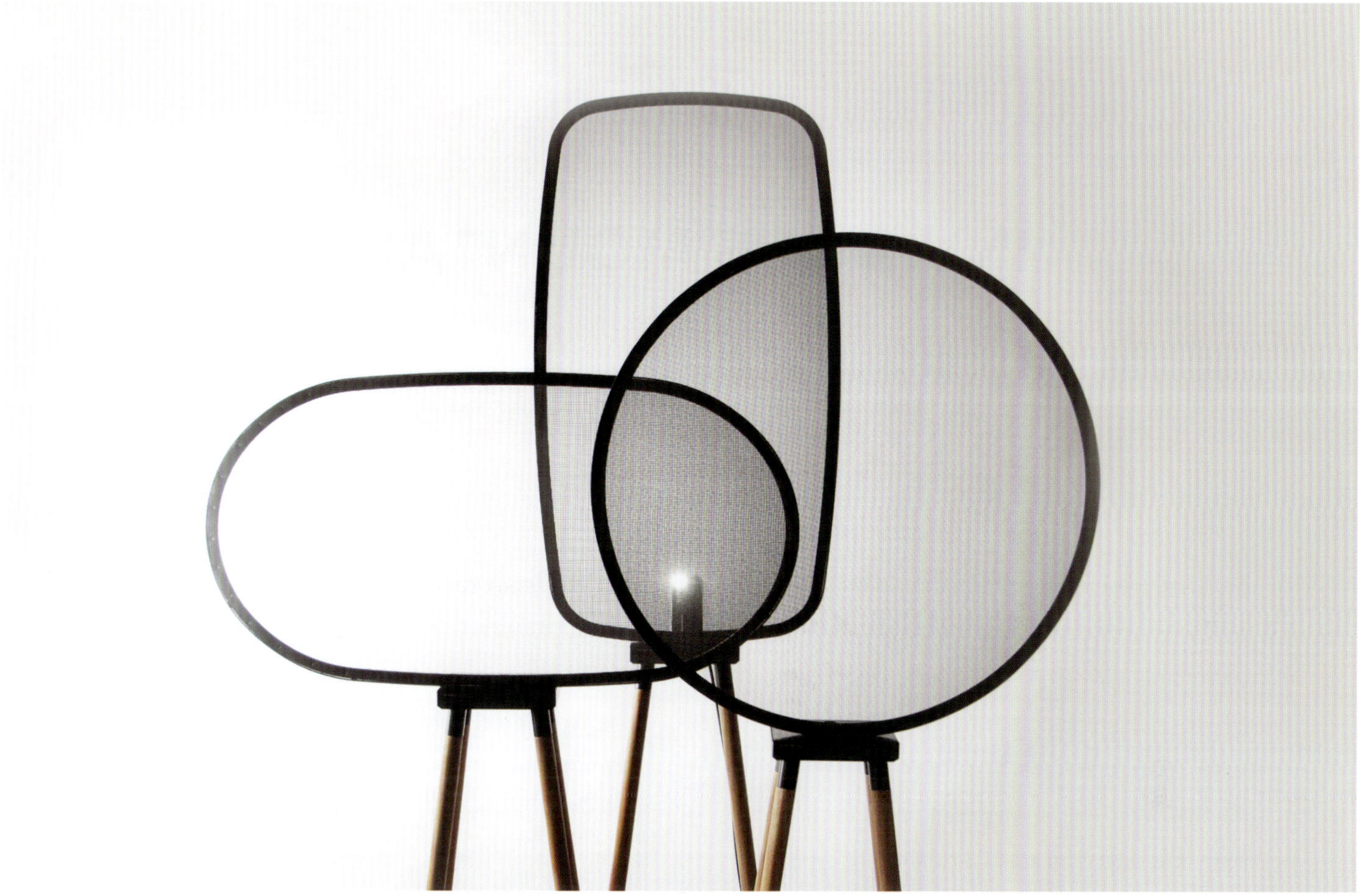

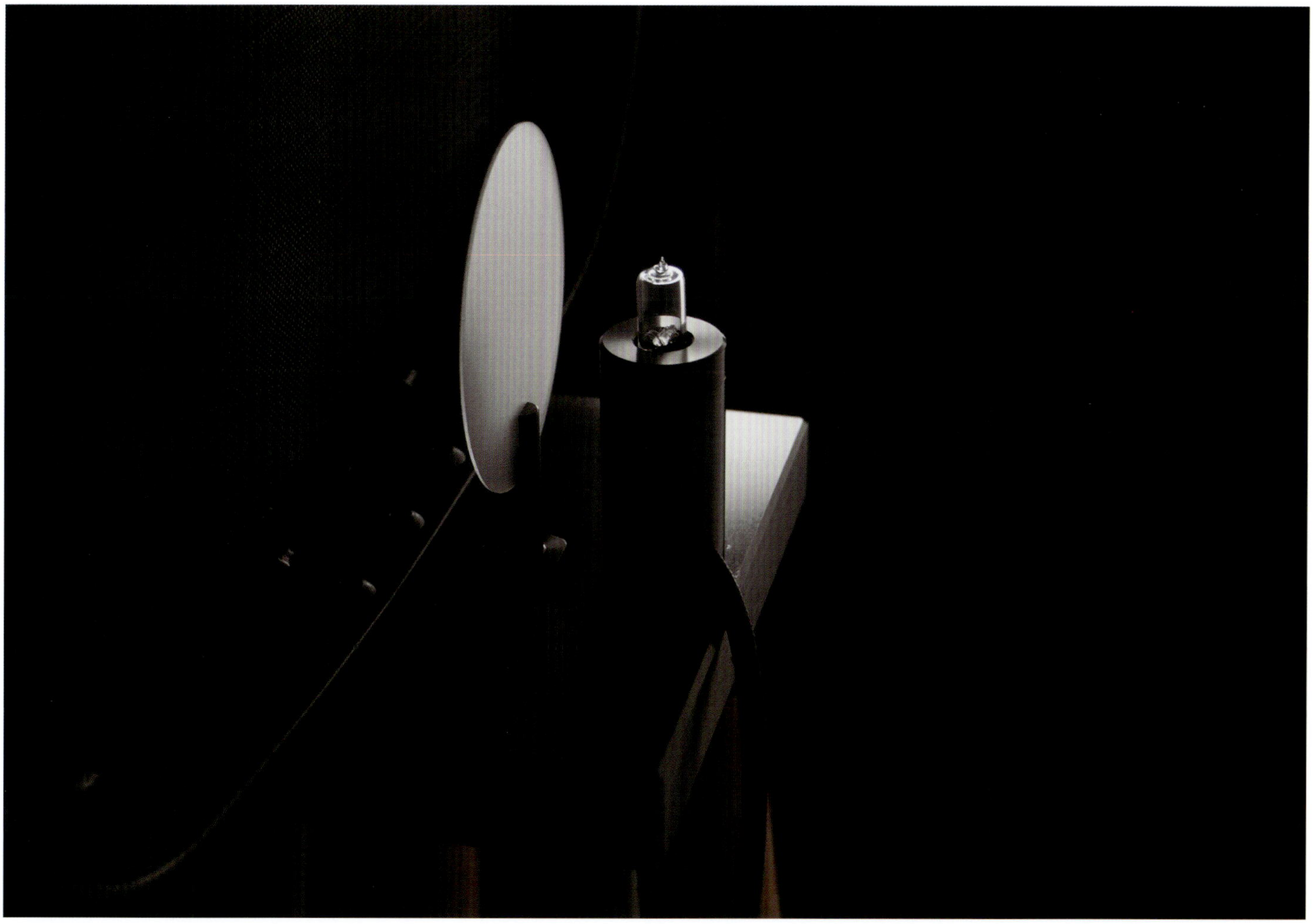

36

INVISIBLE MOUNTAIN

Reversible Glasses

Gina Hsu | DHH Studio

The idea that prescription drugs should be served as a delicious dessert might surprise, but Gina Hsu's set of reversible glasses proves good design can turn taking bitter pills into something fun. Shaped into corrugated glass cylinders, *Invisible Mountain* is an attractive set of measuring containers for liquid medicine and pills. The special dual function is possible due to a deep indent made in the base of each glass. Water and syrups can be poured into the regular glass but when inversed the hollowed out base becomes a tiny serving tray for tablets and capsules.

Growing up in a family of medical practitioners—both her grandfather and father are doctors—Hsu recalls playing with apothecary jars since she was a little girl. In her childhood, meeting sick people was a daily occurrence and at one time she even lived amongst her father's patients.

'Our family owns a small hospital in Taichung. In 1999 there was a devastating earthquake that flattened many homes to the ground, including ours. We had no choice but to move to the hospital because the building was still intact. One of the surgery rooms became my refuge. I often helped my dad scrape his instruments and had my own collection of laboratory glass', says the designer as she recalls the experience.

Observing that it was the little gestures of kindness that helped a patient's speedier recovery, Hsu wondered if the daily taking of prescription drugs could be made more 'happy'. 'Sick people often feel forced to take medication, which is usually kept in some sterile container and delivered by the nurse at meal times. But what if medicine was presented enticingly ... the way we do it with sweets and cakes', she questioned.

To test this concept Hsu started modifying the designs of chemistry glassware used at the hospital. She set herself the goal to reinvent the medical containers so they could hold both liquids and solids. She also wanted them to look attractive. With the help of a glassblower from Hsinchu a reversible vessel was made. The three variations are for different kinds of rationed medicine. The glass is solid enough to allow the object to stand alone even when holding up a small bunch of flowers.

The corrugated decorative element gives the glasses their special soft edge to resonate with a quiet feeling of transience. Hsu is very satisfied with the outcome, because whether used for delivering medicine or not her delicate objects add a touch of loving care to a dining ritual.

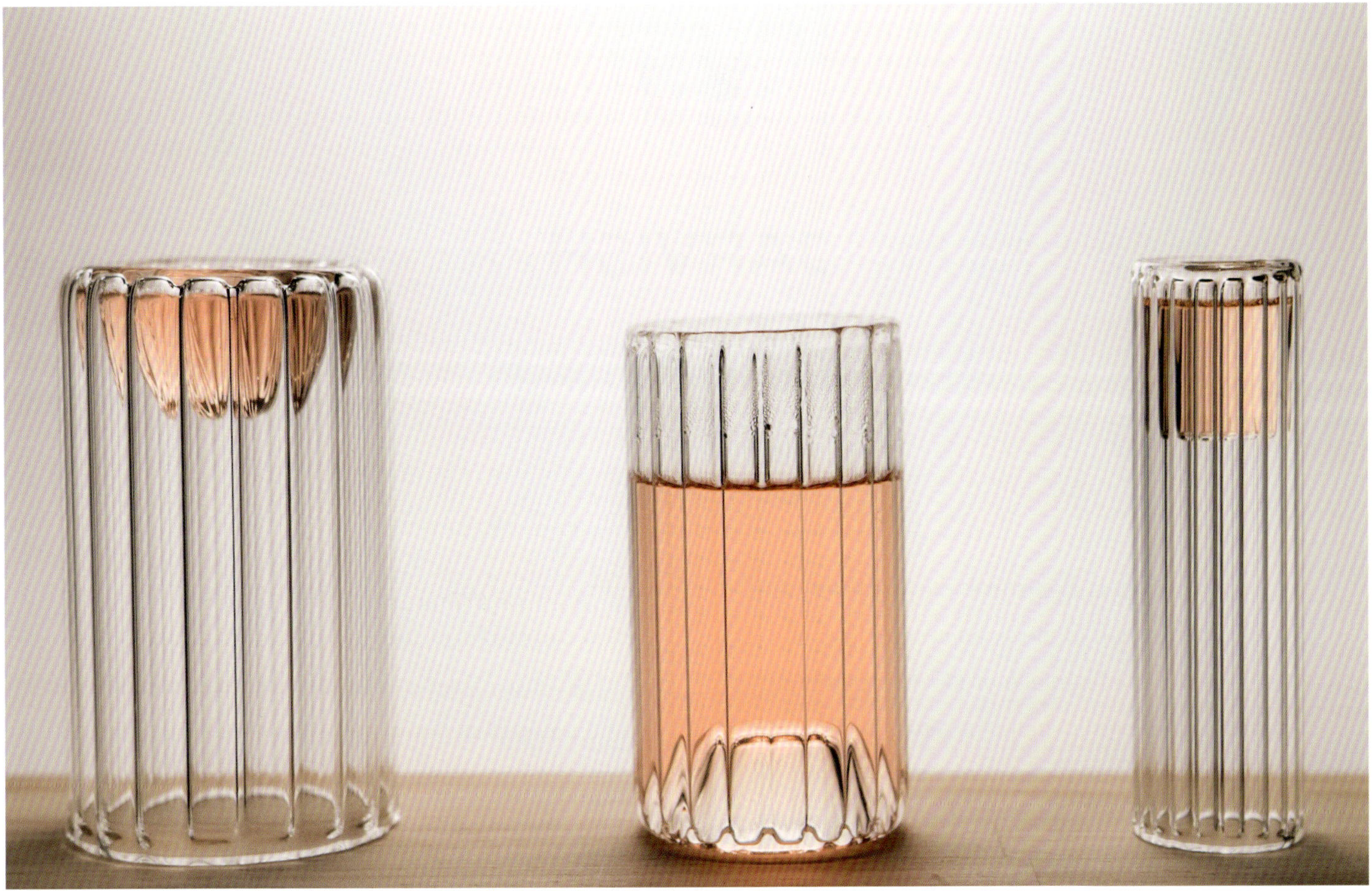

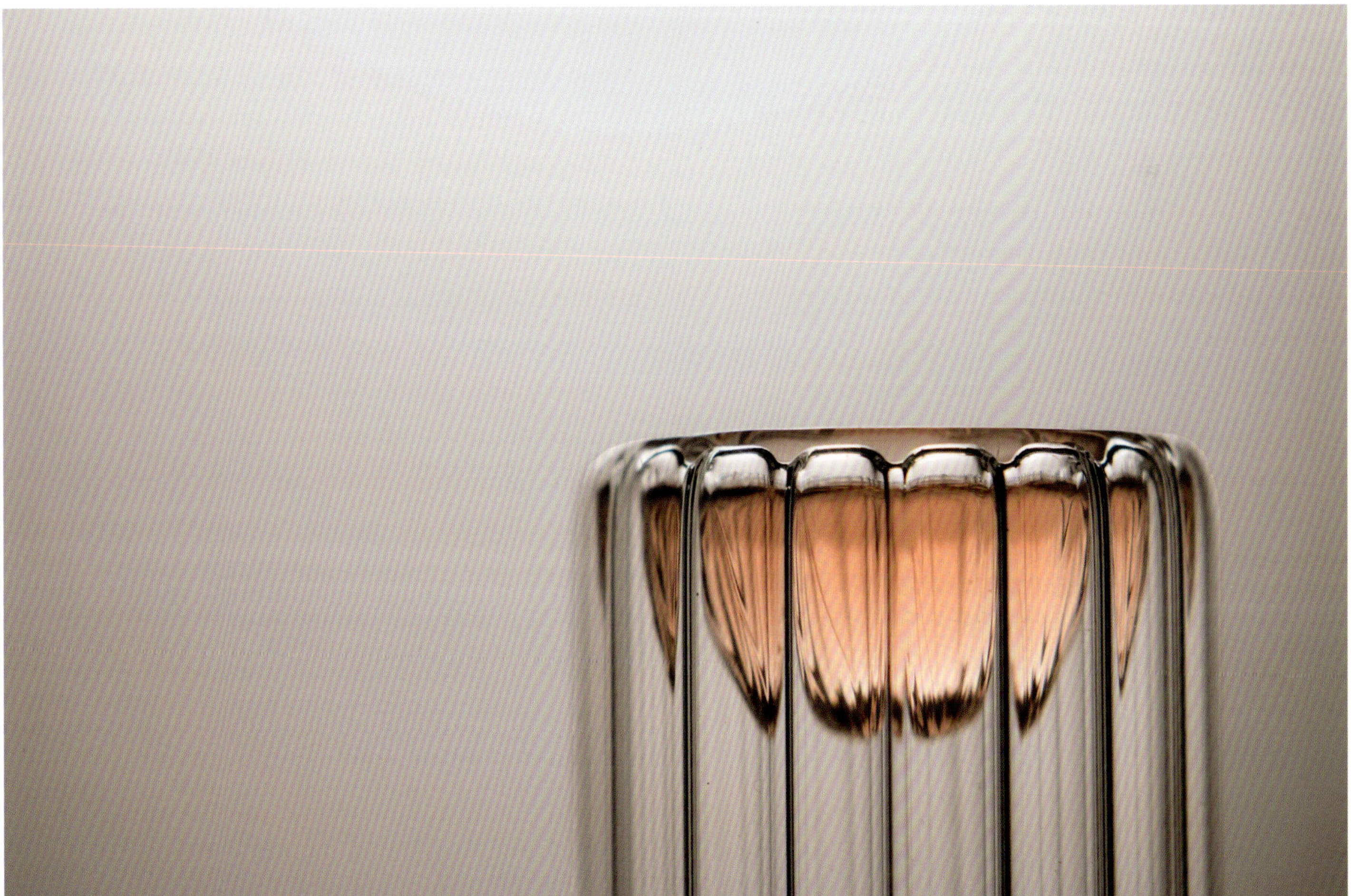

37

JARVISH

Smart Motorcycle Helmet

JARVISH INC.

The *Jarvish* helmet is a personal totem of safety and a stylish companion of the smart scooter. It is of a new generation of high-tech products engineered to calibrate and predict traffic hazards. 'In Taiwan there are too many vehicles now and this is making a scooter ride evermore dangerous. Delivery trucks and taxis are notorious for taking shortcuts and not thinking about the vulnerability of riders,' exclaims Jeremy Lu, one of the lead entrepreneurs behind JarvisH design and manufacturing group.

'Yet it's better for the environment if more people went about on a two-wheeler ... As designers of protective gear, our primary concern is how to maximise safety. We've analysed countless situations in order to better understand the kind of helmet functionality a rider best benefits from. This product not only suppresses impact in the event of an accident, but it can detect potential danger ahead of time. It can be lifesaving!'

Hidden inside the smart helmet, the Internet of Things (IoT) is as complex as the digital ecosystem of a smart phone running an upgradable Android operating system with Bluetooth. Via the seamlessly hidden electronics, sensors and network connectivity, the helmet collects road safety and location data. The information is then rendered into to a 'hazard map'

and, when necessary, a warning beep is given. A rear vision camera helps the rider be better aware of the road situation. The camera can also capture videos of traffic scenes that could be used as evidence, should there be an accident. Other smart features include a built-in noise reduction system and voice recognition capability for commands given to the IoT navigation.

'Optimising the electronics while simplifying the styling of the helmet was a huge challenge. Even though some of the head-up display functions are borrowed from an Apache fighter-pilot helmet, we didn't want it to look like cyborg gear. The technology is made as invisible and intuitive as possible. The look is classy, almost organic', adds Younger Liang, chief tecnology officer and co-founder.

Jarvish is rechargeable via USB and it has become a perfect partner for *Gogoro* (page 90). It snuggles well under its seat and it can be connected to the scooter's battery to recharge while the machine is parked. The two companies are eager to cooperate to revolutionise Taiwanese motorcycle culture by promoting greater safety and more sustainable modes of mobility.

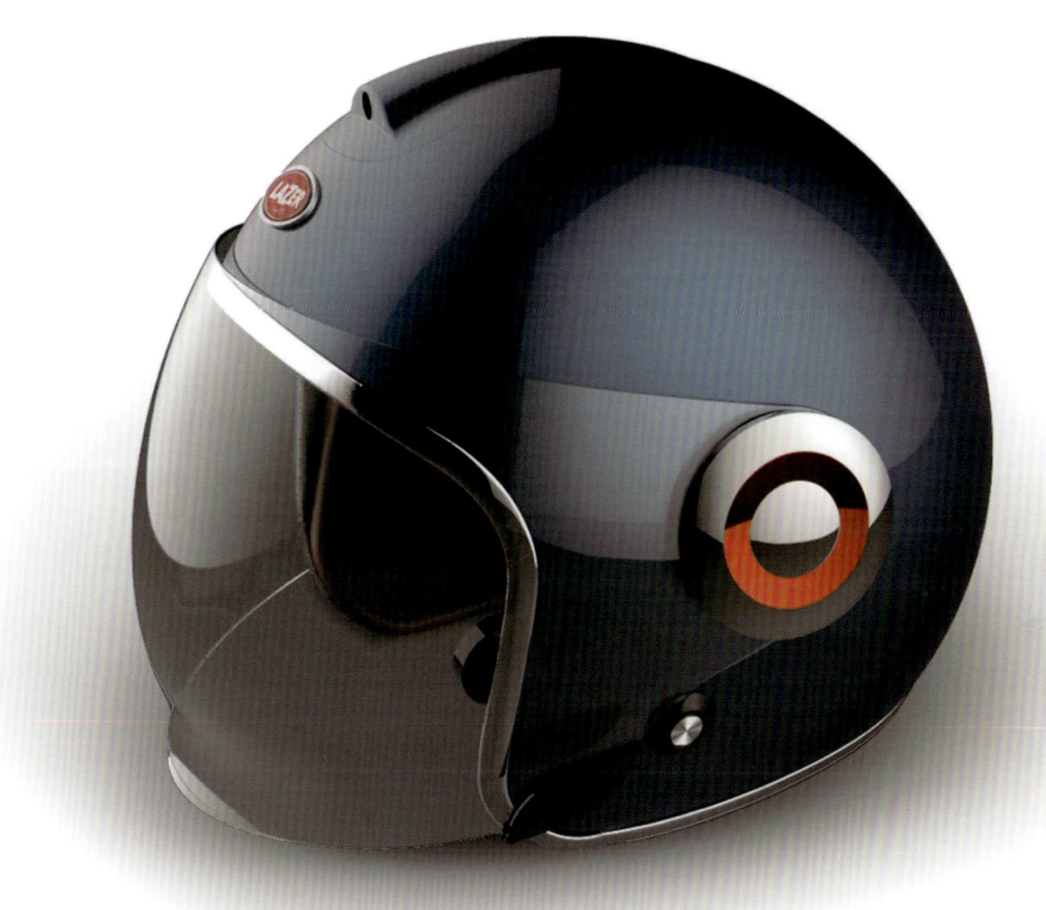

38

JING SI

Multipurpose Folding Bed

Tzu-Chi Foundation

Tzu-Chi is a Buddhist Compassion Relief Foundation, the charitable projects of which involve disaster relief efforts worldwide. From its humble beginning fifty years ago when 30 housewives committed to save small change every day to support the work of Master Cheng Yen, its founder and spiritual leader, the Foundation has grown into an international institution. Marshall Siao works in the technical division responsible for building hospitals and high tech facilities as well as designing for disaster survivors. 'What we do is humanitarian industrial design. It is our belief that out of true compassion grows wisdom ... in a design sense too', he says.

'Our front line volunteers have accumulated many valuable insights about the special needs of survivors of floods, typhoons, earthquakes and epidemic outbreaks. It's an extremely challenging environment. As this is non-commercial aid work, the solution response must be immediate. Only after the pressure subsides do we have the time to consider how to make temporary shelter long lasting.'

The origins of *Jing Si* multipurpose folding bed go back to the summer of 2010 when Pakistan was devastated by severe floods. Distressing footage of a baby girl wrapped in a rag and left lying on the wet ground had reached Master Cheng Yen. Feeling deep care for the survivors, she motivated her team to expediently devise a portable structure good for resting. Nearly 10,000 first generation folding beds were shipped to Pakistan.

'Oh, this was only the beginning! Many elements had to be improved. The bed needed to be inexpensive to transport in large quantities, thus the idea of folding ... When there is no shelter, people are forced to sleep outside so it had to be stable as well as provide ventilation. It had to be made of a material that can be scrubbed down and disinfected as these kinds of facilities get used by many people, including during medical emergencies.'

The product integrates all of these considerations. It is manufactured of easy to clean polypropylene. The fretwork on the top and sides provides ventilation and keeps the weight as light as possible. The folding sections are joined together by plastic hinges so no tools are needed for assembling. The specially designed cardboard box packaging opens flat and fits perfectly along the length of the bed, doubling up as a cushioning mat. A simple pictorial instruction manual is printed on the box so anyone anywhere can put it together quickly. It is a thoughtful piece of comfort the blessings of which could last a lifetime.

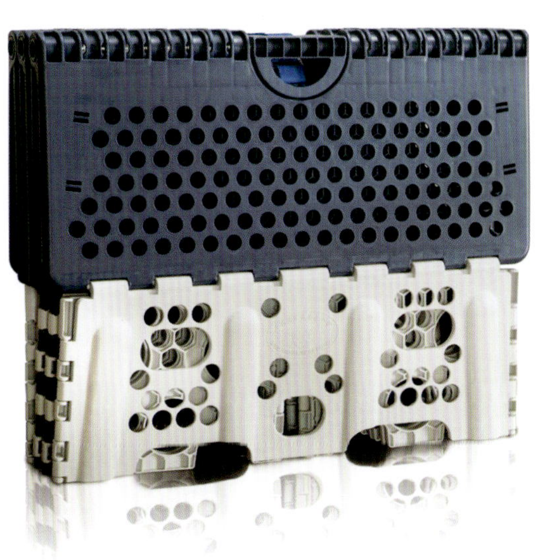

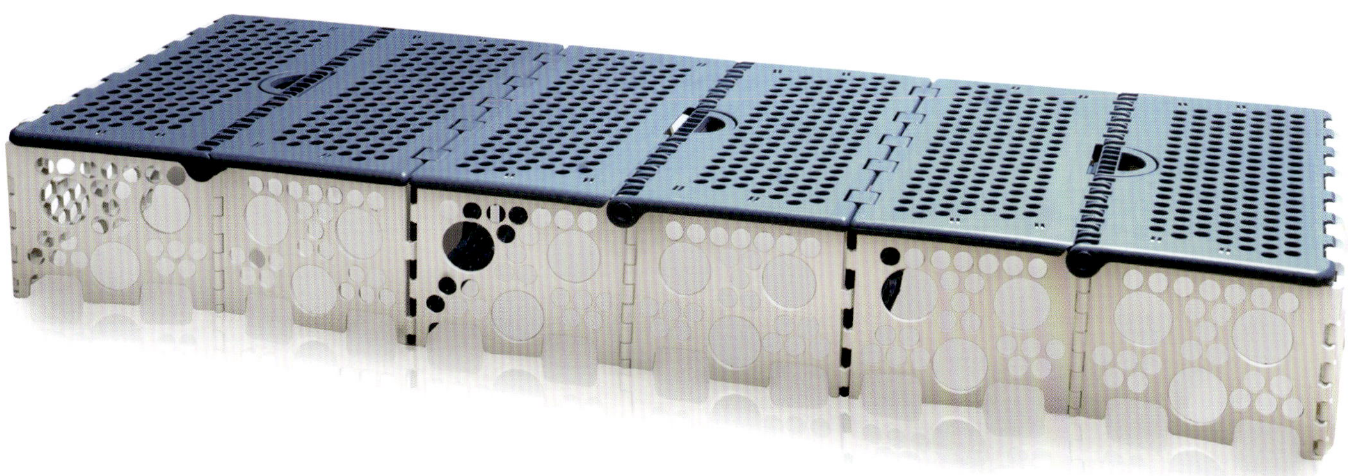

39

JUMP FROM PAPER

Bags

Chay Su & Rika Lin | Pinzaan

Taipei-based designers Chay Su and Rika Lin create playful accessories that look like something out of a Looney Tunes cartoon. Their motto is simple: 'Nothing quite like a bag with an attitude for seriously ridiculous fun!' Trained in communication design, the two first experimented transferring 2D perspectival illustrations into 3D objects for their participation in the International Young Designers Expo (YODEX) at Taipei World Trade Centre.

'YODEX is a great event for young designers because it can be a launch pad for an amazing career. Instead of stressing about it, we approached it as something exciting. Luckily Pinzaan spotted potential in our crazy concept and asked us if we wanted to work with them to develop a new product line. Of course we did! We really want our bags to lighten up the day … make people burst out laughing. If work feels too hard or the world is too much, this might be a cure.'

Poking out their colourful tongues the *JumpFromPaper* totes, satchels and handbags subvert fashion conventions of what is wearable and what is not. Confessing to occupying much of their teenage years on animations, comics and manga, the two girls have a habit of imagining the world around them as if it were a cartoon.

The unique feature of their bags is that they are constructed to give the illusion of the side and front being on the same plane. According to the designers, the black graphic outline and the signature angle that gives the bags the 3D effect have been particularly challenging to implement in a production line. The bags are made of polyester fabric and padded with a zippered pouch tucked behind the front flap. To complete the graphic illusion, the flap is flatly secured with a small magnet. Although slim in appearance the bags can fit all daily essentials.

Each *JumpFromPaper* collection is developed around an entertaining experience the friends have shared. For example, the 1950s retro-themed Time Machine collection was conceived in a small Taipei bar filled with smooth jazz and groovy atmosphere. Individual products have their own nicknames like Scooter: *Let's get lost* and Martini: *Whatever happens tomorrow, we've had today.* Such bags make a bold and vibrant accessory suitable for any occasion. The only other thing one needs is a good sense of humour!

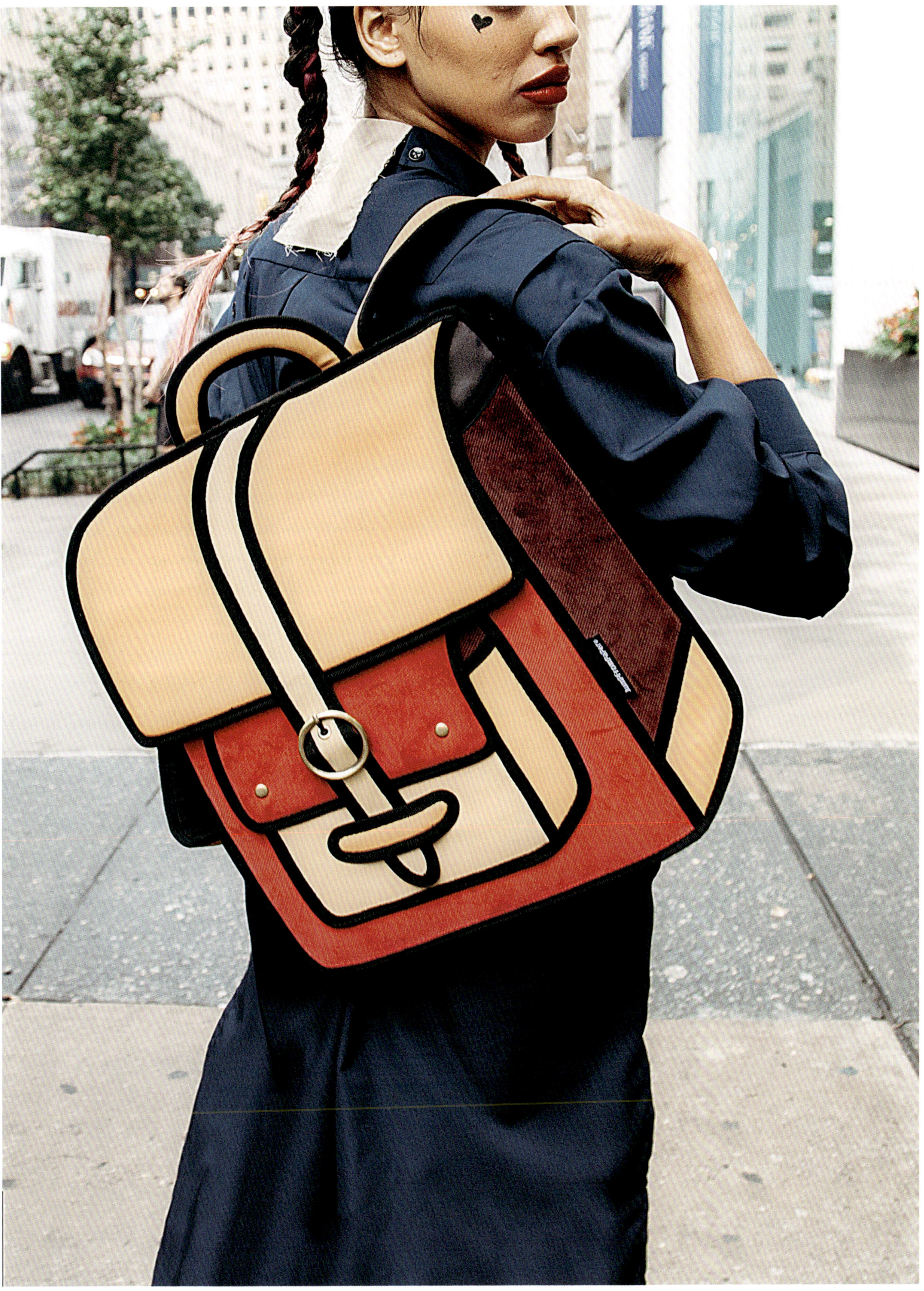

40

JUN

Pull Out Faucet

Awa Faucet

The pronounced slim appearance of *Jun* introduces to the modern kitchen a new type of faucet that is versatile, powerful and economical, while also very elegant. Engineered and manufactured locally, the product is imbued with 40 years of industrial know-how and the high precision machining available to designers in Taiwan.

Most striking about *Jun* is the refined arch of the hose, which has replaced the springs and tubing typical of the average shower tap still widely used in Taiwanese commercial kitchens as well as the home. This reductive structure is due to the specially engineered counter leaver that secures and steadies it in place. The larger than usual shower handle can be grabbed and pulled out easily. The anti-twist system of the hose makes it convenient even for kids to clean their own dishes using a smooth 360° spray motion. There is no danger of their little hands getting burned as the shower handle is designed to remain cool when hot water is running. Once washing is done it is simply clicked back onto its stand.

The handle is another innovative feature. Its two-stage adjustable ceramic cartridge controls the amount of water flowing from the tap. Using this facility can save up to 50% of water each time the tap is turned on for a rinse. The saving may not be noticeable for a single person, but in larger households it can make quite a difference to the family budget.

'These days most people here understand the English term *eco-friendly*, but that doesn't mean they know how to organise their lives around this concept. There is still resistance towards investing in smart products. We are amongst the pioneers who have to educate the end user about how to be eco-friendly by investing in good design. Our faucets encourage everyone in the family to become mindful of their washing habits. The product is also safe, made of brass and fibreglass composites that meet USA regulations on lead free materials', explains Gia To who, together with her engineer husband, founded Awa Faucet.

Curiously the product's form, coupled with the principle of designing to avoid damage, finds its roots in *kung-fu*, which To enjoys. 'The principle in the *crane style* kung-fu is to cause no harm', she explains. Martial artists following this style have a graceful stance whilst their movements are light and swift. One needn't be a practitioner to appreciate the references vested in our product. The faucet presents incredibly smooth movement, and its gracefully curved shower arch introduces a touch of artistry.'

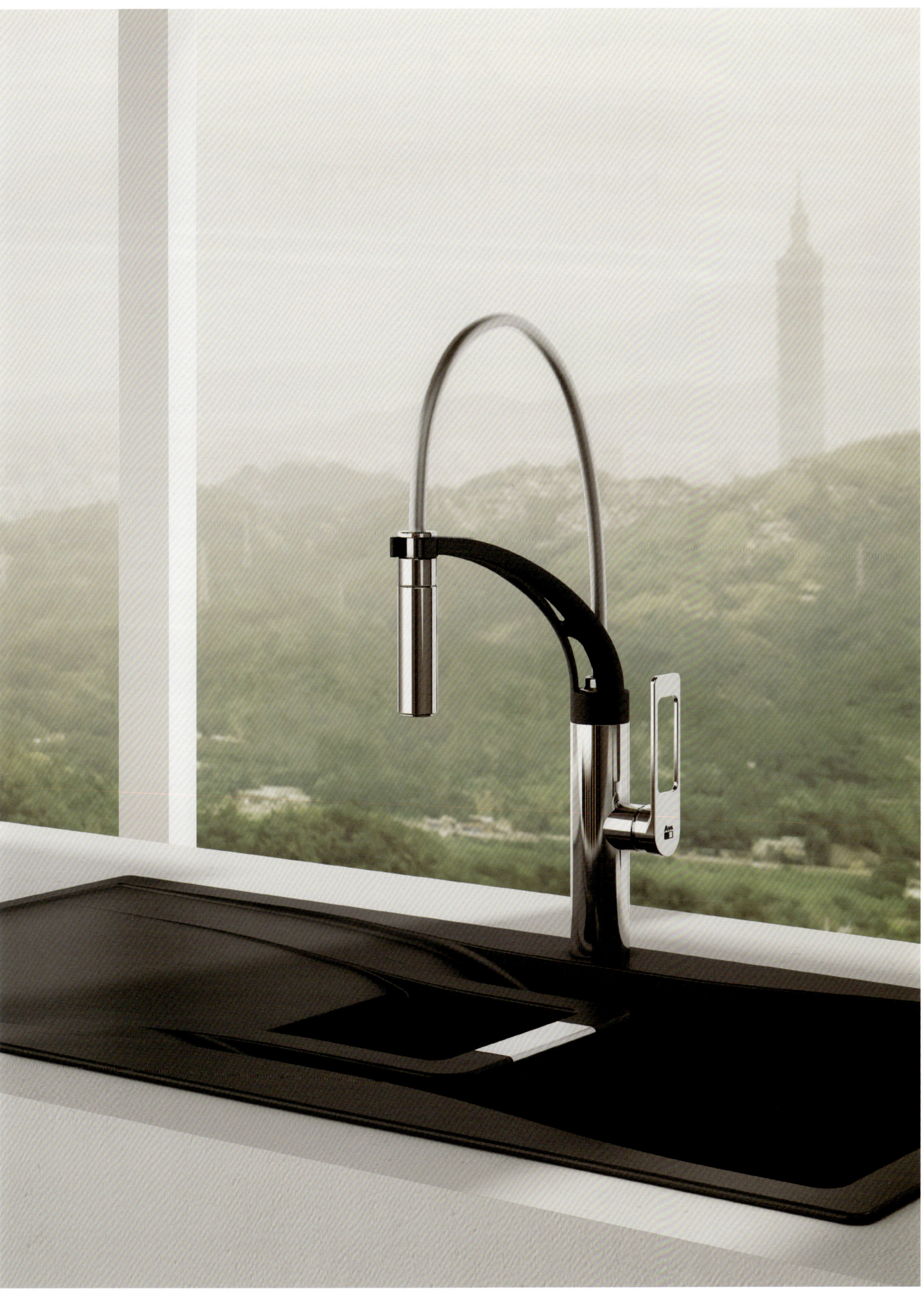

41

KUNG FU MASTER

Flash Driver

Reads Lin | Bone Collection

Timing is everything, as Reads Lin has learned from his long career in design. In 2003 he designed a novel Mp3 player using a single sheet of aluminium, cut and bent into a hot new product. Unfortunately the excitement about his future business venture was short lived: six months later Apple released its first version of an aluminium Mp3 player, the iPod mini, and 'the rest was history'.

Rather than feeling defeated Lin decided to be philosophical about it, and with time a simple but effective strategy emerged in his mind. 'Obviously we could not compete with a giant but nothing could stop us from attaching ourselves to it', he comments cheekily. After two years of intensive market research, Fruit Shop International was established as the company of Bone Collection, making accessories for PC and mobile devices, including iPhone and iPad!

The second business concept came from observing consumers' relationship to their mobile devices. Decorating a cell phone with charms is an Asia-wide custom though these days the silk pouch amulets and coloured knots are replaced with cute icons from popular culture. Taking this practice in a new direction, Lin started producing adorable tiny figures with the dual function of gadget accessories and good luck charms with universal appeal.

Amongst Bone Collection's hundreds of products is the patented dual driver for direct transfer of data between smartphones, tablets and PCs. The *Kung Fu Master* is one of numerous cool characters in a series of ornamental flash drivers with a coat constructed from separable parts for users to play. It is made using microinjection technology that transforms silicone compounds into unique shapes with a soft surface. Only high-grade, fully degradable silicone is used. The USB cap is attached to the figurine's body so it can never be lost. When it is not in operation, the *Kung Fu Master* driver is disguised as a stand-alone mini toy.

The coats of flash drivers can be interchanged with those of any other character from the collection so users can enjoy new styles without having to purchase additional drivers. 'They are addictive like yummy sweets—once you try one you'll want to try them all', laughs Lin. This funky spirit of design is the secret to his company's success: its cute little characters bring on a smile wherever they go for business or leisure.

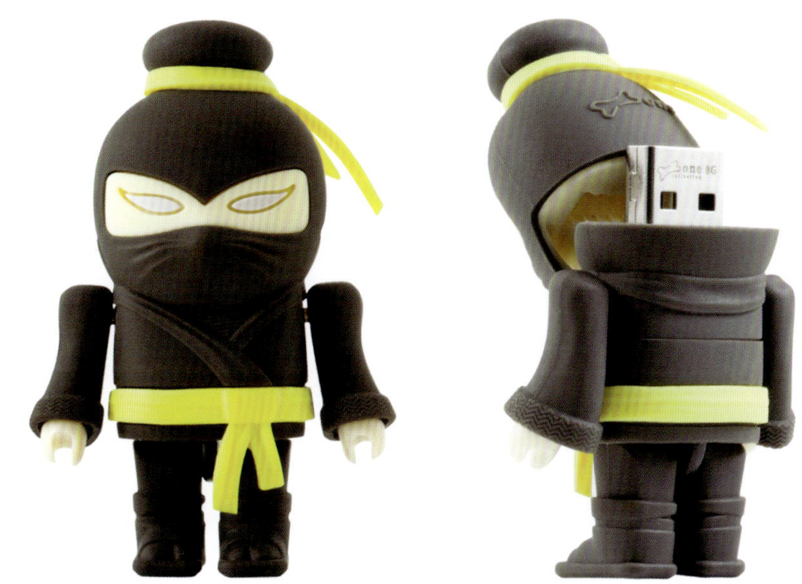
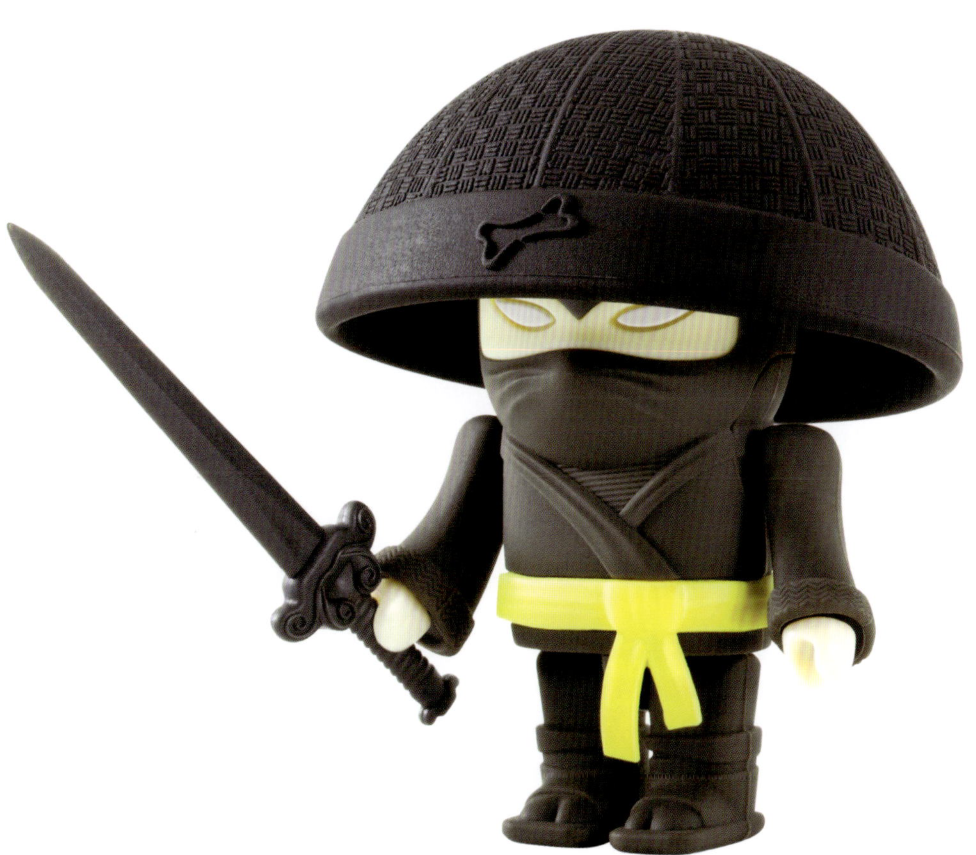

42

LITTLE QIANLONG

Single Serve Tea Set

Tales | Artilize Worldwide

In the early 20th century mass civil unrests swept across the mainland, leading to the abdication of the last emperor of China and the end of dynastic rule. Many of the imperial treasures of the Forbidden City were evacuated to safety and eventually relocated to Taiwan. Today they form the permanent display of the National Palace Museum.

Amongst the Museum's treasures is the lavish collection of Emperor Qianlong (1711–1799), patron of the arts and connoisseur of fine teas. With a passion for ceramics, he commissioned artisans to engrave poetry into fine porcelain as a way of recording his aesthetic virtue. He also loved to play with ceramic miniatures so much that curio boxes with secret compartments were made for him to carry his precious figurines wherever he went.

Tales has an exclusive contract with the Museum to develop ceramic products that interpret its collection. 'We are not just a gadget island; we are custodians of an incredible world heritage. Few, even in Taiwan, reflect on the significance of this. Designers need to find ways to make old things accessible, not only for the tourists but also our own kids who tend to dismiss them as old fashioned. I'd like to think of our products as off-springs of masterpieces', says Tony Tseng, the company's CEO.

Commissioned designers spend months researching the Museum's vast collections to find stories for new products. *Little Qianlong (I Am Qianlong: The Emperor's Treasure)* is a single serve teapot, cup, and lid set which when stacked together form a small figurine. The solid yellow colour glaze teapot references the Emperor's robes as recorded in imperial portraits, while the delicate floral patterns are direct renditions of original designs from his fine porcelain collection. The series comes in five lucky teapot colours, each with an individual decoration. The cup is white with an ink-black band around the rim. When displayed together with the red lid they resemble the emperor's hat.

'Exchanging gifts is a way of wishing someone well, so the shape of the set was designed to allude to the auspicious number eight', explains Tseng. The bottom of the teapot has a seal inscribed with the characters for *guxi tianzi*, derived from the original seal of Qianlong, meaning 'long life blessed by the heavens'. To savour a fragrant cup of tea from this adorable little set is to wish for many blessed experiences.

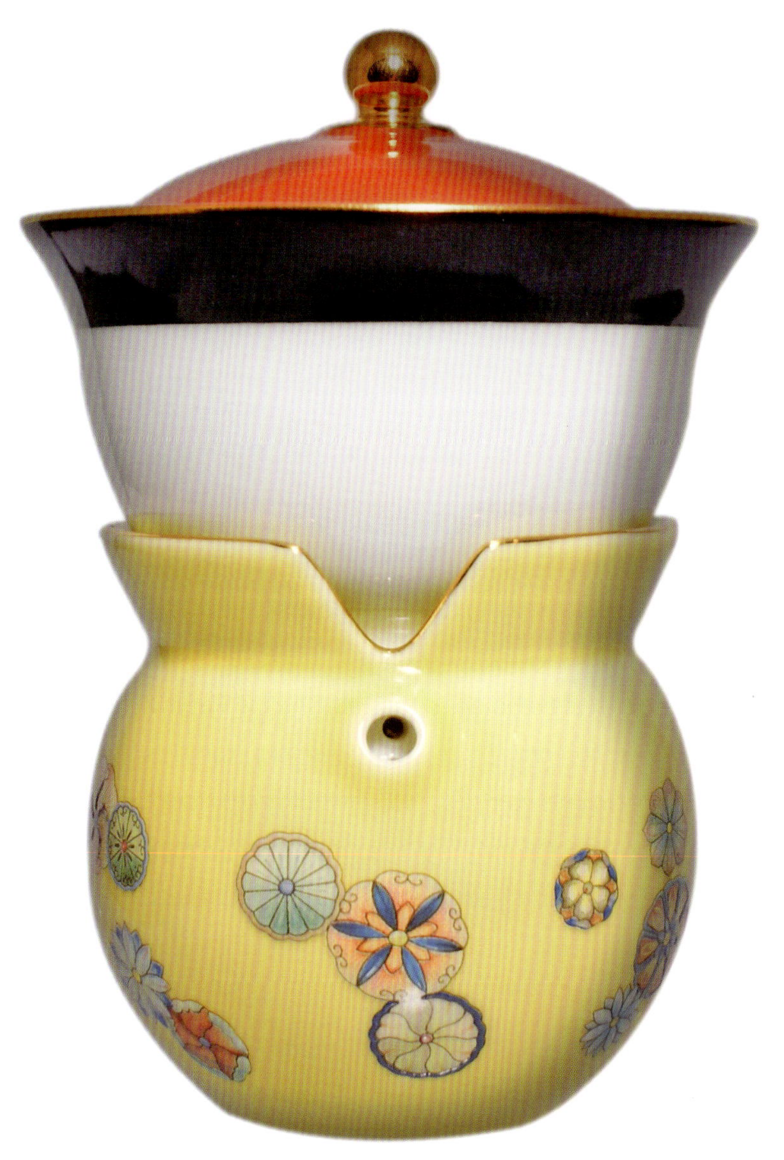

43

LONG PURSE

Leather Purse

Greenroom Ideas Cooperation

In Taiwan, scouting for special offers is an art form everyone is good at—which is understandable given that it was a manufacturing island, and consumers are spoiled for bargains. Despite this, the many mass-produced items rarely bring lasting satisfaction so the search for the next cheap thrill is relentless.

Specialising in hand-made leather goods, Greenroom Ideas Cooperation was founded in 2010 by two industrial designers who had had enough of 'cheap ugly stuff'. They were making cases for friends when Taiwan Designers' Week extended an invitation to participate in its 2011 exhibition.

'At that time a lot of industry events were happening in Taipei and it was a good opportunity to launch our business. We had no stock for a trade show and worked around the clock to come up with a new product line. Visitors loved the authenticity of our goods and we made some sales', reminisce the designers. 'We now employ a small team skilled in making luxury goods using hand-cutting and stitching techniques. An experienced maker might need a whole day to complete one complex item from pattern to object.'

Made of quality Italian leather, the versatile *Long Purse* has strong geometrical lines and special folding that form a rectangular box when it is opened up. Its front compartment functions as a pocket or a small tray. It is suitable for holding business cards, travel size makeup, and a cell phone. The stitching along the edges feels wonderful to touch. It is available in all signature brand colours and it can double as a clutch.

'All our products have a soft texture, but the shapes have a particular industrial styling of bold block colours, strong geometrical lines and defined stitching. We have plastered mages from the Italian Futurists and Russian Constructivists all over our studio as a reminder of our "look". We want our products to celebrate the dignity found in manual labour the way it was in the days of our grandparents', say the designers of their art inspirations.

There is a regenerative quality about such hand-made objects for they encourage care. They bring to us something lovingly touched by the hand of its maker. It is this sense of connectedness that gives the products made by Greenroom Ideas Cooperation their lifelong appeal.

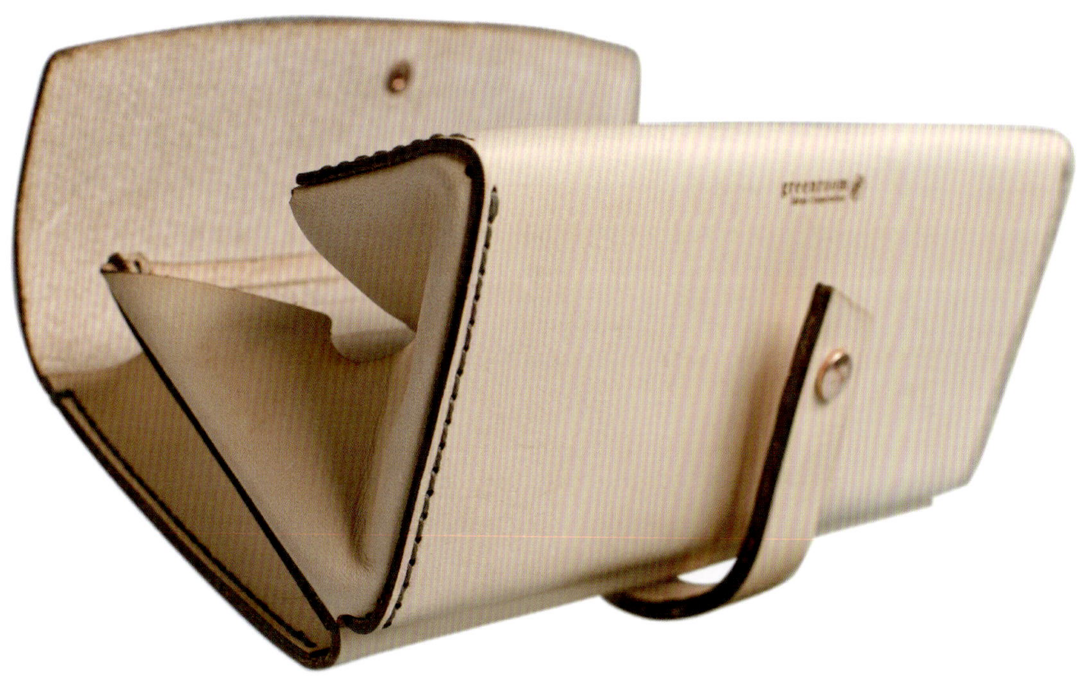

44

LOOP CHAIR

Chair

Pilli Wu & Tain-Chang Jian

Pilli Wu makes fantastical hybrid products that are local in flavour and global in appeal, mixing the handcrafted with the mass-produced, the rare with the commonplace. He became internationally known for his lacquered *Loop Chair* that merged elements from two popular pieces of furniture: the slender lines of the 'horseshoe' armrest of a Ming Dynasty chair and the stump of a plastic stool.

The refined style of Ming furniture is universally admired as one of the most graceful forms of the period. Classical portraits often feature the sitter resting on a Ming chair as a way of asserting an image of sophistication and authority. Nothing can be more different to it than a cheap plastic stool that is now so commonplace in every noodle shop, street and market.

Wu thought that if these two pieces of furniture are iconic of Taiwanese culture, then they should be combined to make one statement. To realise his quirky vision he collaborated with master artisan Tain-Chang Jian, with whom he created the first hybrid. They made a limited edition of 99 chairs in lacquered wood, which displayed the lustre of the natural material and the skill of master Jian. The technique of hand lacquering objects by applying layers of natural lacquer is time-consuming and costly. Today such products are commonly manufactured through machine processes with synthetic resins, but the designer insisted that his chair must have a hand-made finish.

'We used to be nicknamed "plastic kingdom". But the fascinating thing about this place is that we've become a safe haven for craft traditions vanishing elsewhere in Asia. I wanted to highlight this phenomenon of extremes. I wanted the craftsman's mark to be left visible in the grading of the lacquer. It is important to show the product was touched by the human hand.'

True to his original concept of creating cultural hybrids, Wu also released a *Loop Chair* in plastic, further challenging value conventions of what is precious and what is not. By fusing the distinguishing features of such contrasting furniture, Wu hopes to have created an enduring neo-classical chair that transcends materials, time, and tradition.

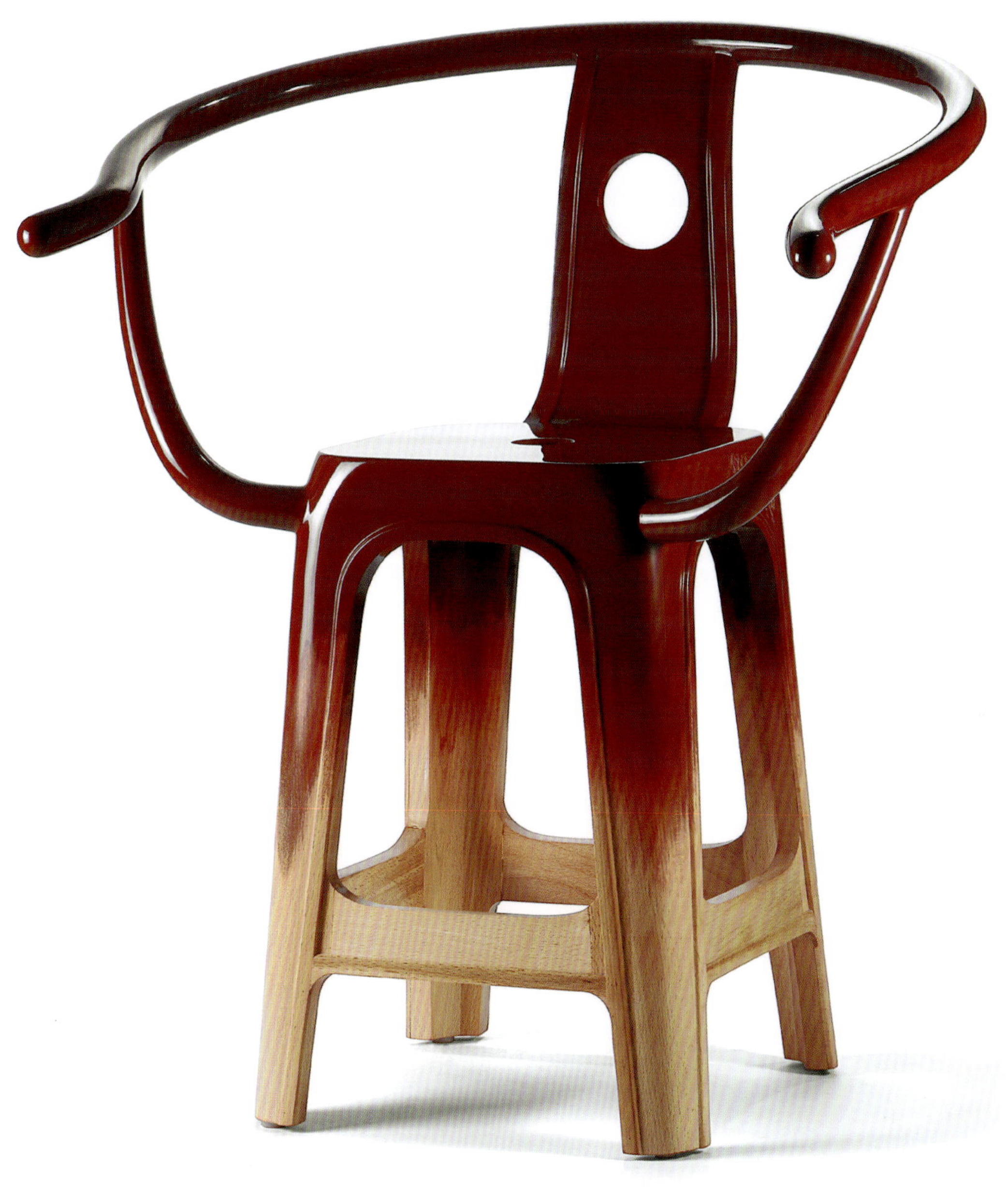

45

LUNA

360° Camera

Memora

Ju-Chun Ko is the first Taiwanese to train at Singularity University, Silicon Valley's pioneering institution where thought leaders experiment with technology to address some of the most pressing issues of our times. 'At Sin we were pushed to think in thirty-year time spans, which inevitably poses the question of how impactful and lasting our work is going to be … Maybe because I am an interaction designer, I quite often tinker with my gadgets to test if I can extend their lifespan.'

Together with collaborators Servanto Calvares and Gaurav Gupta, they mused on what might happen if the life-logging function of the Narrative Clip camera were combined with those of GoPro. 'We set up a design brief to make a new camera out of the wearable device by adding a 360° virtual reality option. We wanted people to have a more complete view of their experiences in still images and video clips. We knew how to do it technically, but it was industrial designer Fon Chiang who developed it into a product. In three months *Luna* was born.'

Held in the palm *Luna* feels the size of a *bao-ding* medicine ball (6 cm in diameter), and it is as easy to manipulate with one hand. Its dual, front and back, 190° Fisheye lenses pull together spherical panoramas of 2K resolution. The camera comes with an auto-stitching function and an inbuilt gyroscope so a stable footage can be produced even if it is recorded while the camera is flying. The switch button is positioned on top: one click takes a single shot; a double click records moving images. Data captured by the camera is Wi-Fi transferable and it can be previewed on any connected smart phone. To recharge, one simply leaves it on its magnetic charger stand.

Luna is a tiny and fun device good for anyone with an adventurous spirit. The camera comes with a range of accessories that make it convenient for it to be attached to something like a drone for aerial shooting. It also can be used underwater as it is built in a waterproof enclosure. As Ko says 'It's a go play camera! With *Luna* we can fully document our experiences and re-immerse ourselves in the memories of some happy times. We all get to be legends in our own stories.'

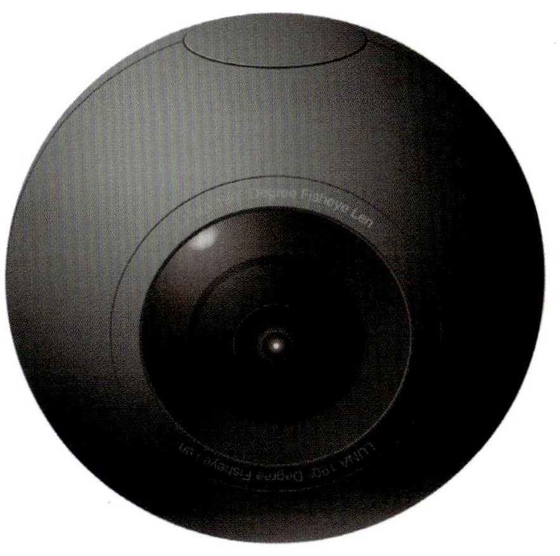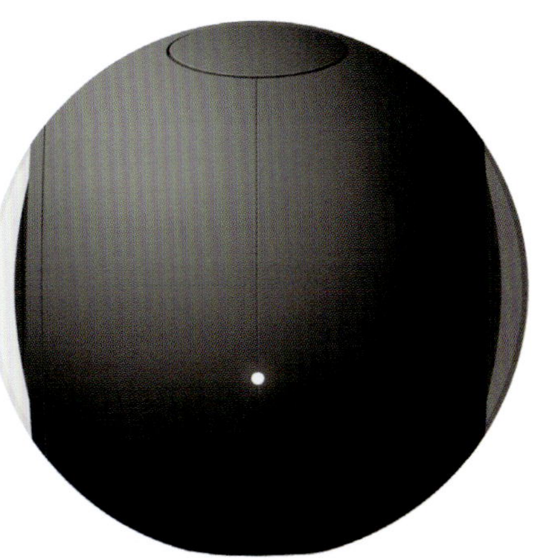

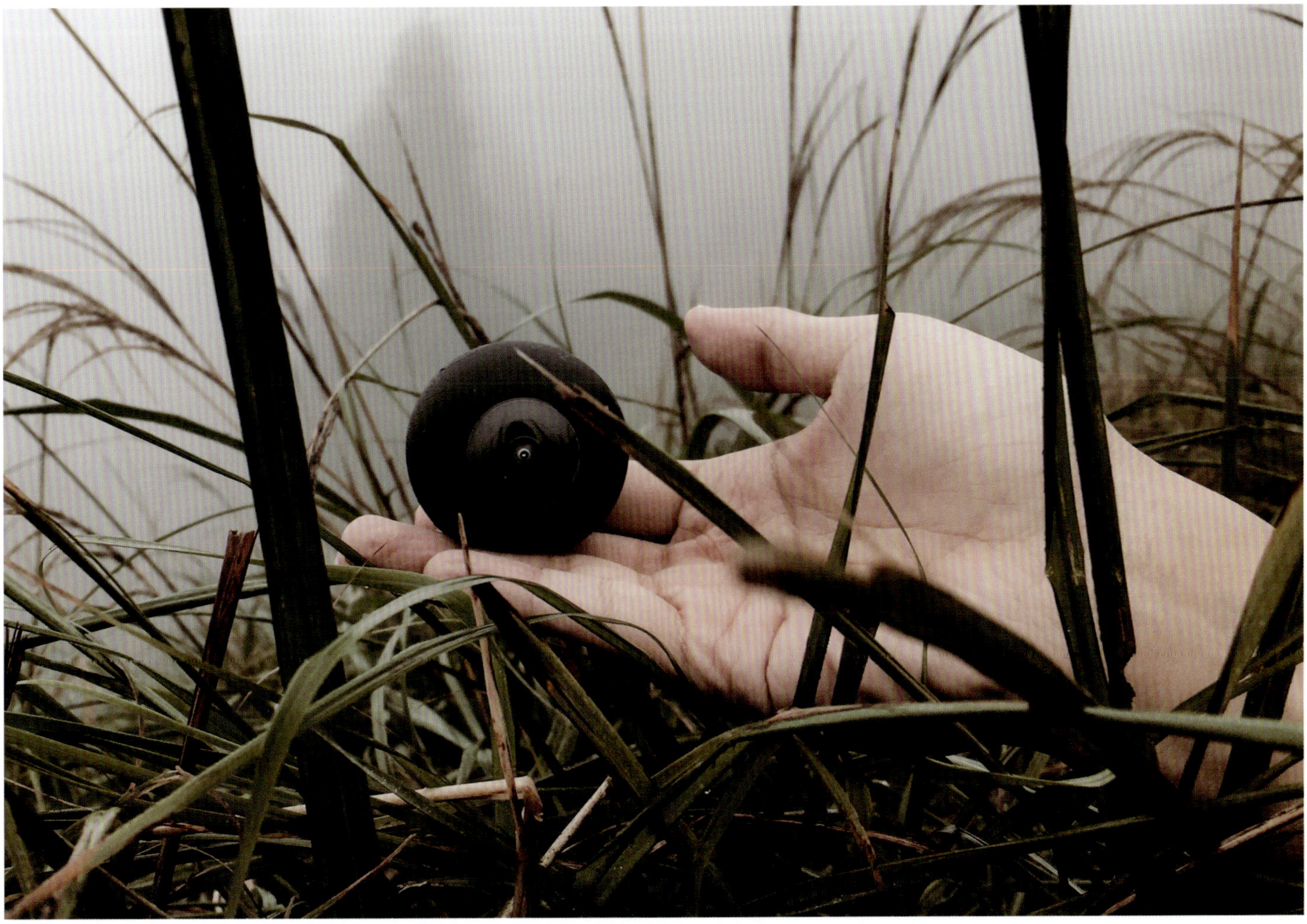

46

MACARON

Mini Sweeping Robot

AsiA One Design

In Taiwan, the aesthetic of *kawaii*—cuteness that draws on people's attraction to juvenility and innocence—is almost as popular as in its place of origin, Japan. From advertising images of cute people and things that greet citizens at metro stations to embodied gestures, everything is kawaii. Which explains why in photos people like making a 'V' sign, why women dress 'petit', and pastel coloured sweets are the flavour of the day.

'I really enjoy designing happy objects. Cute is good!' says William Liu, with a smile. 'A lot of my ideas come from pop-culture and from having creative playtime with my team, which is as essential as solving design problems. We strive to make products that can be appreciated not so much for being smart, which they are, but being adorable. If users treat them like pets, it means a job well done.'

The famous Italian macaron has become a huge hit amongst the fashionable crowds of Taipei. It also tantalised Liu's design tastebuds, as he was trying to define 'cute' for a new house-cleaning robot. *Macaron* is a hard working machine that can perfectly sweep a floor on its own as it roams around the house like a cute baby bug. Embedded proximity sensors detect obstacles to be avoided on its path, and a 360-degree auto-steering function ensures that

the spinning brushes reach all corners of a room. Dust is collected in a plastic container that can be easily removed, washed and reused. A special anti-tangling mechanism prevents the wheels of the robot being caught in the cables.

'There are similar products on the market but they are unnecessarily high-tech and expensive. We designed our machine specifically for compact apartments that need regular sweeping but which are, otherwise, quite clean. It's how most of us live anyway!'

Macaron is suitable for people who are time poor, who might be physically unable to do housework, or who are just lazy. And, because it uses minimal electrical power (0.01 kW per usage), enough for a light sweep, the robot is economical on the budget and gentle on the environment. The designers are working on making the product available for purchase at any one of Taiwan's ten thousand convenience stores. How sweet!

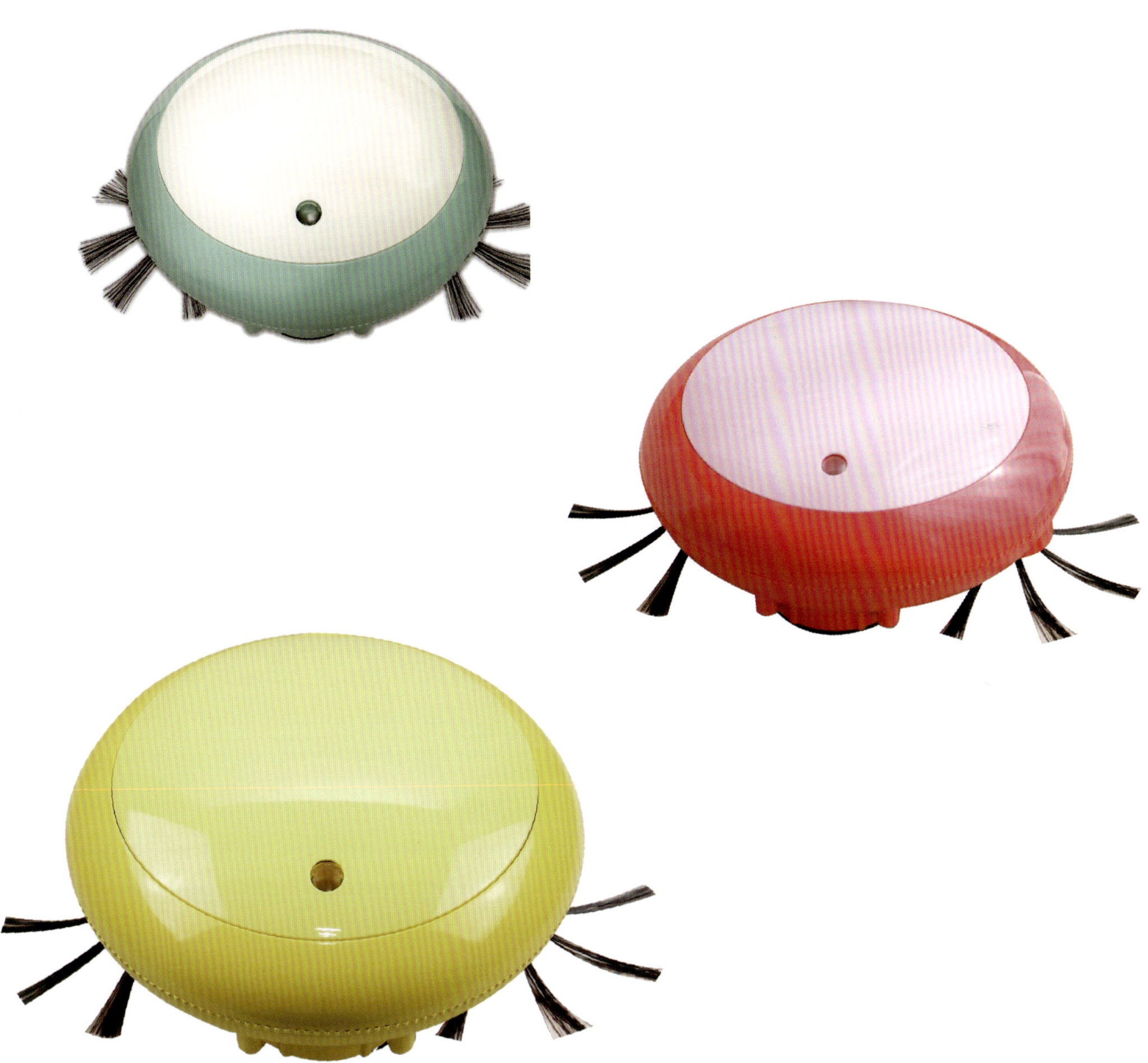

47

MEET THE FAMILY

Serving Tray

Zi-Hui Lin

Created by the collision of the Eurasian and Philippine plates, Taiwan's alpine mountain ranges stretch along the entire length of the island. A place of spiritual nourishment and a home for the indigenous people, the beauty of this breathtaking landscape is steeped in local legends. In the Buddhist and Taoist traditions, secluded mountain sites are venerated as sacred, with countless temples built into the hills all over the country. Tea plantations, too, benefit from growing at high altitudes, soaking up the fresh air to produce world famous tea varieties.

Unsurprisingly, the iconic mountain image finds its way onto many souvenirs but Lin decided it should be taken to a whole new level. 'Our living spaces are often crowded but we also enjoy drinking tea and sharing snacks with visitors. I wanted to design an unobtrusive object that can enhance such rituals by evoking the serenity of the mountains. We need to find more ways of inviting nature into the city', reflects Lin.

The concept for *Meet The Family* evolved from old ink-brush paintings depicting the landscape as an expression of a mood or a sense of nature. She could see that if the outlines of the mountains were abstracted into sculptural shapes they could form a miniature-scape décor. By incorporating a round tray at the base Hui developed a set of serving trays that double as a contemplative interior decoration. 'If people are too busy to go the mountain, the mountain can be brought to them', she says joyously.

The outlines of the peaks are hand-welded from thin iron rods and coated in black paint. Against a white wall they appear more like sketch marks than 3D objects. The tray is made of unglazed clay in three vessel forms. The use of clay was significant as in Taoist thought the earth element is believed to bring opposing forces to balance and draw everything together in harmony, which is particularly important when extended family gather in the home.

Meet The Family is always engaging as the objects can be rearranged into countless landscape combinations. And, one of the trays has a small vase for placing a bouquet of fresh flowers as a way of enhancing the ambience of a room.

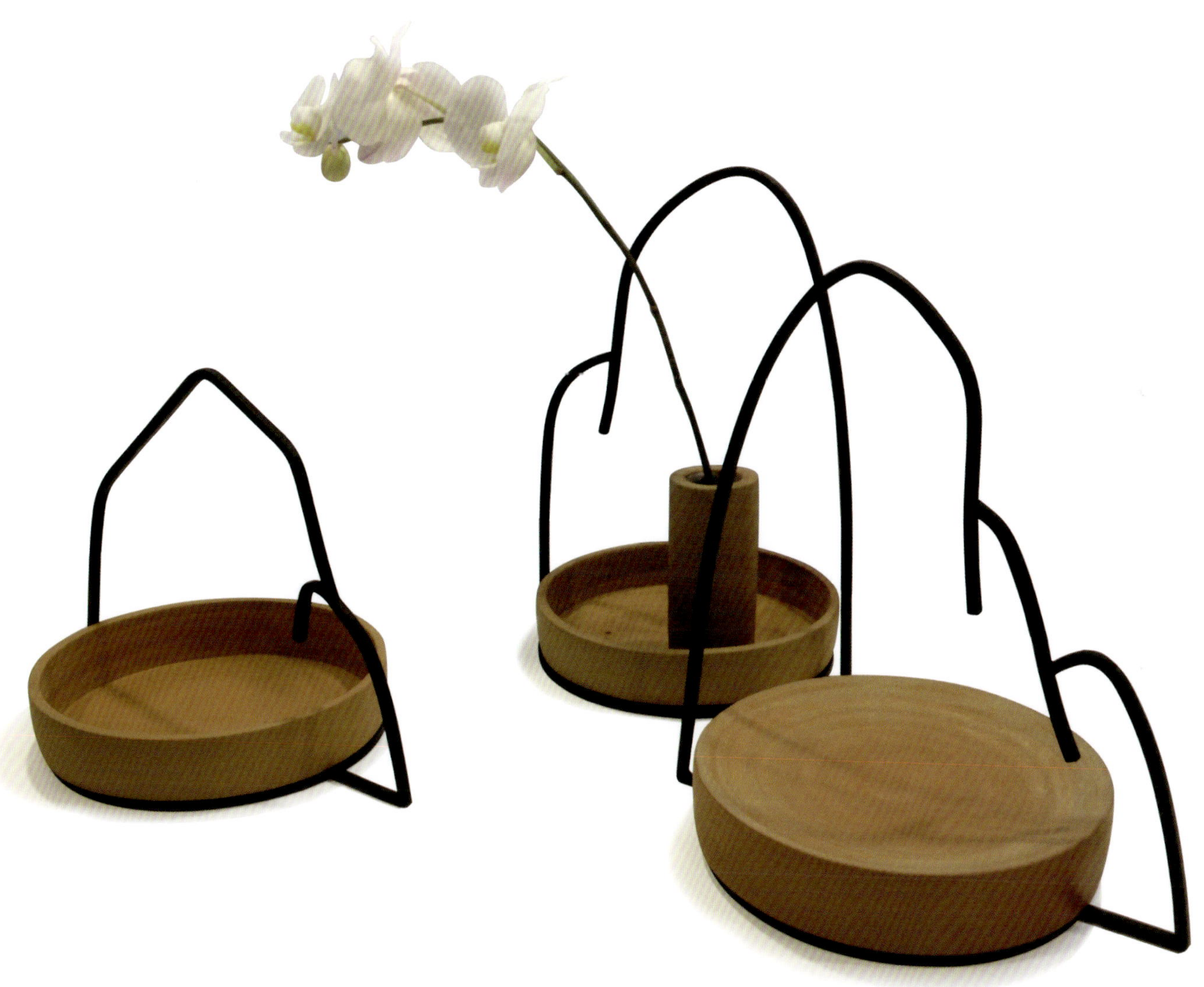

48

MING BAMBOO GLASSES

Spectacles

Chun-Hao Chen | Zen Tao

Spectacle frames are generally manufactured from plastics or metal, but the unconventional *Ming Bamboo Glasses* exemplifies the great versatility of bamboo, one of Taiwan's most abundant renewable resources. The appeal of bamboo is that it is a resilient as well as flexible material. It also grows rapidly without pesticides and it can absorb large volumes of carbon dioxide, so it is an excellent choice for eco-products.

This was the primary concern for Chun-Hao Chen, who collaborated with artisan To-En Huang to fabricate frames with a cultural impact. The distinctive feature of the frames is that it combines the functionality of spectacles with stylistic elements from the Ming period, expressed in bamboo.

'As a budding intellectual I read the works of Zhi-Mo Xu, an early 20th century poet renowned for his verses about love, freedom and beauty. He favoured the vernacular and was one of the first writers to adapt Western romanticism into modern Chinese poetry. Somehow I associated intellectual rigor and elegance with Xu's signature round glasses. When I graduated from college I purchased my first pair of round designer frames as a right of passage', recalls the designer.

Like Zhi-Mo Xu, Chen constantly searches for ways to balance global fashion trends with Asian cultural traditions. For the *Ming Bamboo Glasses* he revisited the aesthetic principles of the Ming period without being nostalgic. The temple-ends are shaped into a 'Ming curve' detail and padded with a barely noticeable silicone that prevents slippage and adds extra comfort. The patented bamboo hinges is an innovation drawn from traditional furniture techniques. The frames are hand-polished and can be customised to fit the individual requirements of the wearer.

The glasses add to the growing movement of making trendy accessories sustainably. As most consumers change their eyewear much less frequently than clothing, the product is suitable for anyone who appreciates tradition while making a bold statement about fashion and green design.

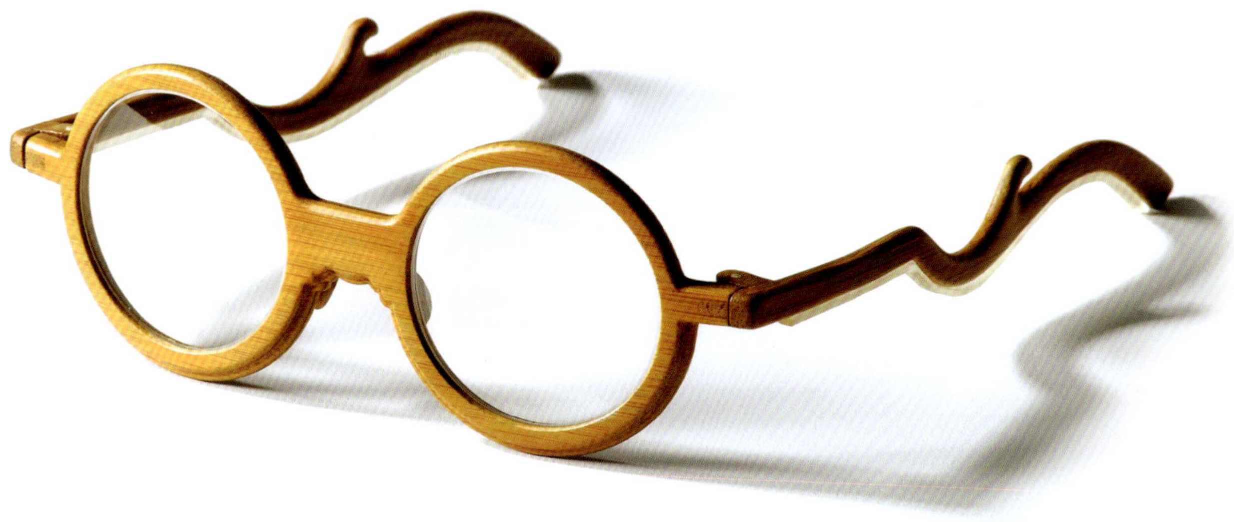

49

MOORE DOLL

Interactive Doll

Leo Guo | Mooredoll Inc.

The *Moore Doll* is a wonderful example of how two concepts can be brought together through technology in order to solve a social problem. When Leo Guo graduated from Stanford University he landed a dream opportunity to join a multinational company as a senior scientist. He could not have predicted that in the following 8 years he would be working and living mostly overseas. 'The job became a huge sacrifice. I've had qualms about it for a long time. I missed my daughter's special events ... the things she was learning. Quite honestly, I felt guilty', he confides.

The issue continued to bother him as he became increasingly aware of the global army of dislocated working parents longing for closeness with their faraway children. Guo saw a direct correlation between that need and the immediacy of social networking, which he thought could be adapted to be more kids-friendly. His inspired idea was to create a 'communication doll' through which parents and children can interact.

Moore Doll is an IoT (Internet of Things) device hidden inside a plush doll, available in a girl, boy and teddy variations.The doll has an embedded speaker and microphone, and each of its hands function as a button for specific commands.

Children can hear the comforting voice of Mum or Dad speaking through the doll and reply back to them as they are playing. 'From my own experiences with my daughter I learned the doll should talk back even when the parents are not available. We have achieved this by adding a *Siri*-like function that makes the child think the doll can 'hear' and 'understand' them in real time.'

To set up remote communication a free *Moore Talk App* needs to be downloaded and installed in the parents' or other family members' mobile phone or tablet. For an enhanced role-play experience there are options for voice alteration that sound like a robot, monster or cute baby. A group of dolls may chat together, and, if desired, wake up calls or other messages can be scheduled ahead of time. The App also accesses cloud-based audio books and songs that are playable through the doll.

Moore Doll is currently programmed in five languages. It is styled with an endearing *kawaii* personality, with a large head, black button eyes and happy grin. As the youngsters associate interacting with their favourite doll as though their parents were beside them, it becomes an affectionate security blanket for kids and grown-ups alike.

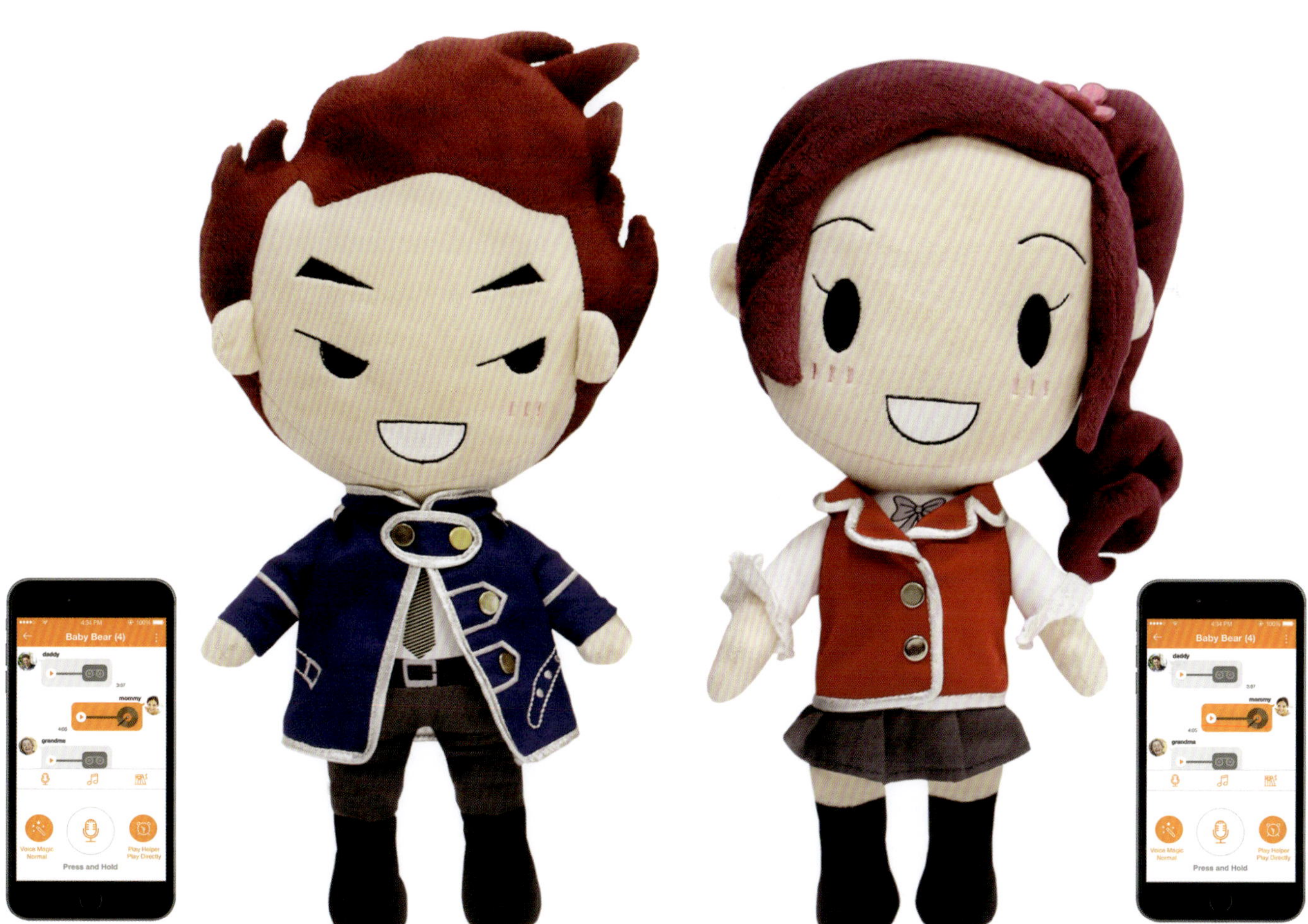

50

MOXOR

Pouch case

Chic Design

Millions of people and vehicles are crammed into just one third of this tiny island so it is not surprising that motorcycles are so popular. Although they are efficient and convenient they actually pose a huge challenge for recycling. Tapping into Taipei's vibrant bikie subculture Chin-Chin Yang of Chic Design discovered an interesting raw material to *up-cycle* for a new line of accessories appropriately named *MOXOR*.

A rider herself, Yang was at her neighbourhood garage one day when she spotted the lovely texture of some retro seats hanging around. She asked the mechanics if they would mind her taking them home. The guys were a little bemused but gave her the seats as it helped them clear up the shop. Thrilled with the discovery, she made hunting for raw materials a regular adventure until she had collected enough to create her products.

'End-of-life bikes are collected by mechanics for parts but the seat covers are thrown away even if the leather is in perfect condition. Older style seats are especially interesting because the fibre is already prefabricated with an interesting woven texture. Sometimes they may have diamond patterns on top or a glossy sheen. What I like about the fabrics is that another designer styled them. My job is to appropriate them creatively ... up-cycling them into something new.'

Once collected the leather is thoroughly cleaned and primed before it is sent to a factory in Taichung for tailoring. To maintain the high quality of styling, only the most perfectly preserved sections of the fabric are cut into wide strips from which the bags are made. Two contrasting textures are matched so that the upper part is soft to touch while the bottom half is more embellished. This combination and styling makes each piece unique.

Motorcycle imitation leather is extra tough and durable, and it is an ideal alternative for those who choose not to wear animal leather. The complete collection includes bags, wallets, and pouches, with new items created as the business grows. Yang is pleased with her work as she has found a clever way to produce useful commodities of better quality from existing products. She is aware that her collection may not be able to beat the obsession with branded bags, but the value of her work is in introducing cool eco-conscious alternatives.

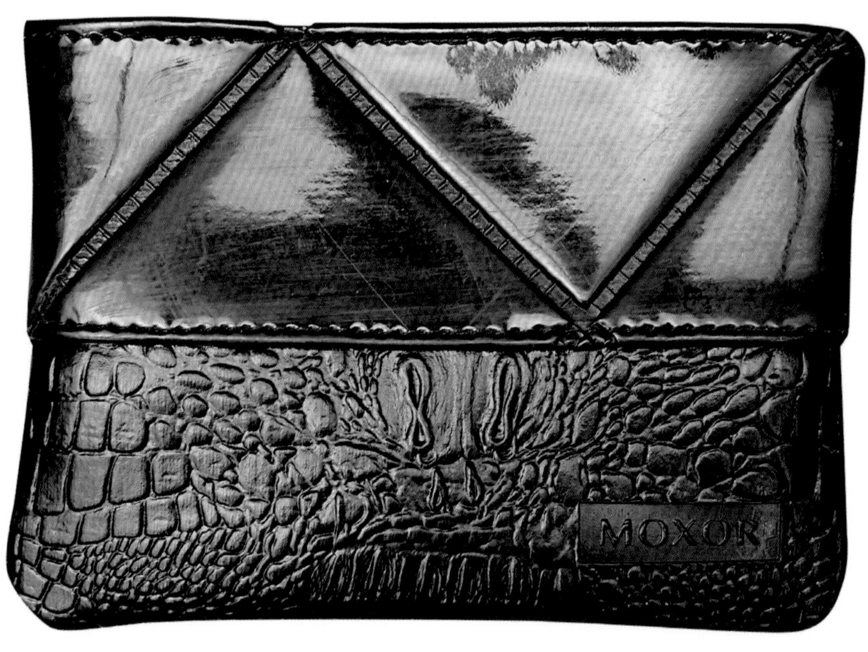
MOXOR

51

MUSE

Chair

Han-Yi Huang | Sitpls

Few locals would know that the benches around Taipei Main Station or those rusty folding chairs—now making a comeback as retro-hip décor—are made in a small factory in Kaoshiung. For four decades Shiang Ye has been manufacturing iron chairs and plastic seats that have gradually populated the island and become a part of everyday life. The family-owned operation has kept up with the times and expanded trade to over 90 countries. In 2010 it launched its own brand Sitpls, with sustainability and simplicity at its core.

Muse is a collapsible chair that effectively balances stability and lightness, weight and size, material efficiency and style. It features a curved armrest seat contoured in the shape of the letter M. The back is sturdy with a comfortable swing. The legs can be easily screwed on at an adjustable length—without the need of additional tools—allowing the chair to be stabilised when placed on uneven surfaces. The product is made entirely of recycled polypropylene mixed with glass fibre and it comes in several fresh colours. To better blend the piece with its surrounds, the legs appear to be made of natural wood: the visual trick of printed veneer!

As a second-generation owner Han-Yi Huang considers herself fortunate to have an entire factory as her studio. 'It's a luxury for most designers, I know. When I graduated from Domus Academy in Italy I wasn't thinking of joining the business. Obviously my father had other plans: his wish was for me to lead the new brand. It's a very hands-on job. I have to integrate design thinking into traditional manufacturing, which is not easy … The old guard always care for the process first, improving style later', she recalls.

One reason why Sitpls chairs are all made of durable plastics is that in Taiwan outdoor timber furniture tends to rot quickly due to the high humidity and relentless rain. 'Even public recreational areas have started adopting imitation wood fencing and steps. It may seem the antithesis to what it means to go for a 'nature walk', but when it's done sensitively it's a better solution than cutting down trees', adds Huang with concern. 'Long gone are the days when companies could just spew garbage. We all understand what it takes to live in the 21st century.'

Huang has recently brokered a partnership with material innovators Miniwiz (page 142) and is experimenting mixing plastics with bamboo fibre. Solving such engineering challenges keeps her spirits high because she knows that the possibilities of doing good through design are limitless.

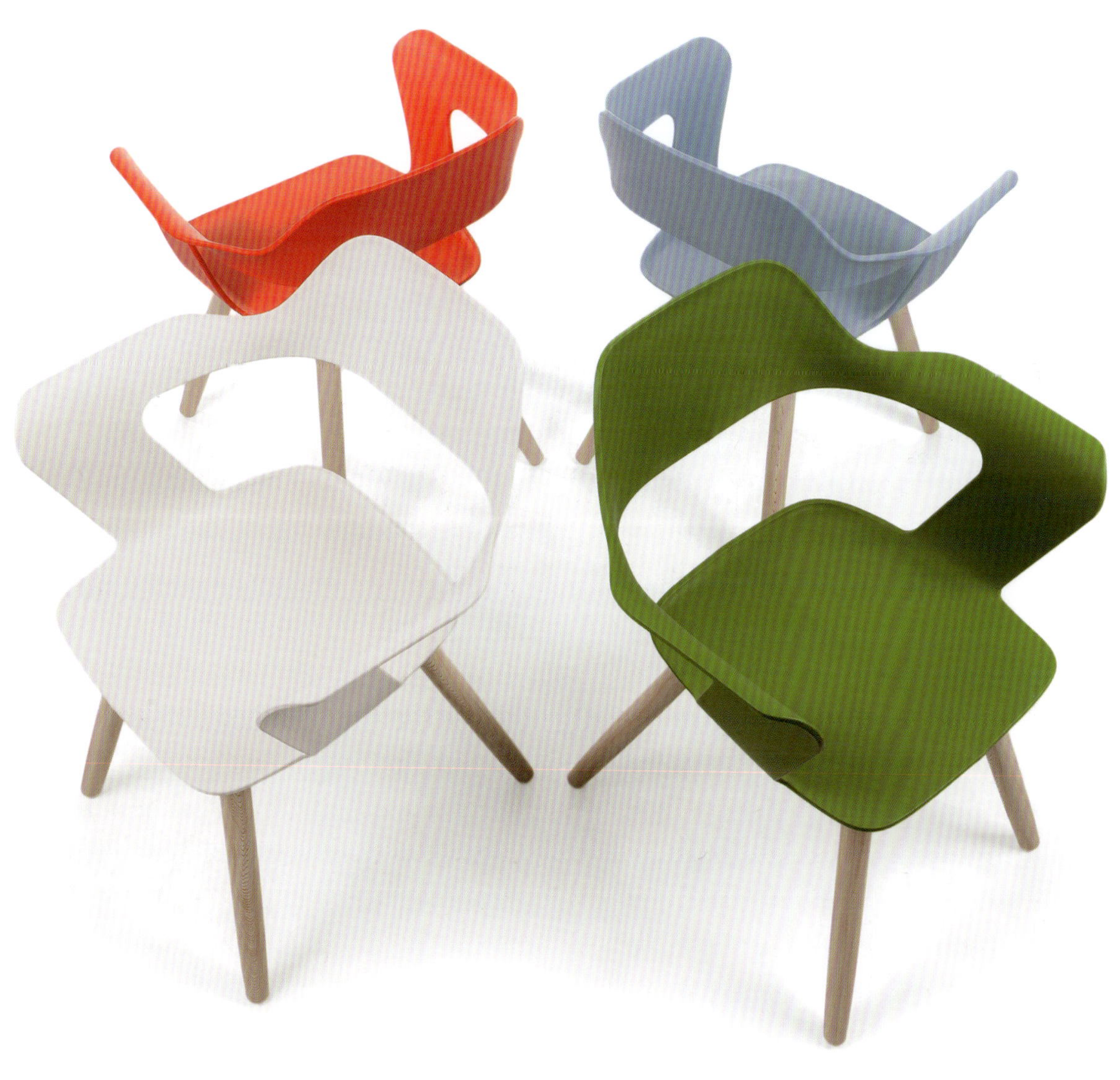

52

O-KEY

Alcohol Detection Device

Balance Wu Design

O-Key is a clinically tested device for drivers to administer an alcohol intake test before setting off on the road. It was developed by Balance Wu as one of the products in the government-sponsored Dechnology initiative. It is an excellent example of how a designer can collaborate with scientists and the community to create a culture of safety.

'Drink driving is a growing problem here', Wu says with concern. 'It's in our culture to entertain, but after an all-nighter at KTV or some banquet people get into their cars as if they're invincible. It's a bit of a stupid bravery, really. We see the horrific consequences on the news too often. Our laws are somewhat dated because offenders can get off the hook quite easily. Something has to change!'

O-Key may not be the cure to all road ills but it is a step in the right direction as it offers drivers an immediate self-assessment. The device is made of two components: a disposable capsule with a microchip, and a reader. All a driver needs to do is lick the free end of the capsule for a tiny bit of saliva to be sampled. The chip end is then slotted into the reader, which measures the levels of alcohol oxide detected in the saliva. If these are within the legal limits pre-set in the machine, a green light flashes. If the light turns red, precaution needs to be taken.

The capsule is made of super soft and safe silicon to be gently bitten or squeezed in the mouth. Because it is the size of a large pill, Wu considered manufacturing capsules in foil packets like those that dispense medicine. His next step is to find a solution to keep the cost down, otherwise the product may become redundant.

'Wouldn't it be great if we had a detector for every invisible hazard like a lie detector, smoke detector, radiation detector', ponders the designer who once developed a pesticides detector, which could accurately measure the pesticides levels in the run off water from washed fruits and vegetables. He named his device *O-Key,* from the English okay. It is universally applicable as it can be programmed to measure the permissible alcohol intake for drivers based on the laws of any country. With this little device in one's pocket, no matter whether taking the scenic road or the highway, all passengers can have peace of mind when travelling.

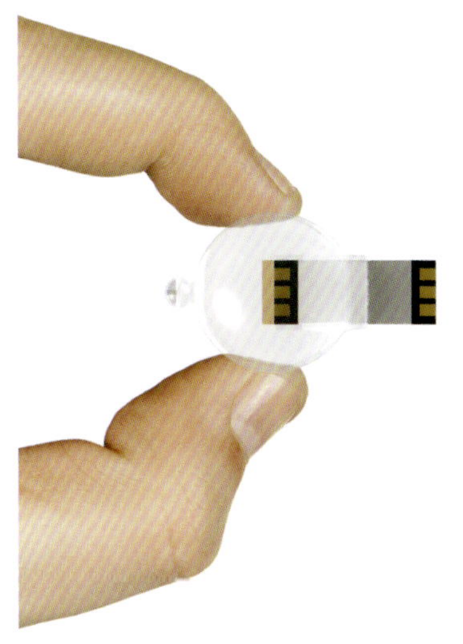

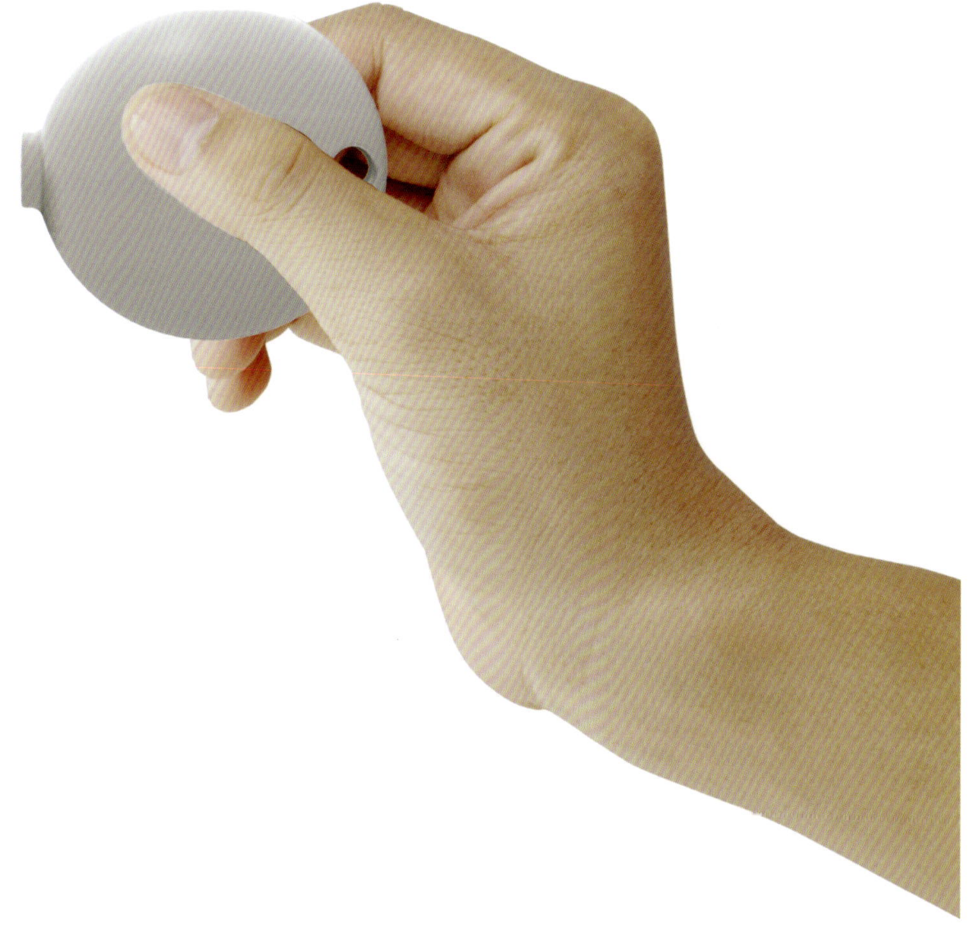

53

OCEAN LIFE

Desalination Straw

Tom Cheng | TWO+ LAB

Ocean Life is considered to be the world's first portable desalination water dispenser. It is a life-saving tool that can effectively remove excessive sodium chloride from seawater. It can also take out the bitter taste of magnesium sulphate while retaining the electrolytes needed for the body's proper function.

In situations of extreme physical distress a person's survival chances are dependent as much on environmental conditions as on preparedness. The basic rule of search and rescue is that an average body can live for about 3 hours without shelter, 3 days without water, and 3 weeks without food. A person lost at sea could perish due to extreme dehydration despite being surrounded by a vast amount of water.

'What if the life jacket was equipped with something that makes sea water drinkable?' asks Tom Cheng, whose studio researches niche opportunities for assisting people in times of distress. From his perspective there is already too much technology in the world. 'Everyone is good at it', he says, 'the challenge is how to apply it to solving real life problems. We need to design products for the common good and make living conditions better for everyone.'

Prior to setting up TWO+ LAB Cheng worked for a big innovation and design firm where he learned first hand the value of user satisfaction. While developing a self-powered showerhead with a special feature for removing chlorine, he had the idea of fabricating a similar filtering system for use in disaster situations.

Having evolved from a straw to a straw-pocket, *Ocean Life* is a half-folded aluminium foil bag with valves. For use, the cap is untwisted to enable the bag to unfold flat. Then, by simply being immersed in the sea the pressure will push a small quantity of water through the inlet valve into the lower unit: the filter. Once the filter is filled up the water automatically passes one-directionally through a carbon core and into the upper unit: the storage pocket. A person can drink from the outlet valve or keep it closed to store the filtered water. Despite its compact size the desalination straw can filter up to 2 litres of seawater.

Essentially, *Ocean Life* is designed to assist in saving lives by extending a victim's survival time until rescued. Lightweight and foldable, it can be easily integrated into a life vest or the aid kits of boats and airplanes.

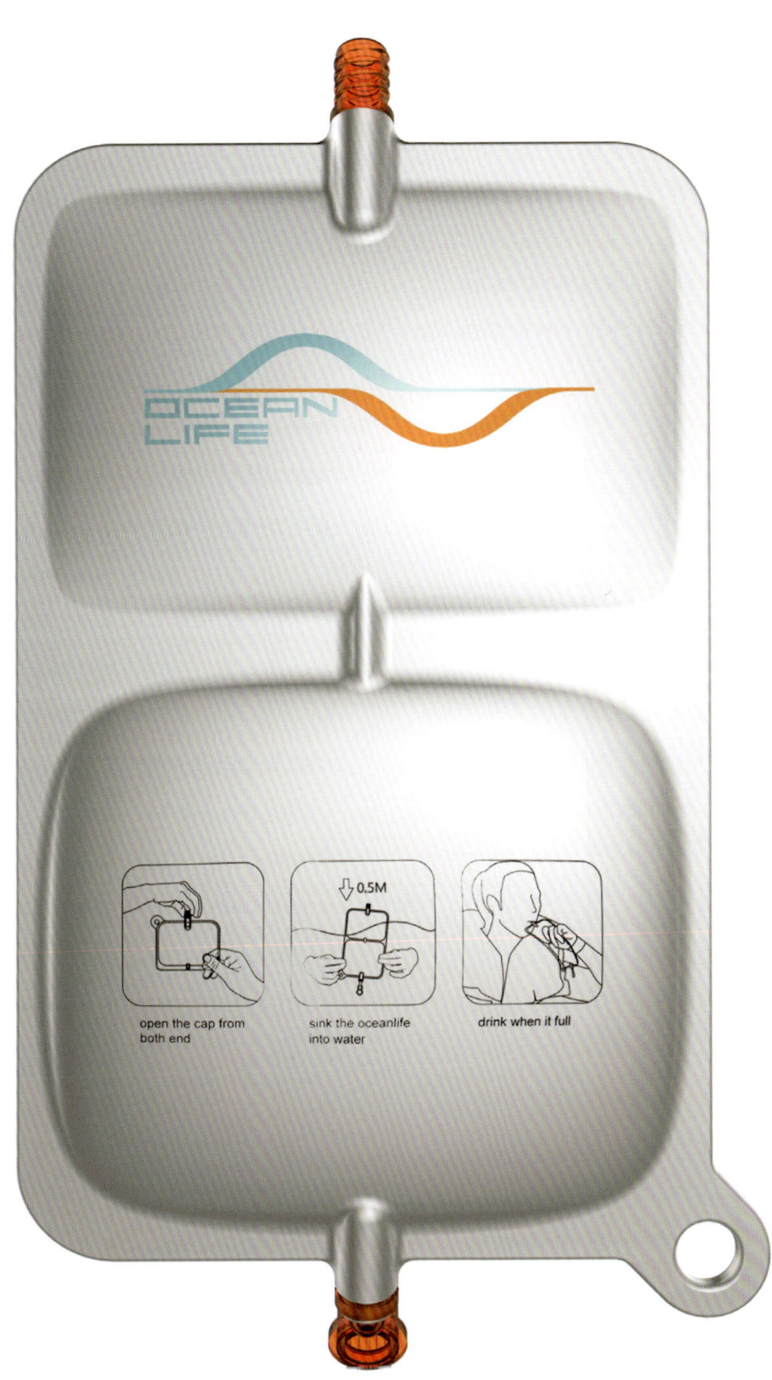
OCEAN LIFE
0.5M
open the cap from
both end
sink the oceanlife
into water
drink when it full

54

POLAR ICE TRAY

Ice Cube Tray

U-Cube Creative

Polar Ice Tray is the first icemaker that can produce a clear sphere of ice under ordinary home refrigeration conditions. An ice tray is essentially a mould to set frozen water. The designers at U-Cube Creative aimed to develop a deluxe version of the common tray: one that produces ice so brilliantly clear it looks like a crystal.

Crystal clear ice occurs widely in nature, forming in lakes and rivers when temperatures drop below zero. The team looked into how water freezes downwards, pushing air and any contaminants to lower levels and leaving the surface purified. The team spent a few years testing ways of replicating this natural process inside the home freezer and eventually came up with this clever dual-chamber solution.

The top two halves of the *Polar Ice Tray* are the sphere-making ice mould. The inner bottom half is designed to capture air pushed down during freezing. Its outer soft cocoon functions as an insulator that keeps the lower part of the water slightly warmer. Unlike the regular trays that make ice form from the outside in—causing the cube's centre to become cloudy—the new invention forms ice by layering it from top to bottom. The result: pure and clear ice spheres!

A delightful bonus of the ice made with this product is that it doesn't absorb odours of the leftover foods, which are usually kept in the freezer. The tray is designed to separate water molecules from impurities so that it will not only produce a fantastic ball of ice but it will also improve the taste of drinks.

The designers recommend that the freezer is set at -18°C and the water is left overnight to set. Warmer temperature may require a longer freezing time, while colder temperature may cause needle-like bubbles form in the ice. Once the tray is taken out of the freezer, one should allow 3 minutes for the surface to melt slightly before the ice sphere is taken out of the tray. The tray is large enough do hold a piece of fruit or a flower, thereby turning the crystal clear ice sphere into a beautiful decoration.

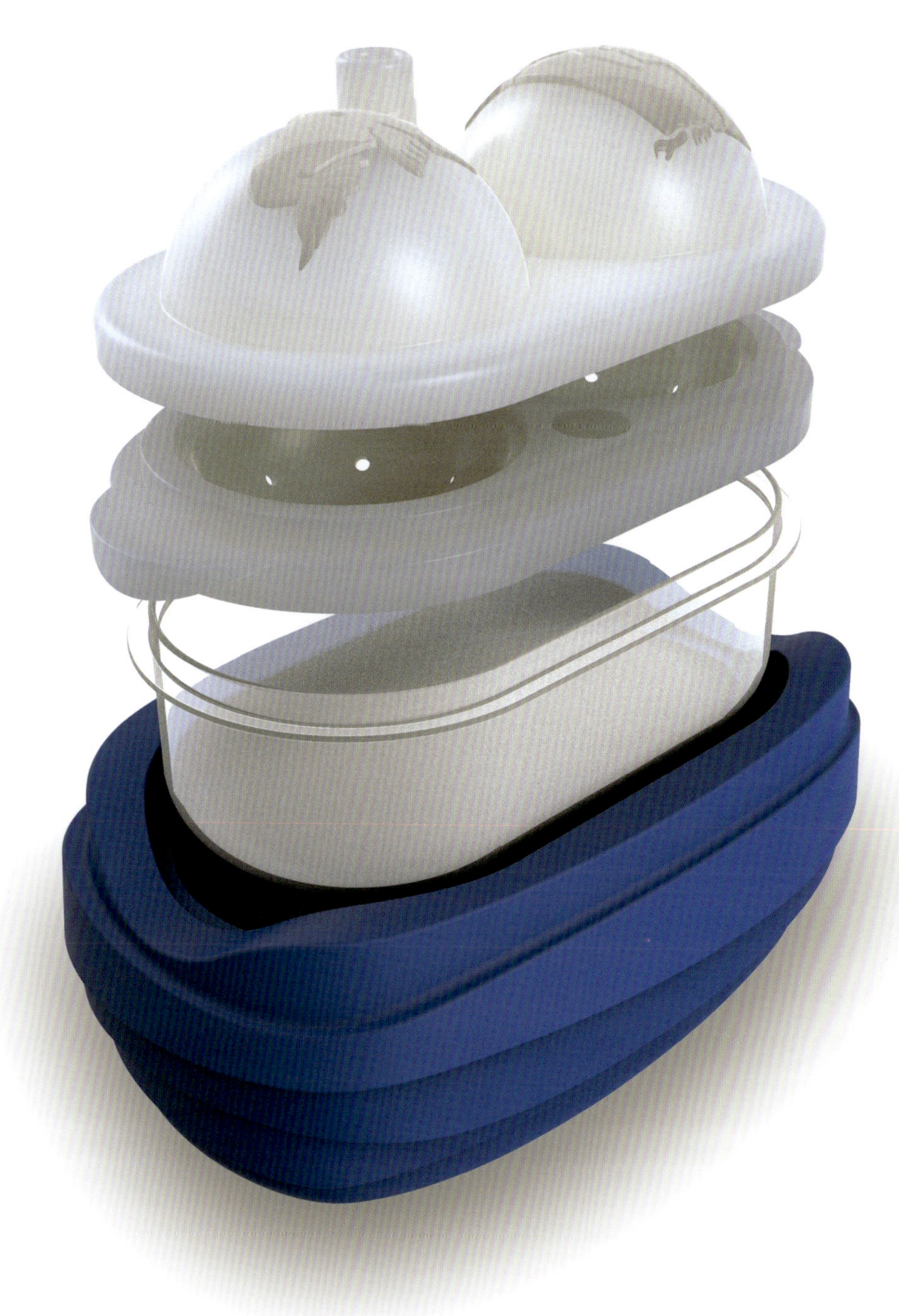

55

POLLI-BER BRICK

Building Block

Miniwiz

This semi-translucent building block belongs to a new class of composite polymer materials manufactured from recycled plastics enhanced with agricultural waste. It is not surprising that such a product would make its debut in Taiwan, which has one of most advanced trash collecting, sorting and recycling systems in Asia. Even the daily food scraps are collected from households and used either as animal feed or compost.

Primarily an engineering company, Miniwiz recycles materials into end-user products such as modules for interior design. Its founder Arthur Huang is a Taiwanese architect and Harvard graduate who won the Financial Times' 2010 Earth Award for his contribution towards building a 'new economy'.

One of the challenges of recycling is that the original material loses some of its performance during the process. Manufacturers tend to strengthen it by mixing in chemicals—a toxic and hazardous practice. Miniwiz has taken recycling plastics into a different direction by reinforcing the polymer matrix with bio-fibre.

The structure of the *Polli-Ber Brick* is formed of several rows of tubes encased in a honeycomb like lattice. Each brick has an interlocking side rim that slots into one another when bricks are layered horizontally, similar to the way the teeth of a zipper lock together. Bricks can also be stacked vertically, in which case one needs to use some special pegs that tightly fit into the bricks and hold them together in place. No bonding agents, nor cement or plastering! Well, maybe a rubber hammer to nail the pegs into position would be helpful, but that is all that is needed.

Assembling a partition wall, a bar-top table or a bench out of these building blocks is fast and easy. The trick is to plan the desired structure in advance and think of how to use natural light. The *Polli-Ber Brick* shows its best features when sunlight makes the specs of rice husks shimmer, creating a warmer ambience for an interior space. Custom colours and grades of transparency can also be manufactured to specification to suit themed interiors.

According to the engineers at Miniwiz, the manufacture of this building block requires two-thirds of the energy used for the production of raw materials. It is UV-stable and has flame resistant grading. And, if over a period of time one wishes to take a wall down, the bricks can be fully reused.

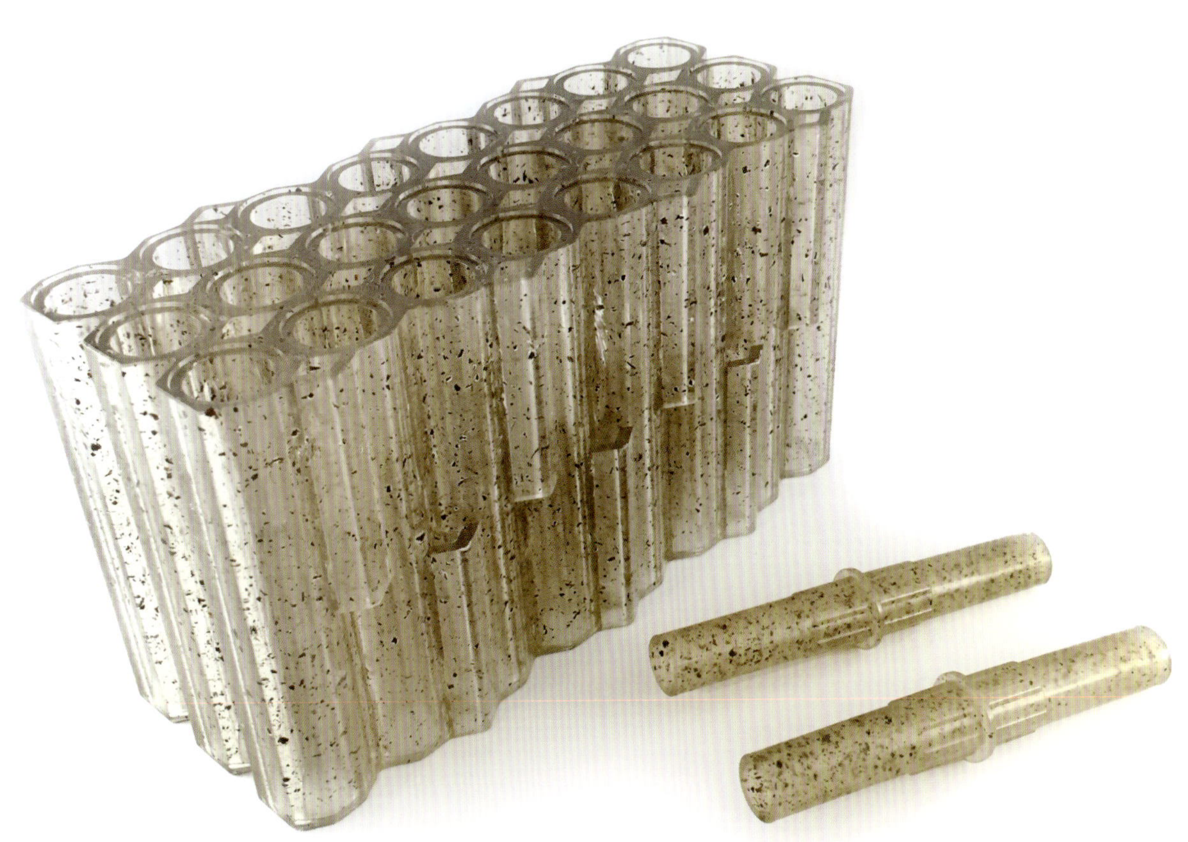

56

PRECIOUS

Doorknob

Ya-Wen Chou | Anthropologie

According to the ancient belief system of the Taiwanese aborigines, spirits inhabit all animate and inanimate creations of Nature. Therefore humans are bound to live harmoniously with the natural world. The aborigines also believed that if people guarded Nature's sacredness they would become spirits in the afterlife and could watch over their off springs. This was what paradise meant.

Ya-Wen Chou learned this story from her grandparents, who in the 1960s were in the rare business of trading butterflies. As they travelled around the island to capture exquisite specimens they formed close bonds with the aborigines and gathered precious artefacts and wisdom. 'I grew up surrounded by mysterious objects; each with its own unique story. Although I'm not an aborigine myself it makes sense that my work is influenced by indigenous culture as I have been immersed in it since childhood.'

It was only after relocating to London to study art that she truly understood its unique place in the world. She felt the indigenous approach to life was restorative and worth grounding her practice in it. As it happened, her way of thinking perfectly fitted the curatorial brief of the Paradise exhibition that she participated in Milan in 2012. Chou created

several objects as offerings of gratitude to nature, amongst them a curious casting of a garlic bulb. 'I was thinking about how to contrast something that is rooted in the ground with something boundless like the sky. I was more interested in the organic shape of the plant.'

Chou made a casting of a real bulb using a mixture of fine glass particles and resin powder. She then sanded it layer by layer to achieve a natural looking texture, coated it with enamel paint and finished it by adding small dabs of shimmering colour. In her mind, the colours reference pristine natural landscapes and the presence of the sun in every living thing.

In Milan the work was spotted by fashion brand Anthropologie, and an invitation for collaboration soon followed. Much admired for its bohemian style, the company gave Chou her first commercial break by commissioning her to make a series of home décor details based on the bulb-cast. With an additional screw and a bolt, Chou's object became a trendy doorknob. It is a small item, but a fortunate one because it gave the talented designer the satisfaction of professional success while being true to her dreams.

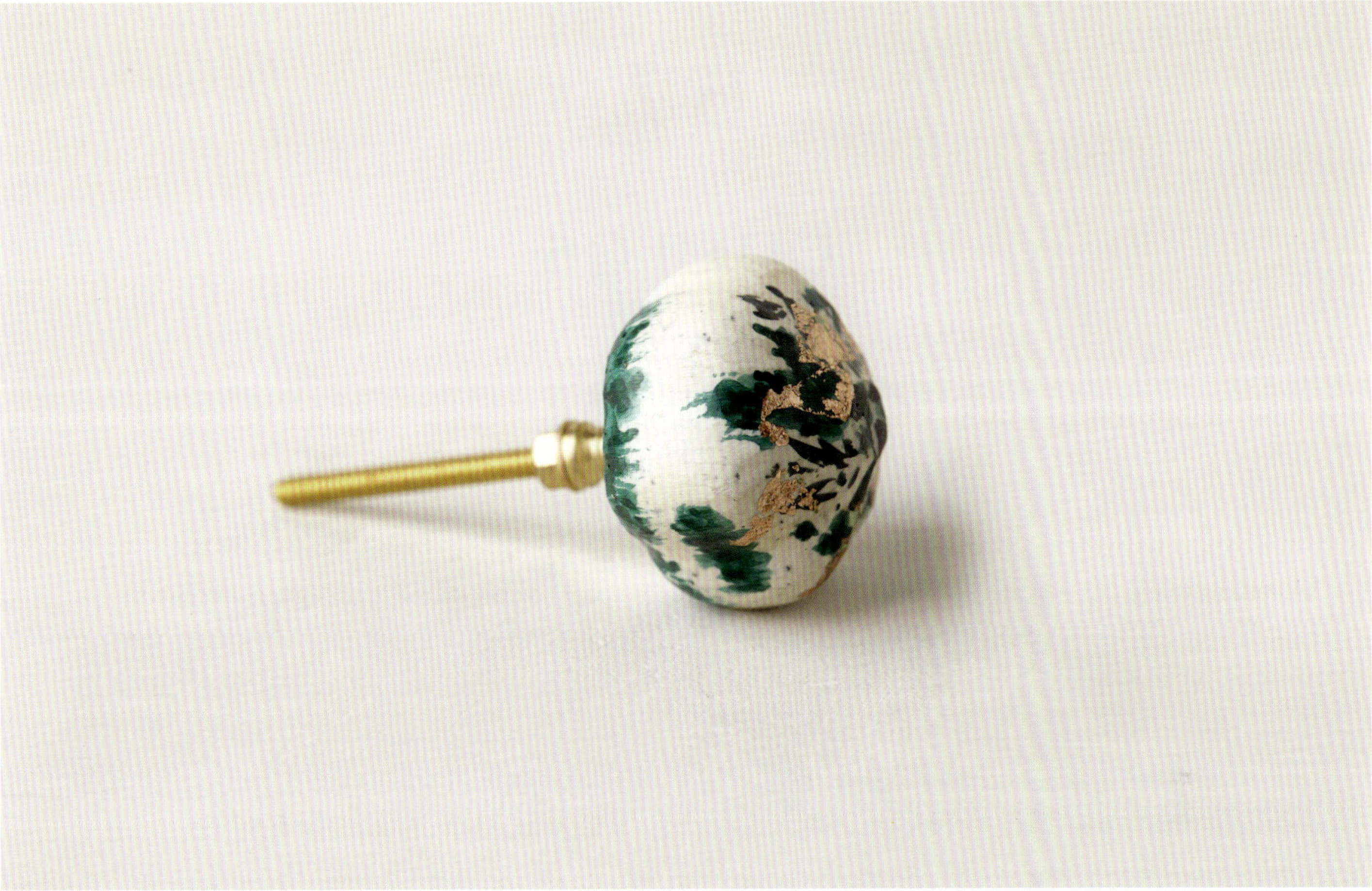

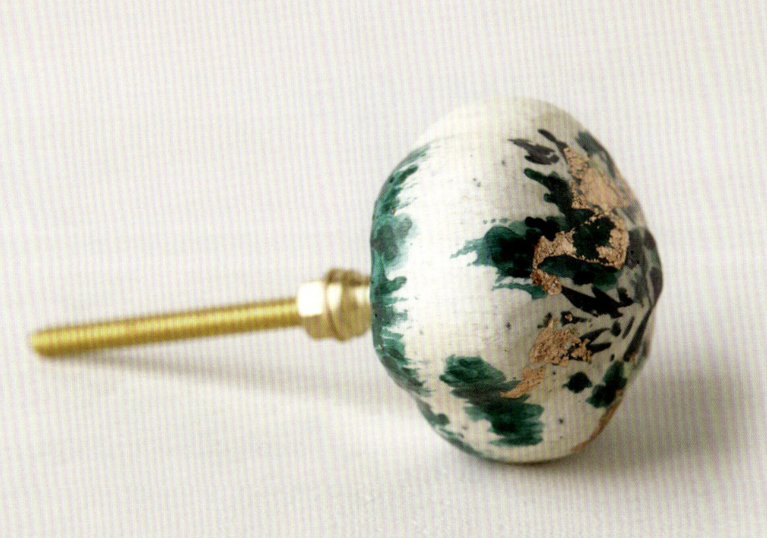

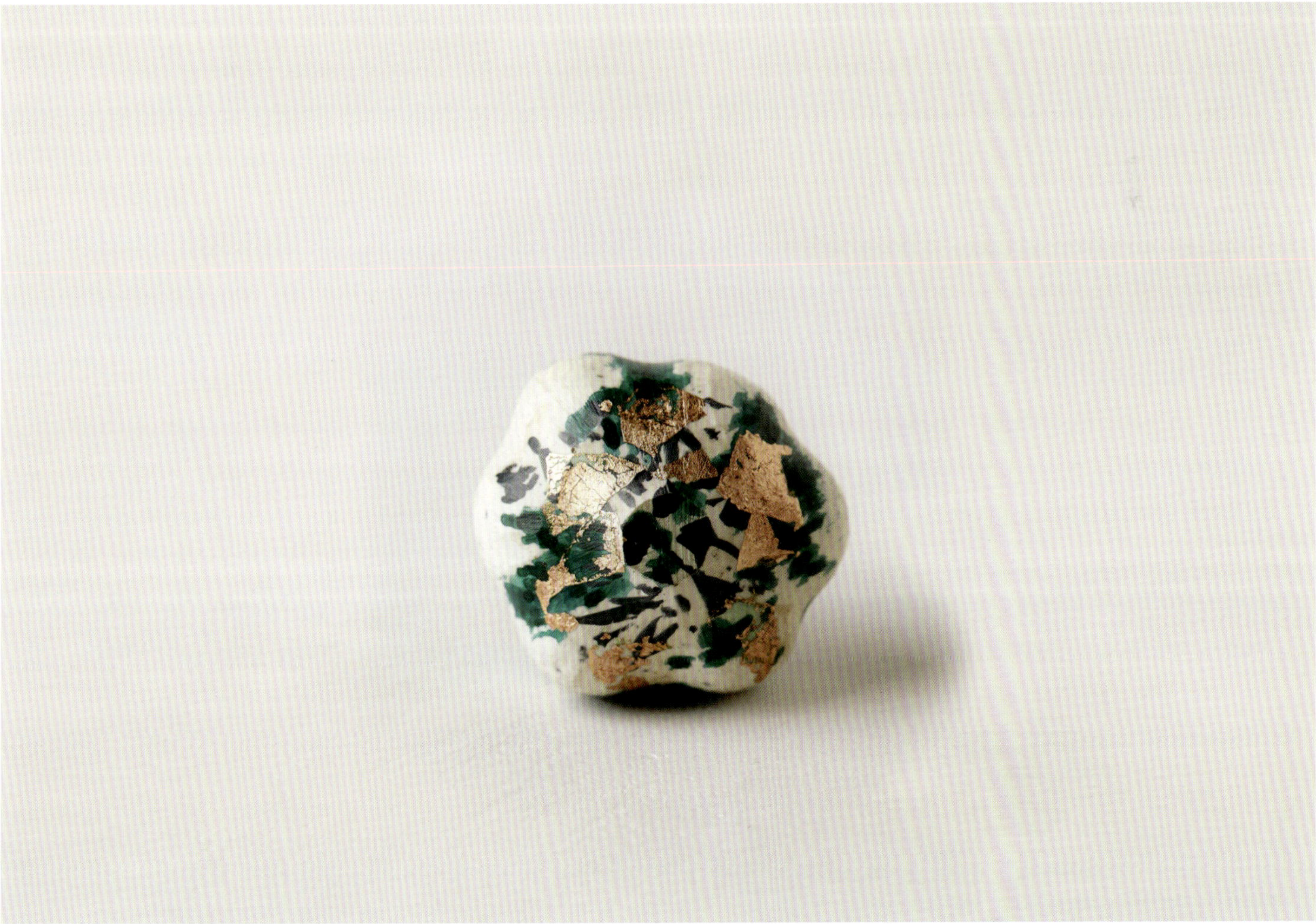

57

QUMI Q6

LED Pocket Projector

Jeff Chang, Andy Lin | Vivitek

Vivitek is a brand of Delta Electronics, one of the world's largest manufacturers of high-end powerful projector equipment for digital cinema screenings, public spectacles and stereoscopic projections. Unlike the mother company, Vivitek focuses on developing digital projection and display devices suitable for everyday, business and home, use.

Launched in the fall of 2015, *Qumi Q6* is a super portable LED projector—the size of a paperback weighing just 475g—that delivers HD quality images while it can be conveniently carried in a briefcase. Its multi-connectivity ports are suitable for a wide range of multimedia players making it a suitable companion for business presentations, video gaming, and media sharing. Touch sensitive buttons and an intuitive on-screen display offer easy control panel navigation.

One of the major challenges for projector manufacturers is developing energy efficient products without compromising image quality. In addition to its excellent portability, *Qumi Q6* integrates an environmentally friendly LED light source that beams rich colors with a brightness of up to 800 ANSI lumens. This means it can deliver the clearest image available for a projector this small.

Styling the product into an elegant object was a lot of fun for the team: 'We're big fans of race cars! We love their high performance and the excellence of their designs, especially of the Italian models. The design of *Qumi Q6's* cooling vents and the colors of the product range somewhat followed our sporting passions', joke the designers.

The company's relatively flat management system and its values of teamwork and business agility create an environment conductive to innovation. Its industrial product designers are encouraged to explore unorthodox ideas and be ready to respond to new trends. 'Once we designed a one-eyed, smiley face projector in the shape of a green apple! The product did not make it to market but being allowed to try out new concepts makes us better prepared to respond to emerging consumer needs', recalls Andy Lin.

The change to original design manufacturing has given Vivitek greater control over its product development and design strategy to optimise the user-experience for each individual application. All projector software is developed in-house and each design process is executed holistically with a full overview of the market demands and the needs of the end user.

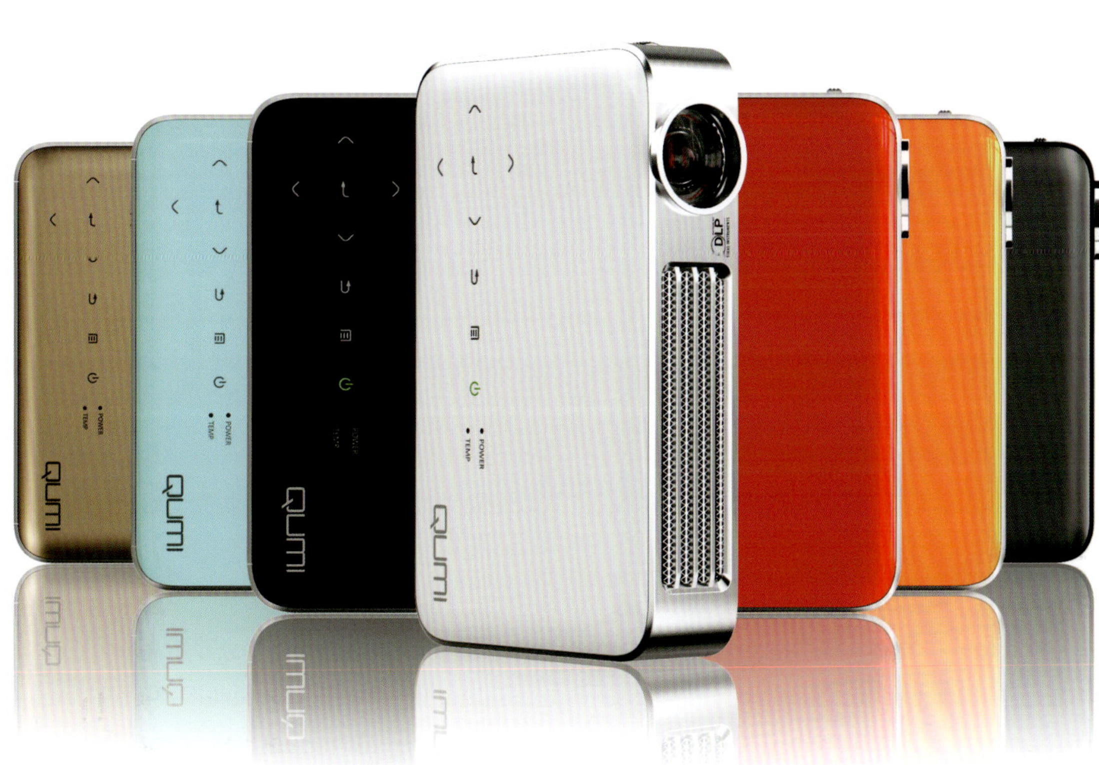

58

RANDOM

Pendant Light

Chia-Ying Lee | studio if

Chia-Ying Lee is a young designer already making a mark in Taiwanese creative circles with her interactive projects. The strength of her practice lies in her ability to seamlessly blend digital technology and structural aesthetics. In her mind, the novelty of any 'next technology' eventually fades away: a new gadget quickly becomes a throwaway thing. She therefore invests effort in creating a product experience of lasting satisfaction whereby technology is made intuitive for the user.

Random is a pendant light that plays with the concept of serendipity. This is determined by the pull of one of two strings suspended from the light's centre point. Each time a string is tweaked the light bulbs switch on, one by one, randomly. The nearly infinite number of lighting combinations makes each interaction a unique moment and each setup unexpected. Pulling the second string dims the light in the reverse order until all bulbs are switched off.

The idea for the pendant light is based on visualising the transmission of electricity, which Lee had been tinkering with for a while. 'A few years ago I designed another product made of two sets of light bulbs: one responsive to an on/off switch, and another to be activated when the first set is lit. Light would then spread virally through the object', she explains. 'Similarly, the uncertainty of which way the light would turn on creates a fresh experience: each light-pattern possibly appearing only once. Will this prolong the enjoyment of having this object … I'm curious to find out!'

The 22 glass balls, each with an attached light bulb, are suspended evenly from the ceiling, looking more like an inverted and weightless bunch of balloons than a light feature. The micro-controller switch is hidden in the strings. All glass balls are changeable and can be safely attached to the pendant via a silicon cap-top.

Each glass ball is hand-blown by Master Rui-Dian Liu, who was delighted to collaborate with a designer on something novel. 'Master Liu is like a walking encyclopaedia of glass making. He knows some incredible techniques so every time I visit him I learn something new. We strived for the lamp to reveal the magic of glassblowing but still to match a techno-style', says Lee with fond admiration for her teacher. Anyone who appreciates smart products would admire *Random*.

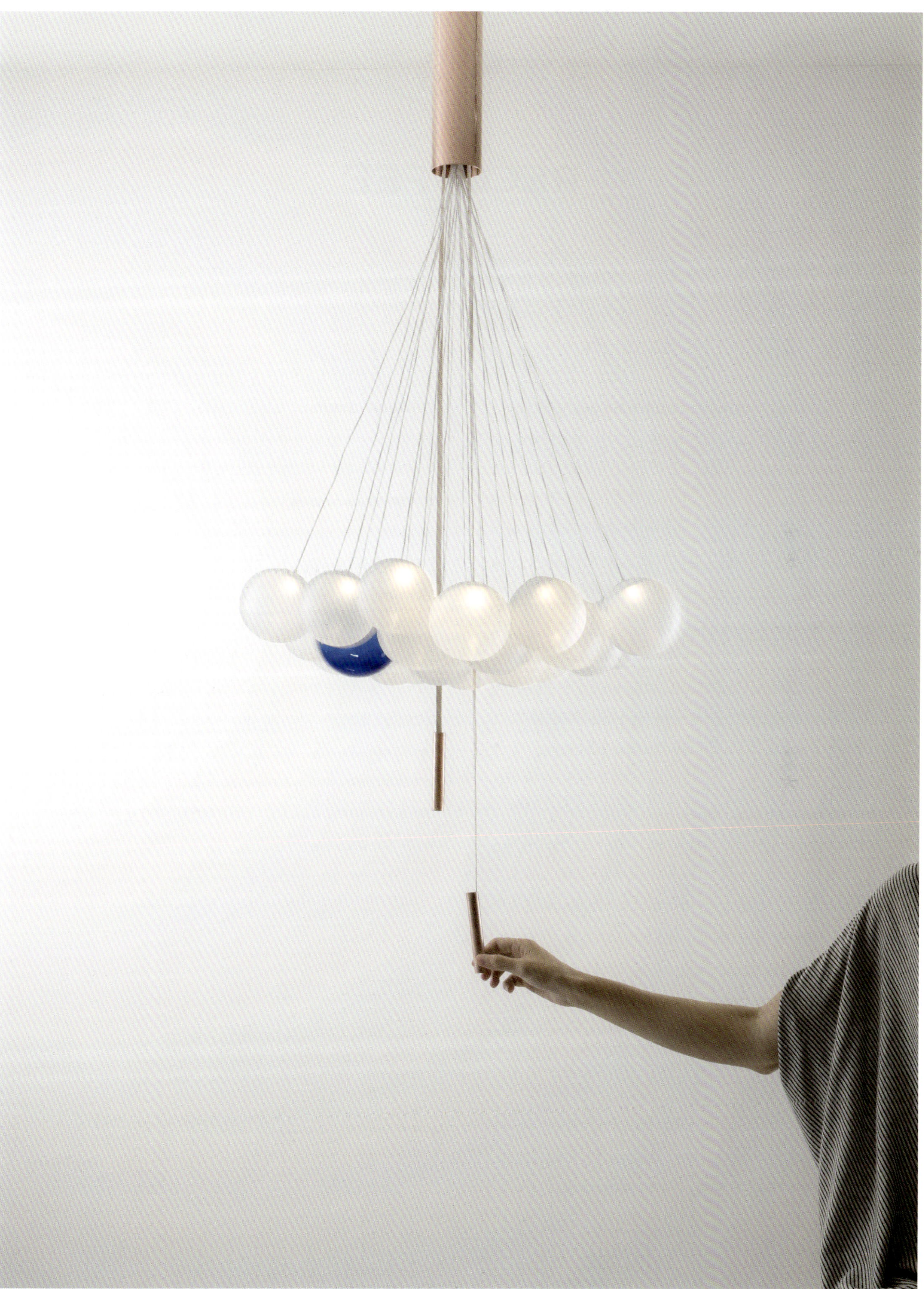

59

RECOFFEE

Hair Care

Hair O'right International

With a mission to inspire consumers to care for the Earth, Hair O'right creates organic cosmetic products that contribute to a more sustainable future. The company was founded by Steven Ko, CEO in 2002, when both of his parents passed away from cancer believed to have been caused by excessive exposure to pesticides. Feeling overwhelmed by the family tragedy, Ko made a pledge to support protecting the Earth from poisons, one product at a time.

Adopting Cradle-to-Cradle green engineering principles across all its operations, Hair O'right manufactures SGS-certified hair care products and proudly claims to be Taiwan's first carbon neutral medium size enterprise. All employees zealously work on turning waste into raw materials and products into renewable resources. They also endeavour to create a completely self-sustaining manufacturing process, and to influence consumers to be more environmentally conscious when shopping for cosmetics.

RECOFFEE: Coffee Tree in the Bottle is the latest hair care product based on the zero-waste principle. Discarded coffee waste is collected from several café chains. With the application of Supercritical Fluid Extraction technology, extra-pure coffee oil and coffee bean fibre are extracted in a contamination-free environment. Coffee oil has UV-protective and anti-oxidation properties that are well suited for cosmetic products. The leftover bean fibre is reused as a compound in the biodegradable PLA (polylactic acid) material used for the bottle. The coffee essence gives a pleasant aroma to both the shampoo and its packaging.

A coffee bean seedpod is planted at the bottom of the product. By placing the bottle in garden soil the bean can sprout and grow into a coffee tree, while the biomaterial of the bottle decomposes and acts as a natural fertiliser. The product is in fact a message in a bottle: consumers are supporting a design concept of living in harmony with the biosphere.

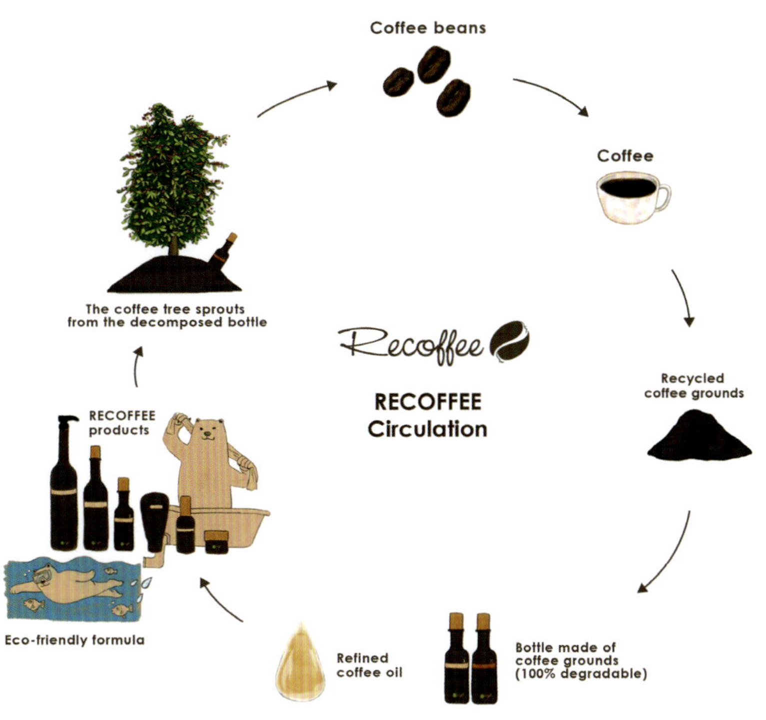

Coffee beans
Coffee
Recycled
coffee grounds
Bottle made of
coffee grounds
(100% degradable)
Refined
coffee oil
Eco-friendly formula
RECOFFEE
products
The coffee tree sprouts
from the decomposed bottle
Recoffee
RECOFFEE
Circulation

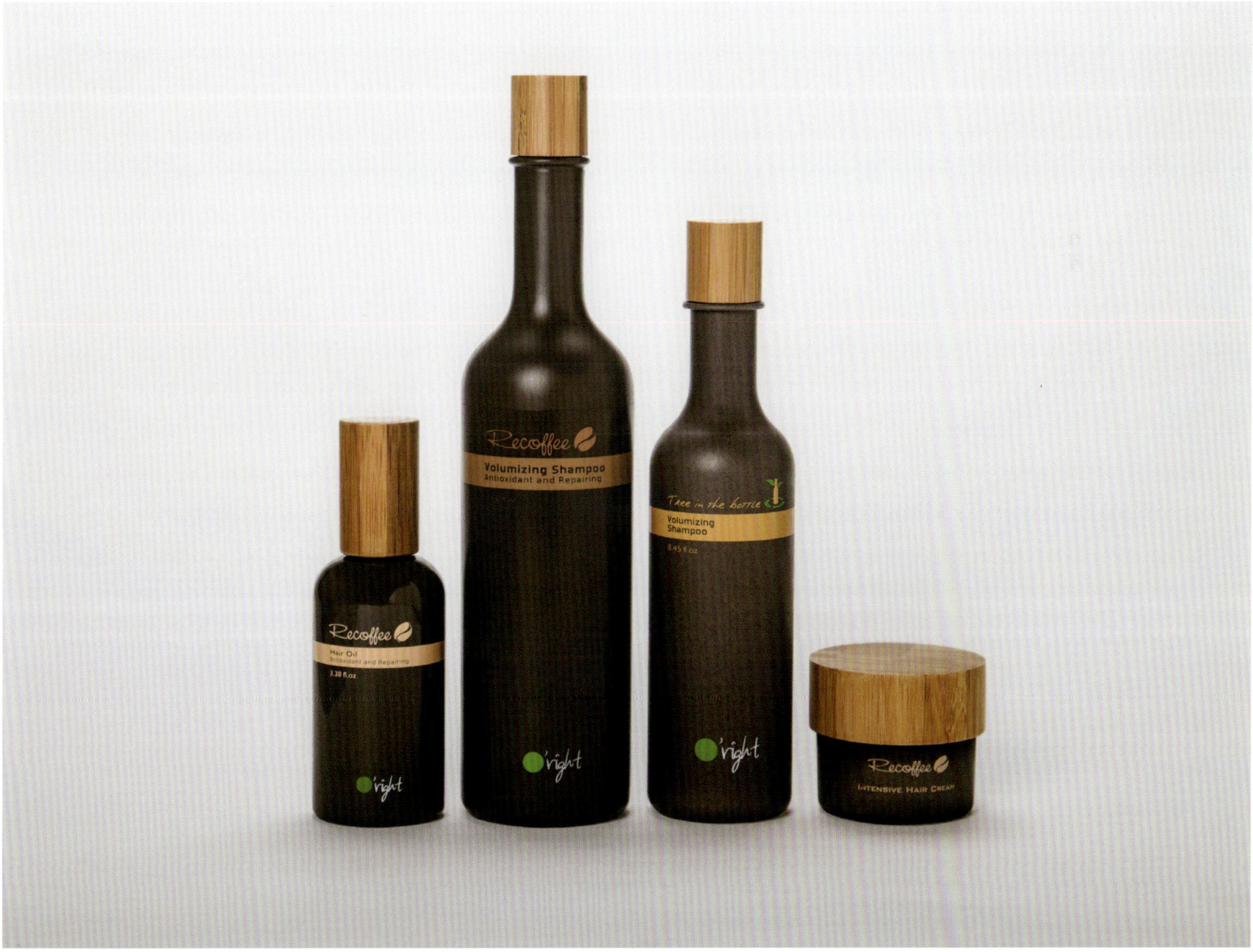

Recoffee
Hair Oil
Antioxidant and Repairing
3.38 fl.oz
O'right
Recoffee
Volumizing Shampoo
Antioxidant and Repairing
O'right
Tree in the bottle
Recoffee
Volumizing
Shampoo
8.45 fl.oz
O'right
Recoffee
INTENSIVE HAIR CREAM

60

RETURN

Burial Urn

Sally Lin | Sa'Bella Design

According to tradition, to be recognised as a master one's skills must illustrate an unsurpassable command of techniques and materials. Only then would the artisan guild accept a master's knowledge as virtuous. Sally Lin set herself the ambitious challenge to master classical object making by acquiring 36 crafts skills over a period of ten years.

As a way of planning her work ahead, Lin decided on key events that have had a significant cultural impact on Taiwan, and selected a material with which to create objects to illustrate them. Her aim was to design 36 sets of new products utilising glass, ceramic, gold, lace, bamboo, and so on, and in the process go deeper into traditional knowledge by working alongside master-artisans.

Return is an alternative burial urn reflecting upon the relationship between disruptive human activity, catastrophic acts of nature, and the evolution of society. It is a commemorative product, which Lin designed in response to the effects of the 921 Earthquake: the deadliest natural calamity to hit the island in living memory. In its aftermath, many burial sites were destroyed by landslides. Local custom dictates that hill sites with specific orientation should be reserved as burial grounds. These are cleared from trees and larger bushes for the ancestral tombs to be built. However, once the vegetation is uprooted, there is little left to hold the ground together and the sites become prone to sliding.

Lin created a synergy between the burial object, the burial ritual and its natural surrounds. The urn consists of a biodegradable core containing the ashes of the loved one, and a honeycomb urn-shaped object made from recycled paper populated with fresh seeds. The idea is that once placed in the ground, the urn would gradually disintegrate and in the process plant the seeds into the soil. As the ashes are absorbed back into the earth they become nourishment for the seeds helping them grow into a beautiful bush or a tree.

'This design is very close to my heart. I visited some of the cemeteries affected by the landslides. They are like deep wounds carved into the hills, not places of eternal peace. I've spoken with my mother about it and she's supportive of this "reformed" way of thinking of our final resting place. Perhaps it's how she'd return to the afterlife … in harmony with nature.' In Lin's mind, the urn is an expression of a person's profound gratitude for the gifts of life, and surrenders us to the fact that we are all an inseparable part of the Eath's living organism.

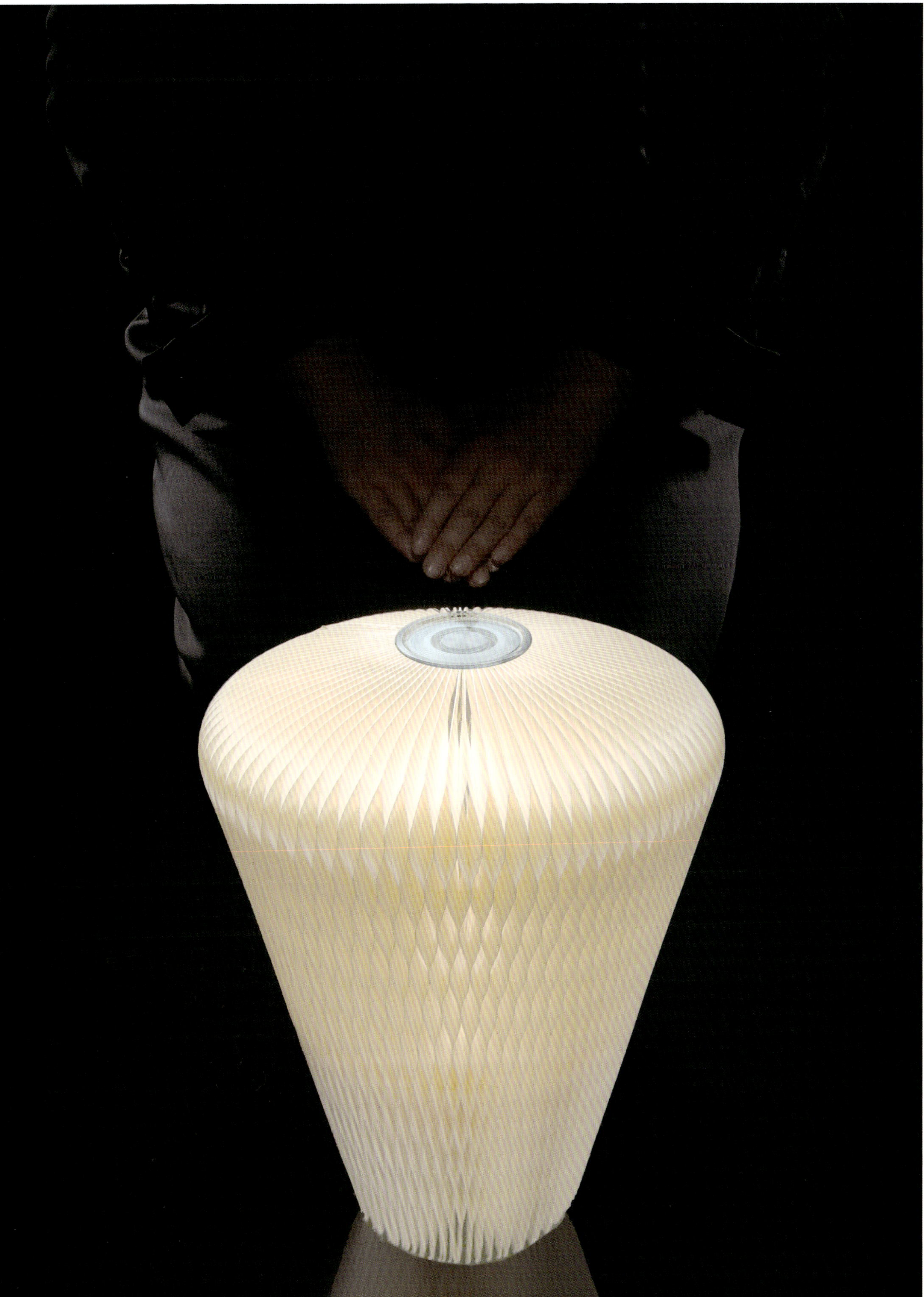

61

RICE

Tea Box

Wuba Yang | JIA Inc.

With the world becoming increasingly interconnected, new dining customs and entertainment rituals naturally evolve, especially within families of blended heritage. This melting pot of cultural experiences is pushing tableware designers to take a broader and more hybrid perspective, a trend that is beautifully illustrated by *Rice* tea box from JIA Inc. The thinking behind this gorgeous product combines two social customs: the Eastern *gong-fu cha*, traditional serving of tea, and the Western afternoon picnic.

Wuba Yang came up with an adorable idea of introducing a mini picnic basket to gong-fu cha. 'It's for people who would like an elegant yet highly functional setting to serve tea while on the move: at a picnic, a family outing, may be even during a business trip. The product has two functions. It is a storage box for all the necessary teaware, which when unfolded becomes a miniature tea-serving platform', explains Yang.

The structure is reminiscent of a vintage wooden box with expandable compartments, sometimes called a 'foldout sewing craft basket'. To un-fold the portable *Rice* tea box one just holds the two handles and gently pushes them downwards until an even base is created. The tea set is stored in the middle compartment, with the left and right sections joined to it with antique brass hinges.

Small bamboo platforms are stored at each side of the box. In order for a table surface to be created, they need to be placed on top of the box with the tendon facing downwards. Yang points to the lattice grid on the top: 'Usually when we prepare tea we like pouring a tiny amount of hot water over the teapot to keep the brewing temperature consistent. Typically the traditional serving tray, or small table, has a lattice grid with tiny holes in the wood. This is to let spilled water run off. All key elements of how tea is served and enjoyed for hundreds of years have been incorporated into the new product. But we upgraded its function.'

The box is made of bamboo and maple timber finished with a fine veneer. Teaware can then be delicately arranged for a visually enticing presentation. By making the setting elegant yet portable, traditional culture can find a new place in a modern context.

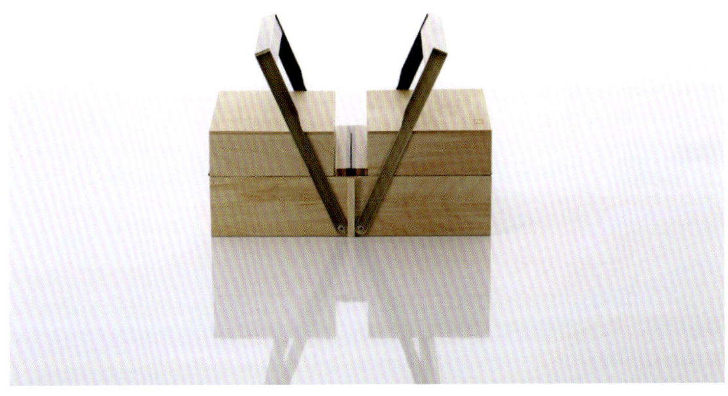
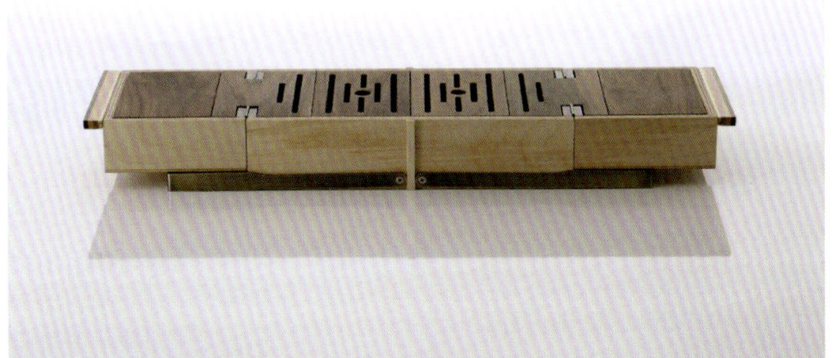
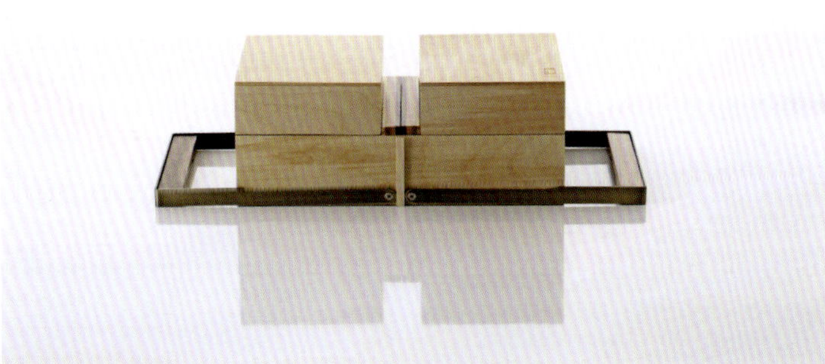
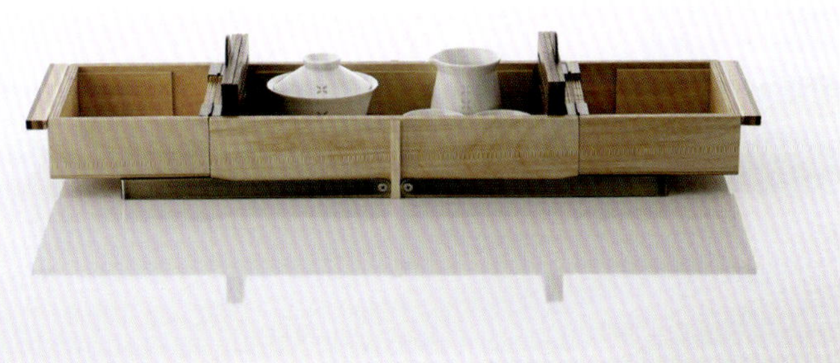
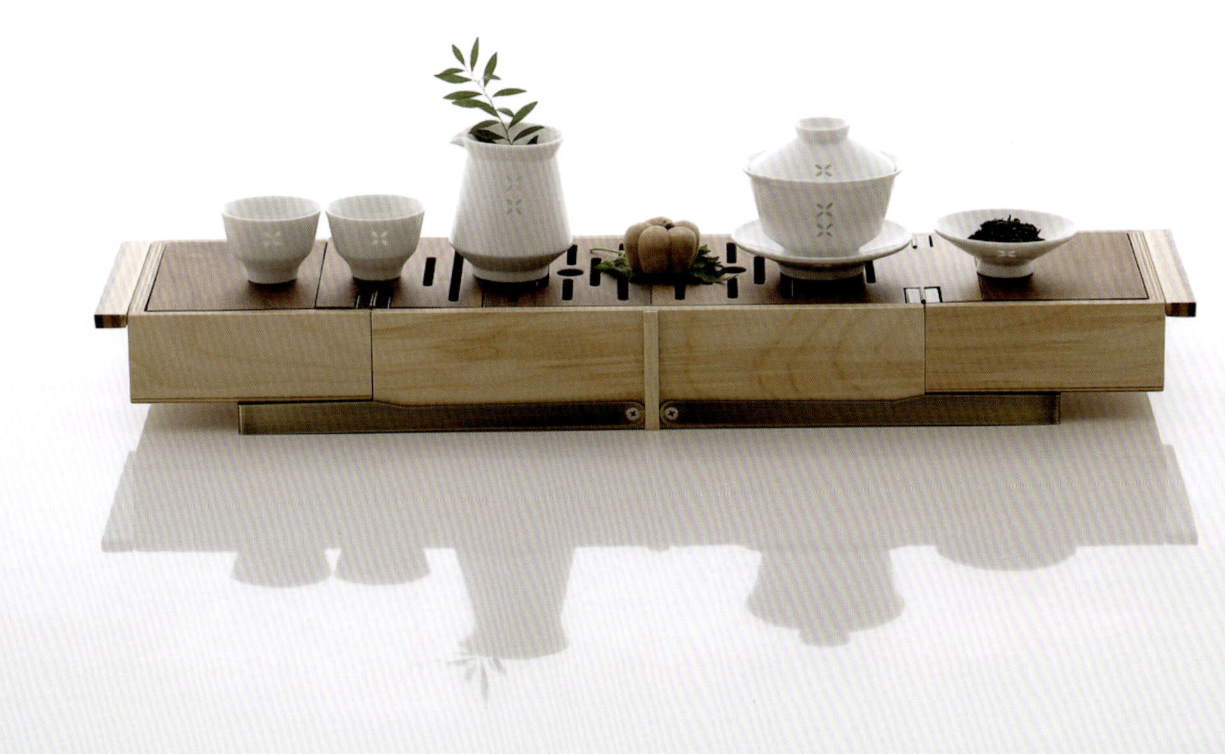

62

RIPPLE

Moving Crystal Light

Poetic Lab | J. & L. Lobmeyr

Founded by brothers Josef and Ludwig in 1823, Lobmeyr is one of the oldest businesses in Europe dedicated to the creation of exquisite vessels and light objects in Bohemian crystal glass. Each piece emerges from the personal sensibility of its maker. World-renowned designers have collaborated with the company over the decades, including pioneers of the Modernist Movement and famous architects and artists, each of whom has added their aspirations for everlasting beauty into its collections.

Still new to European culture, Poetic Lab could not let themselves dream that they could soon be collaborating with Lobmeyr. Yet their mesmerising light captivated the attention of its buyers at a sideshow in Milan and invited them to produce *Ripple* under their brand name. 'It all started with in a swimming pool at a Roman baths in Torino!', laughs Shi Kai Tseng. 'We were two gaping Taiwanese guys who've never seen anything like it before. The pool had all these dancing light reflections of water ripples projected onto the Roman ceiling. The effect felt so soothing, it was like a magic show. It was all new and fascinating, so we became obsessed with the idea of recreating the effect for the home.'

The first obstacle the designers had to overcome was figuring out how to create a reflective surface that could produce light ripples. They played with combining light and actual water, which was unsafe and ended disastrously. They realised that it should be the light not the water that should create the ripples. A glassblower friend suggested that the light body be made as an irregular crystal glass sphere with an unevenly polished surface.

'Half the problem was solved. But we still needed to figure out how to recreate the calming ripples without actually using liquids. Eventually we engineered a motorised mechanism attached to a small LED light so that it rotates the glass bubble around the light source. The light and shadows thrown around the walls of a room are stunning ... They do appear as real as those we experienced for the first time in Italy. Our hope is that *Ripple* captures the special quality of crystal glass in an imaginative way, and that people feel peaceful in the atmosphere of this light.'

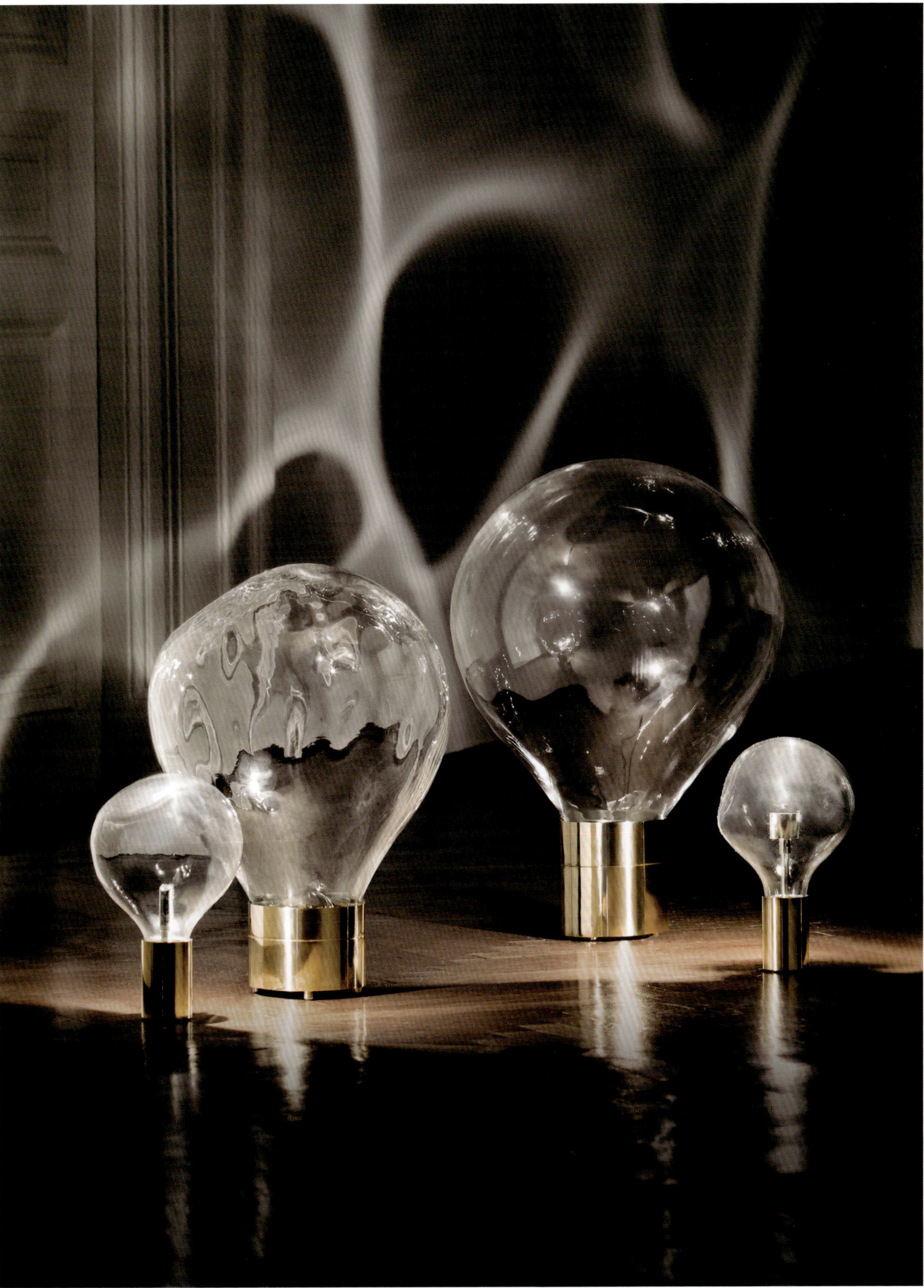

63

RIVER STONE

Tea Set

Tong Ho | Lin's Ceramics Studio

From a humble beginning in 1983 when it made just one small teapot, Lin's Ceramics Studio has grown to become an industry leader in tea culture products much loved for their superb quality. With a mission to popularise the art of tea, the studio commissioned Tong Ho to develop its first concept collection for the youth market.

From the outset the designer understood that it would require particular sensitivity. 'Ritualised tea making is an art as it is a science. To make a perfect brew tea masters carefully choose the water, the temperature and the pottery. So the design brief wasn't simply to make fashionable teaware; the product had to be true to the core principles of brewing and serving tea. The pottery had to balance these three factors.'

Ho did not want to challenge but rather 'take care' of the old designs. As he was not sure where to begin, he decided to go for a walk in the mountains, something tea masters often do. 'While I was hiking, I had to cross a gentle stream running over black pebbles. The water was creating interesting negative spaces around them and this caught my attention. I saw it in a symbiotic way: tradition is solid like a rock; the new is flowing like a river. It was a strong image to work with.'

In the *River Stone* series the new is represented by an ultra modern outer layer with circular holes, which encases a classical tea set. The casing insulates the vessels whilst keeping their forms partially revealed. Visually, the inner black objects evoke things weathered with time, while the outer white surface references the flow of new energy.

The designer also observed that young people enjoy holding teapots with two hands. To match this comforting gesture he reengineered one of Lin's Ceramics teapots iconic shapes by adding a cantilever handle and significantly shortening its spout. '*The River Stone* version looks like a decorative basket, big enough to be held between the hands. The shortening of the spout altered the pouring line significantly. If it is displaced even a millimetre during the firing process it could make the teapot dribble. This was a major production problem we had to resolve to make it function perfectly.'

The complete *River Stone* set includes: teapot, pitcher, sniffing and drinking cups, and matching utensils. The product was launched at specially choreographed Tea Party events accompanied by nature sounds and performative style pouring of tea.

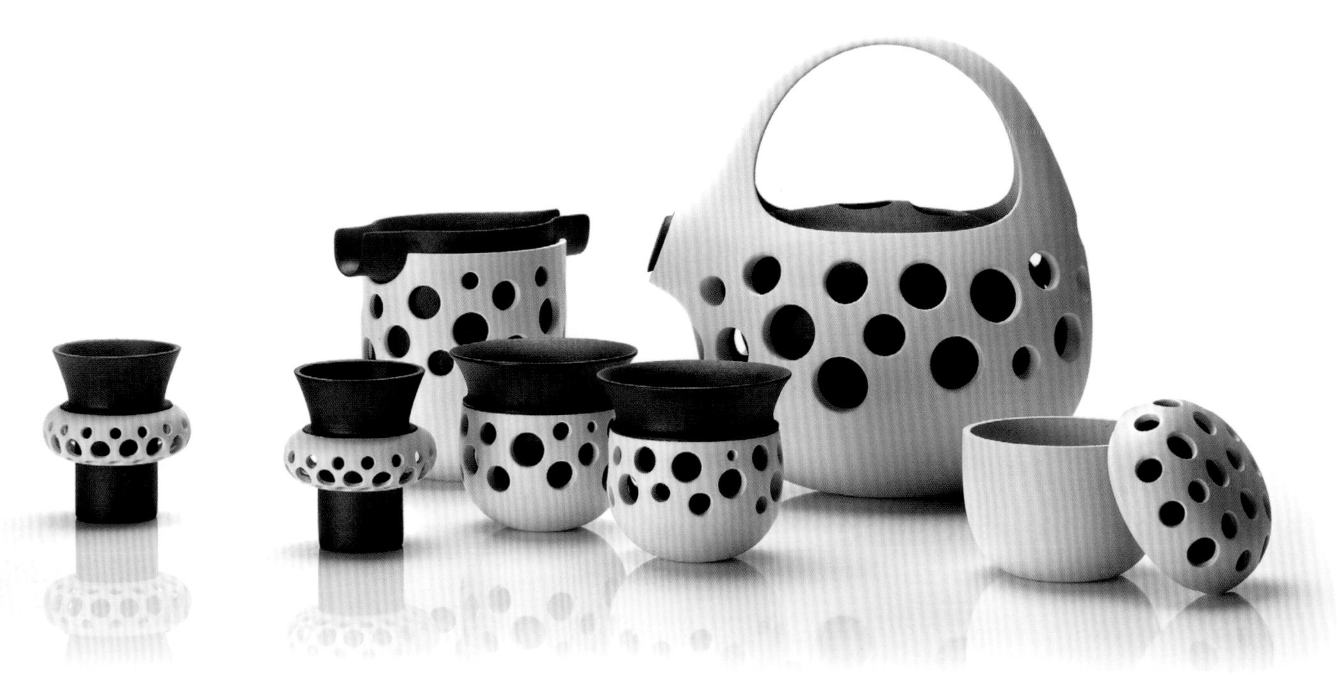

64

ROLLERBALL PEN

Stationery

Y Studio

Taiwan abounds in cultural treasures, amongst the most significant of which is the preservation of the traditional characters of Mandarin Chinese. Derived from logograms, the script is formed by a lattice of strokes that gives its calligraphic form. Kids spend innumerable hours practicing the correct stroke sequence in square-grid notebooks. This helps them memorise the characters and also trains them to hold a pen correctly, vertically. However, technology has reduced the practice to shortcut texting.

Despite being of the digital generation, Y Studio has set itself the goal to reconnect people with the fine art of stroke-by-stroke character writing by designing collectible writing tools. 'It all started when I wanted to send an appreciation note to my parents. In our culture it's hard to show affection towards the elders, so I didn't know how to express my feelings. I couldn't just text them. I spent an afternoon composing a message, which I wrote on a special card I made. It was so endearing for them to receive it, it's been on display in their kitchen ever since', recalls Yihsien Liao. 'This heartfelt gesture of my parents made me realise just how warm and touching handwriting can be.'

With a dream to make fine objects that can accompany people on their life's journey, in 2012 Y Studio released its first collection of pens, pencils and containers made primarily of brass. 'We were very particular about our signature material. Brass has weight, so a pen like this is for writing words with weight. That which is put on paper should be meaningful and lasting. We found a small factory in New Taipei City specialising in brass—they might have been manufacturing bullets at one time! — which agreed to fabricate our products', adds his colleague Yanko.

The weight of Y Studio's *Rollerball Pen* makes the writing tool rest firmly, yet snugly, in the hand. This enhances its grip and rotation control. It is steady when held vertically for character writing, but also glides effortlessly along the page for smooth Western style handwritten letters. To maintain the high quality of the product, only Faber-Castell tips are incorporated into the pen. Over time the pen's surface may slightly oxidise, giving it an individual patina. Each product is packaged for safekeeping in its own wooden box that encourages the user to treasure their writing tools.

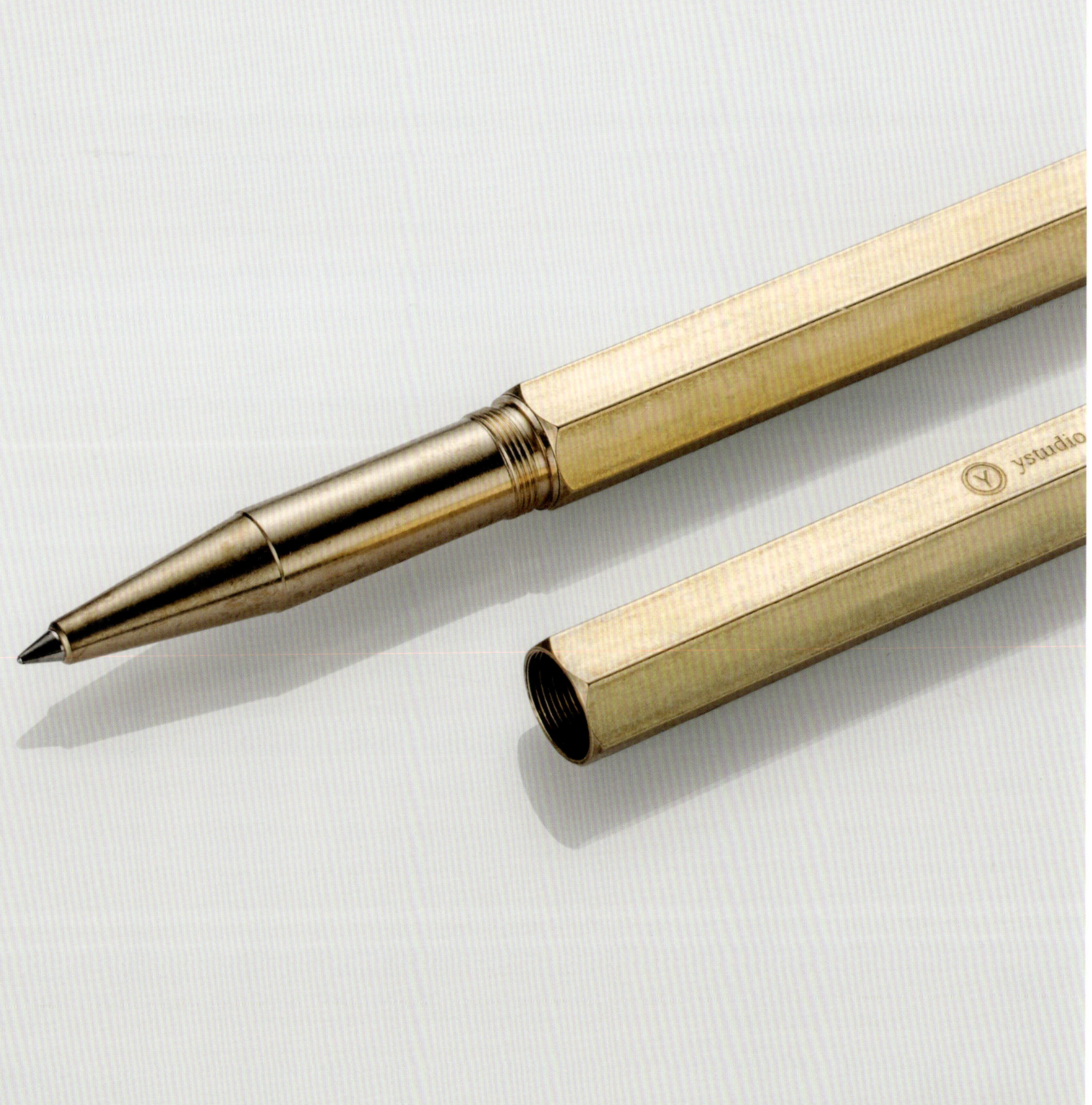

ystudio

65

SENSALIGHT

LED Lamp

Meijun Liu | Wolkeland Design

Sensalight is a table lamp with a dual function of atmospheric and directional lighting interchangeable via a touch panel. It is created by Meijun Liu in partnership with the Industrial Research Institute, renowned for its expertise in smart materials. The institute is located in Hsinch Science and Technology Industrial Park—Taiwan's Silicon Valley—home to more than 300 high-tech companies. This collaborative project was made possible by the *Dechnology* initiative, which aims to connect designers with local engineering know-how.

Given free access to the institute's test laboratories, Liu was eager to experiment with the special properties of LED lighting. 'I set myself the objective to research and design a light that can intuitively encourage better rest time. We may not like to admit it, but our nocturnal habits are alternating around the use of cell phones. It's quite common for people to sit in bed in the middle of the night checking their phones and chatting on social media. But if this turns into a habit it could be detrimental for the eyes. Such habits also interrupt the body's natural biorhythms, robbing it from a good night's sleep', explains the designer.

Sensalight deals with the problem by emitting ambient light suitable for using digital devices. At the same time its directional light stimulates the production of melatonin: the natural hormone secreted from the pineal gland at night that regulates deep sleep. The product incorporates two ball joints for angle adjustment so light can be emitted up, down or in both directions along a horizontal or vertical axis. The lighting element is made of two separate LED panels, with the bottom part being the melatonin sleep inducer. The colour, temperature and luminosity of the light are also adjustable.

When thinking about the form of the light Liu chose to work with the image of the moon. 'Because of its fullness and brightness during a cloudless night, the moon is associated with peacefulness and gentleness. I wanted this reference to be subliminally felt when turning the light on. The clean and unobtrusive round form of the object, with its soft lighting, makes *Sensalight* a gentle companion for a relaxing night in.'

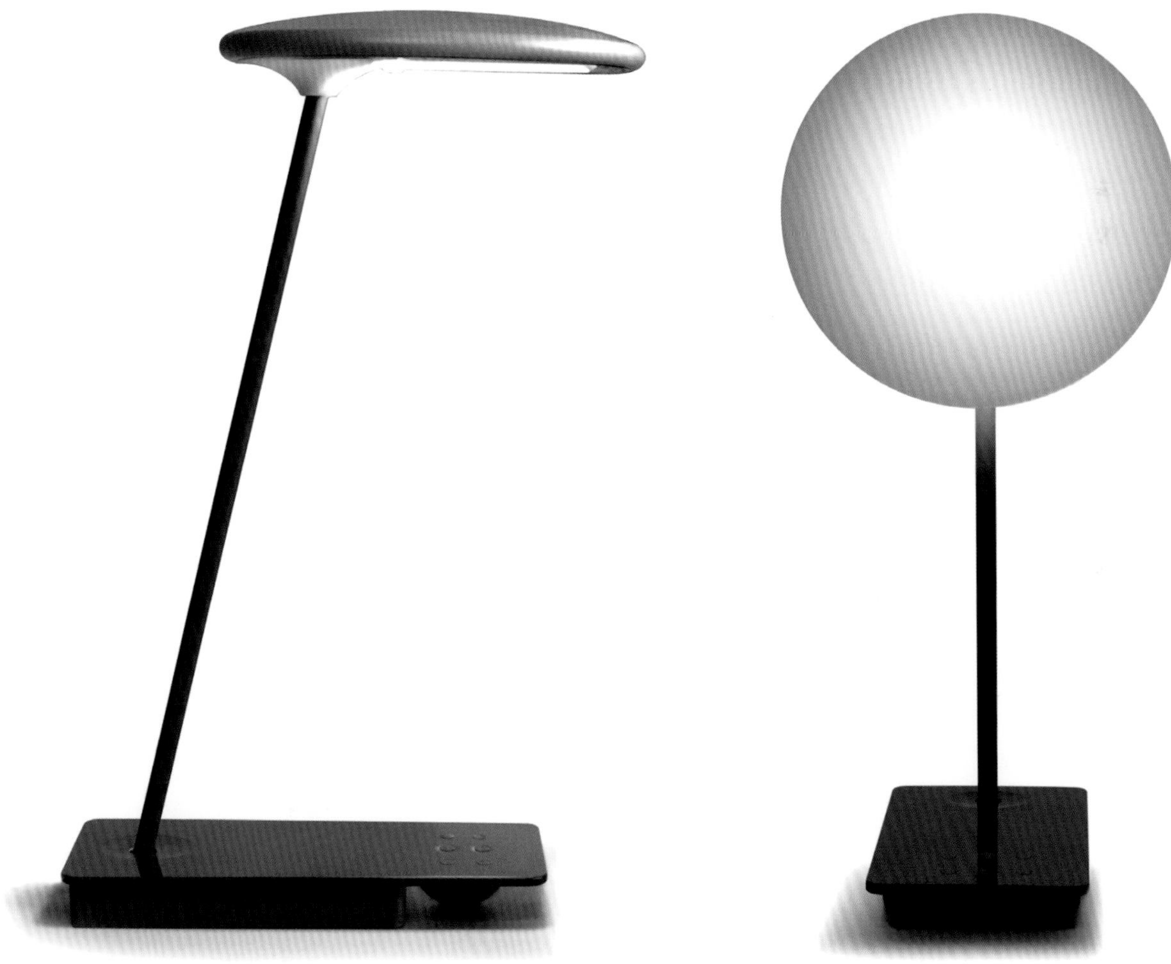

66

SHAKE WEIGHT

Spring Dumbbell

Nova Design | DYACO Inc.

Shake Weight took the US market by storm a few years ago when infomercials featuring sexually suggestive movements by pretty girls exercising with the new dumbbell went viral on the Internet. Popular TV show hosts could not resist the parody, and did their own risqué spoofs pumping the object to entertain their large audiences. Despite the hilarity, the hype helped the product become best-selling fitness equipment, with triple millions of units dispatched.

Nova Design researched and developed the dumbbell but the patented new sports tool was not to see the light of day during its first year. Anecdotally, it was Michelle Obama's well-toned arms that started a new trend: all of a sudden biceps training became a widespread fitness pursuit amongst women wishing to sport strong bare arms like the first lady's. The product found its faithful following.

Shake Weight functions on the principle of 'dynamic inertia' integrated into a regular dumbbell. It has a hard plastic shell with a hollow core in which a spring coil joins each bell end. For an effective workout the equipment needs to be held with both hands vertically, then shaken up and down vigorously and uninterruptedly for 6 minutes. It is the resistance of the spring coil that provides the training.

The dumbbell can be shaken in front of the chest or above the head with both arms raised. As the body needs to maintain balance during the exercise, the abdominal muscles are also given a kinesthetic workout.

Roger Lin, one of Taiwan's fitness equipment design gurus, makes a strong argument for the research and logic behind the product. 'This is a good and practical tool. Most ladies don't do heavy weights because they don't want their arms to bulk up—they like looking toned yet feminine. For that, the muscles of the arms, shoulders and chest need to be trained differently. We based the function of *Shake Weight* on existing vibration technology that makes the muscles contract several times per second. This is believed to make fitness training more impactful. Only that this product is a no-power/no-plug equipment; it requires human energy to operate.'

Whether the bouncy dumbbell enters the design hall of fame or fad, time will tell. What this product has done is to present enthusiasts with an everyday, easy to follow fitness routine, which might well be all that one could manage.

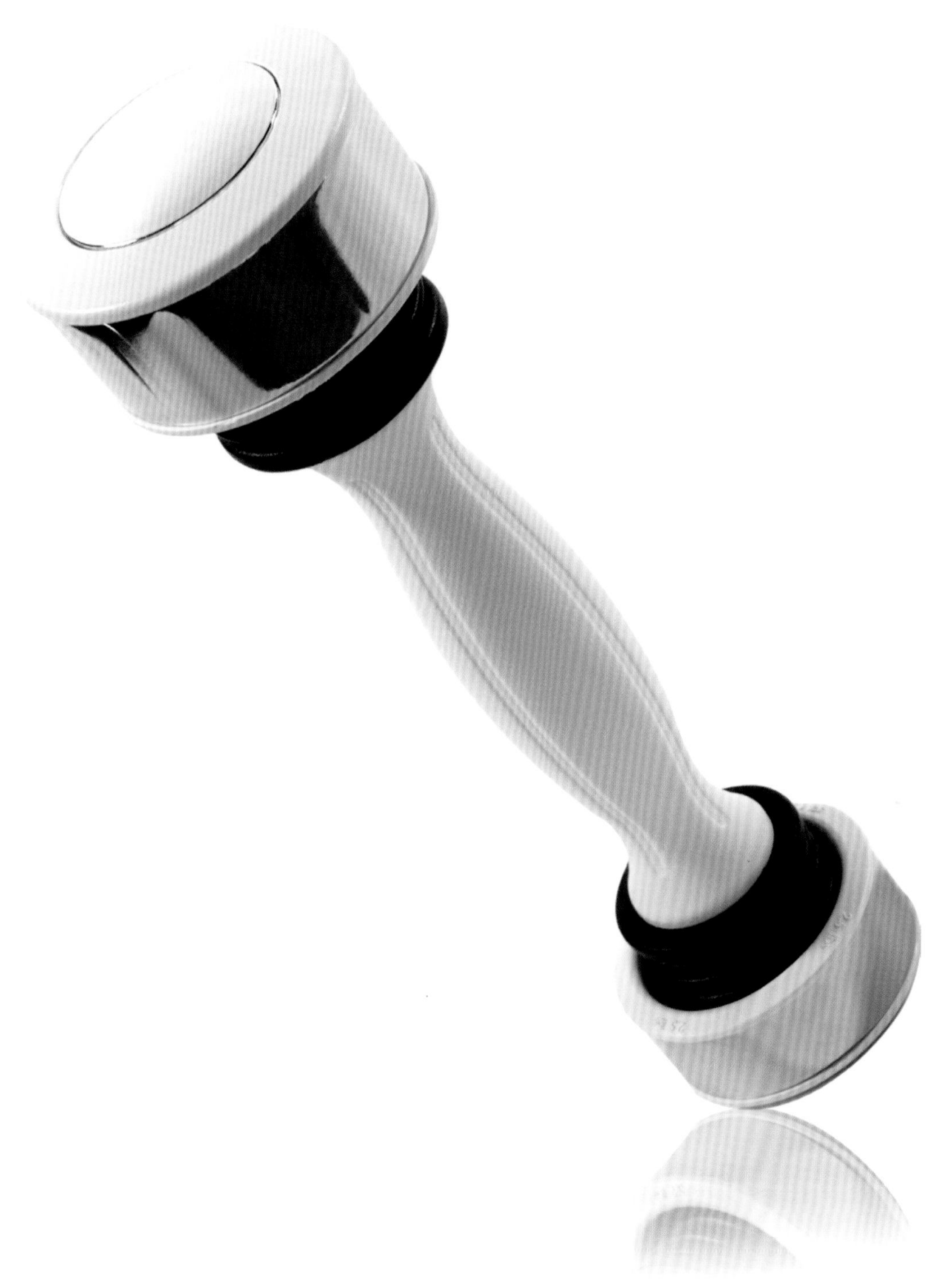

67

SKOG

Aroma Oil Diffuser

Sean Lin | Toast Living

When Sean Lin started his company in 2007, his vision was to build a brand that fused the hip New York homewares he enjoyed whilst living in the US with elements from Taiwanese culture. He felt strongly about the role of design as a connector between different traditions. Asked what made him choose the name, he recalls: 'I was thinking everyday living should be like a piece of toast: it can be appreciated in its simplicity or it can be flavoured with tasteful décor.'

To date Toast Living has created over 30 products, though Lin is reluctant to boast about its success. 'A big steppingstone was our first order from The Museum of Modern Art in New York. Its design store selected one of our products. They carefully curate their collection to feature gifts "made for people to love" so it affirmed we had something unique to offer. Though remaining relevant and lovable is hard work.'

The company is no stranger to enduring market pressures. As the only manufacturer of ultra sonic aroma oil diffusers in Taiwan, it has been bombarded with cheaper versions from other places and so it has had to significantly rethink its range. One way to stand out from the crowd was by improving the user experience. Woody Hsieh,

team leader for the development of the new model diffusers, describes it through an analogy with home furniture: 'People appreciate natural timber for the warm feel of the grain and the tranquillity associated with the forest. In a similar way we wanted the new model to bring the visual and tactile feel of nature. This was the starting point for *SKOG.'*

SKOG is an up-market diffuser with a forest jinnee personality. It merges the design of an early model with a signature wood bark texture developed by Toast. The original surface of the porcelain body is created from the imprint of real pulp and etched by a skilful potter. The inverted cup is balanced onto a stumpy base, which comes in terracotta orange and forest green colours. The product uses 2.5 million ultrasound vibrations per second to release uplifting and soothing essential oils. Simply add water and a few drops of a favourite scent to enjoy.

In the imagination of the designers, unadulterated experiences of nature now exist only in fairy tales and far away places like the Arctic Circle, and so they named the product after the Norwegian word for forest: *skog.*

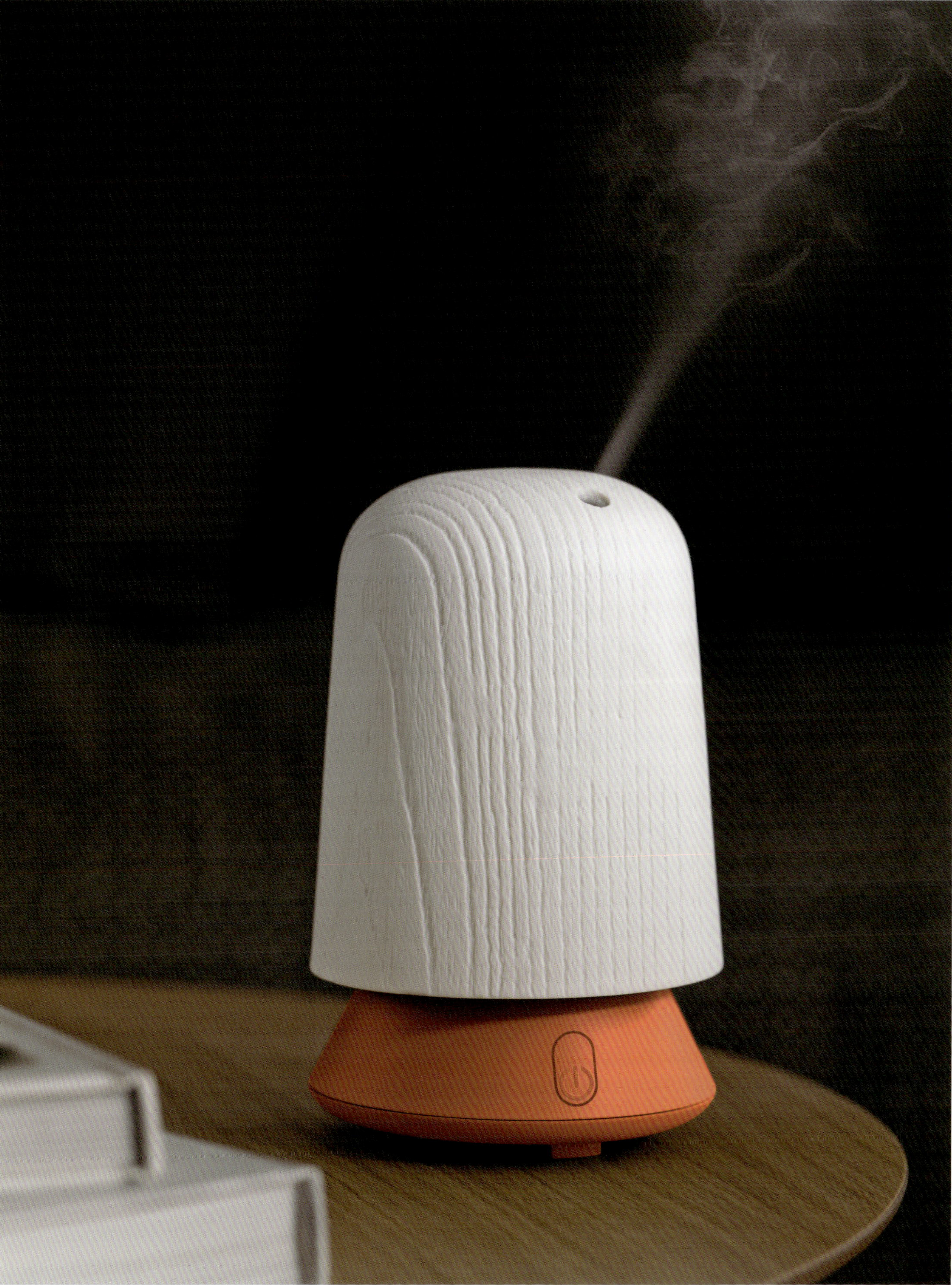

68

SONICMAZE!

Noise Absorbing Panel

GIXIA Group

Research indicates that the lack of sound privacy in open and semi-partitioned offices is the most despised problem at work. It is one of those annoyances no one can control yet everyone is made to suffer. 'Now imagine what happens when the cacophony from the streets also beams into the office. The problem multiplies exponentially even though it is a stressor that could be minimised through sensitive design.' Such is the topic of conversation with the enthusiastic creative team at GIXIA, who are convinced that noise pollution is as bad as acid rain. 'Excessive exposure to noise can dampen a person's motivation to work. Everyone knows what it's like to feel drained for no particular reason: noise might well be the culprit.'

SonicMAZE! is a pioneering product that reduces indoor noise easily and elegantly. It is an acoustical wall panel manufactured of lightweight plastic with highly effective sound absorbing properties. Using a patented plastic-formed perforation technique, microscopic holes are punctured into the panel modules to create an even lattice. The holes are designed to absorb sound signals of different pitch and frequency.

'There is a range of similar products available on the market but they all have their own shortcomings. For example, the sound absorbing cotton or mineral wool sponges are good but difficult to clean; the perforated metal panels are heavy and not very affordable; the wood-based panels won't withstand humidity well in the long run. We have addressed these problems by inventing a panel that is durable and ultra light without any in-fills. It weighs around 180 grams, as light as paper', explain the designers.

In effect, what the team has strived to achieve with *SonicMAZE!* is structural versatility that can be extended into the overall design of an interior space. The traditional panels tend to protrude from a wall by up to 100 mm and do not have visual appeal. In GIXIA's method of making a competitive product out of plastic, the panel extends from the supporting wall only slightly, with a small air chamber at the back of it. The chamber is adjustable to deal with the effects of different acoustics.

The product can be made in customisable colours and patterns via digital painting, and the designers reassure us it can be easily installed disguised as a decorative panel configuration. Few would suspect that the pretty picture on the wall is visually and acoustically perfect for the interior.

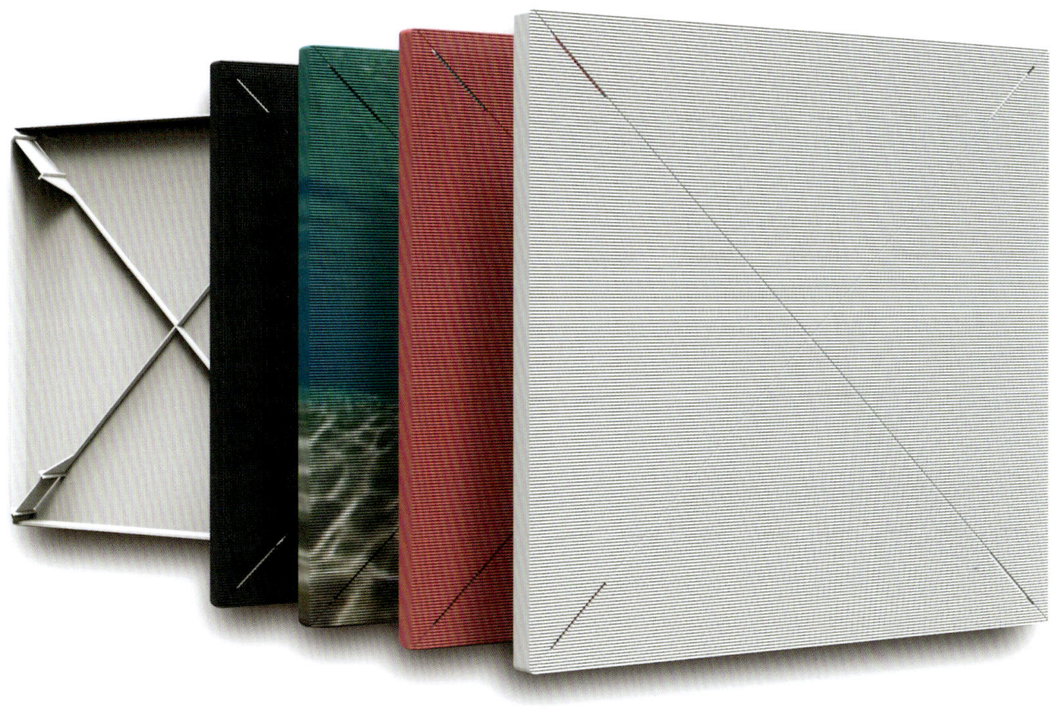

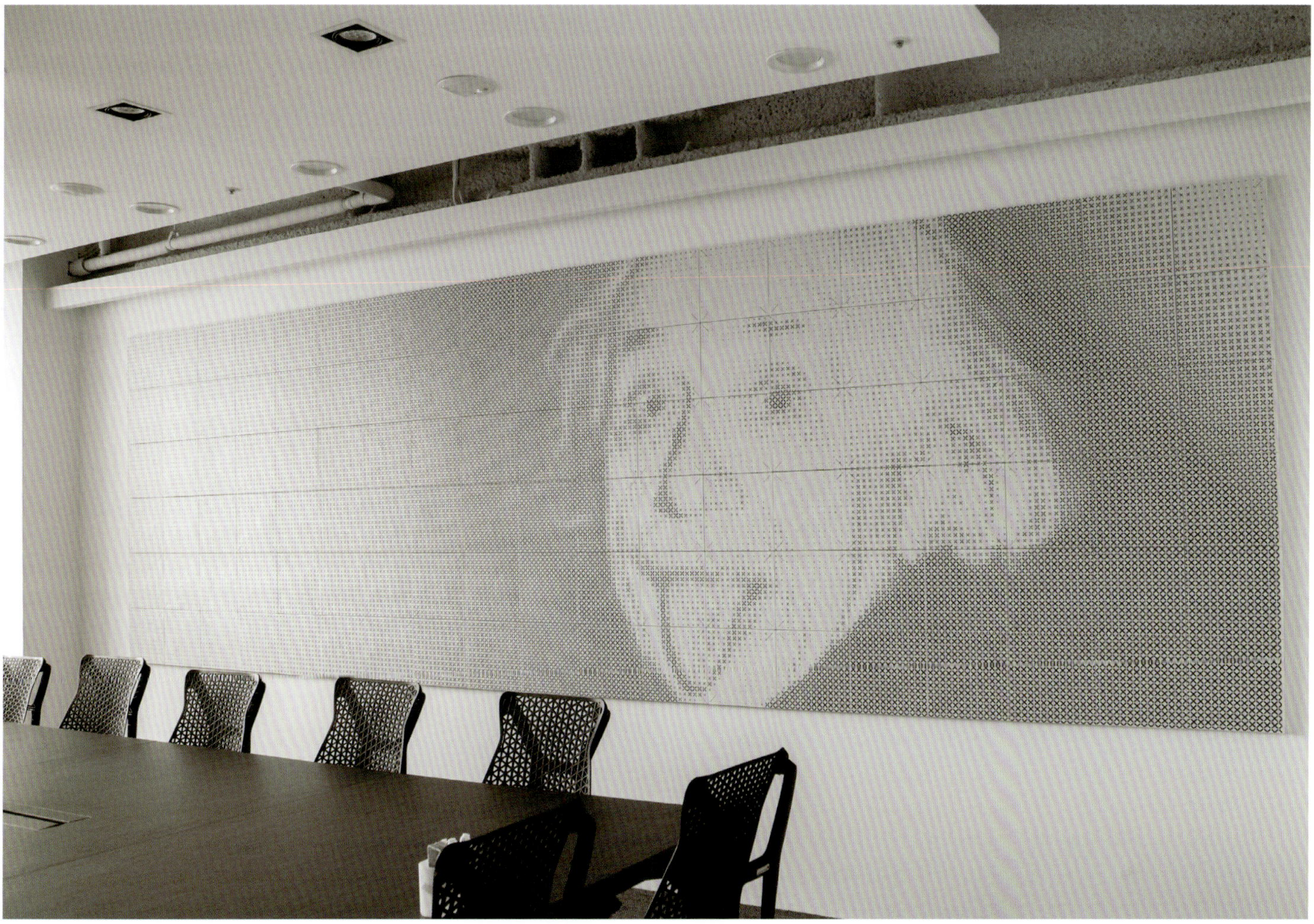

69

SPREADTHAT!

Butter Knife

THAT! INVENTIONS

'Happy time in the kitchen means cooking with least effort by using smart appliances', remarks design director Jung-Ya Hsieh while waiting for a colleague to bring ice cubes from the freezer as part of a product demonstration. Once the ice cubes arrive, Hsieh chops them up with a hand knife as if cutting vegetables for a salad. 'It's wonderful isn't it?', he says with a twinkle in his eyes. 'This is how we think, we use technology to make everyday life that easy for people.'

With its core company philosophy of 'Imagination breeds infinite possibilities', THAT! INVENTIONS is a spinoff brand of GIXIA Group; the top independent design company in the Chinese-speaking region according to IF ranking. The designers spend considerable time testing novel applications of smart materials. At the studio they map out how these could give life to 'hassle-free' kitchen tools. As Hsieh puts it: 'technology is magic when it is invisible'.

The ingenious *SpreadTHAT!* knife has solved the age-old problem of cold butter being nearly impossible to carve and spread. The knife is made of a thermo-conductive material that instantly transfers heat from the user's palm to the blade. It can also be used to cut hard chocolate, cake icing, even ice.

The blunt edge and round point of the knife make it safe even for little kids to butter a piece of toast by themselves.

The patented knife is the result of a yearlong product development partnership between the design team and science advisors based on three continents. They solved the problem of engineering a knife that could heat up without creating electronic waste. Unlike the lithium AA battery-powered butter knives—operable on the basis of a circuit board and heating elements hidden inside the knife's handle—*SpreadTHAT!* draws heat from the self-replenishing reservoir of naturally occurring human energy.

The series also features the *ThawTHAT!* defrosting tray that can defrost cold meats in minutes just by coming in contact with the tray's surface, and *ScoopTHAT!,* a revolutionary product with a thermo-ring heated edge that rolls a perfectly round scoop of ice cream.

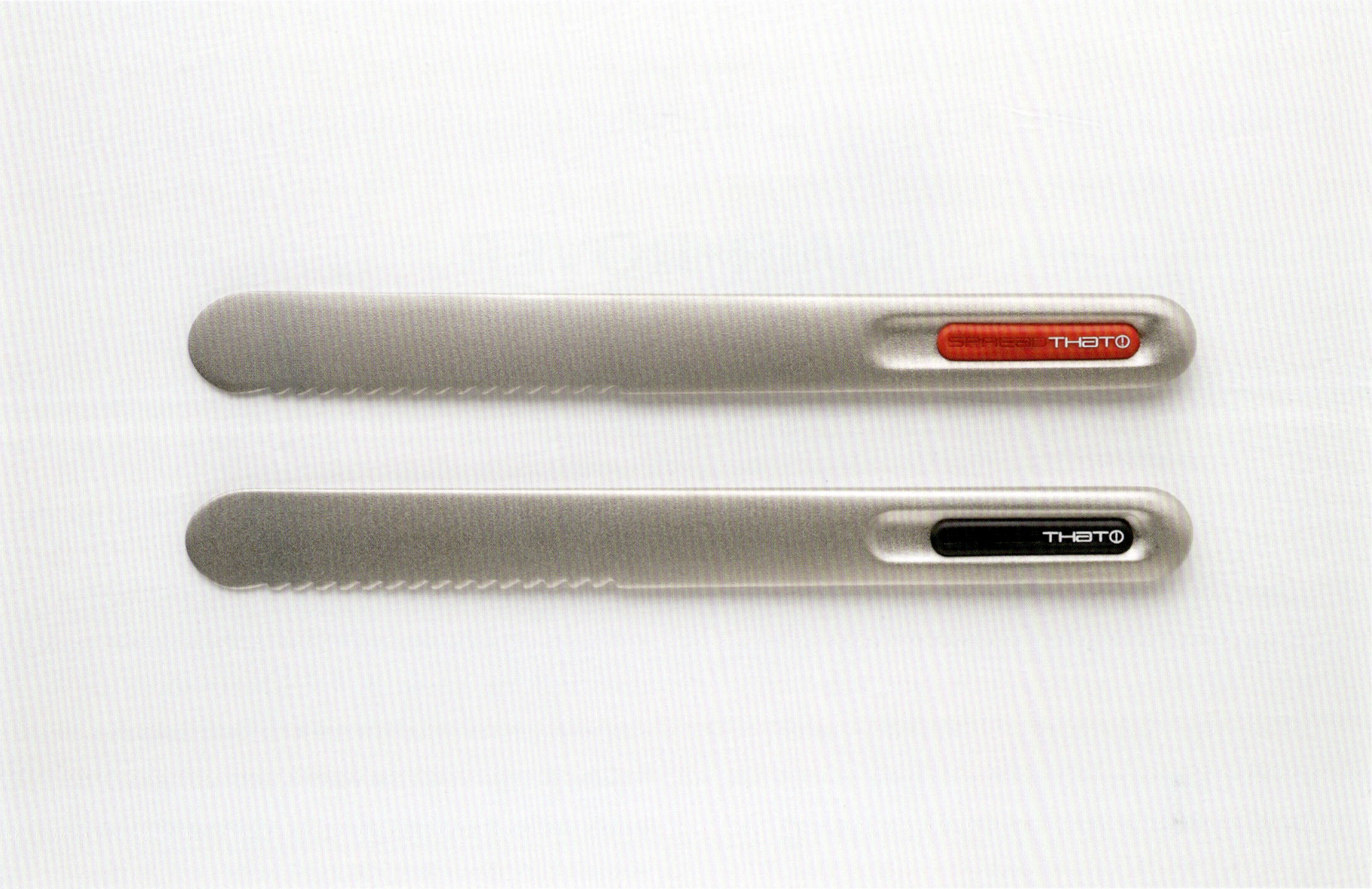

spread THAT
THAT

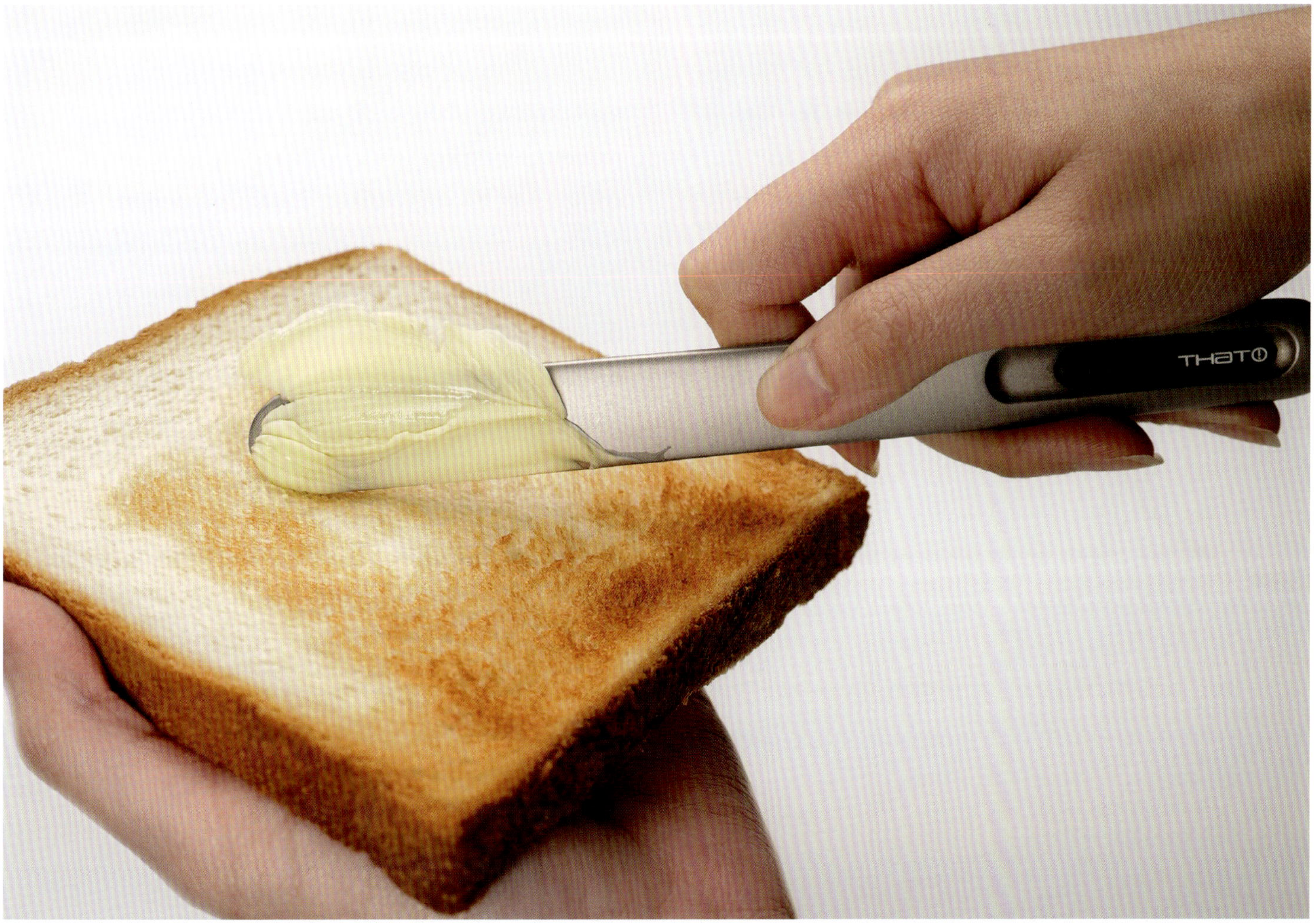

THAT

70

STAIR-ROVER

Skateboard

Po-Chih Lai | Allrover

From a wood plank on wheels fifty years ago to a powerful rover, the humble skateboard has earned its place in design history's hall of fame. Fads and failures aside, and countless broken bones, skateboarding has become a worldwide sport. Having mastered the labyrinthine maze of Taipei's alleys like a pro, Po-Chih Lai regarded himself as 'one of the tribe'—until he moved to Europe and got unexpectedly challenged by cobblestones! 'It's what makes the old streets so charming, but skating around them is another story', he shakes his head in disbelief. Instead of practicing new stunts to tackle the uncertain terrain, he decided to match his beloved board to it.

At first glance the *Stair-Rover* appears to be like any other sporting equipment of its kind. However, the engine underneath hints that this skateboard is in a class of its own. Based on four pairs of wheels attached to V-shaped frames and two straight bars, the patented double deck mechanism enables the wheels to move independently while clambering down stairs. 'Watching it roll for the first time was like watching a crab going down the steps with a fantastic sense of orientation. It was awesome! I only wished the design journey was as fast', jokes the inventor.

In fact, it took two years and 17 product iterations until the desired mobility and balance could be fully realised. By the eighth prototype Lai came up with the two bar solution, and fixed the stopper that prevents the wheels from going over a safety angle. It worked perfectly during a test drive. A short clip about the prototype went viral on the Internet and all of a sudden the designer was flooded with requests for the actual skateboard.

'The community interest in my little experiment pushed me to quickly learn about manufacturing efficiency and sporting value so I could bring it to the market.' Friends supported him drive a crowd funding campaign, raising close to 1.2 million US dollars of start-up investment—unprecedented in Taiwan. For his invention Lai returned home to be closer to the manufacturers. It was a smart move: the factory replaced the iron bars with industrial strength plastic and made further improvements to the wheel. This made the skateboard less costly to produce and lighter to carry.

Due to its unique safety features, *Stair-Rover* is suitable even for people who are not confident riders. Lai dreams of the day when his beloved skateboard is taken up en-mass as an alternative mode of urban mobility.

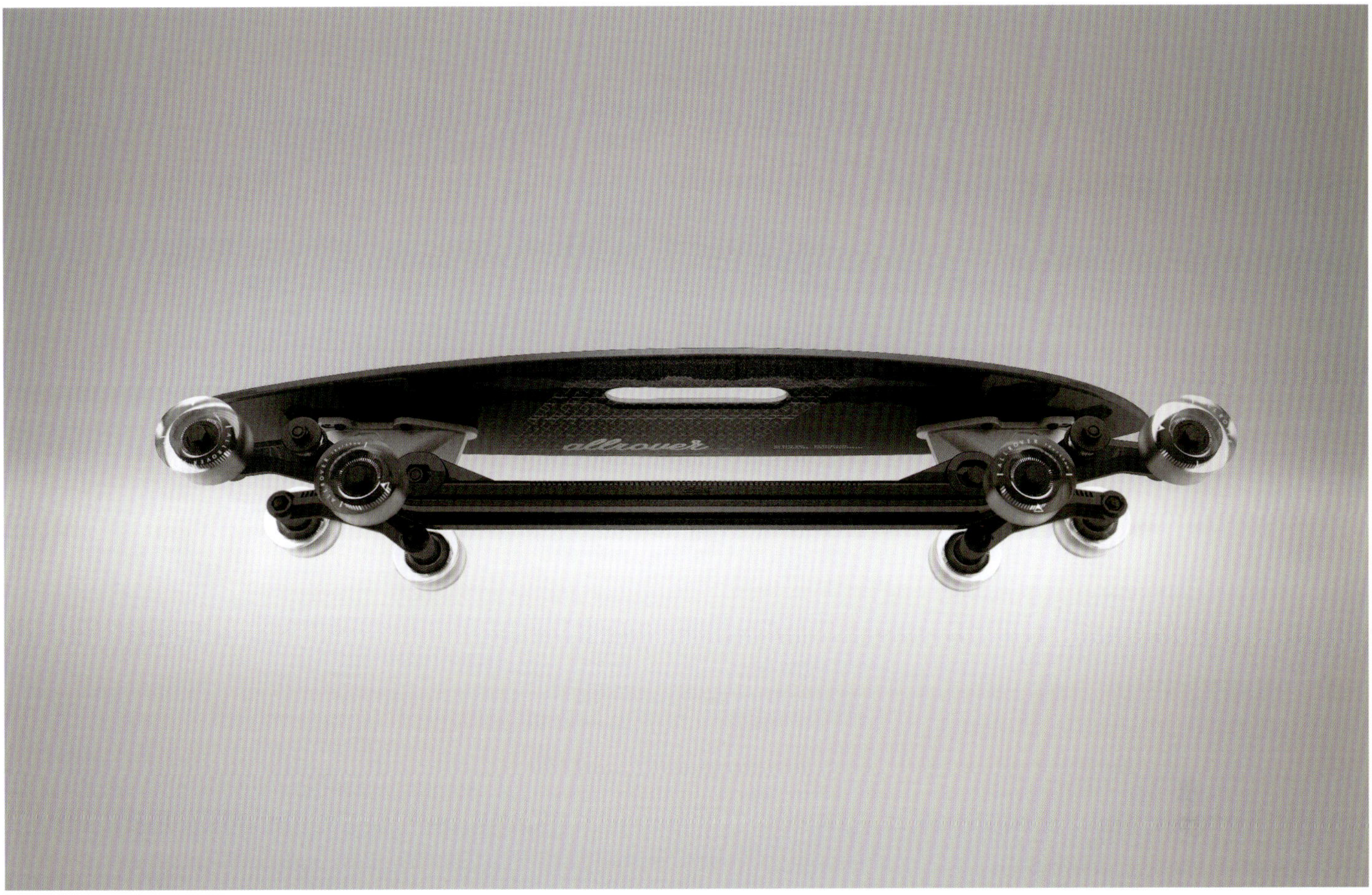

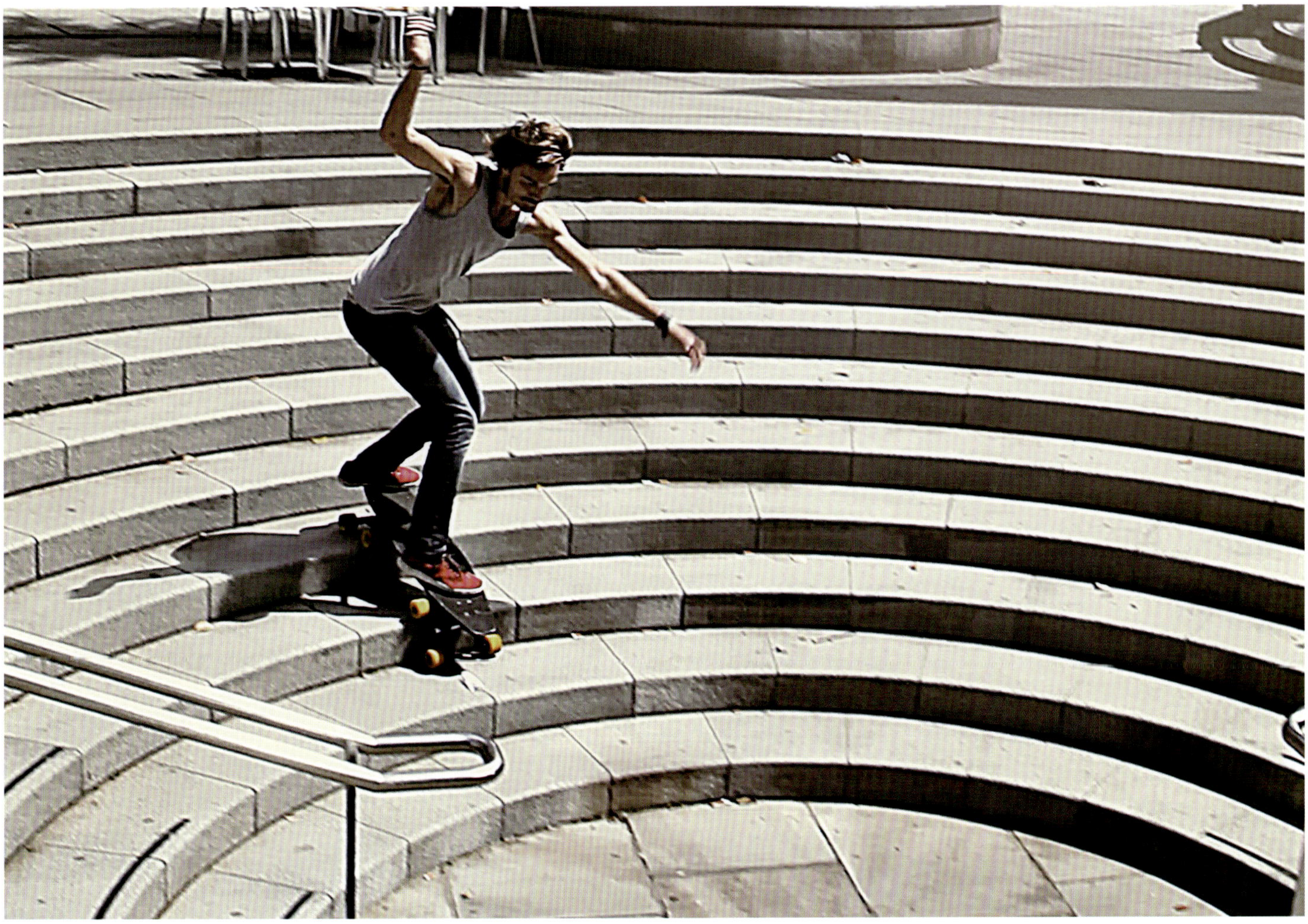

71

SUKORI

Dual-use Filter Bottle

William Yang | Fan Bao

Sukori is a pioneering personal filtering bottle system offering convenient access to safe drinking water, any place and any time. It was created in the aftermath of the devastating Japanese earthquake of 2011. 'The enormity of the crisis was heartbreaking', recalls William Yang. 'I was very concerned because my daughter was living in Tokyo at the time. With the electricity being out of order, people had no access to drinking water. If their personal refillable water bottles had a filter, they could have used them during the emergency.'

An interior designer by trade, Yang explains that his skills are transferable. *Sukori* is the first industrial object he has designed, turning his idea into a functional product through a single-minded sense of purpose. It was only after a year the original prototype was completed that he started researching the market for similar goods to gauge how his bottle's unique features compared. 'I was a little stubborn. I didn't want to be dissuaded. I had a gut feeling I was onto something that could improve the quality of people's lives and wanted to see it through to completion', he admits.

Sukori's patented filter mechanism allows for an easy interchange between it being a portable bottle and a filter bottle. The product consists of an outer and an inner body fitted together with a silicon ring and a lockable filter in between them. Once the outer bottle is filled up with water, the inner is pressed slowly down to the bottom.

The inner spiral of the filter ensures sufficient time for purification. NSF certified high-grade activation carbon is used to effectively remove impurities, while absorbing chlorine and bad odour. Depending on the chemical compounds of the original source, for best results it is recommended that the filter is replaced with a new one after 400 times of use. A 12-month dial that keeps track of usage is located at the base of the bottle.

The bottle is a valuable aid not only when the normal water supply is disrupted, but also when traveling or hiking. Its dual-functionality makes a saving on the budget, and reduces tonnes of energy that would be otherwise wasted in the production and recycling of bottled water.

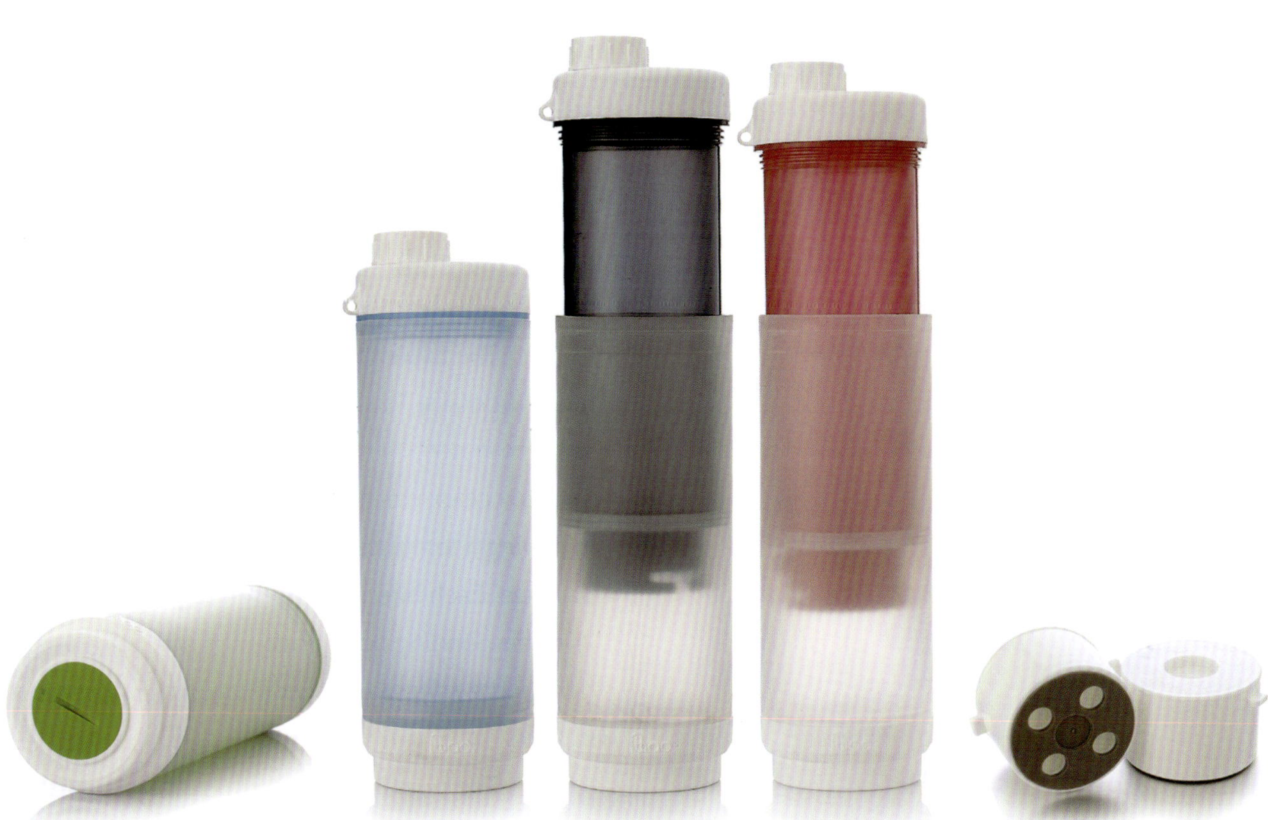

72

SWALLOW

Wall Clock

Griffin Yang | Haoshi Design

Swallow is a wall-mounted clock displaying time through a stop-motion like sequence of 12 small birds flying around a clock mechanism. When its maker Griffin Yang was pondering how to represent the seasonal rhythms of nature in a timepiece, the little swallow captured his imagination. Since ancient times people have been aware of the migratory instincts of swallows as they watched them return to their nesting places each spring. The beloved bird, regarded in some places as 'birds of freedom', is widely worshiped as a good omen that signals the coming of regenerative energy. Also, a flock of swallows always moves forward, which is how we experience time.

Yang was excited about the idea of representing time as a carefree bird: 'not to complain that it flies away, but to relax about it as something naturally passing'. In his mind the swallow was a strong universal image to work with. But in order for the user to have a warm connection with the birds they had to appear as realistic as possible.

The secret to the exquisite detailing of the feathers and wings of the little swallows rests with a master-carver from Taichung whom the designer befriended for the project. 'I found a craftsman who specialises in restoring stone carvings in temples.

Because spiritual insights are often derived from observing nature, temple images of flowers and birds have specific meaning and need be carved with a particular expression. When I gave the master my models he tended to them so carefully one would think he was holding real birds in hands.'

The two worked together on creating the realistic details. The birds are cast in resin, a robust yet light material suitable for wall mounting. The *Swallow* clock can be arranged in a circular pattern following a template included in the product package. Each bird is numbered on the back with its corresponding hour placement and has a semi-permanent adhesive sticker for fixing onto a smooth surface.

The swallows can be freely choreographed to form countless flying configurations. They can chase the direction of sunlight to throw intricate shadows on the wall, flock together, or form mating pairs. Whichever the choice, with these lovely little friends one could hardly feel a captive of time.

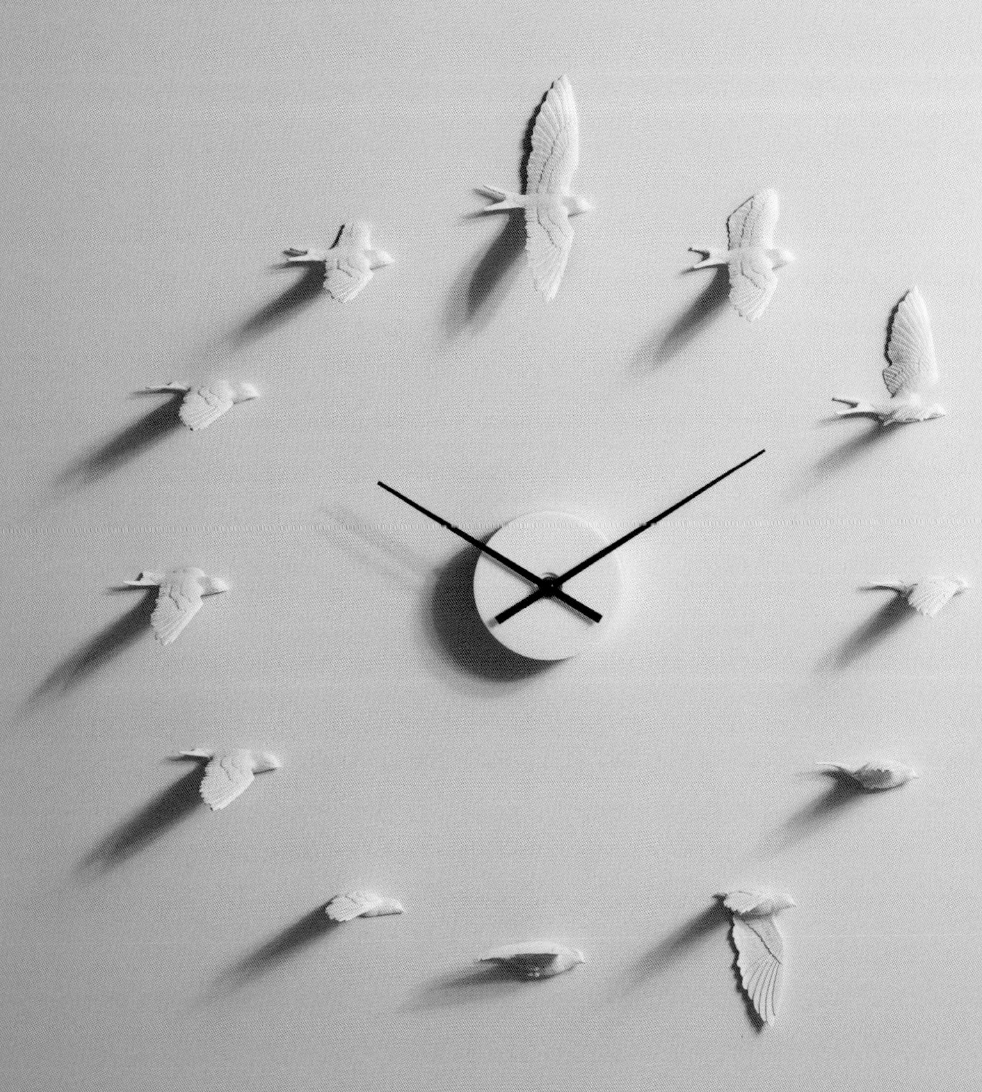

73

TATUNG RICE COOKER

Electric Cooker

Jung-Ya Hsieh | Tatung

With nearly a hundred-year history, Tatung is one of Taiwan's founding corporations that has spearheaded key industries and provided employment for generations of families. In the 1960s it played a pivotal role in the women's liberation movement. Traditionally, housewives would have had to spend hours preparing meals but the advent of the *Tatung Rice Cooker* afforded them precious time away from such duties. Back then it was considered so valuable it was gifted as a wedding dowry.

To celebrate the product's 50th anniversary the company collaborated with leading Taiwanese designer Jung-Ya Hsieh (page 170) to release a limited edition cooker and packaging. 'It is an incredible honour to be a part of design history, which made the task all the more difficult', recalls Hsieh. 'The approach had to remain in line with the classical form and functionality of the cooker, yet the outcome had to be innovative.'

Over the years the cooker has evolved into a versatile appliance suitable not only for rice cooking, but also for steaming and stewing a wide variety of dishes. The improvements Hsieh made were in the application of new materials. The outer layer of the pot was made of aluminium alloy whilst the inner layer of rugged stainless steel. This high-grade dual material composite conducts heat evenly at 65°C and ensures meals retain optimal nutrition and flavour.

The side handles were redesigned and manufactured as a single rim made from anti-bacterial and non-toxic silicon with heat-resistant coating. The up-curve of the handle pays homage to ancient clay pots dating back some two thousand years. Using Physical Vapour Deposition process, the lid was coated in rose-gold plating—a touch of collector's value.

The award-winning packaging was manufactured with 3D imprinting technology to generate a perfect paper-pulp mould of the product. Because pulp moulding is prone to fracture, Hsieh developed a new structure that can support up to 5kg of weight without buckling—a breakthrough design that enables stacking for retail. Finally, to showcase the cooker's iconic form, the packaging is contained in a black box opened at one side.

A total of 999 anniversary cookers were released, and sold out within three months. And while Tatung is enjoying a legacy as an internationally leading home appliances brand, its much loved rice cooker continues to shape food culture in Taiwan.

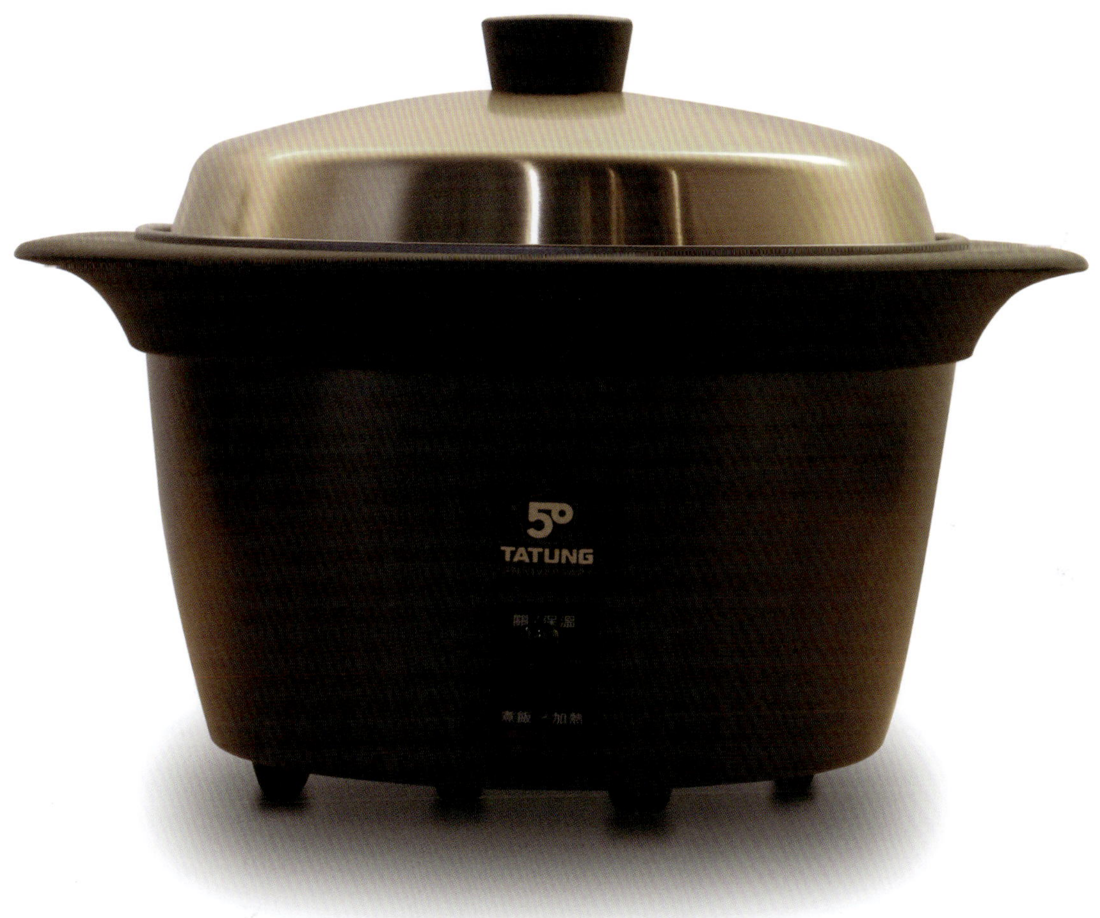
TATUNG
5°

74

TEALEIDOSCOPE

Tea Infuser

John Lan | LANTO

Tealeidoscope is a curious contraption for making tea, which combines a scoop, infuser, and spring mechanism. Educated in Canada with a degree in computer science, John Lan returned to Taiwan in 2006 to work for his father as a product developer. Since the early 80s the Lan family has been manufacturing plastic components for the electronics industry. The company was among many others that had to restructure its business due to pressures of trade liberalisation. The son took on the challenge of helping to turn its operations around by designing original products.

Lan's idea for his tea infuser was a typical eureka moment: it took minutes to formulate and months to prototype. He enjoys telling the story of how it came about: 'Asian tea drinking rituals are incompatible with Western work habits. In Canada we make green tea in our comfort-totem mugs. Everyone sips it at the desk; no one has patience to wait for a pot to brew. Loose leaves may be even eaten from the mug!' Observing this common sacrilege, the designer wondered if he could simplify the making of loose-leaf tea in his office. The click of a ballpoint pen pointed to the solution.

The challenge was to make a tool that scoops the right amount of tea for an individual mug.

Borrowing from a pen design, Lan repositioned the spring to fit in the handle of the infuser. The ballpoint part of the pen was transformed into a measuring spoon tucking into the main body of the product. 'It's easy. Click once to open and scoop the tealeaves, click twice to close it, then dip it into a mug of hot water and brew away. It's completely safe: our engineers know plastics well. We made it from BPA (Bisphenol A)-free materials with a high range of temperature tolerance. It's dishwasher-safe, easy to clean, and recyclable.'

The designer humours about his product. 'Taiwanese tea is very flavoursome and there is a great variety to be appreciated. What I did was introduce convenience: it's like serving a wholesome Asian meal fast-food style. The measuring spoon and the infuser are all-in-one.' *Tealeidoscope* has received international recognition for its inventiveness, but for his father what matters most is that the family's business goes on.

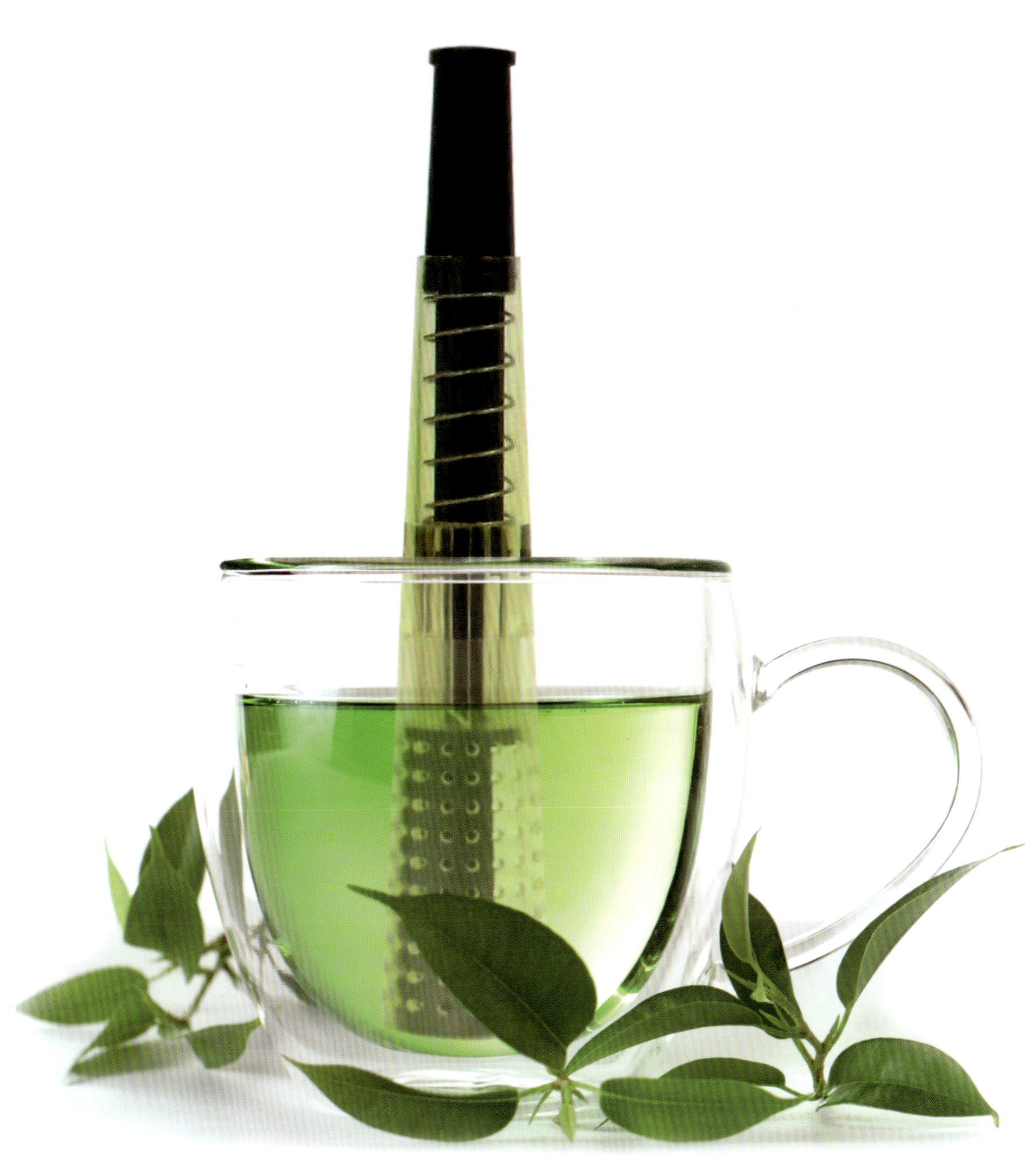

75

TEYEWARE

Frames

Vincent Chuang | TenXion

For the Taiwanese, it is often a challenge to find well-fitting designer glasses. This is because leading eyewear brands tend to cater for the average Caucasian face-types that are anatomically different from the Asian. Having traded in the industry for years, Vincent Chuang got to know this problem through his clientele. 'Customers were paying a premium yet complaining about their misadventures with European spectacles: the frames felt too narrow or would slide down the nose because the nose bridge is a little high and needs to be pushed into position. Ill-fitted eyewear alters the line of vision and can cause headaches. The frames must fit the face, not the face fitting the frames.'

Even though Vincent Chuang had no prior experience of industrial design, he embarked on a quest to produce 'the optimal eyewear fit'. The aim was to engineer a frame that had such dexterity it could guarantee 100% fit between the temples of any face-type while the focal point of the lenses remained unchanged. He wanted to achieve this without the use of screws.

After a year and a half of testing, failing and starting over again, he uncovered solutions for many design and manufacturing challenges, getting ever so close to achieving his goal. He chose to work with 0.5mm beta titanium from Japan, not only for its lightness and flexibility but also because the material could be cut to within the nano-millimetre precision necessary to get the correct frame thickness.

'The key hurdle was attaching the lenses to the frame without using a screw lock. This problem was solved with two innovations. First, an ultra-thin incision was made along the middle of the one-piece flat frame, making it possible for the frame to fold into a 3D shape, similar to paper cutting. The lens is inserted into the groove and held into position using only a nose pin, the second idea. 'The breakthrough was inventing the *shark lock* mechanism for the nose arm. The tiny teeth clip tightly together and are then locked into place only with the nose pin. No screws needed! It's one of the distinct characteristics of our eyewear. We've reduced the use of materials to the bare minimum, which is difficult to do with glasses.'

Every model in the collection has the same qualities of lightness, comfort and flexibility. Depending on styling, the frames weigh between 3.5 and 8 grams, and are guaranteed not to cause pressure or leave sore marks on the nose and behind the ears. Indeed, they feel so natural that one simply stops noticing they are wearing them.

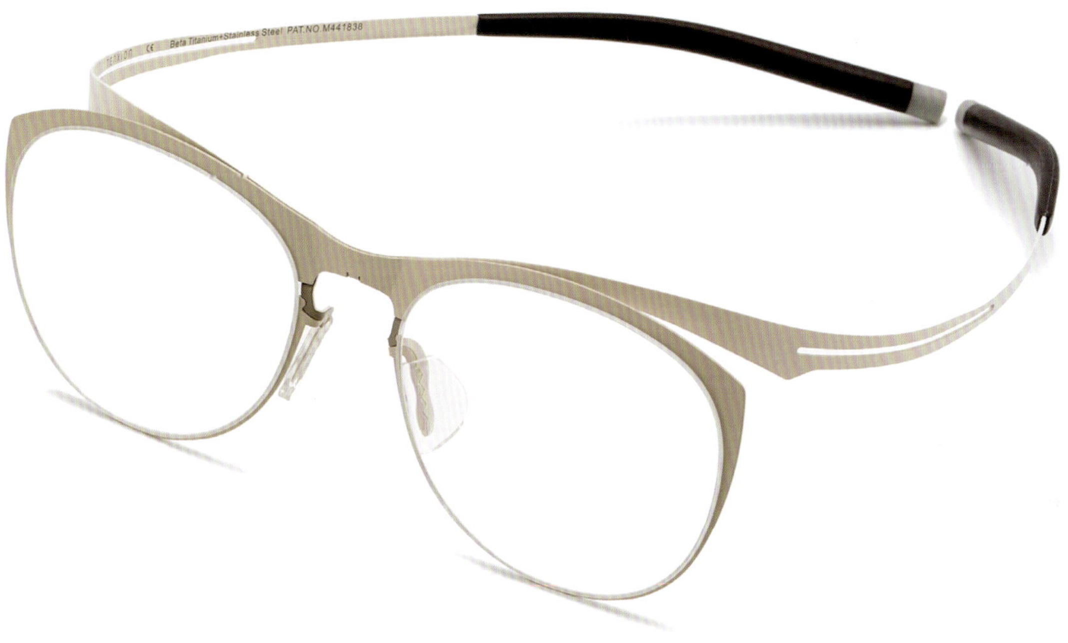

Beta Titanium+Stainless Steel PAT.NO.M441838
CE

76

THE CHANGE

Bike to Work Cycling Pants

SLO'O

The CHANGE is dual wear bike-to-work cycling apparel with a unisex fit. Unlike the popular Lycra shorts, these pants are tailored for discerning cyclists who need their sportswear to be functional yet acceptable in a range of social situations.

In effect the pair is fashioned from two halves: knee-length trouser legs made of regular fabric on the front and stretchy shorts on the back. The two halves are designed, cut and sawn as one piece that introduces a multifunctional style. Importantly the cut is structured around the peddling activity. The three quarter length version is tailored with a knee fold, which makes a roomy shape when the knee is bent. The designers go as far as suggesting that their special 3D pattern cutting method keeps the pants in good shape while giving the wearer a slimmer silhouette.

The secret to the pant's convenience is the removable cycling pad, which can be buttoned on the inner side along the crotch seams. The pad provides good cushioning comfort when seated on the bicycle. Once the end destination is reached, it is simply detached and put away until the next ride. This special feature of the pants is available in several thicknesses suitable for long distance cycling or leisurely peddling around the city.

As the name hints SLO'O promotes slow living as a lifestyle choice. Husband and wife team Mark Peng and Joan Huang came to the world of design via advertising and TV sales: 'We founded our business as a PR agency. When our clients stared relocating overseas we knew we had to reinvent ourselves to survive. We inversed the direction of our work from doing sporting events that promoted big business to doing business that promotes sport... We focused on cycling because it's good to encourage people to be active, especially around the city.'

Joan Huang recalls that when they were searching for creative stimuli the decided to go to Japan. 'We noticed the cycling apparel over there was really funky. It made us think more about the needs of city riders as a sub-culture. In the early days we only made fitted windbreakers, all the while developing the pad system... Trying different ways to fit-and-fix it to the pants for maximum comfort.'

In sportswear performance is key, which is also true of this product. The fabric used doubles as a sun block and temperature regulator due to the fibre being breathable and moisture-absorbent. The pants stay in shape and do not bulge or go baggie even used over a long period of time. They do not let down at impromptu meetings, either.

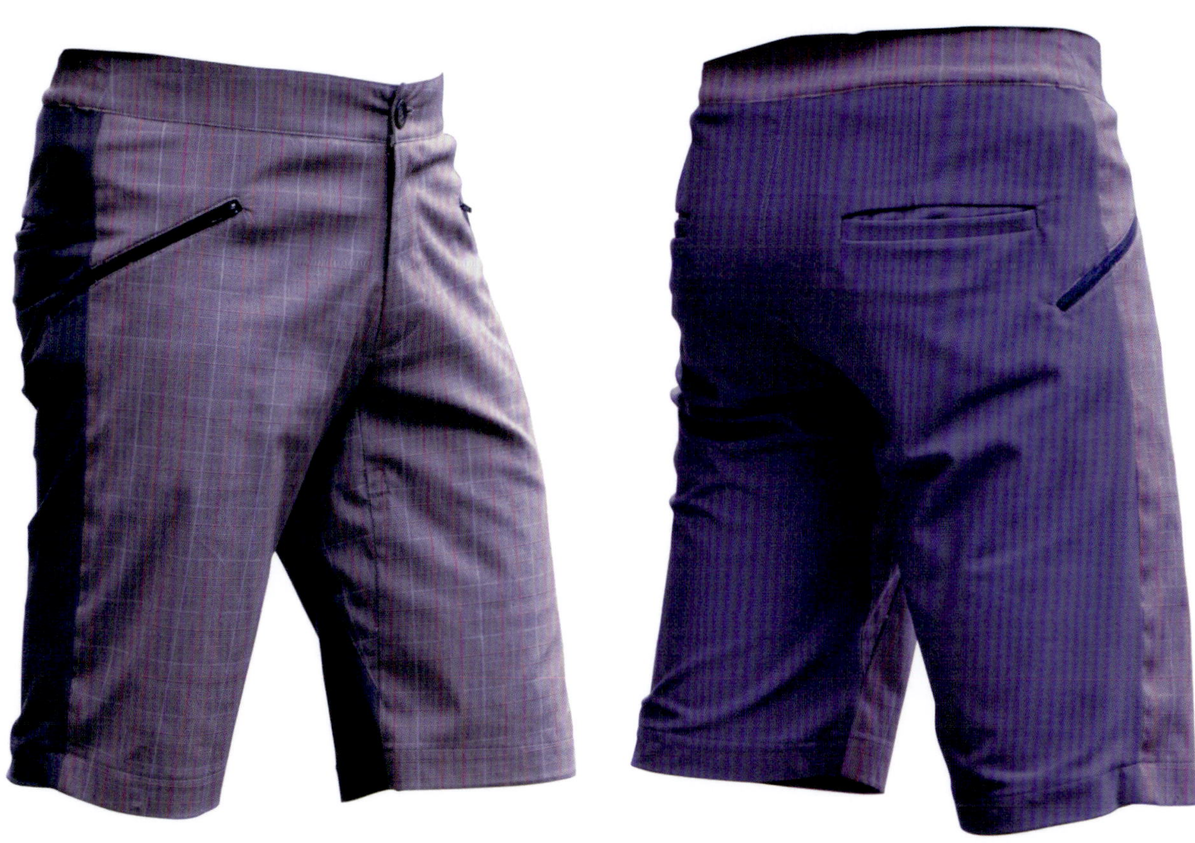

77

THE NEW OLD LIGHT

Pendant Light

KIMU Design Studio

The New Old Light is an elegant pendant lamp that merges traditional and modernist Eastern and Western design. It is based on paper lanterns popularly used in Taiwan as a good-luck blessing during various festivals.

The distinct white lantern is snugly fitted into a retro Bauhaus lampshade made in polished copper or ceramic. Based on paper folding techniques borrowed from lantern crafts, the lamp can be expanded or collapsed like a concertina. This enables different types of lighting to be created: by gently pulling it down the light can be altered from a single beam, to half shade, to diffused glow. Small magnets hidden in the inner side of the top secure it in place when folded. Suspended from a single cord, the lamp has a visually quiet presence.

Initially, the designers were ambivalent about how to position their practice. 'In attempting to bring a bit of Taiwan into our work we questioned even the most iconic products created by famous designers', recounts Kelly Lin, one of the team members. 'It was like trying to construct our own language from existing vocabularies. Just like this lamp.'

Researching the cultural context of lighting, the team visited Pingxi, an old mining township north of Taipei famous for its Sky Lantern Festival. The event is a magical occasion when visitors congregate in the old quarter carrying bell-shaped lanterns with special messages written on them. As night falls, hundreds of lit lanterns are released into the indigo blue skies in the hope that the heavens will make everyone's dream come true.

Soon after visiting Pingxi, KIMU met a 'helpful uncle', one of a few remaining craftsmen still making lanterns using a variety of old techniques. In the lounge room of his home that was also his workshop, the young designers learned how to fold their dream product into being. Combining a traditional aesthetic with a new concept *The New Old Light* was created. The lamp is appreciated as a culturally authentic object with a universal appeal.

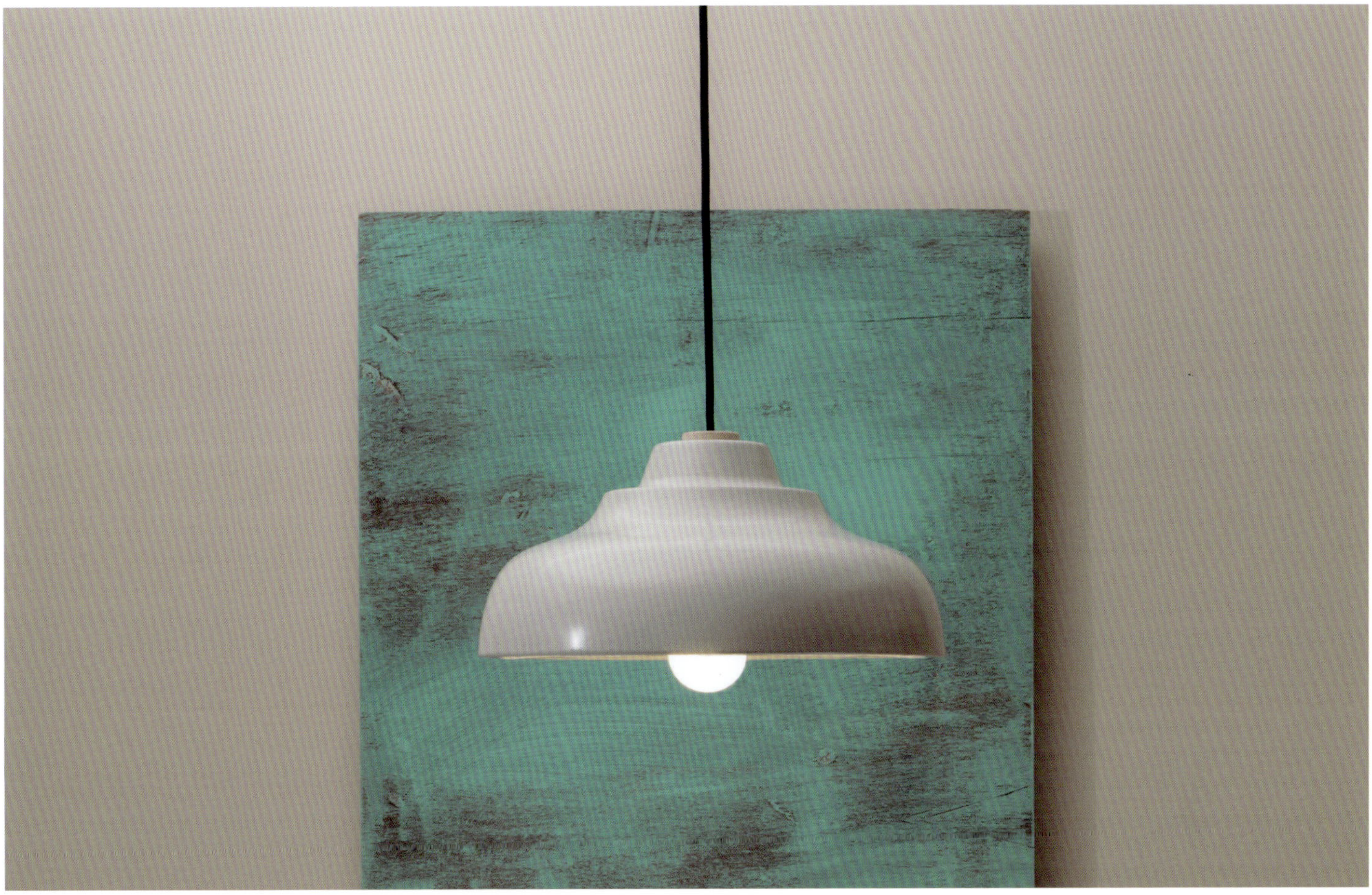

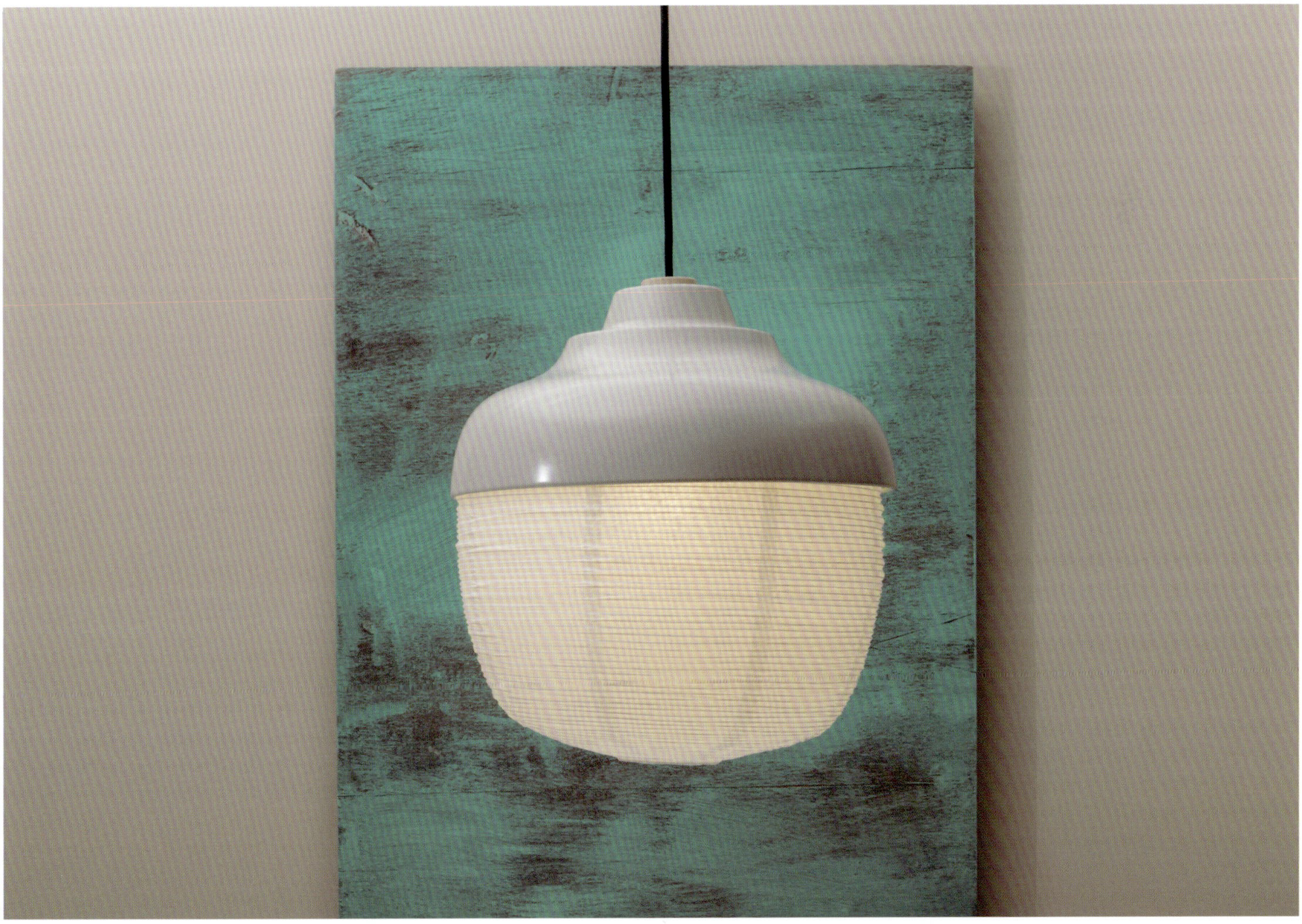

78

THE PRIME GOD

Gift Vessel

Stony Image | Good Gold

When Stony Cherng founded her company Stony Image, she searched for a name that would convey resilience. Indeed, in many cultures the Earth element represents stable feelings and sureness of mind. Something 'rock solid' is considered to be long lasting. 'It also means something grounded in tradition', she comments.

'Like *The Prime God*, I make image-objects of expressive or sentimental value. This is especially important for the creation of gifts. I must have been thinking about it all along, because when I was a little girl I loved traditional storytelling. Now, as a senior designer, most of my objects are like little fables, telling stories and spreading wishes for something wonderful to happen: best luck, nurturing friendship, everlasting love.'

Steel manufacturer Good Gold commissioned Stony Image to devise a strategy to revitalise its business and keep its ironsmiths employed. With plenty of steel at her disposal, the designer decided to match old skills with old treasures, and create a new product line of ornamental vessels.

The Prime God is drawn after a rare bronze held at the National Palace Museum. The original vessel, from the Early Western Zhou Dynasty, is vertically sectioned in four with the middle part being its most iconic. It depicts a relief of a fierce animalistic face with pronounced eyebrows, fixated gaze, and a strong nose line with fire-breath coming from each nostril. Feather-decorated ears protrude at either side of the face. Two fret rims run along the full length of the object. The face's expression is not only arresting but also tricky: if a replication is poorly executed, it ends up looking like a disastrous imitation. Not the way Cherng visualised it!

In her masterful rendition, the original is dissected into five sheets of pattern-cut steel plates of various heights, each prepared with a special patina surface. 'It's a secret old man's technique of making it look antiquated', jokes Cherng. The plates are stacked together, with two in the middle being hand-curved to join at the top rim and form a container shape. Impressions of the original form are layered three dimensionally and stylishly presented on a black wood base.

'We have brought a 3,000-year-old image back into being. It can be placed outdoors or indoors, and it will weather beautifully with time. Depending on personal taste, it be a vase, a jewellery keeper or other functions. But to me it will always stand as a reminder of our primordial spirit.'

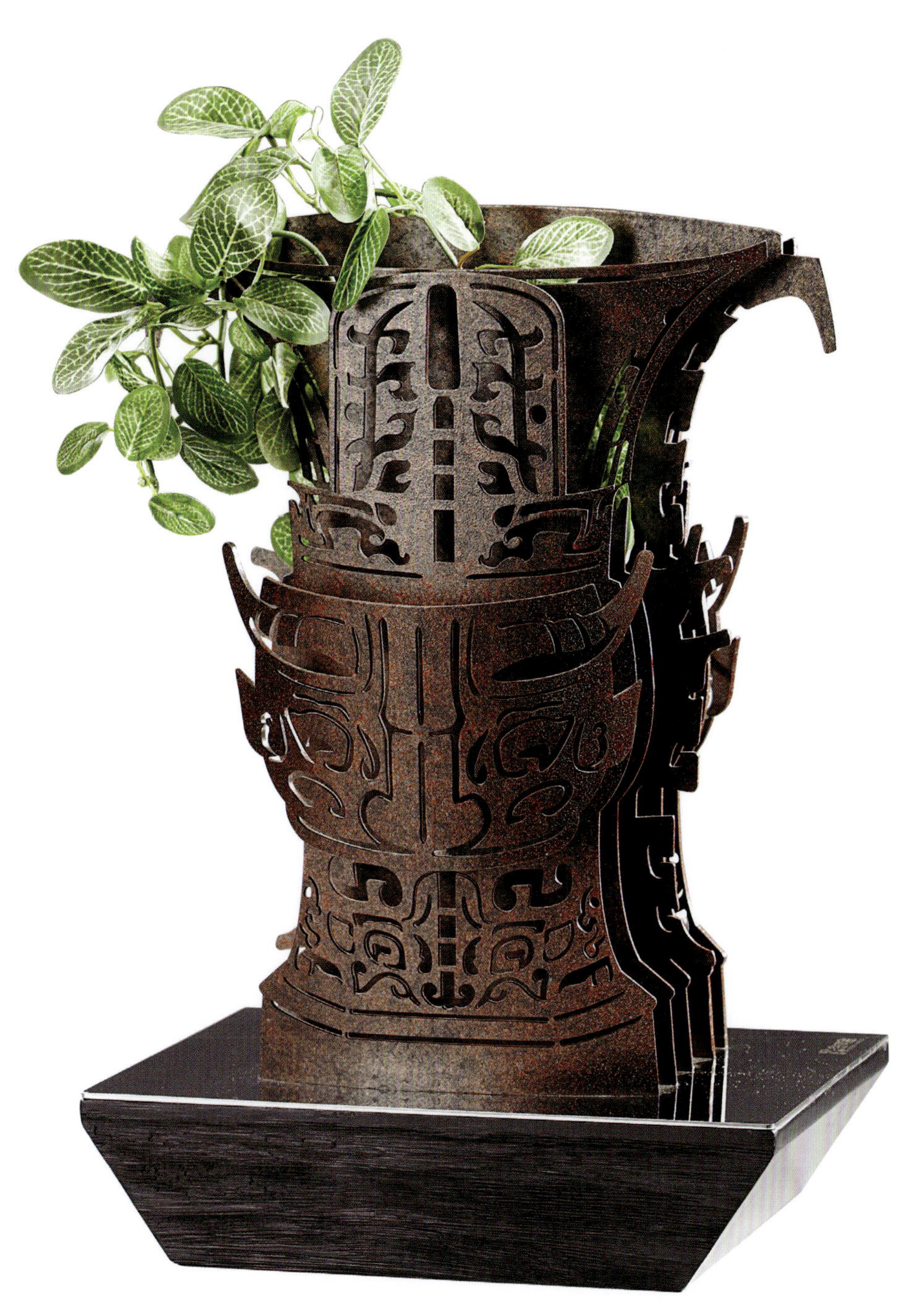

79

THE SEA IN GOLDEN LIGHT

Porcelain Vase

Kuang-Yuh Lee | Franz Collection Inc.

Amongst Franz Collection's 3,000 products, *The Sea in Golden Light* is perhaps its most adventurous. Unlike previous designs, researched and constructed from imagery found in classical works of art or sketched from nature, the concept for this intriguing vase was inspired by a photograph.

Taken by renowned Taiwanese photographer Si-Chi Ko, the original artwork depicts an early morning scene along a seashore illuminated by the golden rays of the rising sun, with tiny boats offsetting the vastness of the seascape. 'It's a mesmerising picture that struck a cord with me. I've long held the belief that we need to cultivate reverence for nature ... meaning to respect Heaven, Earth and people', explains company founder Franz Chen as he sips tea from a butterfly cup. 'It was worth experimenting to see if such a sublime moment captured through the camera lens could be transformed into an equally touching object. The team knew it'd be a difficult, but not impossible, job to do.'

Each product made by Franz requires a process of more than 100 stages to complete, from initial concept through to kilning and packing. One of the major challenges in creating *The Sea in Golden Light* was sculpting its surface to closely resemble the scene in the photograph. Lumps of clay were layered dot-by-dot and built up into a relief of miniature waves of rippling water. But to achieve the optical illusion of depth of field and light, the surface had to be gilded—another test for its designer Kuang-Yuh Lee.

Franz's products are hand-coloured through spray painting and brushwork. When the final thin layer of glaze sets in the second firing, the succulent hues it produces bring the objects to life. The problem with golden paint, though, is its opaqueness. If applied to large areas, it could make the delicate porcelain appear heavy and looking more like a lacquered vessel.

Drawing on his thirty years of skills, Lee imbued the vase with an expression of *light and lightness*. He developed a pallet of warm yellow, orange and brown paints and, grain-by-grain, recreated a micro-depth of surface of reflective golden highlights and shadows. In the final product, the *miracles of creation*—sunlight, air, water, earth, and peaceful presence—shimmer under the spotlight with a near-holographic quality.

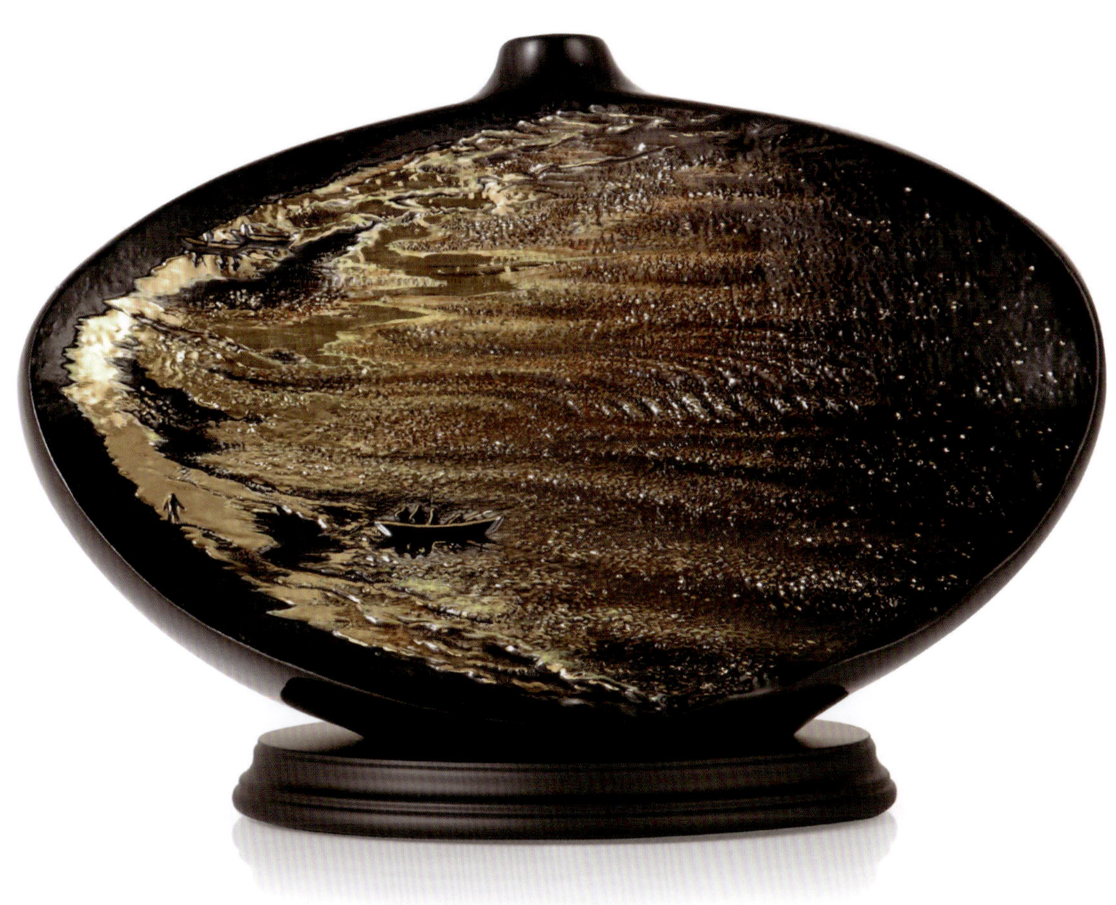

80

TOGETHER RICE

Rice Gift

Green in Hand Food Bank

With the introduction of Western style foods, the dietary preferences of the Taiwanese have become more adventurous and their consumption of rice has decreased considerably. In response to this trend, the agricultural cooperative Green in Hand Food Bank was established with the mission to support the livelihoods of farmers by matching their produce with the changing lifestyle.

One of its benchmark farmer-to-consumer initiatives is *Together Rice/Spring Flowers and Dreamy Dew* package, a brand of organic rice marketed as a special occasion gift. Its name is more evocative in its original version than the English translation. It is more of a blessing for 'all to enjoy the flowers of the Gods when celebrating happy occasions of togetherness'. Not surprisingly the product has grown in popularly as a good-luck gift for newlywed couples.

As part of its survey work, the cooperative's creative team often travels to the east coast rice country to undertake cultural mappings of the area. The colours of the fields, the farmers' garments, and the materials used for packing the crops are all local impressions that are filtered into the stories and presentation of farming produce.

A distinct feature of *Together Rice* is the fabric of its packaging. Although widespread in Taiwan, nobody is certain of the origins of its distinct floral patterns. In the West, the designs are perhaps best known from the works of Taiwanese artist Michael Lin, who paints expansive architectural surfaces in bold flower motifs derived from the cloth. In the collective memory of many locals, these lush patterns are widely associated with joy and the wholesomeness of a good country life.

For the rice product, a special cloth was painted with an original background colour: a grasshopper green reminiscent of sprawling rice paddies. It is dyed and screen-printed as an exclusive edition at one of the few remaining factories that specialise in printing these fabulous blooming fabrics. The package incorporates an award-winning folding technique and a woven handle, which have become a signature mark for the product.

The entire life cycle of *Together Rice*—from cultivating the rice, harvesting it, gifting it, and sharing it as part of a meal with family and friends—encourages positive consumer choices supportive of local agriculture, and enjoyed by the whole family.

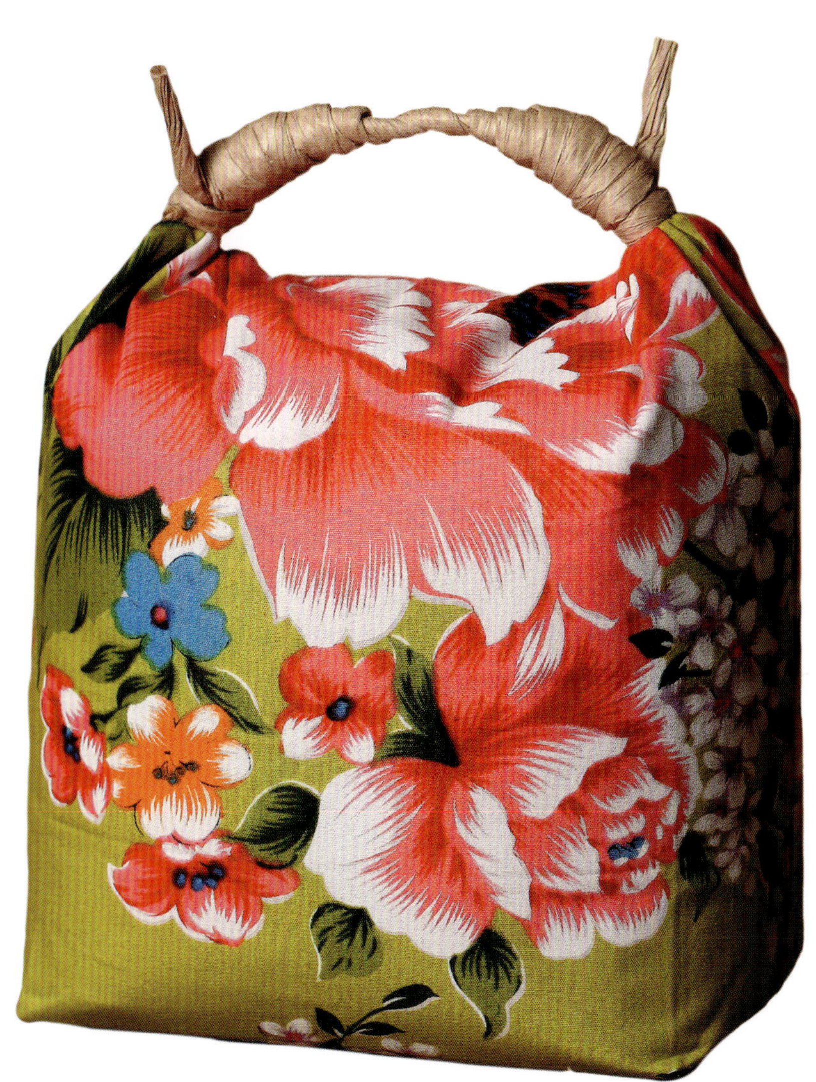

81

TRIP VIEW BOWL

Bowl

Hsi-Yi Peng | Arty Design

Seeing the universe in a grain of rice might be difficult to grasp, but taking an imaginary trip to far away places by contemplating the bottom of a rice bowl is within anyone's reach. An avid cartographer since childhood, Hsi-Yi Peng had the spirited thought that he should turn his love for drawing maps into distinctly Taiwanese products. 'I wish for tourists to have a souvenir which reminds them of the flavours of this wonderful place long after they've returned home. I think a good designer is one who is a responsible citizen not just a product maker. If my bowls can establish meaningful connection between disparate people, I feel purposeful about my work.'

In 2009 Hsi-Yi Peng, or Arty, made the bold move of leaving commercial design circles to collaborate with local communities. He established a new business for the design and manufacture of tableware products about historically significant places from around the island. Descriptively named *Trip View Bowl*, the story-image inside each of his signature bowls is key to his idea of 'cultural sustainability'. A total of 17 series have been released, including: *Design at the Edges Bowl*, official souvenir of the 2011 World Design Congress; *The Bowl of Regeneration*, commemorating the 10th anniversary of the 921 Earthquake; and *The Tainan Bowl*, the drawings for which were created together with 120 eateries from Tainan, all now using the bowl at their premises.

Each item presents an aerial view of a real location, rendered in blue ink around the surface of a porcelain bowl. Accurate photographic panoramas are captured and processed in 3D mapping software to create the sweeping 360-degrees illustrations. Graphic elements are then added as signposts along original tourist trails. The Chinese symbols for East–West–North–South accurately align the picture with the four cardinal directions. All bowls are made in under-glaze blue porcelain, which produces fresh blue colour and clear images that can remain sharp for posterity. The delicate etchings carry on the hallmarks of traditional water ink and non-linear landscape painting.

Trip View Bowl comes in its own packaging designed for maximum protection, and it can be safely posted as a gift. Even if dropped from as high as five metres, the packaging will prevent the bowl from breaking. The accompanying poster of the inlayed image and a small magnifying glass complete the bowl's fascinating virtual glide over the beautiful island.

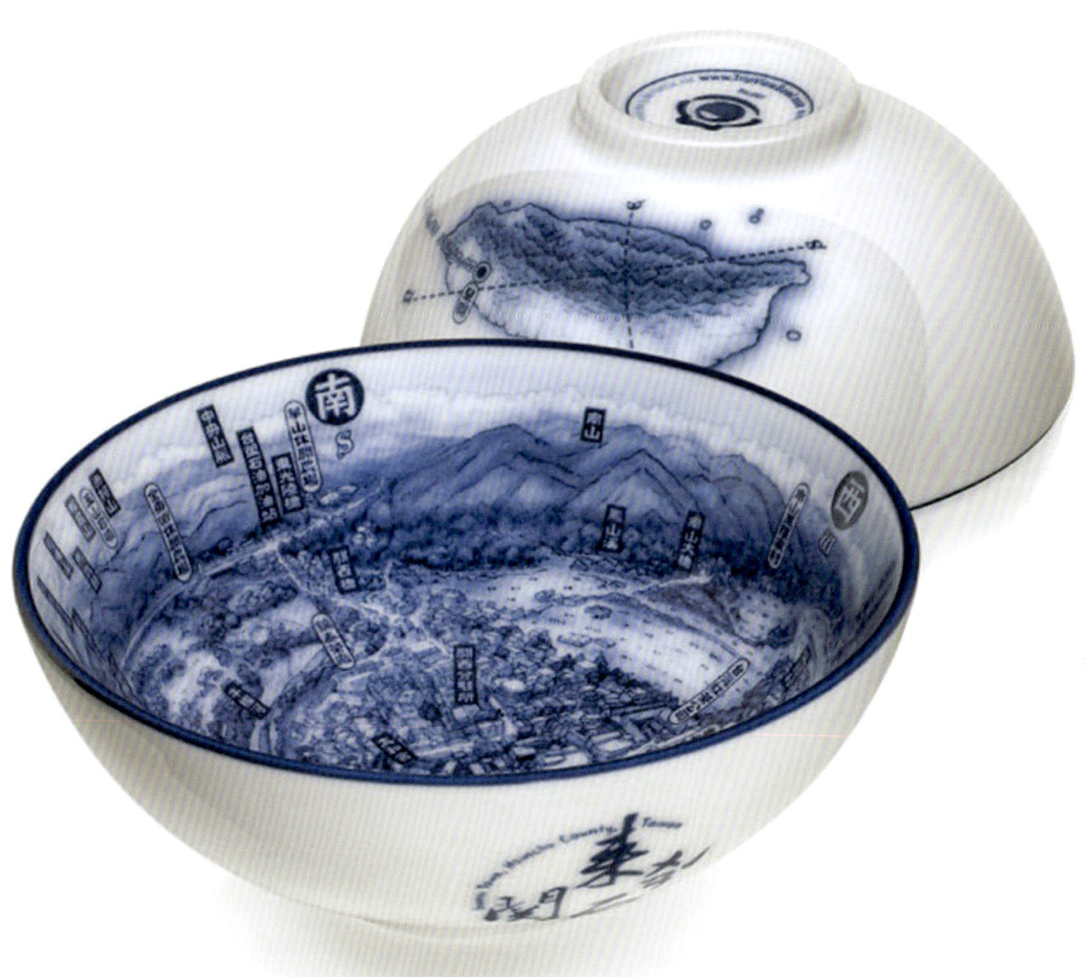

82

UNDER THE SEA

Jewellery

Cai-Xuan Wu

Created by contemporary jeweller Cai-Xuan Wu, *Under the Sea* is a series of brooches that propose a sustainable alternative to accessories made of precious coral and gems. It is hard to believe that these are actually transformations of acrylic and not reworked translucent nautilus shell or preserved plankton!

Each object begins as a clear flat sheet of acrylic, which undergoes several processes to make the thermoplastic pliable. Firstly, it is laser-cut into a circle. Small incisions are spliced at regular intervals with the resulting strips being left joined around the rim. The material is then 'cooked' through fabric-dyeing techniques. 'I do the final grading of the dye myself because I can control the vibrancy of the hues. I want the colouring to highlight the lightness of the structure', explains Wu.

Once dried the cut and coloured acrylic is heated until it is soft enough to be woven. Working quickly from the middle outwards, Wu twists and loops the strips into a new form. 'I am exploring the potential of techniques such as cutting, expanding, rotating and knitting to turn an industrial material into something that looks deceptively natural. Sometimes a pearl is also incorporated for a more striking effect, and I have added three tiny pins on the back so each

brooch can be discreetly attached to a garment.'

Besides being attractive, the accessories posit an uneasy dialogue between the organic and the synthetic. *Under the Sea* may take inspiration from the natural treasures found in deep waters, but it also alludes to their extreme exploitation for trade. Red coral jewellery, for instance, is still popular in Taiwan and praised as a sign of wealth. But coral harvesting has become a contentious issue in the region. Some fishermen illegally drag for coral, uprooting the seabed and thereby destroying major marine ecosystems.

In some respects, *Under the Sea* challenges consumer conventions of material value by offering stylish alternative adornments. Distributed as a limited edition, the collection is as rare a find as the elusive marine specimens found in a Jules Verne novel. It is this sense of the exotic and precious that has fascinated Wu's clientele.

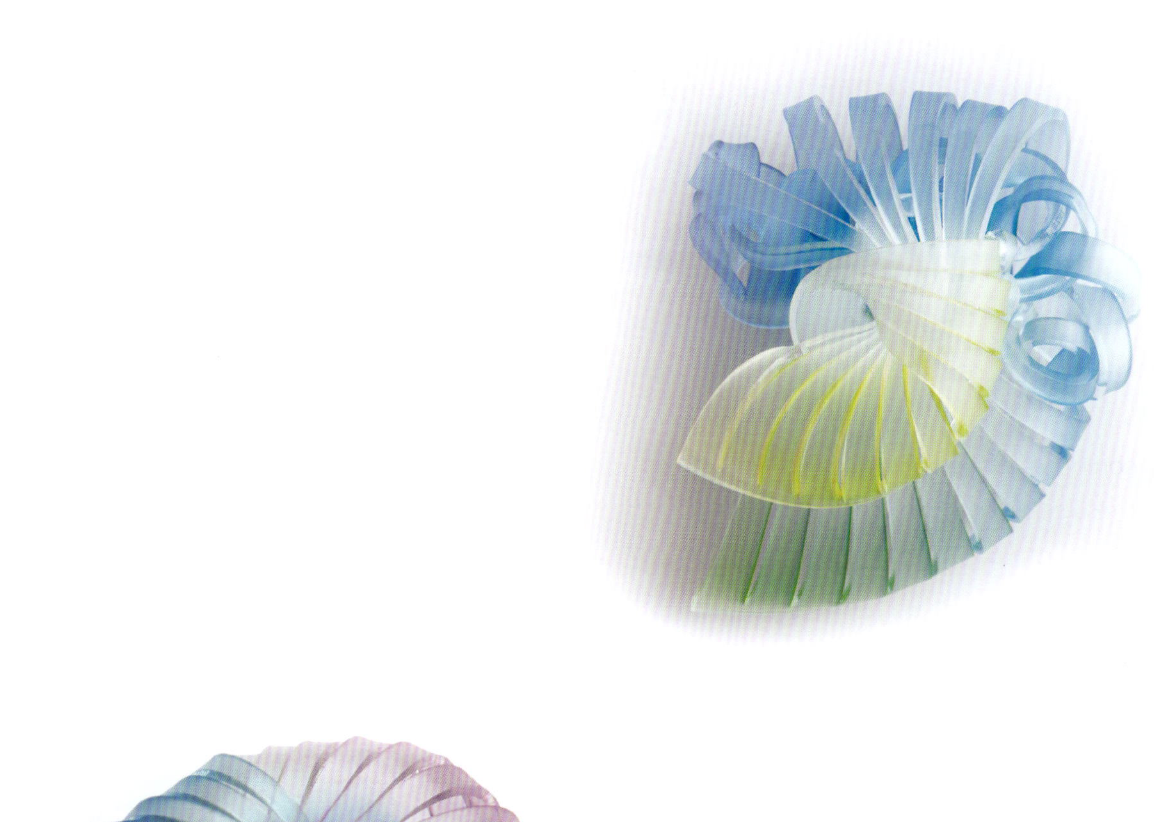

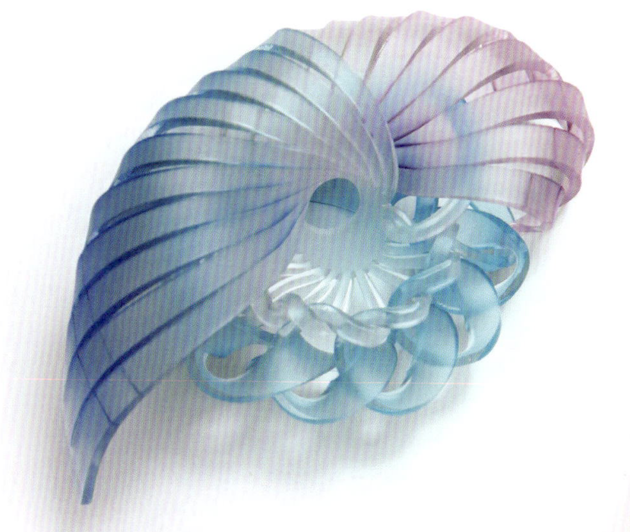

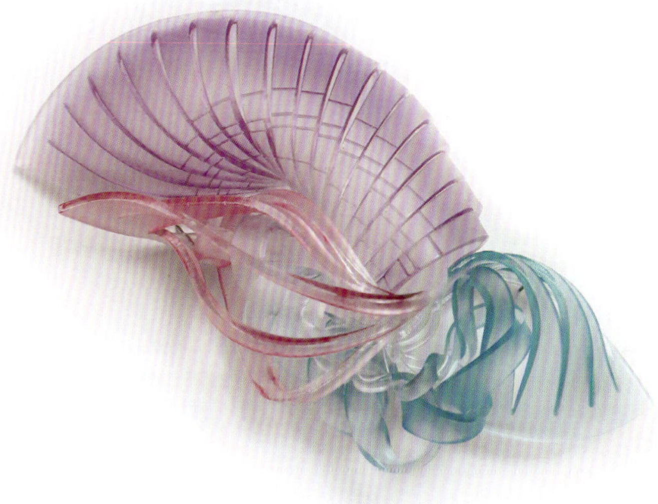

83

ÜPON

Bicycle Tent

Kuandah Union Trading

There is never rest for the energetic Doris Cheng, senior product developer of *ÜPON*. Now in her sixties, she is excited she can still keep up with the trendy youngsters as she launches her new single tent for cyclists. 'Attitudes are changing. The roads around the island are much better now than when I was growing up. Even seniors like me get on their bikes for group outings. It's healthy and it's wonderful. We designed this product in the hope more people enjoy spending time outdoors.'

New recreational activities generate the need for new items. Cheng identified that carry-on shelter would improve the comfort of cyclists. In Taiwan, it can rain unexpectedly and bugs are rampant, so taking a rest on the road is not always a pleasurable experience. 'The question was how to make shelter light in weight and quick to assemble. It had to be smaller than the usual tent, but more substantial than an umbrella', she explains.

Having manufactured sports shoes for years, the smart businesswoman saw a correlation between the lightweight nylon fabric used in trainers and its possible adaptation for the tent. The first *ÜPON* prototype was rectangular in shape, with the challenge of getting it down to about 1 kg. After two years of development, a solution was found—literally in the air. By adding a triangular air pillar to the structure the tent could be made lightweight. When inflated the pillar props it up at one end, while elastic ropes fasten it to the bicycle at the other. In this way, the system secures the upright position of the tent and it locks the bike in place.

To keep the product ultra-light, the material itself is not waterproof but rather it is sprayed with a special water repellent coating that makes moisture run off the fabric, keeping the inner shelter dry for resting. Two mosquito-netted windows, sealed with a waterproof tape, generate sufficient ventilation. The larger window functions as a zipped up entry point. With dimensions of 80 cm wide, 220 cm long and 100 cm high, *ÜPON* provides sufficient space for a single person.

Walkers can enjoy the tent too by purchasing a second air pillar to use in place of the bicycle. A ribbed air mattress made of knitted soft fabric can be spread on the ground for extra comfort. The mattress is sold separately with its own easy-to-use hand pump, and it can be inflated in no time. With its bright yellow and green colours, this new product promises enjoyable recreation by taking care of the basic needs for shelter.

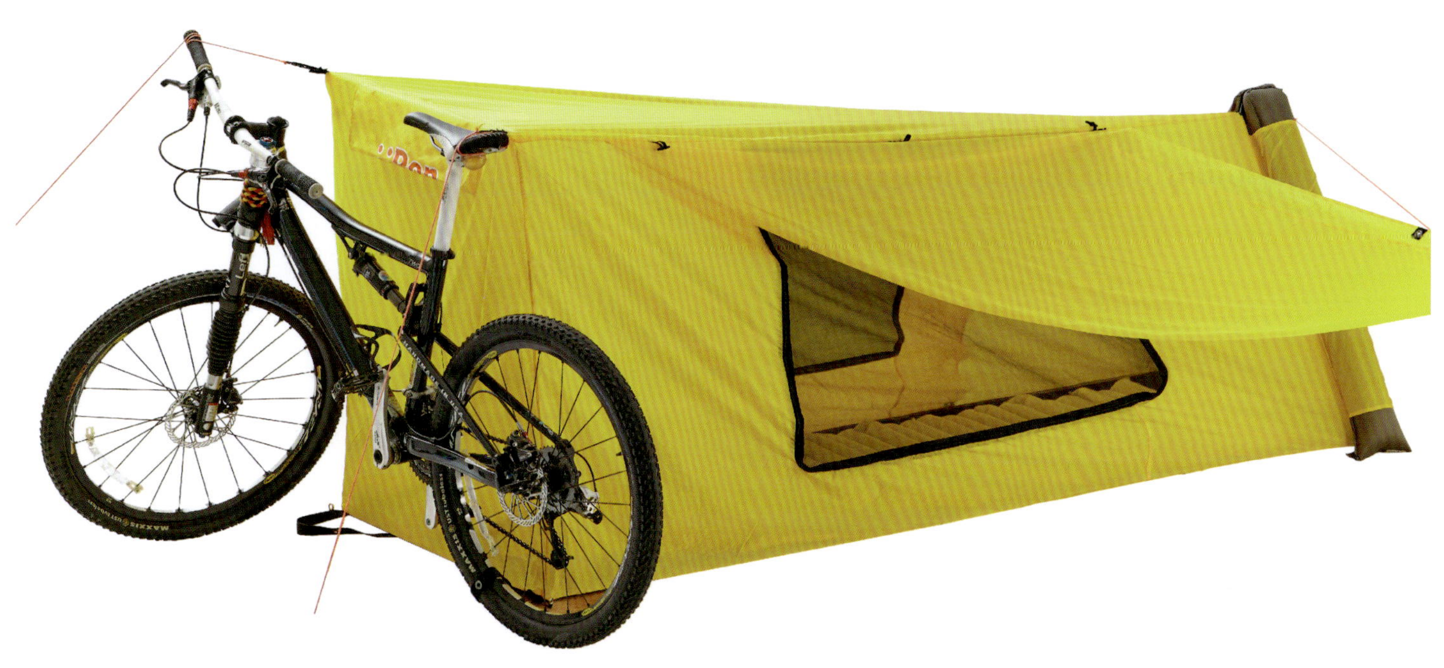

84

URBANCAGE

Sound Speaker

Yi Ting Chen

There is an old street in Taipei famous for selling all kinds of birds, birdcages and pet accessories. In the recent past, having songbirds as decorative pets was fashionable amongst the wealthy, who commissioned artisans to craft ornamental cages as a way of displaying their social status. People loved their exotic pets so much that they would carry them around. Today, preserved as part of Taipei's cultural heritage, Bird Street is more of a tourist attraction than a thriving market. Perhaps surprisingly, a designer born in the digital age is taking a closer look at the street's treasure trove of curiosities.

Yi-Ting Chen's *Urbancage* is both a sound speaker for digital devices and a homage to life on Bird Street. The designer made countless paper models, testing his concept with a welder to adapt the stylistic elements of a birdcage into a flat form speaker housing digital devices. The base and hook replicate original designs, and the minimalist wire frame superimposes classical with contemporary lines. The actual speaker is hidden in the base of the stand with all wires cleverly tucked inside the frame.

In explaining his concept, Chen observes that 'We live in an age when technology is destroying innocence. Gadgets are inhibiting our sense of wonder and all the fun we can get from discovering

something no matter how trivial it might be. I want my product to bring a humanist dimension to the emotionless techno-pets we carry in our pockets.'

Urbancage is accompanied by its own iTunes App, and it can be also appreciated as a stand-alone artwork that plays nature sounds to bring warmth into a domestic space. In the designer's view the product is a subtle criticism of the current state of the world, whereby replacing the natural environment with the technological one is making us more impoverished not wealthier.

'Culturally our minds are becoming like encaged birds, imprisoned by the latest fashions and disconnected from our true nature', says Chen. His lovingly made sound speaker is a lament for a return to innocence. It also suggests that we can enjoy our techno world whilst taking care of nature and remaining close to our human origins.

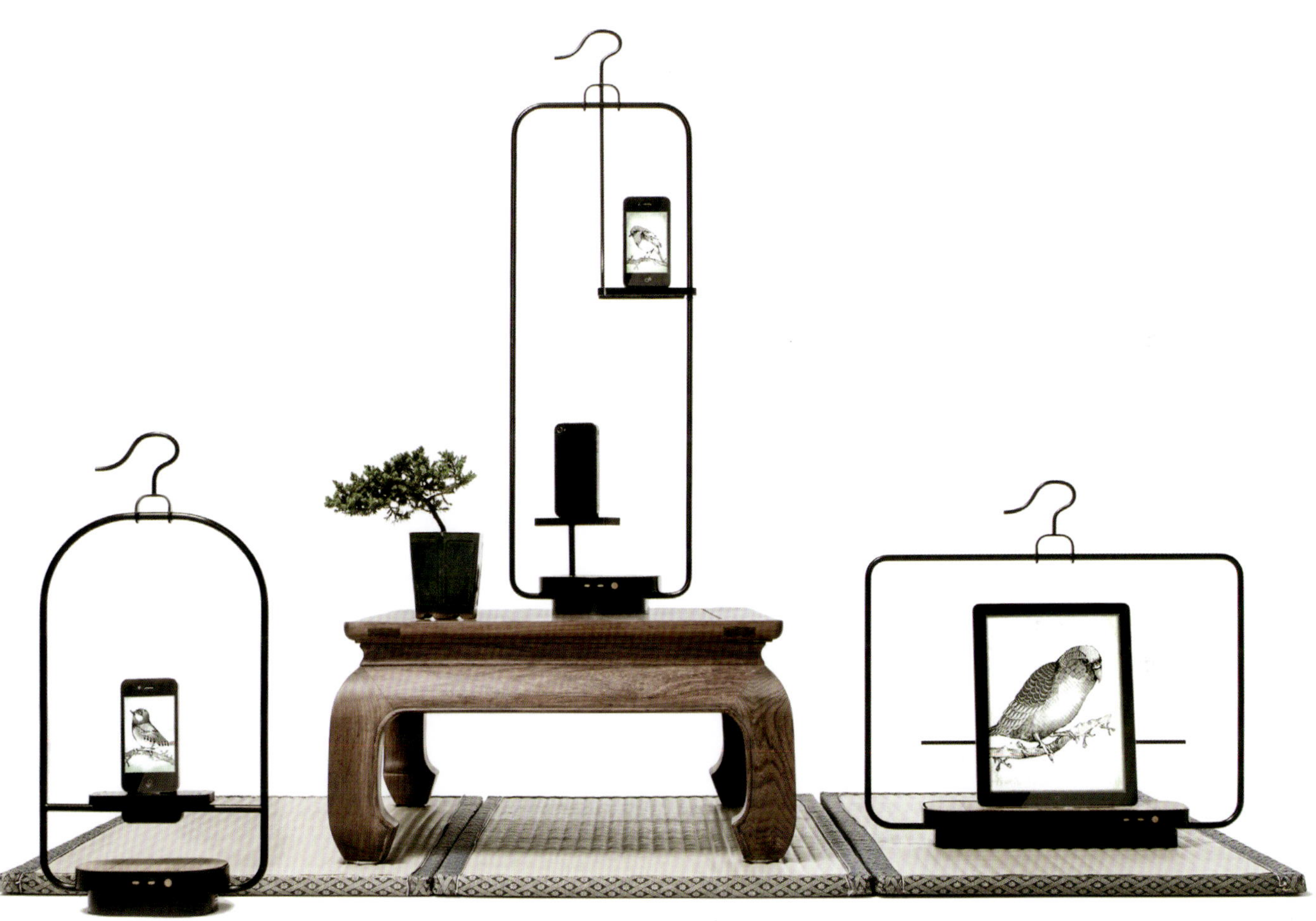

85

USEFULESS TABLE

Dining Table

Jacky Wu Design

The ancient philosopher Zhuang-zi had a theory by which he interpreted the concept of functionality as something to be based on flexibility rather than utility. In accordance with the Taoist way of thinking about the interdependence of opposites, Zhuang-zi regarded an object with no specific purpose to be superior as it can override the limitations of a specific form. 'Something useful is useless, something useless is more useful', he had famously said.

This appealed to Jacky Wu who enjoys taking care of old things not by fixing but by reinventing them. Typically when working on a prototype, the starting point for Wu is to deconstruct, even destroy, an existing object. 'The challenge of having to rebuild something anew encourages inventiveness', he observes. 'This is how the *Usefuless Table* came about. I was trying to salvage some quarter pieces of porcelain vases and placed a plank of wood on top of them. The materials did not match and the broken pieces did not balance, but I could see a brilliant concept evolving.'

Although initially it looked more like an art installation than a piece of furniture, he digitally rendered the construction as a basis for a new product. From Wu's industrial model, a factory produced the mould and cast the table in hard plastic with a gloss finish: a visual reference to the original glazed ceramics.

The legs are hand painted in the style of 'blue and white' porcelain. This mode reached its height during the Ming and Qing Dynasties, when artisans decorated porcelain ware with thin blue outlines then filled in the shapes in a range of patterns. The table's top is painted on the underside. The overall inverted effect appears as if a piece of cloth has been left hanging on the inside.

Some have suggested the painting should be reversed, but Wu remains adamant. 'The product should be authentic to the philosophy that drives its creation. When my job as a designer is done no further changes are necessary just to make an object appear more "normal". More than this, it's a little bit simplistic to think of my products as an expression of an East-West hybrid style. What I am trying to achieve with these repurposed fragments is to reveal the greater possibility hidden inside existing forms.' He does, however, hope that by adopting Zhuang-zi's principles as part of a broader design practice, a distinctly Taiwanese style could be defined.

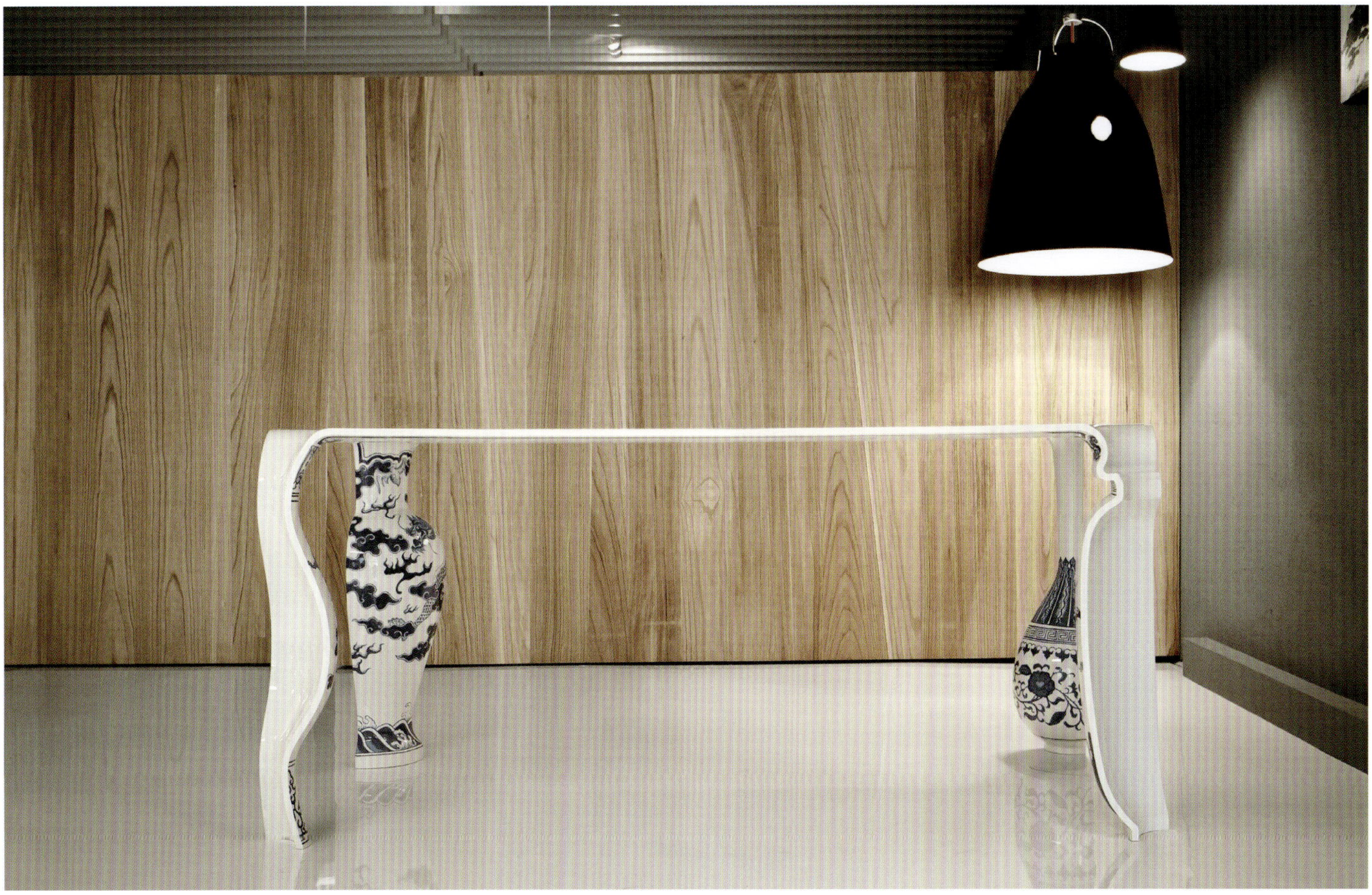

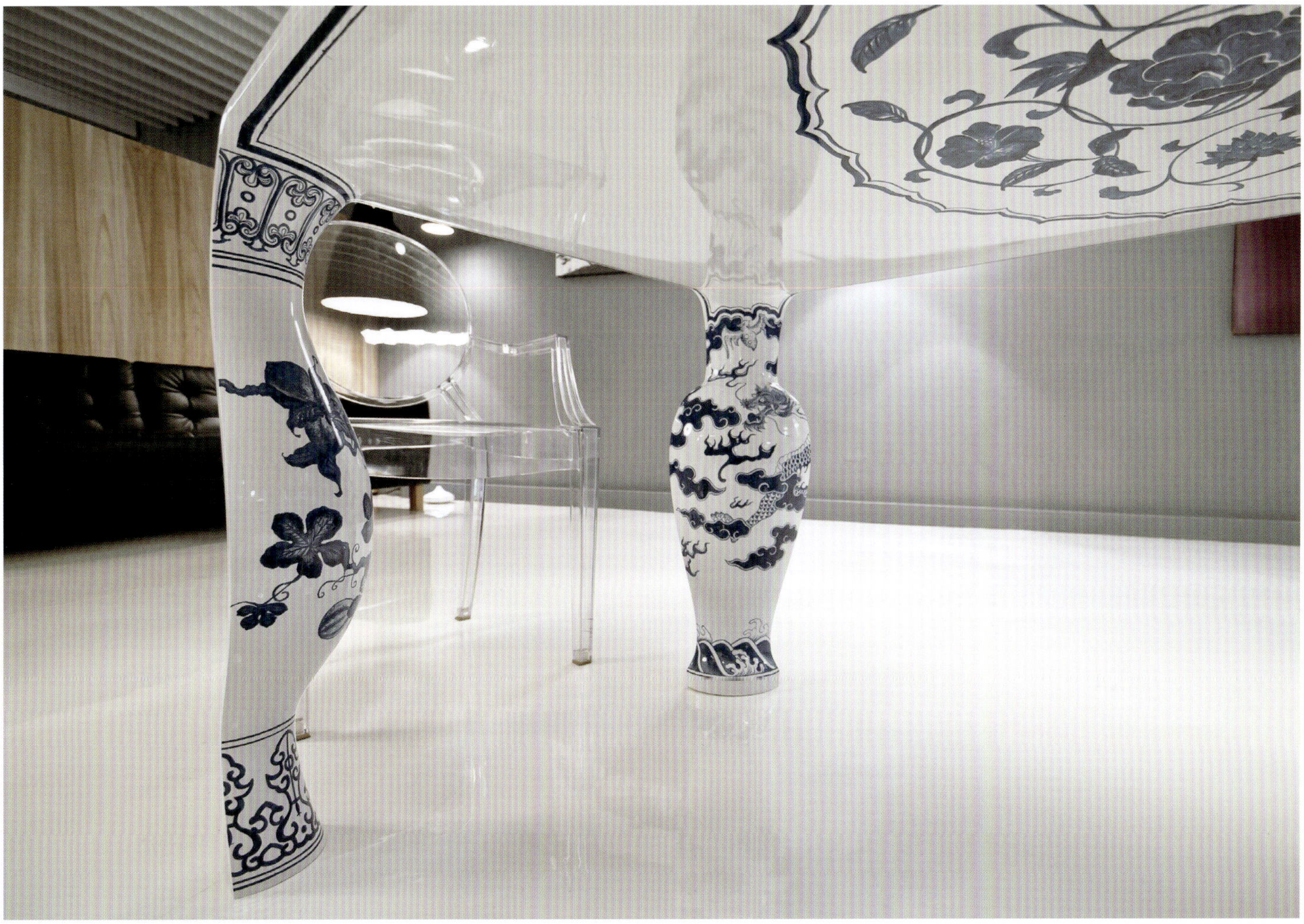

86

VINAERA

Electronic Wine Aerator

Yeh-Yi Chung | Mercuries Asia

Vinaera is the world's first electronic wine aerator capable of decanting wine at the push of a button. It helps reduce the amount of tannins and sulphides when wine is poured into a glass directly from the bottle. Unlike the traditional glass decanter this product offers wine lovers the convenience of wine 'breathing' instantly: its flavours and aromas can be savoured immediately after a bottle is opened.

'Until not so long ago—may be ten to twenty years—the popular drink at the Taiwanese banquet table was whiskey. Wine was thought as something medicinal, more like a food, particularly red wine because in traditional medicine red is believed to be a good-health colour. This is so unlike Europe where for centuries wine has been deeply engrained into every aspect of its culture and religion.'

True to his place of origin, Yeh-Yi Chung decided to solve this cross-cultural discrepancy by introducing some technological ingenuity to the wine drinking experience. Knowing people on the island have no patience for decanting, he wondered if wine could be aerated while it is being poured. His idea came courtesy of a friend's fish tank! 'Well, fish need air, which is why fish tanks have a water pump to bring in the oxygen. It was worth trying to apply the same principle to wine. It seemed logical to me.' Chung looked into the mechanics of the pump and then worked on remodelling it so it could be attached to the top of a wine bottle.

His innovative *Vinaera* aerator comprises a main body (housing a 6 AAA battery compartment and electronics), a spout, and a plastic tube for pumping the wine from the bottle. The aerator needs to be pushed gently down over the bottle mouth and clicked into place. All that is left to do is to place a glass under its spout and press the dispensing button for the wine to flow. Approximately 250 bottles of wine can be aerated before changing the batteries.

'I designed it with a sophisticated stainless steel finish, but actually the material we used for the main body is ABS plastic, nickel-plated and brushed. The lightweight material is better so that the aerator won't topple the bottle over. Besides it's more practical for travelling.'

Sceptics unsure of his invention are encouraged to pour two glasses of wine from the same bottle, one using the pump, and taste test to compare. 'I even took it to a professional sommelier to produce a degustation report. Of course the result was excellent. Air is air! This product takes the waiting time for the wine to breathe out of the equation ... here, enjoy.'

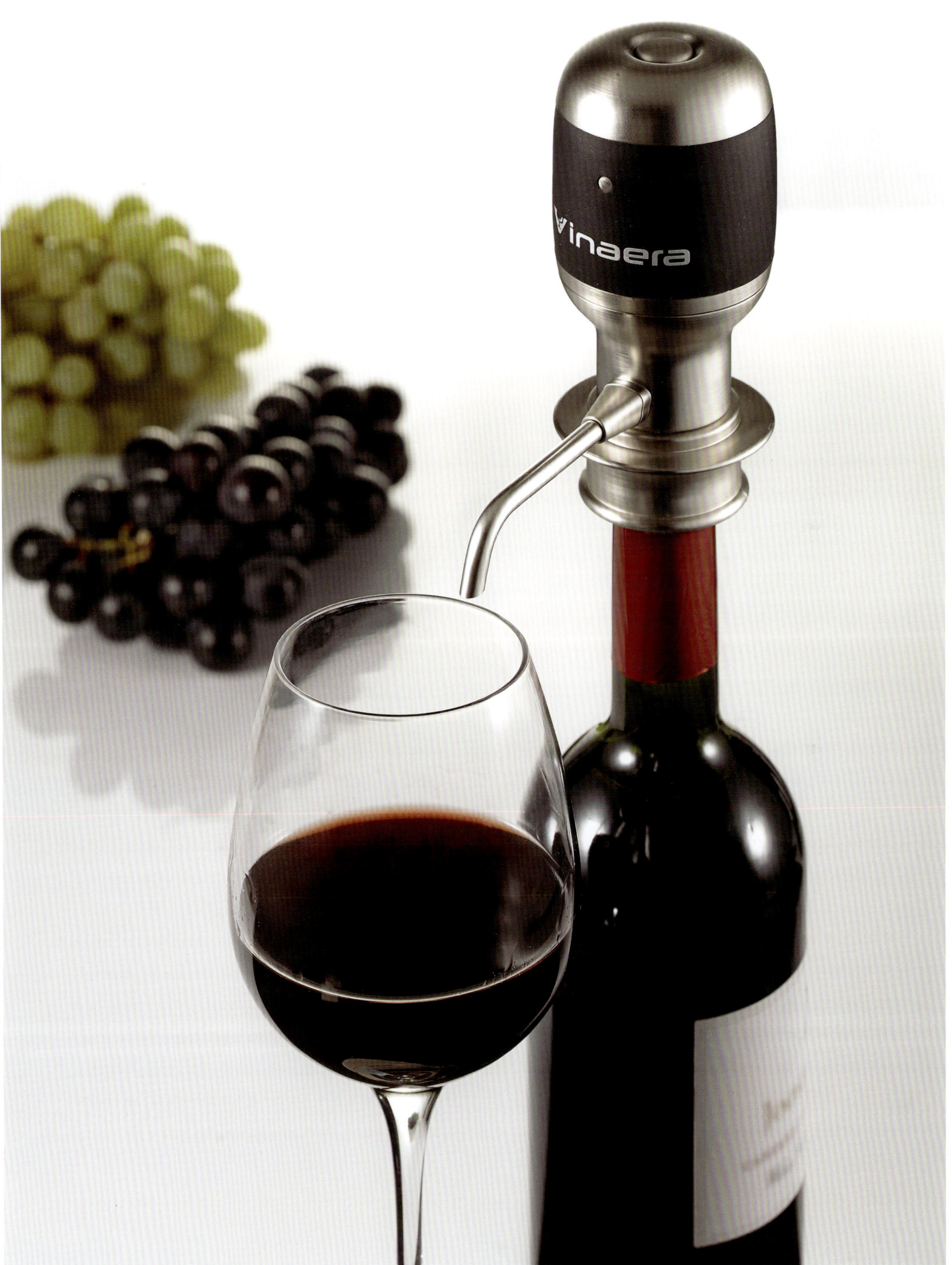
inaera

87

WOLF 300 CLASSIC

Motorcyle

Nova Design | Sanyang Motor

The motorcycles manufactured by Sanyang Motor, and sold under its brand SYM, have sustained a 60-year reputation for quality, reliability and good price. Amongst them, the legendary *WOLF* has a special place in Taiwan's cultural heritage.

The iconic image of the naked bike is etched deeply into the memories of many grandpas who crisscrossed the island on it in their youth. It has been a faithful working machine for many farmers whose only access to their lands is usually via narrow paths best accessed by bike. Even the postal fleet services have adopted a specially modified version of the motorcycle: every day, green uniformed postmen do their delivery rounds speeding on a 'green wolf'!

'Its origins go back to the early 1980s, when Honda started manufacturing its bikes here. The Japanese controlled all design R&D and didn't expect us to be creative. But we smartened up! The local team secretly started redesigning the bike to fit our way of life, eventually breaking away from the mother company to produce our own Taiwanese naked bike. It was nicknamed "wolf", partly because its exposed mechanics look like the powerful muscles of a wild wolf, and maybe it's also a connotation of the lonely rebel rider who was the likely consumer', explains Roger Lin, Vice President at Nova Design, responsible for the development of over 500 products since the company's inception.

The attractive *WOLF 300 Classic* model is enjoying the fashionable come back of the retro naked bikes, with numerous elements from the 1970s small Honda era still on display. Its liquid-cooled single cylinder engine was re-engineered to 278cc, extending the top speed of the bike to 87 mph. It uses a six-speed gearbox and it has very good fuel efficiency for its class.

Another advantage for male and female riders alike is that the motorcycle's dry weight is 169 kilograms, and it is much easier to manoeuvre than a sports bike. Turned on together, the front and rear breaks stop the machine fast with an extremely short break distance. The cast metal accessories add extra stability when riding on uneven surfaces.

Lin speaks admiringly of the *WOLF*'s 'elemental design' as if it were an object of beauty. 'It's a timeless motorcycle made for enjoyment. From the dash and the two retro styled pods of the speedometer and the tachometer to the rear, every part is visible and sturdy. It's designed to be maintained, kept, loved. It's a bike built to last a lifetime. Now, isn't this green design!'

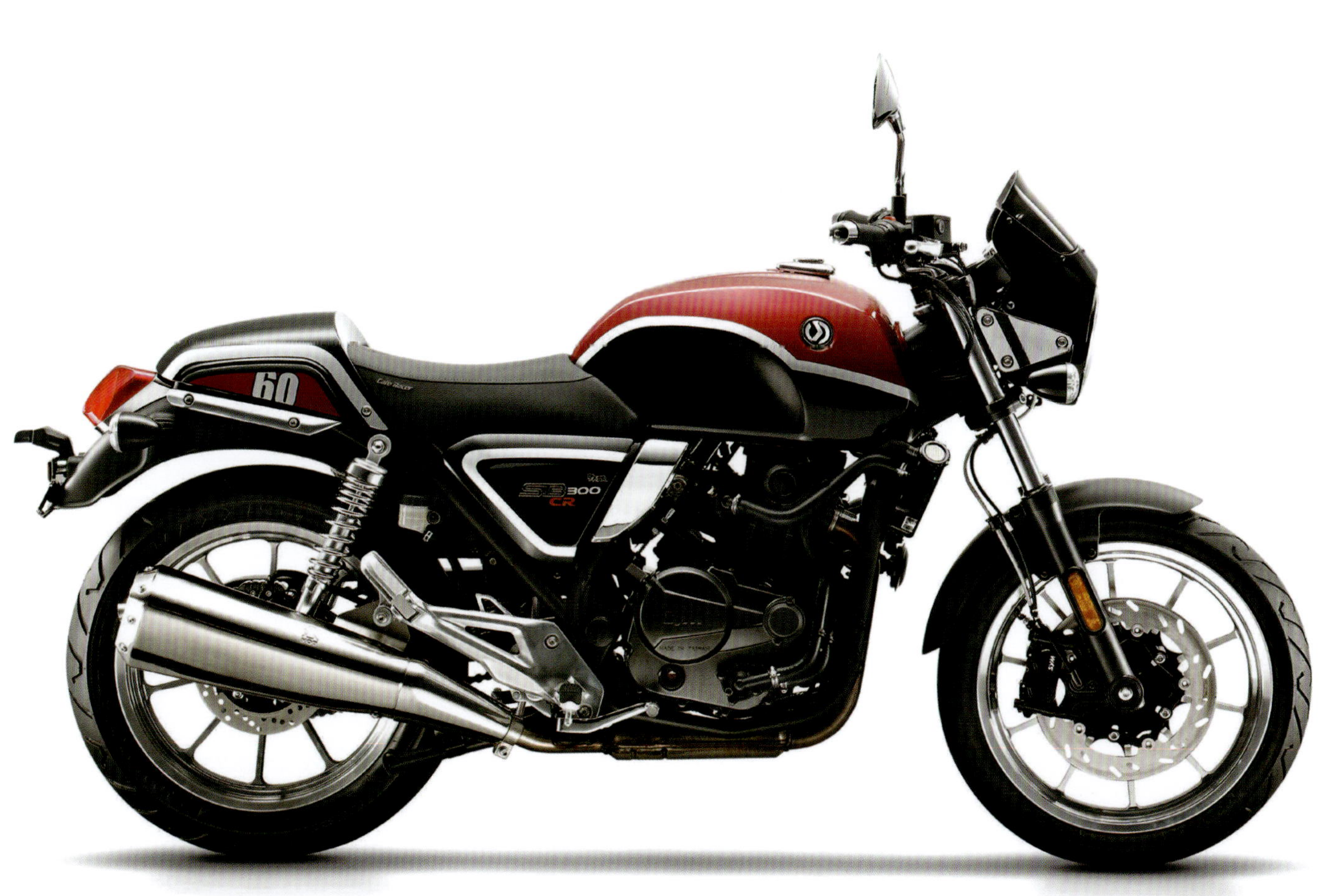

88

ZENWATCH

Wristwatch

Mitch Yang | ASUS

The legendary electronics giant ASUS released *ZenWatch* in 2014, celebrating its first wearable device powered by Android Wear. The most remarkable feature of this next generation wristwatch is the specially engineered user interface.

The device pairs with an ASUS smartphone to provide relevant and useful information on the go. In addition to showing the time and date or displaying updates about the weather, the watch has an embedded sensor which measures the wearer's physiological data. For example, it can track the number of steps made or calories taken, or measure one's heartbeat. The data is readable via the *ZenUI Wellness App*. Users can set personal goals and monitor their daily fitness progress at a glance.

Explaining the development of the concept, Corporate Design Officer Mitch Yang says the work of his team starts with 'people in mind'. 'We want to deliver a digital experience that is smooth running, effortless and enjoyable for the wearer; it should feel like second nature. We strived to achieve a portable device that connects a person to everything that matters to them in their daily routine. Even a virtual wellness manager to keep them motivated to stay healthy!'

The touch screen panel of the *ZenWatch* is operable via gestures and voice commands. This is especially useful when driving: one simply needs to call out specific features or apps. The product comes with over 100 combinations of instantly changeable watch-faces to match the mood and personality of the user. The battery can be easily recharged via a mini USB connected to cable, an adapter, and a nearby power outlet.

The extended range of smart features include *Remote Camera*, *Find My Phone*, and *Presentation Control*. These are designed to make the device a versatile and efficient companion to the many common situations there are in a day.

Although it is adapted to Android Wear, the device is styled after the luxury traditions of fine watchmaking. The interface is elegantly cased in stainless steel, and it wraps around the wrist with a soft, genuine leather strap clasped together with a polished buckle. This smart product is well appointed to please the lifestyle choices of Millennials, who are fast-paced and love their gadgets.

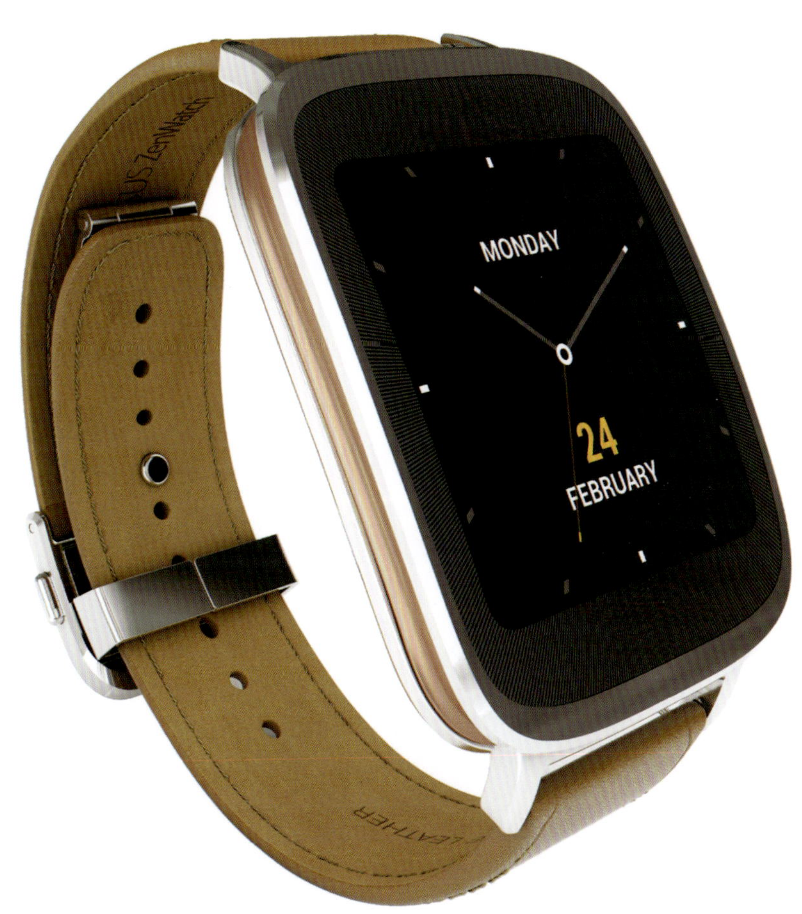

ASUS ZenWatch
LEATHER
MONDAY
24
FEBRUARY

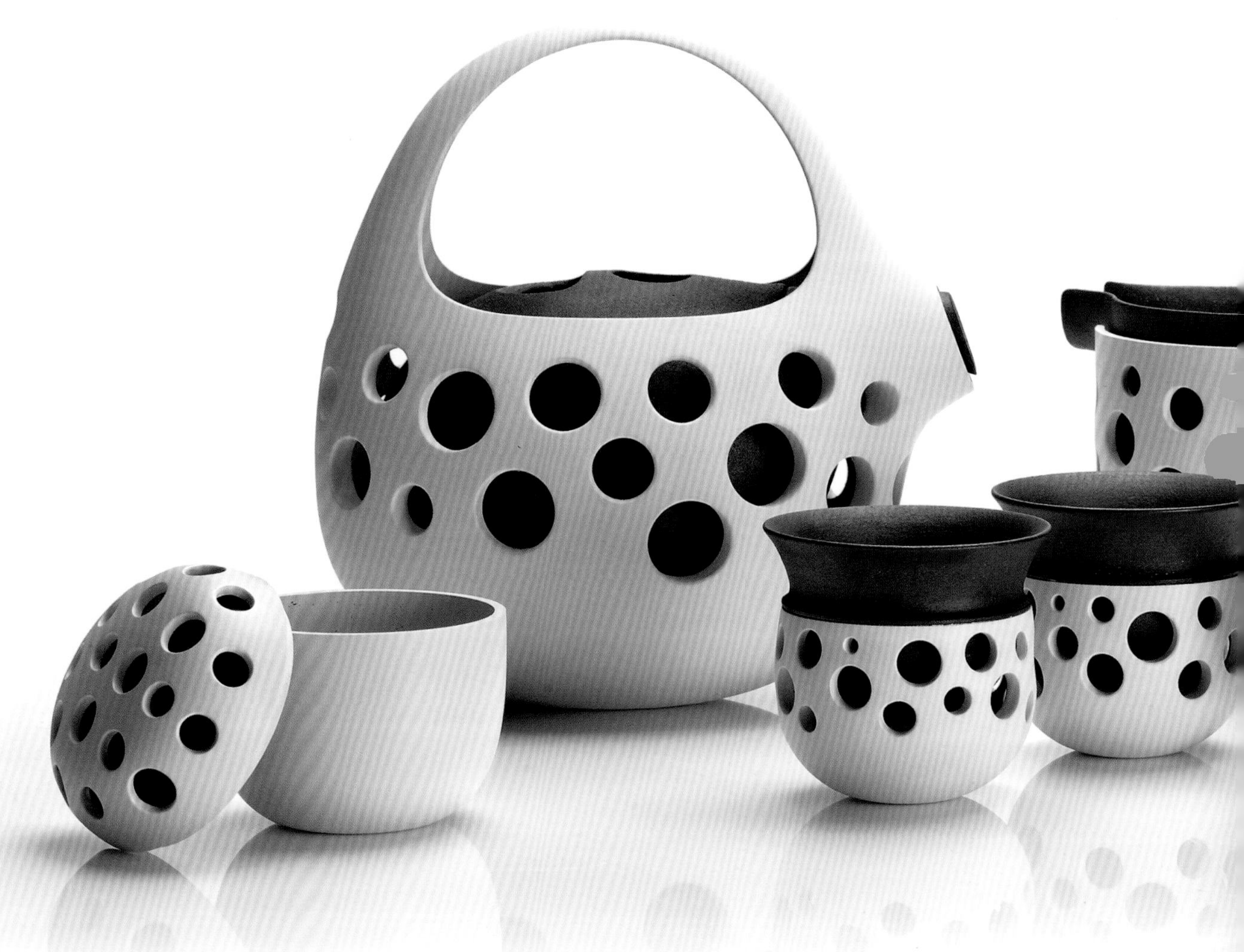

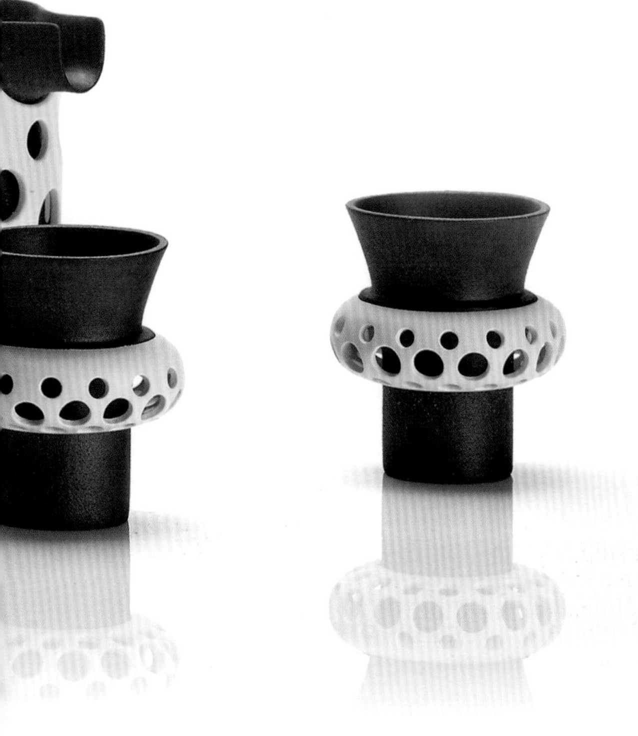

DESIGNER PROFILES

1

22 DESIGN STUDIO

est. 2005

Sean Yu

b. 1982, Taipei

National Cheng Kung University, Taiwan

Yiting Cheng

b. 1983, Tainan

Royal College of Art, UK

Ambiente, Frankfurt, Germany 2013

Design Tokyo, Japan 2013

Inhorgenta, Munich, Germany 2013

Maison&Objet Paris, France 2012

Tent London, UK 2012

100% London, UK 2010

DMY Berlin, Germany 2009

ICFF New York, USA 2008

www.22designstudio.com.tw

3+2 DESIGN STUDIO

est. 2005

Creative Expo Taiwan 2015

Taiwan Designers' Week 2009-2011

Designboom Mart Tokyo 2009

Taiwan Home Style Award 2015

Taiwan Excellence Award

(Industrial Design) 2015

iF DESIGN AWARD, Germany 2015

Good Design Award

(Packaging, Product), Japan 2014

Red Dot Design Award, Germany 2014

www.3add2.com

A

ALLROVER

est. 2014

Po-Chih Lai

b. 1985, Kaohsiung

Royal College of Art, UK

ISPO New Top 50, Germany 2014

Taipei 101 'Gifts from the Star' 2014

Biennale Int'le Design Saint-Étienne, Cité Du

Design, France 2013

Musée de Design et d'Arts Appliqués

Contemporains, Switzerland 2013

Italian Cultural Institute, UK 2012

www.pochilai.com

anLIVING

est. 2014

Yang-An Lin

b. 1984, Tainan

Ming Chi University of Technology, Taiwan

Salone Satellite, Milan Design Week, Italy 2014

Maison&Objet Paris, France 2014

Taipei 101 'Gifts from the Star' 2014

www.anLiving.com

ARTILIZE WORLDWIDE

est. 2004

Tokyo Design Products Fair, Japan 2015

Asian American Expo, USA 2014–2015

Creative Expo Taiwan 2014–2015

Interiorlifestyle Tokyo, Japan 2014

BICF&BIH, Thailand 2014

Taiwan Excellence Award 2015

C-S Industrial Design Award (Gold), China 2015

Good Design Award, Japan 2014

Most Successful Design Award, China 2014

www.talescasa.com

ASIA ONE DESIGN

est. 2000

William Liu

b. 1967, New Taipei City

National Taiwan University of Science &

Technology, Taiwan

Taiwan Designers' Week 2015

Cultural & Creative Expo, Taiwan 2014

A Zone Design Show, Taiwan 2014

IDA Congress Taipei, Taiwan 2011

OTOP Design Award, Taiwan 2015

TIDA Design Award, Taiwan 2010

Golden Pin Design Award, 2009

Red Dot Design Award, Germany 2008

Good Design Award, Japan 2002

www.asiaone.biz

ASUS DESIGN CENTER

est. 2000

Taipei World Design Expo 2011

Taipei Int'l Flora Expo, Taiwan 2010

CES, USA 2009, 2010

Taiwan Designers' Week 2007

Milan Design Week, Italy 2007

iF DESIGN AWARD (Product), Germany 2015

IDEA (Finalist), USA 2015

iF DESIGN AWARD (Gold), Germany 2015

Good Design Award (100), Japan 2013, 2014

IDEA (Bronze), USA 2012

www.asusdesign.com

AWA FAUCET

est. 2011

ISH Messe Frankfurt, Germany 2009, 2013, 2015

Red Dot Museum Taipei, Taiwan 2015

Red Dot Museum Essen, Germany 2013, 2015

Red Dot Design Award (Product), Germany 2010,

2011, 2013, 2015

www.awa.tw

B

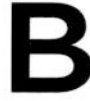

BALANCE WU DESIGN
est. 2010

Balance Wu
b. 1981, Tainan
National Taiwan University of Science &
Technology, Taiwan

Taiwan Designer's Week 2014, 2015
Creative Expo Taiwan, 2014–2015
Bangkok Int'l Gift Fair, Thailand 2015
Project, Las Vegas, USA 2014

Inter'l Council of Societies of Industrial Design,
ICSID World Design Impact Prize, Taiwan 2015
Golden Pin Design Award 2011, 2013

www.balance-wu.com

BIAUGUST CREATION OFFICE
est. 2005

Jui-Hao Chuang
b. 1975, Kaohsiung
Musashino Art University, Japan

Chen-Yun Lu
b. 1975, Kaohsiung
Tama Art University, Japan

Maison&Objet Paris, France 2014
Gewerbe Museum, Switzerland 2013
Hermès Window Design, Taiwan 2011
DMY Festival Berlin, Germany 2011
100% Design London, UK 2011
Royal T Gallery Los Angeles, USA 2010
8th SICF Exhibition Tokyo, Japan 2007

Cultural & Creative Award (Product), Taiwan 2015
Golden Pin Design Award 2013
1st Xue Xue Awards, Taiwan 2009
4th Ceramics Golden Award (Silver), Taiwan 2008
Good Design Award, Japan 2008

biaugust.com

BONE COLLECTION
est. 2005

Reads Lin
b. 1974, Taichung
Da Yeh University, Taiwan

Maison&Objet, France 2012–2015
NY Now, New York, USA 2012–2014
Ambiente, Germany 2011–2013
Tokyo Designers Week, Japan 2012

iF DESIGN AWARD, Germany 2012
iF DESIGN AWARD, Germany 2011
Red Dot Design Award (Product), Germany 2011,
2013, 2014
Design Plus, Germany 2012
Computex D&I Award, Taiwan 2012

www.bonecollection.com

BONNSU
est. 2011

ICFF New York, USA 2015
NY NOW, USA 2015
Creative Expo Taiwan 2015
Tent London, UK 2014
Tokyo Interior Lifestyle, Japan 2014

Red Dot Design Award, Germany 2015
De'chnology Taiwan 2011
Franz Award (Gold), Taiwan 2011

www.bonnsu.com

C

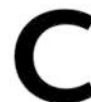

YI-TING CHEN
b. 1987, Taipei
Shih Chien University, Taiwan

ADC Young Guns, New York, USA 2015
Taipei 101 'Gifts from the Star' 2014
Design Exhibition Madrid, Spain 2013

Tokyo Designers Week, Japan 2013
Taiwan Designers' Week 2011-2013
iF DESIGN AWARD, Germany 2014, 2011
Taiwan Int'l Design Competition (HM) 2013
Red Dot Design Award (Best of the Best),
Germany 2012
iF DESIGN AWARD (Top 300), Germany 2012
IDEA (Bronze), USA 2012
Gold Pin Design Award, Taiwan 2012

www.facebook.com/fomstudio

YA-WEN CHOU
b. 1983, Taipei
Royal College of Art, UK

Heal's Modern Craft Market,
London, UK 2014
Basel Art Fair, Switzerland 2013
Milan Ventura Lambrate, Italy 2012
Royal College of Art, London 2012

www.yawenchou.com

D

DA.AI TECHNOLOGY
est. 2008

Taipei in Style, Taiwan 2015
Tianjin Taiwan Trade Fair, China 2015
Zhejiang Taiwan Trade Fair, Ningbo, China 2015
Taipei 101 'Gifts from the Star' 2014

GCCA Later Stage Award 2014
23rd Environmental Protection Award, 2014
Common Wealth Magazine CSR Award, 2014
2nd Environmental Education Award, 2014
Taiwan Excellence Award 2014
Cradle-to-Cradle Certification (Renewal),
USA 2014

www.daait.com

DHH STUDIO

est. 2002

Gina Hsu

b. 1976, Dungshih

Design Academy Eindhoven,
The Netherlands

'Cross-Design+ x Art+' MOCATaipei, 2016
Basilica Palladiana, Vicenza, Italy 2015
Adaptive City, Taipei, Taiwan 2013
Salone del Mobile, Milan, Italy 2010, 2011, 2013
Dutch Design Week, The Netherlands 2013
London Design Week, UK 2012
DMY Berlin, Germany 2012
Salone Satellite, Milan Design Week, Italy 2012
Ventura Lambrate, Milan, Italy 2012
Maison&Objet Paris, France 2009
Huashan Cultural Park, Taiwan 2006

www.dhhstudio.com

DRII DESIGN

est. 2012

Camo Lin

b. 1986, Tainan
Southern Taiwan University, Taiwan

Ping-Hsin Huang

b.1984, Taipei
National Taiwan University of Arts, Taiwan

Maison & Objet Paris, France 2014
Design Int'l Furniture Fair, Shenzhen, China 2014
Int'l Industrial Design Fair, Shenzhen, China 2013
Taiwan Designer's Week, 2013
Creative Expo Taiwan, 2013
Triennale Design Museum,
Milan Design Week, Italy 2011
Beijing Design Triennial, China 2011
DMY Young Design Festival, Germany 2010

Red Dot Award, Germany 2015
Golden Pin Award, Taiwan 2014
Taiwan Good Craft, Taiwan 2014

www.drii-design.com

F

FAN BAO

est. 2010

William Yang, Wen-Der

b. 1953, Chiayi
Cheng Chi University, Taiwan

Giftionery Taipei, Taiwan 2015
Giftionery Taipei, Taiwan 2013
Taipei Int'l Invention Show & Technomart 2014
Red Dot Design Award, Germany 2013

www.fbao95.com

CHENG-TSUNG FENG

b. 1987, Hsinchu
Yunlin University of Science & Technology,
Taiwan

Maison&Objet Paris, France 2015
Asian STAR Showcase, Singapore 2015
Ambiente, Frankfurt, Germany 2015
Asia Talents: Ideas for Tomorrow, Bangkok,
Thailand 2014
Taiwan Contemporary Chairs, la Triennale di
Milano, Italy 2013
Salone Satellite, Milan Design Week, Italy 2013

iF DESIGN AWARD, Germany 2010–2013
Red Dot Design Award, Germany 2009–2011
IDEA (Silver), USA 2010

www.chengtsung.com.tw

FOLDnFOLD ENGREENEERING

est. 2010

'Good Design in Taipei', Taiwan 2015
Golden Pin Design Award, 2013
iF DESIGN AWARD, Germany 2013
Good Design Award (Best 100),
Japan 2013

www.FOLDnFOLD.com

FRANZ COLLECTION

est. 2001

Révélations Paris, France 2015
Creative Expo Taiwan 2015
Porzellanikon Selb, Germany 2012
National Museum Adrien Dubouché,
France 2008
Maison&Objet, Paris, France 2006
Ambiente, Frankfurt, Germany 2006

National Presidential Innovation Award, 2014
UNESCO, Seal of Excellence for Handicrafts
2006–2012
E&Y, World Entrepreneur Of The Year, 2012
Guild of Specialist Gift Retailers (Best Ceramic),
UK 2003
New York Int'l Gift Fair (Best in Gift), USA 2002

www.franzcollection.com.tw

G

GEARLAB

est. 2008

Henry Chang

b. 1979, Taipei
University of Michigan, USA

Chung-Shih Sun

b. 1975, Taipei
Domus Academy, Italy

Golden Pin Exhibition, Taiwan 2015
Taipei Int'l Cycle Show, Taiwan 2015
Taipei 101 'Gifts from the Star' 2014
Taiwan Designers' Week 2014
Cycling x Photography, Youth Square, HK 2014

Golden Pin Design Award (Best Design), 2014
Good Design Award, Japan 2014
iF DESIGN AWARD, Germany 2013
Red Dot Design Award (Best of the Best),
Germany 2011

www.gearlab.com.tw

GIXIA GROUP

est. 2010

VITRA Design Museum, Germany 2013
Red Dot Museum, Germany and Singapore
2012–2013
100% Design London, UK 2012

German Design Award (Special Mention),
Germany 2015
Good Design Award, Japan 2012, 2014
IDEA (Gold), USA 2011
iF DESIGN AWARD, Germany 2011
Red Dot Design Award,
(Best of the Best), Germany 2011

www.gixia-group.com

GOGORO TAIWAN

est. 2011

Consumer Electronics Show, USA 2015
EICMA, Italy 2015
The Verge Award, USA 2015
eWeek, Consumer Electronics Show, 100
Innovative Products, USA 2015
Gizmag Best of CES, USA 2015

www.gogoro.com

GREEN IN HAND FOOD BANK

est. 2006

Yun-Yi Cheng

b. 1969, Taipei
Fu Jen Catholic University, Taiwan
Creative Expo Taiwan
2010, 2011, 2014
Taiwan Lovely Home, Taiwan 2013
Hong Kong Houseware Fair, 2011
Nanjing Trade Fair Show, China 2011
Beijing Int'l Cultural & Creative Industry Expo,
China 2010

LaVie, Culture & Creative Industry Awards, 2015
Red Dot Design Award,
Germany 2012, 2014, 2015

Good Design Award, Japan 2012, 2013
Design for Asia Awards (Grand Prix, Culture,
Gold, Bronze), Hong Kong 2011, 2012
Cultural & Creative Award (Gold), 2010, 2011

www.greeninhand.com

GREENROOM IDEAS COOPERATION

est. 2011

Taiwan Design Expo, Yilan 2015
RAW Taipei, Taiwan 2015
Taiwan Designers' Week 2015
Taipei 101 'Gifts from the Star' 2014
Back To The Belle Époque, Taiwan/Japan 2014
SimpleLife Taipei, Taiwan 2012

www.grday.com

H

HAIR O'RIGHT INTERNATIONAL

est. 2002

Good Design Award, Japan 2015
Red Dot Design Award
(Social Responsibility), Germany 2014
Red Dot Design Award
(Eco Packaging), Germany 2014
Nuremberg Inventions
(Gold Medal), Germany 2014
Nuremberg Inventions
(Green Invention), Germany 2014
INPEX Gold Medal & Special Award, USA 2014

www.oright.com.tw

HAOSHI DESIGN

est. 2009

Griffin Yang

b. 1979, Taipei
Tainan National University of the Arts, Taiwan

NY NOW, New York, USA 2015
Creative Expo Taiwan, 2015
Maison&Objet, France 2013–2015

Cultural & Creative Industry Award, Taiwan 2015
IDA Int'l Design Award, USA 2011
iF DESIGN AWARD (Gold),
Germany 2006

www.haoshidesign.com

HNH LIVING

est. 2012

Vii Chen, Ju-Wei

b. 1983, Hsinchu
National Taiwan University of Science &
Technology, Taiwan

Creative Expo Taiwan 2015
Maison&Objet, France 2014, 2015
Taipei 101 'Gifts from the Star' 2014
Salone Satellite, Milan Design Week, Italy 2014
Tokyo Interior lifestyle, Japan 2014
Tent London, UK 2013
Beijing Design Week, China 2013
Taiwan Designers' Week 2010-2013

German Design Award, Germany 2015
Tokyo Designers Week, Asia Awards, Japan 2014
Good Design Award (Packaging),
Japan 2013
Red Dot Design Award (Product), Germany 2013
Qualia Cultural & Creative Award, Taiwan 2013
Golden Pin Design Award (Packaging, Product),
Taiwan 2013
BraunPrize (Winner), Germany 2009

www.hnhliving.com

HOMER CONCEPT

est. 2011

Elvis Chang, Hsiu-Ming

b. 1976, Tainan

National Chiao Tung University, Taiwan

Taipei 101 'Gifts from the Star' 2014

Tent London, UK 2012

Maison&Objet Paris, France 2012

HK Innodesign Tech Expo 2012

Taiwan Design Expo 2012

Interior Lifestyle, Shanghai China 2012

Creative Expo Taiwan 2011–2013

Fuori Salone Milano, Italy 2009

Golden Pin Design Award, Taiwan 2012

HK Global Design Award (Silver) 2011

iF DESIGN AWARD (Product), Germany 2009

Taiwan Int'l Design Competition (Bronze) 2008

www.homerconcept.com

J

JACKY WU DESIGN

est. 2011

Jacky Wu

b. 1978, Hualien

Shi-Chien University, Taiwan

Red Dot Design Museum Taipei, 2015

100% Design, Product Guide, Taiwan 2013

SaloneSatellite Milan, Italy 2012

Red Dot Award, Germany 2005, 2009, 2014

Good Design Award, Japan 2011

iF DESIGN AWARD, Germany 2008, 2011

Braun Prize, China 2009

Taiwan Good Design Award 2007, 2009

Lotus Int'l Industrial Design Competition 2008

Red Dot Design Award (Best of the Best),

Germany 2007

IDEA (Bronze), USA 2007

JARVISH

est. 2015

Younger L. Liang

b. 1968, Taipei

National Chiao Tung University, Taiwan

Ideas–Inventions–New Products, Germany 2015

Worldwide Motorcycle Exhibition, Italy 2015

IENA Exhibition (Silver Medal), Germany 2015

www.jarvish.com

JIA Inc.

est. 2007

Kate Chung

b. 1982, Taichung

Domus Academy, Italy

Taipei 101 'Gifts from the Star' 2014

Ambiente, Germany 2011, 2012, 2013

Maison&Objet, France 2008, 2009

Design Plus, Germany 2011–2013

HK Design For Asia Award (Silver) 2011

Good Design Award, Japan 2011

www.katechungdesign.com

Wuba Yang

b. 1987, Kaohsiung

Shih-Chien University, Taiwan

Design Museum, Japan 2011

Taiwan Designers' Week 2010, 2011

Kara-S, Trace of identity, Japan 2010

iF DESIGN AWARD (Top 100), Germany 2011

Taiwan Int'l Design Competition (Gold), 2009

www.jia-inc.com

JUMP FROM PAPER

est. 2010

'The Daydreamers' Launch Event,

New York, USA 2016

Shanghai Fashion Week, China 2015

Agenda Tradeshow, USA 2015

The Diner Crossover Project, Taipei 2015

London Fashion Weekend, UK 2014

PINK Launch Event, London, UK 2014

The Box, Paris Fashion Week

France 2012, 2013

www.jumpfrompaper.com

K

KIMU DESIGN STUDIO

est. 2013

Salone Satellite Milan, Italy 2015

Asia Talents, Bangkok Thailand 2015

Ambiente Germany 2014, 2015

Maison&Objet, France 2014, 2015

Seattle Gift Show, USA 2013

Tent London, UK 2012–2014

Tokyo Designers Week 2011–2013

Design Tokyo (Grand Pix), Japan 2015

Red Dot Design Award, Germany 2014

Golden Pin Design Award 2014

IFFS Asian Star, Singapore 2014

Imm Cologne (D3), Germany 2013

www.kimudesign.com

KYO CHEN

b. 1973, Yilan

National Taiwan Normal University, Taiwan

'Modern Taipei', Taipei City Government, 2016

Chi Sing Eco-conservation Foundation, 2014

'Future Poster' Quanta Culture & Education

Foundation, Taiwan 2012

Beijing 798 Creative Park, China 2011

Mexico Poster Biennale, Mexico 2010

Warsaw Poster Biennale, Poland 2008

Moscow Int'l Foto Awards (Gold), Russia 2015

IPA Int'l Photography Awards (Gold), USA 2014

PX3 Prix de la Photographie (Gold), France 2014

LongXi Awards (Best Illustration), China 2007,
2008, 2010, 2013
AWARD Awards (Bronze), Australia 2007, 2011
London International Awards (Gold), UK 2010
Asia Pacific AdFest Award (Silver), Thailand 2010
MOBIUS Advertising Awards
(Gold & Silver), USA 2008
New York Festivals, Television & Film Awards
(Gold), USA 2007
D&AD Advertising Design Awards (Book
Illustration), UK 2007

www.facebook.com/TheLovelyWorld

LANTO

est. 2011

John Lan
b. 1982, Taipei
University of Victoria, Canada

Maison&Objet Pais, France 2012–2016
Frankfurt Ambiente, Germany 2015
Creative Expo Taiwan 2015
Pulse London, UK 2013
Taiwan Designer's Week 2011, 2012
Tokyo Designer's Week, Japan 2011

Red Dot Design Award, Germany 2011
Golden Pin Design Award 2011

www.lanto.co

LAYER ONE

est. 2015

Lawrence Lee
b. 1981, Tainan
Royal College of Art, UK/
McGill University, Canada

ICT Innovative Elite 2015

www.atom3dp.com

LIBERTE

est. 2013

Lorraine Shih
b. 1984, Tainan
Yunlin University of Science & Technology,
Taiwan

Ya-Wei Wang
b. 1975, Taipei
Yunlin University of Science & Technology,
Taiwan

Creative Expo Taiwan 2015
Hangzhou Cultural & Creative Industry Expo,
China 2015
Cross-Strait Cultural Fair, China 2015
Taipei 101, 'Gifts from the Star' 2014
Milan Design Week, Italy 2014
Shanghai Interior Lifestyle Show 2014
Taiwan Designers' Week 2014
Tokyo Design Week, Japan 2013

Cultural & Creative Award 2015
Asia Awards, Japan 2013

www.libertedesign.tw

TZU-HUI LIN

b. 1976, Taipei
National Yunlin University of Science and
Technology, Taiwan

Taiwan Design Expo 2015
Taipei 101 'Gifts from the Star' 2014
Intermix & Object Taiwan, 2014
Cross-Strait Cultural Industries Fair, China 2013
Taiwan Designer's Week 2013

www.facebook.com/DroDrofreemind

KEVIN LIN

b. 1977, Chiayi
Feng Chia University, Taiwan

Taiwan Designers' Week 2014, 2015
Good Design Exhibition Tokyo 2014
Tent London, UK 2013
iF DESIGN AWARD, Germany 2014

Good Design Award, Japan 2014

www.mr-sci.com

MEI-JUN LIU

b.1974, Taipei
University of Alberta, Canada

Taiwan Designer's Week 2007–2014

Good Design Award, Japan 2008, 2014
Int'l Franz Design Award, Taiwan 2012
Red Dot Design Award, Germany 2009
iF DESIGN AWARD, Germany 2006

www.wolkeland.com

M

MEMORA

est. 2015

Fon Chiang
b. 1984, Tainan
National Taiwan University of Arts, Taiwan

Super Trivial, Taiwan 2011
You Can't See Me, Taiwan 2007
Super Immature, Taiwan 2006
Move! Kinetic Sculpture, Taiwan 2006
Post Documents, Taiwan 2006
Erase Quantity, Taiwan 2005

CES Innovation Award, USA 2015

luna.camera

MICCUDO

est. 2004

Rebecca Chang
b. 1987, New Taipei City

Creative Expo Taiwan 2015
Hong Kong Gifts & Premium Fair 2014
Golden Pin Design Award 2014

www.miccudo.com.tw

MINIWIZ

est. 2005

Boutique Design New York, USA 2015
Northmodern, Denmark 2015

World Economic Forum, Technology Pioneer
Award (Energy, Environment), USA 2015
IDEA (Gold), USA 2013
Make a Difference Award, Ministry of Culture,
Hong Kong 2012
Wall Street Journal, Innovation Award (Finalist),
USA 2011
Financial Times Earth Award, UK 2010

www.miniwiz.com

MOOREDOLL Inc.

est. 2014

Creative Expo Taiwan 2015
Spielwarenmesse Toy Fair, Germany 2015
New York Toy Fair, USA 2015
Realtek Ameba IOT Competition (Silver), 2015
Asia Pacific Entrepreneurship Competition
(Bronze), Taiwan 2014
Ministry of Culture Competition,
Digital Content (Gold), Taiwan 2014

www.mooredoll.com

MOXOR | Chic Design

est. 2014

I-Chin Yang
b. 1980, Tainan
Ming Chuan University, Taiwan

Taiwan Designer's Week 2014–2015
Creative Expo Taiwan, 2014–2015
NY NOW, New York, USA 2015
International Council of Societies of Industrial
Design, World Design Impact Prize, Taiwan 2015
iMatch Award, Taiwan 2015

www.moxor-style.com

N

NOVA DESIGN

est. 1988

iF DESIGN AWARD, Germany 2006–2015
Red Dot Design Award Germany
2006–2009, 2011, 2013, 2014
Good Design Award, Japan 2013
Appliance Design, Excellence in Design Award
(Silver), USA 2007, 2008, 2013
Golden Pin Award, 2010–2006, 2013, 2014
CES Innovations, Design & Engineering
(Gold; Sliver), USA 2010
IDEA Awards (Sliver), USA 2008
Ministry of Economic Affairs, Taiwan 2008
Guanghua Dragon Award, China 2006
National Product Image Award, 2000–2005

www.e-novadesign.com

P

PEGA D&E

est. 2008

Creative Expo Taiwan 2015
Maison&Objet Paris, France 2014
Milan Furniture Fair, Italy 2013
Taiwan Designer's Week, Taiwan 2013

www.pegadesign.com

PILI WU DESIGN STUDIO

est. 2011

Pilli Wu
b. 1986, Taipei
Shih-Chien University, Taiwan

Creative Expo Taiwan 2015
Design Museum Helsinki, Finland 2012
Beijing Design Week, China 2012
Salone del Mobile, la Triennale di Milano,
Italy 2009–2012
Museum Of Applied Arts, Köln, Germany 2008

Good Design Award, Japan 2014
Tokyo Design Week, Asia Award (Nominee),
Japan 2013
Design for Asia (Student, Finalist), HK 2012

piliwu-design.com

PINZAAN

est. 2005

Chi-Shen Chiu
b. 1982, Miaoli
National Taiwan University of Science &
Technology, Taiwan

Paris Fashion Week, France 2015
London Press Day, UK 2015
Design Guide, The Marriott, USA 2015
Taipei 101 'Gifts from the Star' 2014
Milan Design Week, Italy 2014
Facing Pages, The Netherlands 2012
MOMA Material Lab, NY, USA 2011
Clerkenwell Design Week, UK 2010

www.flexiblelove.com

POETIC LAB

est. 2013

Han-Hsi Chen
b. 1984, Taipei
Royal College of Art, UK

Shi-Kai Tseng
b. 1984, Taipei
Royal College of Art, UK
Spazio Rossana Orlandi, Milan, Italy 2014
Salone Satellite, Salone Del Mobile, Italy 2014
Vitra Design Museum, Germany 2013
Maison&Objet Paris, France 2015
ELLE DÉCOR, Young Designer of the Year, 2014
Design Report Award (1st Prize), Salone Satellite,
Milan, Italy 2013
Salone Satellite Award (3rd Prize), Italy 2013

www.shikai.tw
www.poetic-lab.com

Q

QISDESIGN
est. 2009

Jennifer Chen, Jen-Feng
b. 1975, Yunlin
National Taiwan University of Arts, Taiwan

Taipei 101 'Gifts from the Star' 2014
3D Printing Design Exhibition, Songshan Culture
Park, Taipei 2013
Taipei World Design Expo 2011
Masion & Objet Paris, France 2009

Good Design Award, Japan 2015
Red Dot Design Award,
(Best of the Best), Germany 2011
iF DESIGN AWARD (Product), Germany 2010

www.qisdesign.com

R

RICCO ENGINEERING
est. 2004

Ronald Tuan
b. 1960, Tainan
Feng Chia University, Taiwan

Outdoor, Friedrichshafen,
Germany 2015
Maison&Objet Paris, France 2013
Shanghai Interior Life Style, China 2012
Hong Kong Houseware Fair 2011
Mega Show, Hong Kong 2010

Taiwan Excellence Award 2013
Red Dot Design Award (Product), Germany 2013
My Favourite Houseware, HK 2012, 2013
iF DESIGN AWARD, Germany 2012
Cultural & Creative Award, Taiwan 2012
Golden Pin Design Award 2010, 2012

lamare.cc

S

SA'BELLA DESIGN
est. 2007

Sally Lin, Hsiao-Ying
b. 1972, Taipei
Shih Chien University, Taiwan

Design Days Dubai, UAE 2015
Maison&Objet, Paris, France 2014
Taipei 101 'Gifts from the Star' 2014
Salone del Mobil, la Triennale di Milano, Italy
2010, 2011, 2013, 2014
Salone Satellite, Milan Design Week, Italy 2012
Museum für Gestaltung, Germany 2012
Maison&Objet France 2009–2011
Taipei Fine Arts Museum 2007

Yii Design Grant, Taiwan 2007–2013
Top 100 Designers, Taiwan 2011
Franz Award (Bronze), Taiwan 2007
Red Dot Design Award, Germany 2006
iF DESIGN AWARD, Germany 2004

www.sabella-design.com

SITPLS | Shiang Ye Industrial
est. 1978

Int'l Furniture Fair, Shanghai 2016
Imm Cologne, Germany 2014, 2015
Orgatec Köln, Germany 2014, 2016
China Int'l Furniture Fair, Guangzhou 2010,
2012–2016

IDEA (Bronze), USA 2013
iF DESIGN AWARD (Gold), Germany 2011
Design for Asia Awards, Hong Kong 2011
Good Design, Australia 2010
Red Dot Design Award, Germany 2008

www.shiangye.com

SLO'O
est. 2013
Taipei Cycle Show 2015

Interbike USA 2015
Taipei Red Dot Design Museum 2014
Red Dot Design Award, Germany 2015
iF DESIGN AWARD, Germany 2015

sloolife.com

STONY IMAGE
est. 1988

Stony Cherng
b. 1956, Pingtung
National Taiwan Normal University, Taiwan

Autumn Space, Shin Kong Mitsukoshi, 2015
Taoyuan Land Art Festival 2014
Fu Jen Catholic University, Taiwan 2013
National Chengchi University, Taiwan 2011
Kaohsiung Museum of Fine Arts, Taiwan 2009
Brain Magazine, 50 Best Design Companies
(No 1), Taiwan 2011
ICOGRADA, Lifetime Achievement Award
(Graphic Design), 2011
Golden Pin Design Award 2009
Taiwan Design Award (Visual) 2008
MEA Commercial Creative Design Award, 2004

www.stony-image.com

STUDIO CO-FUSION
est. 2012

Che-Chen Kuo
b. 1984, Yunlin
National Yunlin University of Science &
Technology, Taiwan

Pei-Tse Chen
b. 1951, Nantou

Taiwan Designers' Week, 2015
Creative EXPO Taiwan, 2014
Salone del Mobile, Milan, Italy 2013
Tokyo Int'l Gift Show, Japan 2013
Taipei World Design Expo 2011
Maison&Objet Paris, France 2010

cargocollective.com/co-fusion

www.studio-if.com

STUDIO IF

est. 2012

Chia-Ying Lee

b. 1978, Tainan

Ivrea Interaction Design Institute, Italy

Salone Satellite Milan, Italy 2015
Int'l Furniture Fair Show, Singapore 2015
Mint Gallery, London, UK 2015
IDW Hangzhou, China 2015
Maison&Objet Paris, France 2014
Tent London, UK 2014

www.studio-if.com

STUDIO QIAO

est. 2009

Rock Wang

b. 1972, Yilan

Design Academy Eindhoven, The Netherlands

Tong Ho

b. 1972, Cholan

Design Academy Eindhoven, The Netherlands
Taipei 101 ' Gifts from the Star' 2014
Taipei World Design Expo 2011
Salone del Mobile, Milan, Italy 2009-2011
Maison&Objet Paris, France 2008
Lineoid Magazine '100 Most Influential
Designers' (Chinese-speaking), China 2007

DFA Design For Asia Award (Culture), HK 2015
iF DESIGN AWARD, Germany 2013
DFA Design For Asia Award (Gold; Branding),
Hong Kong 2013
Missoni Private Art Collection, Italy 2012
London Design Museum Collection, UK 2010
Vitra Design Museum Collection, Germany 2009

www.qiaodesign.com

T

TAIWAN PHYTOCULTURE

est. 2012

Creative Expo Taiwan 2015
National Farmers Benchmarking Award,
Council of Agriculture, Taiwan 2014
Ministry of Economic Affairs,
Qualia Award, Taiwan 2012

www.green888.com.tw

TAIWAN TEXTILE RESEARCH INSTITUTE

est. 1959

Wei-Hung Chen

b. 1976, Taipei

Tamkang University, Taiwan

Taipei Innovative Textile Application Show,
Taiwan 2011–2015
Taipei Int'l Invention Show and Technomart,
2011, 2012, 2014

Red Dot Design Award (Product), Germany 2015
iF DESIGN AWARD (Product), Germany 2012
INST Award (Platinum), Taiwan 2014
INST Award (Gold), Taiwan 2011

www.ttri.org.tw.

TENXION | Yun San Corporation

est. 1971

International Optical Fair Tokyo,
Japan 2012–2014
Paris Optical Fair, France 2012, 2013
Milano Eyewear Show, Italy 2012

Int'l Optical Fair Tokyo
(Eyewear of the Year), Japan 2015
Good Design Award, Japan 2013
Cross-Strait Industrial Design Award, Taiwan 2013
Red Dot Design Award, Germany 2012

www.tenxion.tw

THAT! INVENTIONS

est. 2014

Jung-Ya Hsieh

b. 1967, Pingtung

Da Yeh University, Taiwan

Int'l Home & Housewares, USA 2014–2016
Excellence in Housewares Awards, UK 2015
iF DESIGN AWARD (Product), Germany 2003,
2005–2013
iF DESIGN AWARD (Packaging), Germany 2013
Red Dot Design Award, Germany 2005–2012
IDEA Award, USA 2006, 2008, 2010
Good Design Award,
Japan, 2004–2007, 2011, 2012

www.thatinventions.com

TOAST LIVING

est. 2007

Sean Lin, Yung-Shiun

b. 1976, Taipei

Rochester Institute of Technology, USA

Ambiente, Germany 2014, 2015
Taipei 101, 'Gifts from the Star' 2014
Tokyo Interior Life Style, Japan 2013
Maison&Objet, France 2009–2015
Salone del Mobile, Milan, Italy 2009
BIG+BIH, Thailand 2008, 2014
iF DESIGN AWARD, Germany 2013, 2015
Golden Pin Design Award 2011, 2013
Good Design Award, Japan 2012

www.toastliving.com

TRIP VIEW BOWL | Arty Design

est. 2008

Arty Peng, Hsi-Yi

b. 1970, Hsinchu

Chinese Culture University, Taiwan

Taipei 101 'Gifts from the Star' 2014
Tokyo Interior Lifestyle, Japan 2013
100 years of Presidential Gallery, Taiwan 2011

'101 OTOP', Taipei, Taiwan 2011
Taipei World Design Expo 2011
Blue & White Wares Competition, Taiwan 2009
921 Ji-ji Earthquake, Community Reconstruction
Exhibition, Taiwan 2009
Red Dot Design Award, Germany 2011
Taiwan Visual Design Award 2010
Good Crafts Award, Taiwan 2009
EPD Green Package Design Award, Taiwan 2009
Taiwan Best 100, 2008

tripviewbowl.com

TWO+ LAB
est. 2012

Tom Cheng, Hung
b. 1981, Taipei
Chang Gung University, Taiwan

Creative Expo Taiwan 2015
Taiwan Designers Week 2014, 2015
MOCATaipei Street Festival, Taiwan 2014
Eslite Concept Exhibition, Taiwan 2014

iF DESIGN AWARD (Product),
Germany 2013, 2015
Red Dot Design Award, Germany 2014
iF DESIGN AWARD (Gold), Germany 2011
IDEA Award (Sliver), USA 2010

www.facebook.com/twopluslab

TZU CHI
Buddhist Compassion Relief Foundation
est. 1966

INPEX, Inventions & New Products Exposition,
Special Humanitarian Award & Gold Medal for
Furniture Category, USA 2015
Good Design Award Winner, China 2015
iENA Intl Trade Fair, Gold Medal, Germany 2015
Kuwait Int'l Invention Fair, Kuwait 2015
Seoul International Invention Fair, Korea 2015
Golden Pin Social Design Award Winner, 2015
Red Dot Design Award (Gold), Germany 2014

http://tw.tzuchi.org/en/

U

U-CUBE CREATIVE
est. 2008

Jack Chu
b. 1964, Tainan
National Chung Tung University, Taiwan

Tokyo Design Show, Japan 2015
Giftionery Taipei, Taiwan 2011
HK Mega Show, Hong Kong 2011
Tokyo Interior Lifestyle, Japan 2011
Creative Expo Taiwan, 2011

udn Design Award, Taiwan 2015
Cultural & Creative Award (Commercial), 2014
Golden Pin Award, Taiwan 2011
Taiwan Cultural & Creative Boutique Award 2010
Red Dot Design Award (Product), Germany 2009

www.polaricetray.com

UPON | Kuandah Union Trading
est. 2007

Outdoor, Taiwan 2015
Taipei Cycle, Taiwan 2014
Techtextil Messe, Germany 2013
Red Dot Design Award, Germany 2014
Taipei Cycle d&l awards, Taiwan 2014

www.upon-smile.com

V

VINAERA | Mercuries Asia
est. 1997

Yeh-Yi Chung
b. 1976, Tainan
National Yunlin University, Taiwan

HOFEX Int'l Food & Hospitality Trade Show,
Hong Kong 2015
ProWine, Int'l Wine & Spirits Trade Fair, China
2013–2015

Int'l Housewares Association, Innovation Award
(Finalist), USA 2015
Asian Catering Equipment Award, HK 2015
Red Dot Design Award, Germany 2014
Golden Pin Design Award 2014

http://www.vinaera-global.com/

VIVITEK | Delta Electronics
est. 1992

Consumer Electronics Show, Las Vegas, USA
BETT Show, London, UK
Integrated Systems Europe, The Netherlands
Computex, Taipei, Taiwan
InfoComm, Amsterdam, The Netherlands
GiTEX, Dubai, UAE

iF DESIGN AWARD, Germany 2016
Good Design Award, Japan 2015
Taiwan Excellence Award (Silver) 2014
Projection Times, Outstanding Product 2013
PC World, Product of the Year 2012
Golden Pin Design Award, Taiwan 2011
Beareyes, Best Product of the Year 2010
Stuff Magazine, 5-stars 2009

www.vivitekcorp.com

W

WEPLAY | Kiddie's Paradise Inc.
est. 1987

Hong Kong Toys & Games Fair,
Hong Kong 2002–2016
American Toy Fair, USA 2005–2016
Spielwarenmesse Nuremberg,
Germany 2002–2016
ABC Kids Expo, USA 2015–2016
Red Dot Museum, Germany 2014
Taipei World Design Expo 2011

Red Dot Design Award, Germany 2008, 2014
Good Design Award (Product), Japan 2002, 2006
iF DESIGN AWARD, Germany 2002, 2006, 2008

Mark of Excellence (Product), Taiwan 2008,
2010, 2015
Taiwan Excellence (Gold) 2010
Golden Pin Design Award (Product),
2002, 2004, 2006, 2007, 2009, 2012, 2015

www.e-weplay.com

CAI-XUAN WU

b. 1985, Hsinchu
Birmingham City University, UK

Contemporary Jewellery & Object Trail,
Melbourne, Australia 2015
Kobeia, Munich, Germany 2015
Mobilia Gallery, Cambridge, USA 2015
Pôle Bijou, Baccarat, France 2014
Alliages Gallery, Lille, France 2014
Itami Museum of Arts & Crafts, Itami, Japan 2013
Int'l Handwerkmesse, Munich, Germany 2013
Itami Int'l Contemporary Jewellery Exhibition,
Japan 2013

www.caixuanwu.com

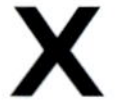

X

XCELLENT PRODUCTS INTERNATIONAL
est. 2001

Creative Expo Taiwan, 2015
Taipei Int'l Invention Show 2015
Hangzhou Cultural & Creative Industry Expo,
China 2015
Shenzhen Int'l Industrial Design Fair, China 2013

IDEA (Finalist), USA 2014
Golden Pin Design Award 2014

www.xcellent.com.tw

Y

Y STUDIO
est. 2012

Interior Lifestyle, Shanghai, China 2015
Maison&Objet, France 2014, 2015
Taipei 101 'Gifts from the Star' 2014
Tent London, UK 2014
Tokyo Interior Lifestyle, Japan 2014
Taipei Int'l Book Exhibition 2012, 2013
Original Festival Taipei, Taiwan 2012

Shopping Design (Best 100) 2012
HK Global Design Awards 2012

www.ystudiostyle.com

Z

ZEN TAO
est. 2013

Chun-Hao Chen
b. 1973, Taipei
Design Academy Eindhoven,
The Netherlands

Taipei 101 'Gifts from the Star', Taiwan 2014
Taipei Design Show, Taiwan 2013
Post Fossil, 21_21 museum, Tokyo, Japan 2010
Good Design Award, Japan 2013

www.zentao.com.tw

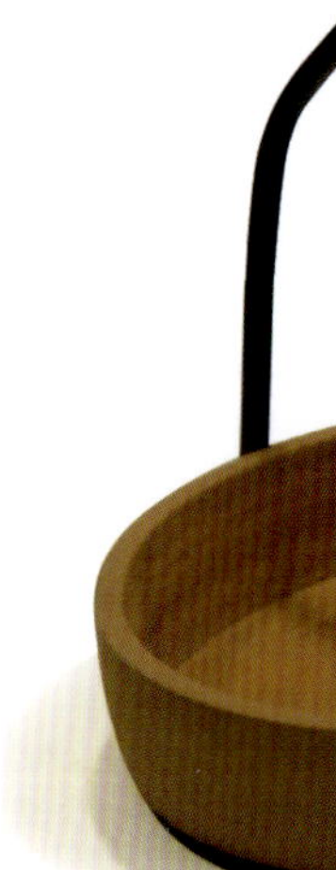

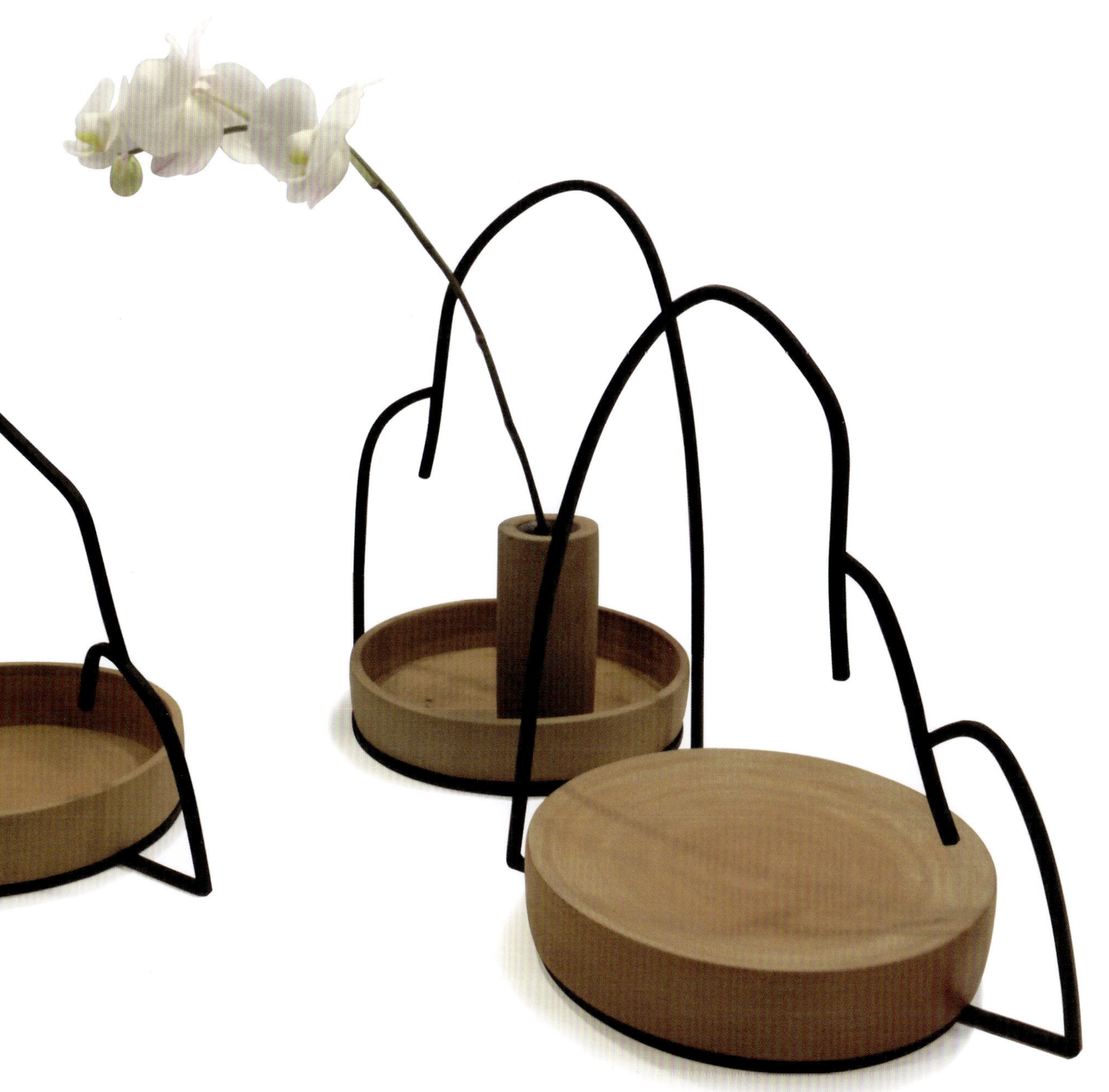

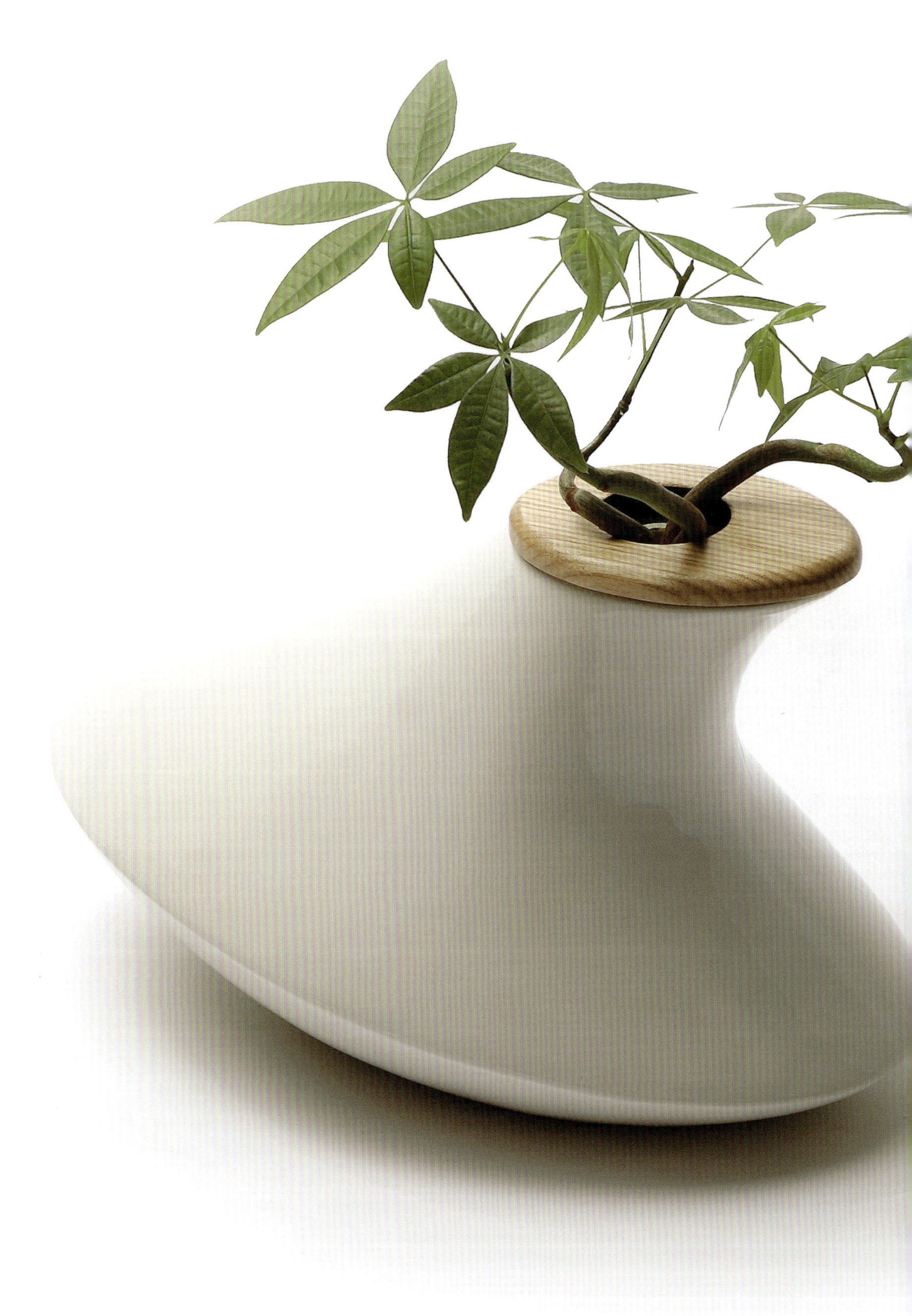

CREDITS

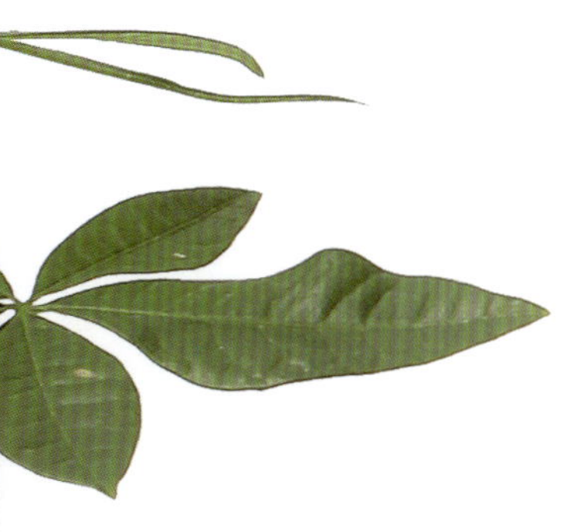

FROM THE AUTHOR

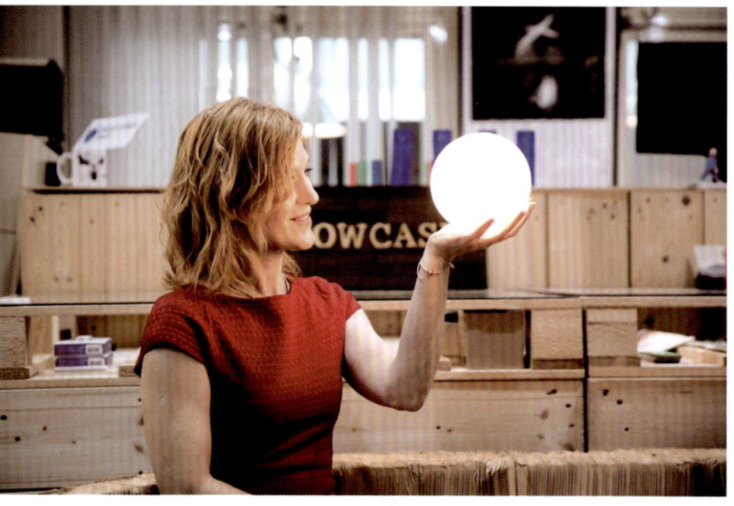

It was in the sweltering summer of 2010 when I first landed at Taoyaun International Airport, wondering how I would survive the humidity. Taipei Art Fair had invited me to curate a media arts exhibition at the World Trade Centre, and it was to be a weeklong visit. I had declined the offer several times yet the organisers could not take 'no' for an answer. It must be destiny, because shortly after I made a pact with myself to return.

There was dynamism and energy being poured into the creative sector, and the thought I could be a part of it was tantalising. I relocated my studio from Melbourne to Taipei with the aim to collaborate with all subsectors of the creative industries as well as to contribute to bi-lateral cultural relations. I frequently travelled around the island to visit design studios and workshops. With time even the magic spell of the language lifted as my comprehension of Mandarin Chinese increased. I am well aware mine is a privileged position and I do my best to put it to good use.

This book emerged from a sense of frustration. Initially I was searching for original concepts to introduce to Australia. To me Taiwan is fascinating for many reasons. Culturally it is a custodian of arts and crafts traditions that have been obliterated elsewhere in Asia. This heritage is a valuable resource for Taiwanese creative people, and it is what differentiates their practice. Local designers also have enviable access to 50 years of manufacturing know-how and one of the world's best electronics industries in their back yard. As a result prototyping new concepts is done efficiently and rapidly. Furthermore, the particular environmental conditions—frequent earthquakes, typhoons, humidity, and high population density—challenge designers to develop a unique sensitivity towards form and function. Products tried and tested here can become solutions for liveability and sustainability problems occurring elsewhere in the world, now and into the future.

But after attending countless exhibitions and trade fairs, and previewing innumerable products and idea-projects, it became apparent to me that there is a serious gap between the cultural context and the marketing spiels that promote Taiwanese design thinking to the world. I strongly believe that the wealth of insight and diversity of Asian design ought to be made accessible through cross-cultural communication not merely through translation of promotional materials. As there is no such resource in English, I made it my mission to produce one.

This publication is the culmination of more than 2 years of surveying the industry, including more than 350 visits to companies and over 120 interviews that informed the 88 product stories presented here. I became adept at building relationships and networking with anyone who was willing to share information. Importantly, my independence from institutional interests allowed me curatorial freedom to select not only *lao-shi*, established designers, but also to include the work of new talent. Within this period I also curated Taipei 101's Gifts from the Star exhibition, its first Taiwanese design showcase based on products featured in this book. Further, I presented my research at academic conferences and gave workshops.

The selection of entries for this book was based on five criteria: excellence, innovation, sustainability, culture, and easy living. Each product had to demonstrate an original approach to at least two of the above. I stayed away from purely technology-based goods because it was important to break away from stereotyping Taiwanese designers as 'geeks'. Instead, I focused my research on finding design gems and stories that I regarded as valuable and intriguing. As a cultural explorer, I longed to discover something to enrich me and make me see the world from different vantage points. I hope that you will also find some new perspectives within these pages.

I am grateful to the girlfriends and wives of designers who helped with translation during the interviews: some 30 wonderful ladies! It was as vital for the success of the book to make friends with 'significant others' as it was to gain access to studios and boardrooms. (I was told that at university the guys would go sleepless playing computer games, while the girls studied hard to pass English exams, which might explain it!) To get past the language barrier we sometimes used Google to find visual cues and word translations, while sipping Oolong tea that soothed the awkward edges. I would scribble notes and draw diagrams for further research, piecing together disparate references and ideas into engaging short stories.

I am grateful to the staff at Taiwan Design Centre's Library for their help in finding yearbooks available in English. Also, to my friends in Australia, Alessio Cavallaro and Andrea Kleist, whose astute observations guided the final draft of the manuscript.

This project could not have happened without the care of my dear friend Eva Fang. She let me write at her cafe on Beiping East Rd, a convenient downtown location where I held some of my meetings. The TAV Café continues to be my writer's sanctuary. Eva generously supported me through the many ups and downs of being a foreigner in Taipei, and made my stay here most enjoyable.

To successfully publish and launch the book I partnered with Backer-Founder, a team of highly motivated young people, and together we run an awesome crowdfunding campaign. To my collaborator Li-Hsin Ho, every team member, volunteer and backer: my heartfelt thanks, we did an incredible job!

With profound gratitude and everlasting love, I dedicate this book to my mother, Margaritta, for instilling in me a deep curiosity about other cultures, and for teaching me to embrace the human family as my own.

Annie Ivanova

IMAGES